T0145335

Lecture Notes in Information Systems and Organisation

Volume 37

Lecture Notes in Information Systems and Organization—LNISO—is a series of scientific books that explore the current scenario of information systems, in particular IS and organization. The focus on the relationship between IT, IS and organization is the common thread of this collection, which aspires to provide scholars across the world with a point of reference and comparison in the study and research of information systems and organization. LNISO is the publication forum for the community of scholars investigating behavioral and design aspects of IS and organization. The series offers an integrated publication platform for high-quality conferences, symposia and workshops in this field. Materials are published upon a strictly controlled double blind peer review evaluation made by selected reviewers.

LNISO is abstracted/indexed in Scopus

More information about this series at http://www.springer.com/series/11237

Concetta Metallo · Maria Ferrara ·
Alessandra Lazazzara · Stefano Za
Editors

Digital Transformation and Human Behavior

Innovation for People and Organisations

Editors
Concetta Metallo
Department of Science and Technology
Parthenope University of Naples
Naples, Italy

Maria Ferrara
Department of Business and Economics
Parthenope University of Naples
Naples, Italy

Alessandra Lazazzara
Department of Social and Political Sciences
University of Milan
Milan, Italy

Stefano Za
Management and Business Administration
University of Chieti-Pescara
Pescara, Italy

ISSN 2195-4968 ISSN 2195-4976 (electronic)
Lecture Notes in Information Systems and Organisation
ISBN 978-3-030-47538-3 ISBN 978-3-030-47539-0 (eBook)
https://doi.org/10.1007/978-3-030-47539-0

This Springer imprint is published by the registered company Springer Nature Switzerland AG
The registered company address is: Gewerbestrasse 11, 6330 Cham, Switzerland

Preface

Digital transformation is impacting all aspects of life, the way we live and the way we work. Due to the pervasive effects of such digital revolution on firms and societies, both scholars and practitioners are interested in better understanding the key mechanisms behind digital transformation challenges. Therefore, this book contains a collection of research papers focusing on the relationships between technologies (e.g. artificial intelligence, social media, and the Internet of Things) and behaviours (e.g. social learning, knowledge sharing, decision-making). Moreover, it provides insights about how digital transformation may improve the quality of personal and work life within the public and private organizations. The plurality of views offered makes this book particularly relevant to users, companies, scientists, and governments. The content of the book is based on a selection of the best papers (original double-blind peer-reviewed contributions) presented at the annual conference of the Italian chapter of AIS which took place in Naples, Italy, in September 2019.

Naples, Italy
March 2020

Concetta Metallo
Maria Ferrara
Alessandra Lazazzara
Stefano Za

Contents

Digital Technology and Individual Behaviour

Digital Social Innovation

Digital Transformation and Human Behavior: An Introduction

Concetta Metallo, Maria Ferrara, Alessandra Lazazzara, and Stefano Za

Abstract Digital transformation is impacting all aspects of life, the way we live and the way we work. The aim of this book is to introduce the current debate on the relationship between digital transformation and human behavior. This volume proposes a revised version of some interesting and relevant contributions presented at the XVI Conference of the Italian Chapter of AIS (ItAIS2019) entitled "Digital Transformation and Social Innovation", which was held at the University of Naples "Parthenope" on September 27–28, 2019. The book contains 24 chapters evaluated through a double-blind review process and provides a plurality of views that makes this book particularly relevant for scholars but also for practitioners, managers, and policy makers.

Keywords Digital skills · Individual behavior · Digital social innovation

---

C. Metallo (✉)
Department of Sciences and Technology, Centro Direzionale, University of Naples Parthenope, Isola C4, 80143 Naples, Italy
e-mail: concetta.metallo@uniparthenope.it

M. Ferrara
Department of Department of Business and Economics, University of Naples Parthenope, Via Generale Parisi (Monte di Dio) 13, 80132 Naples, Italy
e-mail: maria.ferrara@uniparthenope.it

A. Lazazzara
Department of Social and Political Sciences, University of Milan, Via Conservatorio, 7, 20122 Milan, Italy
e-mail: alessandra.lazazzara@unimi.it

S. Za
Department of Management and Business Administration, University "G. d'Annunzio", Viale Pindaro, 42, 65127 Pescara, Italy
e-mail: stefano.za@unich.it

C. Metallo et al. (eds.), *Digital Transformation and Human Behavior*, Lecture Notes in Information Systems and Organisation 37, https://doi.org/10.1007/978-3-030-47539-0_1

The aim of this book is to introduce the current debate on the relationship between digital transformation and human behavior by highlighting the pervasive effects of such a revolution on aspects concerning the way we live and work. In so doing, this book provides insights about how digital innovations may change and improve the quality of personal and working lives within public and private organizations.

As observed by Yoo [1], pervasive and ubiquitous digitalization has brought about new disruptive changes in the economy and society. Therefore, digital transformation can be understood as "the changes that the digital technology causes or influences in all aspects of human life" [2, p. 689]. As such technologies become increasingly omnipresent, the opportunities and challenges they present for people and organizations become greater. Digital technology diffusion has altered the ways in which business processes are conducted, how organizations compete and interact, and how workers, customers and users behave. These changes underline the need to take into consideration the human side of digital transformation, focusing on human-technology interactions both within and outside of organizations. Although technology is a foundation for transformation, digital innovation starts with people and how digital technologies (artifacts, platforms, etc.) interact with innovation agents (be they organizations or individuals) [3, p. 228].

The emphasis on the human aspect, connected with the digital transformation phenomena, is precisely what binds together all the papers contained in this book in relation to skills, behaviors, attitudes, organizational practices, and societal challenges. This volume proposes a revised version of some interesting and relevant contributions presented at the XVI Conference of the Italian Chapter of AIS (ItAIS2019) entitled "Digital Transformation and Social Innovation", which was held at the University of Naples "Parthenope" on September 27–28, 2019. This volume contains 24 chapters evaluated through a double-blind review process and provides a plurality of views that makes this book particularly relevant for scholars but also for practitioners, managers, and policy makers.

The book contains three sections addressing the following topics: (1) digital skills and new forms of learning, (2) digital technology and individual behavior, and (3) digital social innovation.

1 Part I: Digital Skills and New Forms of Learning

Digital transformation increases the need for acquiring new skills but also fosters new forms of learning [4]. New jobs and new ways of working that did not exist until a few years ago and are now emerging due to the digital revolution require "changes in both what has to be learned and how this learning is to happen" [5, p. 403]. Therefore, identifying the new skills needed for managing digital transformation and exploiting digital learning opportunities are necessary for employment and participation in society.

In this vein, Caporarello, Manzoni and Panariello provide both a research and practice-oriented contribution in the field of learning within organizations. Through an online survey involving 245 Italian employees, their study compares the current versus desired use of different learning models and learning methods from the perspective of the employees. From a practical point of view, the authors offer HR professionals suggestions about how to better design effective learning experiences and communicate them to employees. Ivanov, Bednar and Paraskelidis conduct an analysis concerning a project for creating an augmented reality (AR) authoring tool for an organization in the education sector. The authors analyze the usefulness perception of the AR solution as initially designed and prototyped. At the beginning, the tool seemed to have great potential; but as the project progressed, it gradually became evident that although the solution was possible, it was not necessarily a good solution. The authors discuss this important aspect from a socio-technical perspective. Sigridur Íslind, Norström, Vallo Hult and Ramadani Olsson's study primarily aims at better understanding platform characteristics in higher educational settings through a socio-technical and socio-cultural learning perspective. Moreover, the authors consider learning as an exchange within a transaction platform, arguing for platform context transactions that are not monetary. The main contribution of their paper is to discuss several issues about the transactional concept in two-sided markets. Manzoni, Caporarello, Cirulli and Magni explore the preferred learning styles of Generation Z and compare them with those of previous generations. The findings show significant differences between Generation Z and individuals belonging to previous generations concerning their learning style, which conflicts with the common stereotypes from existing academic and practical evidence.

The current workplace requires highly skilled workers to face changing job requirements. Thus, Prezioso, Ceci and Za address the issue of digital skills (DS) related to the digital transformation in an Italian firm operating in the manufacturing sector. The study explores the diffusion of DS across different departments of the firm, how DS are distributed, and what are the reasons for the different perceptions. The results show that the DS described in the job description are often not aligned with the expectations of the managers (interviews). The study offers a taxonomy of digital skills that organizations can relate to in order to obtain a successful digital transformation and increase their absorptive capacity and employees' awareness. Buonocore, Agrifoglio and De Gennaro investigate the relationship between digital competencies and job crafting within the Italian public sector. The study's assumption is that public workers with digital competencies can act proactively on their work by modifying their contents, relationships, and cognitive perception. Svensson's paper analyzes how teachers' competence development in using digital technologies within their pedagogical practice can be supported in a community of practice. Through an action-based qualitative study of a Nordic education project, where inter-professional collaboration and the use of digital tools were of great importance, Svensson shows several pedagogical approaches, curricular structures, digital resources, and organizational conditions required for virtual collaboration within this community of practice.

2 Part II: Digital Technology and Individual Behavior

Digitization has significantly changed personal and work lives both within and outside of organizations. The effects of these changes on individual behavior are evident in every aspect of daily life, in which the individual assumes the role of user, customer or worker. Considering the adoption or usage behavior area, for example, the individual's exposure to digital technologies highlights the dependence on information security issues, as well as the loss of boundaries between work and non-work contexts. Thus, Za, Ceci, Masciarelli and Iaia investigate the role of social axioms in affecting social network dependence, combining the analysis of personal cultural values with media system dependency theory. Using a large dataset composed of 622 observations, the study develops and validates a research model to shed new light on the investigation of dependence phenomena in the context of social network sites, thus exploring the role of individual beliefs.

Traer and Bednar's paper examines the motives behind DDoS (distributed denial of service) attacks as a form of cyberattack, along with attacker personas. This paper finds and discusses several motives behind DDoS attacks, as well as the possible attackers' profiles. Niechoy, Masuch and Trang analyze human behavior with regard to information security (ISC) using the lens of social learning theory (SLT) and rational choice theory (RCT). The proposed research model is analyzed by using partial least squares (PLS). The results reveal that SLT has an influence on RCT; therefore, these two theories can be used to explain ISC. Polyviou, Pouloudi, Pramatari and Dhillon introduce the concept of digital emancipation to refer to the notion of freedom experienced by individuals due to the wide use of digital technology. These tools liberate individuals as they set them free from the time, place and device restrictions of their everyday life. As a result, the tools blur the boundaries between work, social and personal life contexts. The study shows that digital emancipation is associated with both positive and negative experiences within each context (personal, social or work) and with a relevant balancing effort. Thus, the authors propose an integrated theoretical framework for understanding the balancing effort of digitally emancipated individuals.

Regarding customer behavior, digital technologies expose customers to new experience, as highlighted by Kemppainen, Makkonen and Frank. These authors explore customer experience formation in an online shopping context by investigating the causes of customers' positive and negative emotions during their visit to an online store. The study is conducted using survey data collected from 1794 Finnish online store customers, and attribution theory is utilized to explain how individuals make sense of their emotions. The findings demonstrate the complexity of customer experience formation. In the same research area, the paper written by Za, Lazazzara, Pallud and Agostini draws on assemblage theory to propose a research model aimed at investigating the willingness to buy a further smart device to increase the number of devices shaping the personal digital ecosystem. The model considers the continuance intention to use smart devices and smart device dependence as antecedents of purchase intention. Furthermore, the moderating effect of user satisfaction and the number of smart devices already owned are explored. The proposed model may be useful to not only disentangle the drivers of smart device users' purchasing behavior but also explore the negative side of technological possession, such as technostress and addiction. Lunberry and Liebenau focus on anthropomorphism, which is the tendency of humans to apply human-like attributes to non-human objects. Through an empirical study involving the introduction of interactive voice response (IVR) with clients of a savings and loans company in Ghana, the study applies a socio-technical approach using affordance theory to examine the relationship between technology and anthropomorphic perceptions among users. The findings highlight four main ways that IVR technology exhibits human-like qualities within user-technology interactions (as perceived by users).

Moreover, technological changes affect work behaviors, i.e., the ways in which to interact, collaborate, and communicate both within and outside of organizations. In fact, Cochis, Mattarelli, Bertolotti, Scapolan, Montanari and Ungureanu investigate the experience of professionals working in collaborative spaces, such as coworking spaces and innovation labs, created for enhancing individual and group creativity. The authors focus on creative processes in collaborative spaces by explicitly recognizing the fundamental role of collaborative technology use. In particular, the paper explores how the positive resources related to wellbeing and work-life balance in collaborative spaces interplay with the use of collaborative technology in affecting individual creativity. The survey conducted within 27 collaborative spaces reveals that an intense use of collaborative technology with actors who are external to the collaborative spaces can generate perceptions of overload, thus making the impact of work-life balance on creativity not significant. Cipriano and Bednar investigate how people communicate in a company and how this is likely to support knowledge-sharing practices. Their paper proposes an "interaction-context" schema, which emphasizes a practical proposition that is useful for analyzing interactions that underpin real-work practices in context. The proposed model seeks to identify the interactions (focusing on digital enabled interactions) among different business areas and stakeholders concerning a specific company. In building the "interaction-context" schema, the authors focus on the interplay between interactions, technology and ICT competencies, which support or develop business activities.

Pascarella and Bednar's study is focused on sustainable work practices in small and medium-sized enterprises (SMEs) with a sociotechnical and triple bottom line (TBL) approach. The study shows that the lack of management attention given to the systemic integration of employees' work practices could be a main issue that hinders the improvement of sustainability. The authors integrate technology and systemic perspectives in the TBL approach to achieve sustainability from a sociotechnical perspective, thereby creating a systemic sustainability model focused on economic, environmental, social and technological aspects. Finally, Briganti, Mele and Varriale investigate the main implications of new technologies within hospitals in preventing and reducing the verbal and non-verbal assaults, aggressions and violence actions received by healthcare professionals. Through a review of the literature, the study provides a picture of the current state of the situation and gives some useful suggestions about solutions concerning new technologies.

3 Part III: Digital Social Innovation

Digital social innovation refers to the use of digital technologies in building innovations with a strong social impact in fields such as healthcare, education, democratic participation, or environment [6]. In this way, technology can be useful for a wide range of social needs, such as social inclusion, urban development, better governance or a sustainable environment. Badr and Kosremelli Asmar conduct a scoping review of the literature on value co-creation with the use of technology for interaction and social inclusion. Their aim is to explore the potential of technology for improving social interaction and the inclusion of people with learning disabilities in digital society. Through the DART framework, the study seeks to explore how the current literature treats this contemporary topic, suggesting the criticality of including participants with disabilities in user testing for a successful outcome of validation and value-added innovation.

The main purpose of Depaoli, Sorrentino and De Marco's study is to inform readers about and increase the awareness of the complexity of the implications of ICT used by governments and to sketch a range of information policy recommendations for contemporary decision makers seeking viable solutions to ethical concerns. Castelnovo and Romanelli investigate how citizens' involvement as co-producers in smart city initiatives impacts the power relationships between the city governments and the citizens. The authors observe that to take advantage of citizens' contributions for the success of smart city initiatives, interaction-defined and participation-based governance infrastructures should be implemented that return power to the people. The paper concludes that this requires city governments to shift from the traditional power-over governance style to the new power-with governance style. Dima and Maassen's research has the main objective of determining the implementation degree, needs and costs of some of the most important smart city and Industry 4.0 tools in the Romanian market, as well as the expected trends until 2025. The findings reveal that while there is still a significant gap between the needs of the population, the infrastructure and the city and the current implementation level of these tools, significant progress has been made. Finally, Mokaddes Ahmed Dipu and Sultana propose a mobile-based marketing channel (Smart GOALA) for connecting peri-urban marginal dairy farmers with urban milk consumers that will ensure them obtaining a better and fairer price.

References

1. Yoo, Y. (2013). The tables have turned: How can the information systems field contribute to technology and innovation management research? *Journal of the Association for Information Systems, 14*(5), 227–236.
2. Stolterman, E., & Fors, A. C. (2004). Information technology and the good life. In: B. Kaplan et al. (Eds.), *Information systems research, relevant theory and informed practice. Proceedings from IFIP 8.2 Manchester Conference* (pp. 687–692). London: Kluwer Academic Publishers.

3. Nambisan, S., Lyytinen, K., Majchrzak, A., & Song, M. (2017). Digital innovation management: Reinventing innovation management research in a digital world. *MIS Quarterly, 41*(1), 223–238.
4. Voogt, J., Erstad, O., Dede, C., & Mishra, P. (2013). Challenges to learning and schooling in the digital networked world of the 21st century. *Journal of Computer Assisted Learning, 29*(5), 403–413.
5. Za, S., Spagnoletti, P., & North-Samardzic, A. (2014). Organisational learning as an emerging process: The generative role of digital tools in informal learning practices. *British Journal of Education Technology, 45,* 1023–1035.
6. Stokes, M., Baeck, P., & Baker, T. (2017). What next for digital social innovation? Realising the potential of people and technology to tackle social challenges. A study prepared for the European Commission DG Communications Networks, Content and Technology. London: NESTA.

Digital Skills and New Forms of Learning

The Evolution of (Digital) Learning Models and Methods: What Will Organizations and Their Employees Adopt in 2025?

Leonardo Caporarello, Beatrice Manzoni, and Beatrice Panariello

Abstract Today learning within organizations is the most important driver of people attraction, retention and engagement. While "why" we should learn is out of questions and "how" (in terms of options) we could do it is relatively well known, we know little about how individuals learn and especially how they would like to learn in the future. In this paper, we compare how much employees currently use different learning models (traditional or face to face, online and blended) and learning methods and how much they would like to use them in the future. We surveyed online 245 Italian employees and we discovered that respondents predominantly use face to face learning while aiming for more online learning and relatively more blended learning in the future. With regard to learning methods, our data highlight that there is the expectation to use less instructor-led lectures in favor of other more engaging learning methods. These results offer interesting insights for the HR function and the Business Schools that have to design up to date learning programs.

Keywords Learning models · Learning methods · Tech-based learning · Online learning · Blended learning · Face to face learning

1 Introduction

Learning is a hot topic today, being one the most important drivers of workforce attraction, retention and engagement, in the sense of a profound motivation and commitment towards to the job and the employing organization [1, 2]. Engaged

---

L. Caporarello · B. Manzoni (✉) · B. Panariello
SDA Bocconi School of Management, and BUILT (Bocconi University Innovations in Learning and Teaching), Bocconi University, 20136 Milan, Italy
e-mail: beatrice.manzoni@unibocconi.it

L. Caporarello
e-mail: leonardo.caporarello@unibocconi.it

B. Panariello
e-mail: beapanariello@gmail.com

C. Metallo et al. (eds.), *Digital Transformation and Human Behavior*, Lecture Notes in Information Systems and Organisation 37,
https://doi.org/10.1007/978-3-030-47539-0_2

people not only stay longer, they also deliver a better performance, are passionate about their work, and recommend their company as a good place to work [3].

While "why" we have to engage in continuous learning is therefore out of question [4–6], "how" we can do it is currently among the most debated topics in the academic as well as practitioner-oriented literature [7]. This growing interest towards the theme can be also explained in light of the technological shift. Technology is boosting an important learning (r)evolution, determining the rise of many new learning models and methods [8].

Existing research widely conceptualizes and reviews learning models and learning methods. While the map is now relatively clear, despite some persistent confusion especially on tech-based learning models and methods [7], we know little about the most used ones and, in particular, about the expectations people have about them for the future.

Given this, in current study, we compare the past and the expected (desired) use of traditional (face-to-face), online and blended learning models, and a variety of learning methods. In order to do so, we surveyed online 245 Italian employees working in different companies, in different roles and of different seniority levels.

The article is structured as follows: first, we conceptualize learning models and methods, reviewing existing literature on the matter. Then, we present our research methods and discuss the main findings. Results suggest a desired increase of online learning, a slight decrease of traditional (face to face) one, while the use of blended learning apparently remains substantially stable according to respondents' expectations. With regards to learning methods, the use of instructor-led lectures significantly decreases in the future, while, on the contrary, the use of all the others moderately increases. We conclude with implications for both research and practice.

2 A Review of Learning Models and Learning Methods

In the recent literature, we witness to an increasing variety of conceptualizations and interpretations of what learning is. This reflects on one hand what scholars research about, but also what employees adopt and are used to within their organizations. Some recent works shed light on a plethora of terms (methodologies, models, methods, modes, approaches, etc.) that are sometimes confused, in overlap or combinable one with each other [7, 9].

For example, Caporarello et al. [7] categorize many of these terms into learning models and learning methods.

Selecting the learning model implies a choice between traditional (face to face), online and blended learning [10].

The traditional (face to face) learning model is—or at least was—the most common way of learning, yet it is hardly defined because it is somehow taken for granted [11]. Singh and Yusoff [11] are among the few who formally define it as a learning process where learners and experts are physically present in the same place at the same time.

Similarly, both online and blended learning are poorly defined—as many other tech—based terms [7]. According to some authors [12] terms such as online course/learning, web-based learning, distance learning are often seen as synonymous, due to poor or vague definitions. Building on various references, we can say that online learning is a model of distance education that uses the Internet and tech-based devices (computers, tablets or smartphones) as delivery means, eliminating time and space constraints [13, 14]. Blended learning is even more prone to a flawed definition. Some scholars define it as a form of learning using technology [15] or as mix of experiences that are necessarily face to face and online [16], yet according to many the concept remains ill-defined [15]. Caporarello and Inesta [17] emphasized the combination of different learning methodologies. Leveraging on different aspects of previous definitions, we can suggest that blended learning provides a learning experience combining the integration of different learning methods (i.e. face to face lecture, case studies and role plays, web-based simulation, other tech-based tools) which are used in class (on-campus) and outside class (off-campus).

When it comes to learning methods, the array of options is even wider, especially if we refer to tech-based methods [7]. Existing literature studied more traditional learning methods, such as lecture-based [18] and case-based ones [19]. However, in recent years there has been a growing interest towards less conventional and more experiential and active learning methods, such as project-based one [20, 21], cooperative learning [22] and game-based learning [23]. There is also a growing interest towards tech-based learning methods (see Caporarello et al. [7] for a fully comprehensive review). In general, all these studies focus on conceptualizing and defining each different method, reflecting on their adoption, as well as on related advantages and disadvantages, often making comparisons among them.

Given this, while the map of learning models and learning methods is now relatively exhaustive and clear, what we know less is how much they are used and will be used in the future (at least according to employees' expectations). Despite some very practice-oriented contributions [24] research has not fully investigated the future evolution of learning yet.

3 Methods

As part of a broader research project on actual and future learning approach within organizations, in 2018 we surveyed 245 employees via an online platform, asking them how they learn today and how they would like to learn in the future.

With regard to the sample, 53.9% of the respondents are male. All of them are Italian and currently work in Italy. In terms of age the majority of participants reported to be between the ages of 26 and 45, which stands at 66.4%. Average age is 38 years old. In terms of functional role, 47.8% of the respondents work in HR, mainly in training and development (77.8%); the other half is well distributed among administration, accounting and finance, technical and R&D, marketing and sales, general management, or operations, production and logistics. In terms of industry, 49.4% of the respondents works in the service industry, 19.6% in the manufacturing industry, 11.4% in the public government industry and 19.6% in other categories. Half of the sample (51.8%) works for big companies (more than 250 employees). In terms of seniority, the sample is nearly perfectly split between those who reported to have been working for more than 10 years now and those below this threshold. Average seniority is of 14 years. In terms of job level, 33.9% of the sample are professionals with no managerial responsibilities. The rest are managers (senior, middle or junior), and in particular senior and top managers account for 18% of the sample.

Respondents answered how they learn today ("how much have you learnt in this way during the past 12 months?") and how they expect to learn in 2025 ("how much would you like to learn in this way in 2025?"), both in terms of learning models (face to face, online or blended) and learning methods (instructor-led lectures, exercises and case studies' discussions, guest speakers, individual and group assignments, company visits, interactive class activities such as instant polls, web based simulations, forum discussions). They were asked to distribute a total of 100 points to the different learning models or methods depending on how much they use and would like to use each of them.

When analyzing the data, we divided and aggregated respondents' answers according to a meaningful cut-off point to create different respondent categories. We have created three categories for the usage intensity (i.e. low, medium, high) of both learning models and methods. Low use is below 30%, medium use is between 30 and 70%, high use is above 70%. We compared the percentages of responses in the various categories pertaining to questions about past usage to those obtained for questions about future usage.

4 Results and Discussion

4.1 The Use of Learning Models: Present Versus Future

With regard to learning models (see Fig. 1), nowadays respondents' learning opportunities are mainly designed adopting a traditional face to face model. 36.3% of respondents declare a high use of this learning model and 47.3% a medium use.

Looking at the future in comparison with the present (see Fig. 1), respondents aim for face to face learning remaining in use, even if only 21.6% of the respondents say they would like to keep on using it intensively (against the current 36.3%). The percentage of respondents declaring a low use of traditional learning—at least in terms of expectations—will double (from 16.3% today to 30.2% in 2025).

Respondents hope to increase the use of online learning, even more than blended one. While today less than half of respondents (48.5%) report a medium/high use of online learning, in 2025 this percentage will be 61.2%.

With regards to blended learning, 86.1% of the respondents currently make a low use of it. The trend for the future is however more positive than negative with almost

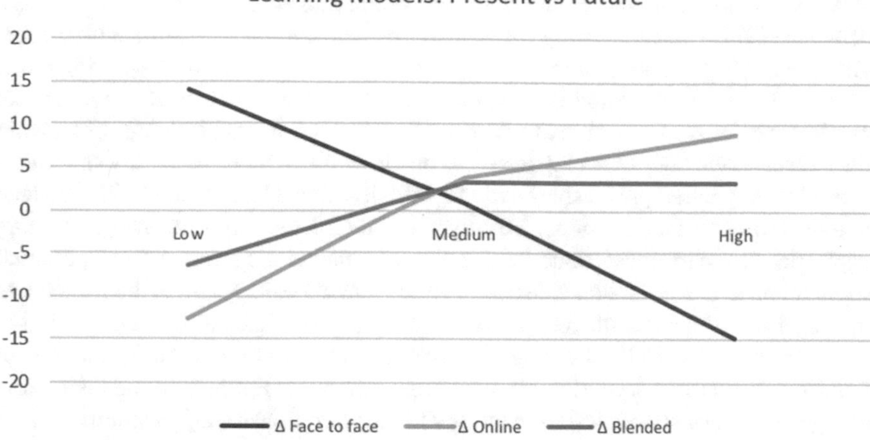

Fig. 1 Learning models: present versus desired future (low use is below 30%, medium use is between 30 and 70%, high use is above 70%). The figure shows the difference between the future use and the present use: a positive percentage implies that the usage will increase in the future compared to the present. The vertical axis expresses the forecasted variation (increase when the value is positive or decrease when the value is negative) in low, medium and high use for each learning model. For example, a +15% of low use of face to face learning implies that 15% more of respondents will have a limited use of face to face learning in the future compared to the present

a 5% increase in terms of high use. Still, only 20.4% of respondents would like to use it at a medium/high level.

These results are overall aligned with the existing literature. A recent qualitative study by Caporarello et al. [2] comparing respondents' perceptions of their current situation and expectations for the future revealed a decrease of class-based learning and an increase of digital-enhanced learning. The same trend is also evident when analyzing the past 20 years of research on learning: tech-based models and methods are increasingly studied, at the expenses of traditional face to face ones [7].

A surprising finding from our results relates to blended learning, whose trend of use for the future is only moderately increasing. Given the undoubtedly advantages of blended learning [10, 17, 25, 26] we could have expected a higher increase in its use. We might infer that there is no common and shared understanding at employees' level of what blended learning is. In fact, it is counterintuitive that respondents, who would like to overall keep on using face to face learning while increasing online learning, do not consider blended learning as ideal solution, being this, by nature, a mix of different learning models and methods.

Another finding supporting the hypothesis that the concept of blended learning is not clear is that respondents working in HR reported a significantly higher will of applying blended learning in the next future in respect to those working in other functions. We could assume that the more respondents know about blended learning and the more they are familiar with it, the more they are willing to appreciate its benefits.

Another surprising and counterintuitive finding emerges when we look at age differences. Individuals working for 10 or more years reported a significantly higher will of applying online learning in the next future in respect to those with lower seniority levels. There could be several reasons for that. First of all, more senior people have (or believe to have) less time to invest on formal training, perceiving themselves as too busy or seeing learning-on-the-job as a more valuable experience. Secondly, they rather prefer short and maybe tailor-made “knowledge pills” instead of longer face to face sessions. Thirdly, they might see online learning as more appropriate to learn those digital skills the job market asks for. A final potential explanation is that they don’t “trust” training anymore in terms of being able to provide them with the skills they need, and they perceive face to face classes as too much theory-based and not enough experience-based to be a good investment of their time. In all these scenarios, relevant implications for HR people and instructors emerge when it comes to design the flow of the different learning programs.

4.2 Learning Methods: Present Versus Future

With regard to learning methods, nowadays respondents predominantly use instructors- led lectures. Half of the sample (50.2%) in fact reports to have used this method with medium to high frequency in the last 12 months. Differently, more interactive methods such as company visits, case study discussions, as well as guests’ presentations, seem to be less applied in the majority of the cases. Overall, experiential learning approaches appear to be under-utilized in organizations as they are in educational environments.

Differences arise among employees with different age and job seniority. In particular individuals with less than 10 years of work experience reported a significantly higher use of teachers’ lectures and a lower use of case studies discussion in the past 12 months in respect to those of higher seniority level. We can explain this finding in light of the fact that HR develops less standard and more experiential learning opportunities (with only a little component of lecture-based teaching) for the more senior and demanding people within the organization.

For the future, overall respondents wish a less intensive use of the lectures carried out by the instructor (see Fig. 2). This is coherent with recent discussions about the greater effectiveness of active learning and experiential learning [1, 2, 27, 28].

For the other learning methods there are no relevant variations. This can suggest that employees are overall satisfied with how they learn or face difficulties in imaging a “new future”. This raises a challenge for the HR function, whose responsibility is also related to the design and communication of a new way of corporate learning.

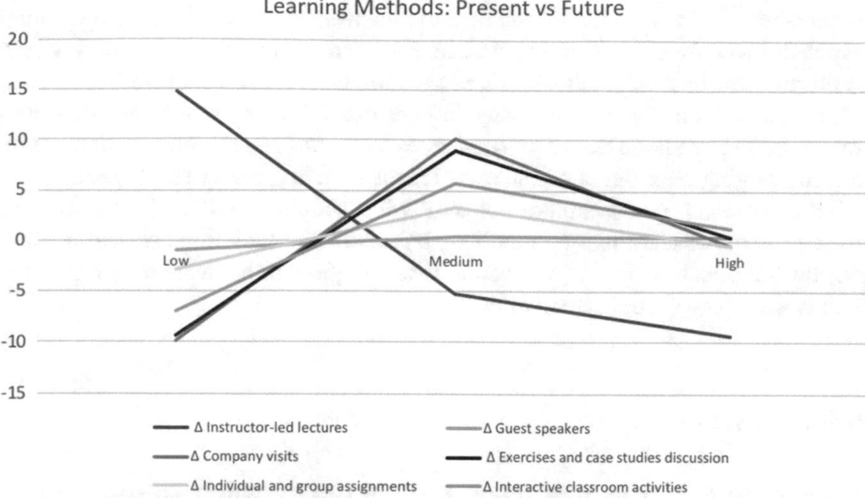

Fig. 2 Learning methods: present versus desired future (low use is below 30%, medium use is between 30 and 70%, high use is above 70%). The figure shows the difference between the future use and the present use: a positive percentage implies that the usage will increase in the future compared to the present. The vertical axis expresses the forecasted variation (increase when the value is positive or decrease when the value is negative) in low, medium and high use for each learning method. For example, a +15% of low use of instructor-led lectures implies that 15% more of respondents will have a limited use of them in the future compared to the present

5 Conclusions

With this paper, we aim to provide both a research-oriented contribution and a practice- oriented one in the field of learning within organizations.

From a research point of view, we compare the current vs. desired use of different learning models and learning methods, from the perspective of the employees. By doing so, we offer insights with regards to the expected evolution of learning within organizations, from the perspective of those who should take advantage of the learning initiatives. Our results confirm, with quantitative data, the existing debate in the literature with regard to the increase of digital enhanced learning models and active and experiential learning methods. Yet our results also suggest that blended learning, despite being among the most discussed terms nowadays, needs additional research to clarify it. Considering the results of our study, we can assume that employees are often not aware of what blended learning really is. They wish to keep on using face to face while increasing online learning, yet they do not take into account blended learning as an option, even if we know that actually it is the learning model that effectively mixes traditional and online learning.

From a practice point of view, we offer HR professionals suggestions for better designing effective learning experiences and for better communicating them to the employees. From a design point of view, our results show that younger participants are more exposed to a lecture-based face to face learning which is less experiential, despite the need for active learning at all levels. More senior employees, instead, aim for more online learning in the future, suggesting that face to face learning for them is not anymore good "value for money". Therefore, HR could reflect on redesigning more engaging hands-on learning experiences for all targets, as well as on embarking on a challenging redesign of online experiences targeting senior employees.

Future research could explore not only what people expect and wish for their future in terms of learning opportunities, but also what they think should be more relevant and effective. In fact, we cannot take for granted that what they would like to do is what they should actually do.

References

1. Caporarello, L., Manzoni, B., & Trabelsi, L. (2020). (Digital) learning models and organizational learning mechanisms: Should organizations adopt a single learning model or multiple ones? In *"Exploring digital ecosystems: Organizational and human challenges". Springer series: Lecture notes in information systems and organisation (LNISO).*
2. Caporarello, L., Manzoni, B., Moscardo, C., & Trabelsi, L. (2020). How do we learn today and how will we learn in the future within organizations? Digitally-enhanced and personalized learning win. In "*Exploring digital ecosystems: Organizational and human challenges". Springer series: Lecture Notes in Information Systems and Organisation (LNISO).*
3. The Open University. (2017). *Trends in Learning Report 2017*. Online at https://www.open.ac.uk/business/apprenticeships/blog/trends-learning-report-2017. Retrieved January 1, 2020.
4. Beer, M. (2011). Developing an effective organization: intervention method, empirical evidence, and theory. *Research in Organizational Change and Development, 19,* 1–54.
5. Fink, L. D. (2013). *Creating significant learning experiences*. Jossey-Bass.
6. Soane, E., Truss, C., Alfes, K., Shantz, A., Rees, C., & Gatenby, M. (2012). Development and application of a new measure of employee engagement: The ISA Engagement Scale. *Human Resource Development International, 15*(5), 529–547.
7. Caporarello, L., Giovanazzi, A., & Manzoni, B. (2017). Reimagine E-learning: A proposal for a 21st learning framework. *EAI Endorsed Transactions on e-Learning, 4*(16), 1–9.
8. Garrison, D. R. (2011). *E-learning in the 21st century: A framework for research and practice.* Taylor & Francis.
9. Moore, N., & Gilmartin, M. (2010). Teaching for better learning: A blended learning pilot project with first-year geography undergraduates. *Journal of Geography in Higher Education, 34,* 327–344.
10. Al-Qahtani, A. A., & Higgins, S. E. (2013). Effects of traditional, blended and e-learning on students' achievement in higher education. *Journal of Computer Assisted Learning, 29,* 220–234.
11. Stewart, A. R., Harlow, D. B., & DeBacco, K. (2011). Students' experiences of synchronous learning in distributed environments. *Distance Education, 32*(3), 357–381.
12. Porter, W. W., Graham, C. R., Spring, K. A., & Welch, K. R. (2014). Blended learning in higher education: Institutional adoption and implementation. *Computers and Education, 75,* 185–195.
13. Kentor, H. (2015). Distance education and the evolution of online learning in the United States. *Curriculum and Teaching Dialogue, 17*, 21–34.
14. Willis Towers Watson's 2017 Global Talent Management and Rewards, and Global Workforce Studies (2017).
15. Puri, I. K. (2018). Why learning from experience is the educational wave of the future. *The Conversation.*

16. Garrison, D. R., & Kanuka, H. (2004). Blended learning: Uncovering its transformative potential in higher education. *The Internet and Higher Education, 7,* 95–105.
17. Caporarello, L., & Iñesta, A. (2016). Make blended learning happen: Conditions for a successful change process in higher education institutions. *ICST Transaction E-Education E-Learning, 3,* e2.
18. Delialioğlu, O. (2012). Student engagement in blended learning environments with lecture-based and problem-based instructional approaches. *Journal of Educational Technology and Society, 15*(3), 310–322.
19. Jensen, J. L., Kummer, T. A., & Godoy, P. D. (2015). Improvements from a flipped classroom may simply be the fruits of active learning. *CBE-Life Science Education, 14,* ar5.
20. Boss, S., Krauss, J. (2014). Reinventing Project-Based Learning: Your Field Guide to Real-World Projects in the Digital Age. *International Society for Technology in Education.*
21. Kolodner, J. L., Camp, P. J., Crismond, D., Fasse, B., Gray, J., Holbrook, J., et al. (2003). Problem-based learning meets case-based reasoning in the middle-school science classroom: Putting learning by design(tm) into practice. *The Journal of the Learning Sciences, 12*(4), 495–547.
22. Capar, G., & Tarim, K. (2015). Efficacy of the cooperative learning method on mathematics achievement and attitude: A meta-analysis research. *Education of Science: Theory and Practice, 15,* 553–559.
23. Hamari, J., Shernoff, D. J., Rowe, E., Coller, B., Asbell-Clarke, J., & Edwards, T. (2016). Challenging games help students learn: An empirical study on engagement, flow and immersion in game- based learning. *Computers in Human Behavior, 54,* 170–179.
24. Sessa, V. I., & London, M. (2015). *Continuous learning in organizations.* Psychology Press, Taylor & Francis Group.
25. Graham, C. R. (2013). Emerging practice and research in blended learning. *Handbook of Distance Education, 3.*
26. Roach, T. (2014). Student perceptions toward flipped learning: New methods to increase interaction and active learning in economics. *International Review of Economics Education, 17,* 74–84.
27. Joksimović, S., Kovanović, V., Skrypnyk, O., & Dawson, S. (2015). The history and state of online learning. *Preparing for the Digital University* 93–122.
28. Singh, A. K., & Yusoff, M. A. (2009). A comparative study between traditional learning and E-learning. In *Proceeding of Teachers and Learning Open Forum 2009* (pp. 1–7). Sarakaw: CSM.

Bedazzled by Technology

Ivanin Ivanov, Peter Bednar, and Athanasios Paraskelidis

Abstract This paper is about the socio-technical findings of a project that was carried out for an organisation in the educational sector. The main aim of the project was to explore the possibilities of developing a mobile Augmented Reality authoring tool that educators would use to create AR experiences in attempt to improve their teaching methods. A novel 'solution' was designed and prototyped, which initially seemed to have great potential, but as the project progressed it gradually became evident that although the solution was possible, it was not necessarily a good solution. The project ended up being a prime example of the nowadays common phenomenon of designing efficacious but ineffective solutions for ill-defined problems. This paper analyses the project in retrospective from a soft systems thinking point of view, reflecting on the problems and limitations of attempting to solve problems with ill-defined boundaries and requirements using hard systems thinking.

Keywords Soft systems thinking · Hard systems thinking · Augmented reality

1 Introduction

Ever since the introduction of computers and the Internet, i.e. the Third Industrial Revolution or Industry 3.0, innovation seems to be all about replacing humans [1]—chatbots, 'smart' assistants and machines making decisions instead of or on behalf of humans. This has been especially prominent in Industry 4.0 where focus was on automation. Since then, there has been a gradual mindset shift focused on the

I. Ivanov (✉) · P. Bednar · A. Paraskelidis
University of Portsmouth, Portsmouth, UK
e-mail: ivanin.val.ivanov@gmail.com

P. Bednar
e-mail: peter.bednar@port.ac.uk

P. Bednar
Lund University, Lund, Sweden

C. Metallo et al. (eds.), *Digital Transformation and Human Behavior*, Lecture Notes in Information Systems and Organisation 37,
https://doi.org/10.1007/978-3-030-47539-0_3

cooperation between man and machine, setting the foundations of Industry 5.0 [2]. However, many modern businesses appear to be forgetting that technology is meant to assist people in doing their jobs more efficiently and to empower them to be more creative and promote focus on important aspects of their jobs, instead of manual and/or repetitive tasks [1, 3]. This hinders their ability to be competitive and sustainable long-term and puts a limit on the advance of society overall. What is more, many of those businesses fail to see that just because a machine can do something that a human can, does not mean it can do it better or even as good. In fact, if a person performed as good as a common household robot vacuum cleaner—i.e. not cleaning the stairs, or under some furniture, or some harder to reach places—that would be called cheating or doing a 'lousy' job. And yet, such 'solutions' see some success mainly due to their novelty factor until people realise they don't really solve the real-world problem they are intended to and are disposed of.

The same phenomenon can be observed in businesses everywhere. Competitive advantage is what everyone is trying to gain or maintain in order to grow and climb or stay on top. Sometimes this is achieved through adopting a new, novel approach that no one asked for, providing a solution to a problem that did not exist—a prime example being the new folding smartphones [4]. Of course, it can be argued that this is what drives innovation and leads to healthy competition, ultimately being a good thing. However, more often than not companies cease to exist or suffer great consequences because of project failures, fallen victim to lack of understanding about the problem, the root cause, limitations of the solution, ambition, negligence or a mix of the above [5].

This paper is based on an exploratory project about creating an Augmented Reality (AR) authoring tool for a client in the education sector. More specifically, by how it was considered to deliver an efficacious solution, without it being effective or contributing to the business overall. The project is used as a means to illustrate the statements of the paper and show the origin of the findings, giving them context. It is not meant to be the main focus of this paper, but rather a real-world example of the points made, which when understood can be applied to a broad spectrum of cases, unfolding similarities and patterns. For this to be possible, a general background of the project is presented without going into too much details about the application itself, as those are not relevant for the main topic of this paper—namely, the issues and limitations of attempting to solve problems with ill-defined boundaries and requirements, using hard systems thinking. Nonetheless, an attempt was made to include the more important technical details that frame the problem domain, without drifting away from the topic.

2 Background

The project client was an organisation that provides accredited training services to both employees and people actively looking for employment in various vocational areas. The core area that the project was focusing on was the mechanical engineering training that the client provided.

The company's general aim in connection to their project was to improve their teaching methods through the use of AR technology. The client's project had a timeframe of three years, each considered an iteration. In the previous iterations of the project, an AR application was created that allowed tracking of mechanical engineering machines and overlaying augmentations with educational content, like videos, text, sound, images and links to external resources. As stated by the client, the objective was to reduce the time spent by instructors with students by allowing students to use an interactive app which would enhance their learning experience. Allegedly this objective was met, and it was reported that the application received great feedback from both students and staff.

However, the client wanted to have more flexibility and independence should they need to expand the AR experiences in-house or create new ones themselves. Although not explicitly stated, this lack of independence was assumed to be driven by the fact that they needed external developers—which they would have to outsource—to amend and extend the application built for them each time they acquired a new mechanical engineering machine.

This led to the client's idea of having a custom-made *mobile* AR authoring tool with their educators as end users, which was the focus of the project.

The client did not know of any other *mobile* AR authoring tools on the market, according to their research, and this was reflected in their requirements—or lack thereof. What was requested was an application to allow their trainers to create AR experiences like the ones on the initial educational app on their own. However, they hadn't seen a similar application that could do that; therefore, they did not know what exactly to ask for. The only explicit requirements were that the application should run on Android tablets and that it should be based on the Wikitude AR engine, for which the company had invested in acquiring a commercial license. This dictated the exploratory nature of the new iteration of the project and required a study on its own. Ergo, a prototyping methodology (a variation of the Rapid Application Development methodology, or RAD) was considered most suitable at the time and adopted, consisting of 4 phases: Analysis and Preliminary Design (i.e. the 'study'), Prototyping Cycles (consisting of 'build-demonstrate-refine' stages), Testing and Implementation.

The first step was to determine whether the AR engine had the capabilities needed for building such application. The main problem was the ability to *dynamically* create a tracker that would recognize a particular scene or an object. At that stage this was achieved through an external program that would create 3D trackers from pictures of an object, taken at different angles. The tracker would then have to be embedded into the application. Obviously, this process required mobile app developers with knowledge in AR and could not be expected from the educators.

Several alternatives were explored in attempt to eliminate the need of this process and using Wikitude's Instant Tracking technology to create trackers on the flight seemed promising. However, that was an immediate step back, because it only allowed tracking of a flat, 2D plane, i.e. a specific angle of an object or scene—it would not recognize a 3D object from different angles or any objects on the plane itself. It was also not nearly as accurate or robust which could be accredited to the fact that the technology was still quite young for Wikitude and not as polished. Nonetheless, it was indeed promising and, evidently, made sense to proceed with the project from a managerial perspective. After all, the assumption was that if the project was successful it could have been a great competitive advantage to the company.

After it was determined that it was indeed *possible* in theory to create an AR authoring tool based on Wikitude, an initial prototype was built as proof of concept and to confirm the hypothesis. It allowed creation of AR experiences and embedding augmentations (sound, text, video, links and 3D models) to the dynamically created trackers, persisting the experiences in storage and allowing them to be loaded in 'view' mode.

The next logical step was to research what are the issues and limitations of other AR authoring tools in education and what are some defining characteristics of successful AR authoring tools on the market, which would influence the further requirements and general direction of the project.

To summarise the findings of the study, there were no well-established Graphical User Interface (GUI) based applications for AR authoring in education at the time. Mobile AR authoring tools seemed to be a very niche topic that did not have much coverage, if at all, especially for educational purposes. There were numerous non-mobile GUI-based solutions proposed and/or prototyped over the years that did not manage to keep up with the quick advances in AR technology. Recently proposed tools employed some novel approaches and attempt to tackle *some* of the issues with GUI-based AR authoring [6, 7]. Yet, issues and limitations still persist or are not fully resolved by any GUI-based AR authoring tool for educators, such as personalisation, assessment, statistics and collaboration [8]. The main bottleneck seemed to be that only so much can be achieved through a GUI without involving coding and the fact that functionality is often sacrificed in favour of simplicity due to the target audience. Arguably the most comprehensive solution that addresses the most, but not all issues is VEDILS [9]. However, it is not a mobile solution, since that would be extremely infeasible from a usability perspective. Unfortunately, it did not seem to be a very popular solution either, giving way to commercial GUI-based AR authoring tools, attempted to be adapted on a per-use-case basis for educational purposes [10].

In terms of current commercial GUI-based products for AR authoring, there seemed to be a great choice on the market but with little variety. Most of them would have the same functionality with slightly different selling points (e.g. Amazon Sumerian, Zapworks, Augment, etc.). All commercial GUI-based AR authoring tools seemed to be either desktop applications, web-based SaaS products or mobile applications, with the latter being most niche and represented by a single iOS-only app—Torch AR. For the characteristics review—a single product of each type was reviewed, based on popularity and success. Great similarities were observed across all products with the main ones being:

- A clean and intuitive interface separated in no more than 3 sections;
- Support for common augmentations like text, images and 3D models;
- Very similar controls for manipulating augmentations;
- The canvas or working area being the main focus of the application;
- Some mechanism for importing 3D models.

There main common limitation of all tools that were reviewed was exporting and sharing AR experiences. There was either a proprietary format involved that required a specialised 'interpreter' or a lack of exporting altogether, ultimately limiting the potential use cases significantly.

The adoption of a prototyping methodology was considered to be of great benefit at the time, because it allowed requirements flexibility. Newly requested or 'thought-to-be-useful' features were rapidly prototyped and presented, leading to a decision of whether they should be adopted or not, which was highly valued by the client. However, what was not considered was the fact that such requirements flexibility did not make much sense for the very short and strict timeframe of the project. Although this did not end up being as big problem as anticipated in the end, there was a very high risk of going over the deadline or budget, which was accepted *surprisingly* light-heatedly. Another thing worth mentioning is that the prototype demonstrations were presented to the project mediator representing the client and not the end users, i.e. the educators employed by the client, due to organisational and logistical constraints. Eventually it turned out that they were not involved in the decision-making process, despite the importance given to requirements flexibility.

Later it gradually became more and more evident that just because it was possible to build such a 'solution', that did not mean it was necessarily going to be a *good* solution. Neither it meant that it would contribute to the business overall, outside of its immediate purpose that it was designed around, which turned out not to be what the educators needed.

3 Discussion

Although the main focus of the study was to explore the possibility and feasibility of creating a tool that would benefit the client, an important aspect was observed from a socio-technical perspective that emerged quite early in the project. It was the common phenomenon of implementing efficacious but ineffective solutions for vague or ill-defined problems.

Such situations are often the product of lack of understanding and distinction between 'soft' and 'hard' systems thinking [11]. The terms are well contrasted in the works of Peter Checkland, and especially in his paper, written two years after the publication of STSP, about the 'crisis' in Operations Research [12]. His critical discussion is focused on O.R. representing a '*systematic* search for an efficient means of achieving a defined objective', rather than being *systemic* in the traditional sense of systems thinking, stemming from organismic biology [12]. In other words, the critique is about O.R. practices where logic about parts of a situation is aggregated to make conclusions about the whole situation that don't really apply to it. The problem originates from the fact that the system can exhibit properties that the sum of its parts doesn't. These are the so called "emergent properties". The term 'holon', suggested by Koestler [13, 14], was adopted as an alternative to 'system' for the abstract idea of a whole having emergent properties, a layered structure and processes of communication and control to enable it (in principle) to survive a changing environment; and also to separate the meaning of 'system' from its common use in everyday life.

The fundamental difference between 'soft' and 'hard' systems thinking is that hard systems thinking assumes that the perceived world contains holons. Hard systems thinking is based on scientific reductionism, assuming the problem situation has exact static boundaries and can be broken down and analysed through its parts *systematically* [11]. On the contrary, soft systems thinking accepts that there is no single 'truth' about a problem situation because of the ever-changing flux of events and ideas that is reality, as coined by Vickers [15]. Soft systems thinking takes the stance that the process of enquiry into a fuzzy, ill-defined problem situation itself can be appreciated [16]. In that sense, hard systems thinking can successfully be used when engaging with rather well-defined problems, whereas soft systems thinking is intended to support people addressing messy, ill-structured problem situations.

In the case of the project that is in focus for this study, initially a 'hard' systems thinking approach was taken to a, clearly, ill-defined, fuzzy problem. It was assumed that a solution could be engineered that would allow non-qualified people to effectively do a job that required highly-qualified people. Logically, this implied that it was also assumed that knowledge can be re-engineered into a technological solution. Naturally, this is not possible, since knowledge is the ability to use information, acquired through experience and thought processes, unique to each individual [17, 18]. Although knowledge can be diffusive—tends to leak and can be reproduced by other people through learning (for example, imitation)—it cannot be isolated and distributed physically; that would be just data. Nonetheless, once data is understood—i.e. attributed meaning in context—it becomes information, which people can then learn to use, becoming knowledge [16–18]. However, that would make those people 'qualified' and the technological solution would not have a purpose. Evidently, the client didn't understand that, since they wanted non-qualified people and a technological solution substituting their lack of knowledge in a particular area, instead of highly qualified people in the same area. This doomed the project from the very beginning.

Assuming that executive decisions for exploratory projects are not made lightheartedly and without solid backing of figures and well-calculated risk, possibly it was estimated that investing in the 'solution' and utilising existing or hiring more human resource with the same qualification level for the job would be more cost-effective long term than hiring highly-qualified personnel. And that appears to be a perfectly valid reason from a managerial standpoint. But it can also be a problem when decisions are made in isolation and solutions are designed based on hard assumptions about reality—i.e. when the context of the problem is not understood. Although the risk of this project appeared to have been accepted, it was evidently misinterpreted, since, as already discussed, the problem was not fully understood to begin with, and neither were the limitations of the solution.

Unfortunately, this is a common occurrence in our technology-driven society, as evident by the high failure rate of IT projects [5]. Technology has become so ubiquitous and easily accessible that it seems to have led to an inevitable mindset shift of the modern-day human. People—especially the recent generations—have become used to having all their questions answered by 'smart' devices, which are usually at a hand's reach and have become part of everyday life; taken for granted. It seems like technology is assumed to be the solution for every problem, and this assumption about reality gets transferred to businesses, as well. More often than not, technology-first solutions are adopted (see agenda for Industry 4.0 [19]), instead of people-first solutions (see socio-technical approach [1] and agenda for Industry 5.0 [2]). Prime examples include robot vacuum cleaners with performance and efficacy issues that a human caretaker would be criticised for; fully-robotised hotels that are more of an inconvenience, rather than luxury or 'the step forward'—like the world's first robot hotel where management had to 'lay off' their 243 robot 'employees' [20, 21]; and, of course, the project in focus here—a mobile application to replace knowledge and qualification. The thing that all of these have in common (along with many other, less apparent examples) is that they attempt to solve a problem that either does not exist, is not understood, or is based on strong assumptions about the problem that don't reflect reality. The 'solutions' that are provided are only 'solutions' in a static, non-changing, well-defined environment; exactly the opposite of the real world—dynamic, ever-changing, fuzzy. This can be considered an example of sub-optimisation and reductionist thinking. As consequence, those 'solutions' simply cannot survive the real world and cause unintended consequences. In return, those unintended consequences can create problems that are not worth the 'solution'. That is the difference between thinking about a problem from a 'soft' and 'hard' systems perspective—hard systems thinking assumes that reality can be predicted and accurately modelled.

The same applies to the AR authoring tool prototype built as part of this project. It proves that it is possible to fulfil the client's *technical* request. However, it is not an effective solution from a trainer's point of view. It addresses the problem from a managerial point of view—trainers can now create their own AR experiences and developers are not needed anymore. But the capabilities of the 'solution' prototype are extremely limited, and what is worse—they cannot be extended much further. The prototype was already pushing the acceptable performance limit of the same device that was used for the initial educational application with minimal functionality. Surely, more powerful hardware can be acquired that would run the authoring application better, but then, as more features are incorporated, usability issues start to emerge. For example, even with just a handful of buttons and sliders, some participants in the usability study of the prototype noted that the sliders were not easy enough to use due to their size and lead to miss-clicks and unintentional errors. Some of them were replaced by two-finger gestures, like pinching and rotating, but it was immediately discovered that those were not intuitive enough and quite performance intensive, causing the device to stutter and make the process even more frustrating. In the end, the sliders were brought back, making them a bit bigger. But then there is only so much that can be displayed on a 10-inch tablet, so it was all about balancing features with usability. And usability would always take precedence, since there's no use of a feature if it cannot be used in a way that ultimately benefits the user.

This opens up discussion on the correlation between 'usable' and 'useful'. In the case of this project, making the application more usable—i.e. easier to use—would reciprocate by rendering it less useful—contributing to a purpose. Again, a bigger device with more screen real-estate could be acquired, but to what extent before a laptop becomes the better and more compact choice? It would always have the capacity for more processing power and would separate the input devices from the working surface, allowing for much more flexibility from a usability perspective.

Another major problem was that the prototyped 'solution' would not contribute to effective teaching, which requires student monitoring, assessment and personalisation of interactions [8]. And that is not because it is not possible to implement those features, but because it would be infeasible from a usability perspective [10]. The cause of this problem was that it was not considered by management to begin with, since its complexity was underestimated. And the root of that cause is that they had fallen victim to hard systems thinking in a situation that does not allow it, leading to the assumption that there are clearly defined boundaries, in which a problem can live in isolation. In that situation it is clear that there was group separation between 'management' and 'the educators' with no effective communication channels between the two. And that is obvious from the fact that the requirements communicated by the 'management' group of stakeholders did not include any that would ensure effective teaching, although it is at the core of the business as a whole. Moreover, unlike in previous stages, in this stage of the company's project the potential students were outside of the stakeholder scope, although they add yet another level of complexity. This is a prime example of the Darkness Principle in Systems Theory. There are some variations of how it is interpreted but the general idea is the same—the elements of a system are ignorant of the behavior of the system as a whole and respond only to local stimuli/information [22]. A different variation of the Darkness Principle by Clemson states that 'no system can be known completely' [23]. Again, this can be interpreted as a condensed statement implying that each element of a system has its own ever-changing perception of reality that never contains the whole complexity of the system; therefore, a system can never be known to its entirety. Nonetheless, it can always be attempted to understand what is studied as a system from as many perspectives as possible, starting with the identified stakeholders. In the context of the project subject to analysis in this paper, it is evident that the problem was analysed from a single point of view, which was proof of an attempt to treat a complex problem like a complicated one by breaking it down and isolating its parts. This led to a false perception about reality and any solution designed for it was bound to fail.

Nonetheless, the failure would usually not be evident until it is already too late, which is normally when the solution is introduced back into the real world. And that is because of the single point of view that was taken into account—see similar discussion in [1, 5, 11, 12, 15]. That way, the particular perception of reality cannot be compared to anything else, introducing 'tunnel vision', which in turn makes judging right and wrong nearly impossible, because there is no alternative. And even if a particular judgement is right in a particular context, it may be wrong for the whole of the problem situation. A similar phenomenon can be observed in statistics under the large class of association paradoxes. One of the better-known ones being the Simpson's Paradox, where trends that appear when a dataset is separated into groups reverse when the data are aggregated [24]—i.e. the 'truth' of the parts is not the 'truth' of the whole. What should also be noted is the use of the word 'paradox' for phenomena that appear illogical from a hard systems thinking perspective but are expected and normal from a soft systems perspective. The problem illustrated with the Simpson's Paradox is obviously transferable to systems theory and is about boundaries. Putting boundaries within and around a *real-life* problem situation—i.e. breaking it down and attempting to tackle each part individually; a reductionist approach—is bound to lead to a solution that will fail in the real world, since those artificial boundaries do not exist there. The limitation of applying hard systems thinking to complex problems manifests as the inability to judge reality accurately, because it is assumed to be static, and that there is a single truth about it, therefore missing out on the real-world complexity.

In the context of the project in focus this could have been avoided by including all stakeholders in the analysis of the problem and any potential solutions—suitable approaches would have been through contextual analysis and SSM [11, 16]. Having multiple points of view and inputs from different parts of the organisation would open up discussions about emerging issues and conflicts that can be addressed before investing resources and committing to the project. It can even be argued that in-house projects have higher probability of success than ones, the development of which is outsourced.

This is partially related to the incentive or motivation of the team executing the project. At the end of the day, the success (or lack thereof) of a project would reflect much more on an in-house team, as opposed to an outsourced team. A failed project may cost an outsourced team a potential client, but not necessarily, if they have delivered exactly what they were asked for and fulfilled their part of the contract, which just happens to not be what the client needed. On the other hand, an in-house team would suffer much greater consequences from a failed project, potentially costing them a budget reduction, a salary cut, or even their jobs if the failure is devastating to the business overall. In that sense, in-house teams have much higher incentive to point out problems, flaws and conflicts of potential solutions so measures can be taken to prevent a project failure.

Nonetheless, it can be argued that failure is what can lead to progress. If people are not allowed to fail, they would never learn from their mistakes, which could gradually lead to a twisted perception of 'right' and 'wrong', caused by the lack of experience with both ends of the spectrum [25]. Furthermore, if *forbidden* to fail, people will try to hide their failure, so they don't suffer the consequences, bound to cause a disturbance in the environment. The 'out of sight, out of mind' principle would not work long-term, and that failure would surface eventually and could cause much more damage than anticipated—and not only to the person responsible, as we know from many historical events [26, 27].

But more importantly, because an in-house team is part of the problem situation—they know and have experienced the *real* environment. In contrast, an outsourced consulting team may attempt to inquire into the problem situation, but the sole act of intervention can lead to a false perception about reality. This is because the process of inquiry can be considered an appreciative system, according to the Appreciative Systems Theory [15], meaning that it contributes to the flux of events and ideas that is reality. Furthermore, such an external stimulus can cause a response from the environment—for example, people may act differently and do things they would not normally do, or in a different way. This ultimately leads to a false perception about the problem situation and can potentially render any solutions engineered for the perceived version irrelevant to the real one.

4 Conclusion

What was concluded from the project was that even though the prototype proved that is was possible to create such an application, it was fundamentally flawed. At the time, it was clearly evident that the AR engine was not meant for the purposes it was attempted to be used for, so it couldn't be used neither effectively, nor efficiently. In fact, the client thought they were innovating because they did not know of any other mobile AR authoring apps on the market for educational purposes. Turns out there was a reason for that—the technology was not mature enough and there were inherent issues with mobile devices related to usability that cripple potential apps of that sort.

Another important finding was that the project was a prime example of the nowadays common phenomenon of designing efficacious but ineffective solutions for ill-defined problems. As with most projects of the kind, the client had fallen victim to hard systems thinking where the real situation would not allow it. As a consequence, that lead to their lack of understanding about the problem, the solution and its limitations, and the boundaries of the problem situation. In turn, that caused them to misinterpret the risks and assume that there was a single root cause to their *perceived* 'problem' for which a solution could be engineered. In other words, they were *bedazzled* by the technology the solution utilised, deciding to proceed with it and outsourcing its development. Ultimately, they got what they *wanted*, but not what they *needed* [28–30].

References

1. Mumford, E. (2003). *Redesigning human systems*. Hershey, PA: Idea Group Publishing.
2. Ostergaard, E. (2018). Factory Automation: Welcome to Industry 5.0. https://www.isa.org/intech/20180403/. The International Society of Automation.
3. Bednar, P. (2018). *Socio-technical toolbox*. University of Portsmouth.
4. Savov, V.(2019). The galaxy fold makes no sense as a consumer device yet. https://www.theverge.com/2019/2/21/18233917/samsung-galaxy-fold-price-features-consumer-worth-buying-editorial.
5. Williams, P. (2007). Make sure you get a positive return. *Computer Weekly*.
6. Yang, Y., Shim, J., Chae, S., & Han, T. (2016). Mobile augmented reality authoring tool. In *2016 IEEE Tenth International Conference on Semantic Computing (ICSC)*.
7. Yang, Y., Shim, J., Chae, S., & Han, T. (2016). Interactive augmented reality authoring system using mobile device as input method. In *2016 IEEE International Conference on Systems, Man, and Cybernetics (SMC)*.
8. Bacca, J., Baldiris, S., Fabregat, R., Kinshuk, & Graf, S. (2015). Mobile augmented reality in vocational education and training. *Procedia Computer Science, 75*, 49–58
9. Mota, J., Ruiz-Rube, I., Dodero, J., & Arnedillo-Sánchez, I. (2018). Augmented reality mobile app development for all. *Computers and Electrical Engineering, 65*, 250–260.
10. Vert, S., & Andone, D. (2017). Zero-programming augmented reality authoring tools for educators: Status and recommendations. In *2017 IEEE 17th International Conference on Advanced Learning Technologies (ICALT)*.
11. Checkland, P., & Holwell, S. (1998). *Information, systems and information systems*. Chichester: Wiley.
12. Checkland, P. (1983). O.R. and the systems movement: Mappings and conflicts. *Journal of the Operational Research Society, 34*, 661–675.
13. Koestler, A. (1978). *Janus: A summing up*. London: Hutchinson.
14. Koestler, A. (1967). *The ghost in the machine*. London: Hutchinson.
15. Vickers, G. (1965). *The art of judgement: A study of policy making*. US: Springer.
16. Checkland, P., & Scholes, J. (1990). *Soft systems methodology in action*. Chichester: Wiley.
17. Langefors, B. (1966). *Theoretical analysis of information systems*. Lund: Studentlitteratur.
18. Langefors, B. (1995). *Essays on infology*. Lund: Studentlitteratur.
19. Sniderman, B., Mahto, M., & Cotteleer, M. (2016). *Industry 4.0 and manufacturing ecosystems: Exploring the world of connected enterprises*. Deloitte.
20. W, A. (2019). *Why the world's first robot hotel was a disaster*. https://www.economist.com/gulliver/2019/03/27/why-the-worlds-first-robot-hotel-was-a-disaster. Washington, DC: The Economist.
21. Gale, A., & Mochizuki, T. (2019). Robot hotel loses love for robots. *Wall Street Journal*. https://www.wsj.com/articles/robot-hotel-loses-love-for-robots-11547484628.
22. Masys, A. (2015). *Applications of systems thinking and soft operations research in managing complexity*. Springer International Publishing.
23. Clemson, B. (1991). *Cybernetics: A new management tool*. Philadelphia: Abacus Press.
24. Berman, S., DalleMule, L., Greene, M., & Lucker, J. (2012). Simpson's paradox: A cautionary tale in advanced analytics. https://www.statslife.org.uk/the-statistics-dictionary/2012-simpson-s-paradox-a-cautionary-tale-in-advanced-analytics. American Statistical Association, The Statistics Dictionary.
25. Bateson, G. (2000). *Steps to an ecology of mind*. Chicago: University of Chicago Press.
26. Medvedev, Z. (1992). *The legacy of chernobyl*. New York: W.W. Norton & Co.
27. Marino, F., & Nunziata, L. (2018). Long-term consequences of the chernobyl radioactive fallout: An exploration of the aggregate data. *The Milbank Quarterly, 96*, 814–857.
28. Albert, T., & Ramis, H. (2000). *Bedazzled*. United States: Regency Enterprises.
29. Cook, P., & Donen, S. (1967). *Bedazzled*. United Kingdom: 20th Century Fox.
30. Goethe, J. (1808). *Faust*.

Socio-Technical Interplay in a Two-Sided Market: The Case of Learning Platforms

Anna Sigridur Islind, Livia Norström, Helena Vallo Hult, and Suzana Ramadani Olsson

Abstract The rise of the platform era changes the way interactions are structured and enables transactions at a distance. The platform phenomena also enables co-creation of content, shifting the way services are delivered across diverse boundaries. This is especially apparent in workplaces, where the developments change roles, relationships and conditions for teaching and learning, creating the possibility of a two-sided market. From a socio-technical and socio-cultural learning perspective, this study primarily aims for a better understanding of platforms in higher educational settings. Using a learning platform as an illustrative case, we argue for platform context transactions that are not monetary transactions. The main contribution of the paper is to offer a discussion where we problematize the transactional concept in two-sided markets. The findings shed new light on emerging challenges and tensions in the interplay between the constant change of technology and what it means to work in such change. This has implications for both teaching and learning and offers insights that can be valuable for understanding the shift to online learning during the recent pandemic of covid-19.

Keywords Two-sided market · Platforms · Learning platform · Transactions · Higher education · Socio-technical interplay · Online learning · Covid-19

A. S. Islind (✉)
School of Computer Science, Reykjavik University, Reykjavik, Iceland
e-mail: islind@ru.is

L. Norström
Division of Informatics, University of Gothenburg, Gothenburg, Sweden

H. Vallo Hult · S. R. Olsson
School of Business, Economics and IT, University West, Trollhattan, Sweden

H. Vallo Hult
NU Hospital Group, Trollhattan, Sweden

C. Metallo et al. (eds.), *Digital Transformation and Human Behavior*, Lecture Notes in Information Systems and Organisation 37,
https://doi.org/10.1007/978-3-030-47539-0_4

1 Introduction

The rise of the platform era is changing the way services are delivered as platforms enable different types of transactions at a distance. The development is rapid and multidimensional, raising various socio-technical questions around issues about trust, ethics, responsibility and privacy that are influenced by transactions enabled by platforms [1]. Studies on workplace technology have historically focused on specific systems and tools provided by the organization, in contrast to private use based on individual choice [2, 3]. Now, the emergence of platforms and ubiquitous technologies are blurring the boundaries between professional and personal use; shifting the focus in the field of IS and related disciplines from organizational, individual or group interactions with single technologies to platforms and artifact ecologies [4–8]. This shift brings diverse challenges and an immense cultural shift that affects various contexts in society. Higher education that enables teachers and students to switch between the classroom and meet through learning platforms is one such context. The context of higher education is changing rapidly, a change which has been especially apperent during the recent pandemic of covid-19.

The socio-technical systems work of Mumford and of Checkland, adopted in UK and Scandinavia [9–11], created an opening for qualitative and critical perspectives in IS research early on [12]. Over the past years, there has been renewed attention to the relationship between the social and the technical, in the light of the ongoing transformation of work and society, and the increased interest in platforms and artifact ecologies. The socio-technical approach, especially the Scandinavian school, is still thriving within modern IS research and, as we argue in this paper, is highly relevant for understanding two-sided markets in learning environments. Conceptualizations of digital infrastructures and platforms in prior literature have emphasized the socio-technical aspects [1, 13], however much of the research on two-sided markets and platforms address large-scale platforms and merely sees the transactional concept as an economical transaction. More insight is needed on socio-technical aspects of how small-scale platforms can be configured within local contexts in order to enable other types of transactions [1, 14, 15]. In this study, we use a learning platform as an illustrative case in order to argue for platform context transactions that are not monetary, which outlines a gap in the literature, addressed as the primary aim of this study. Even though most universities use learning platforms, they are not necessarily supportive of neither the features needed by the students nor the teachers, which brings us to the secondary aim of shedding light on the needs within a learning platform context. This dual aim is addressed herein as little is known about what is needed for learning to be exchanged online on the one hand, and offline on the other hand and how the socio-technical interplay between the classroom and the learning platform is actualized.

The two-sided market perspective is, until this point, applied to economic exchange, whereas we, in this paper, argue for other aspects being exchanged in a two-sided market. Consequently, we argue that *learning* can be such an exchange in a two-sided platform. To elaborate on the context of learning platforms, we see that students in higher education have access to high-quality lectures and expertise from top universities and institutions which include subjects their teachers may not be knowledgeable in. Massive online open courses (MOOCs) and other forms of distance learning compete with traditional campus-based education. It raises questions about how education today can be complemented by MOOCs and the freely accessible learning materials flourishing on the Internet. Similarly, parts of higher education are increasingly digitalized, especially due to changed work situations in the lock-downs following the pandemic, and the shift between online and offline needs to be examined carefully. In traditional higher education, the one does not outweigh the other; instead it is an interplay between the classroom interactions and the learning platform, an interplay that is not always seamlessly fitted.

The main contribution of this paper is to offer a discussion where we problematize the transactional concept in two-sided markets. We also provide a discussion, from a teacher perspective, on how they see their role in engaging students in *learning to learn* and the socio-technical interplay of shifting between classroom and platform interactions. Our research is guided by socio-technical and socio-cultural perspectives, using concepts from the platform literature and two-sided markets, illustrated with examples from interviews with university teachers and the authors' own teaching experiences.

The remaining part of the paper is structured as follows: The following section provides an overview of related literature, where the concept of performance and two-sided markets are elaborated on. In this section, we also present central theoretical concepts guiding this research. Section three presents the results of the learning exchange in the platform, followed by the final section, where learning platforms as two-sided markets are discussed and reflected on from a socio-technical perspective.

2 Related Work and Theoretical Background

Lifelong learning is a concept used to illustrate the will to create the motivation for students to learn in school (in this case, higher education), and to apply the technique through the working life and in that way, continue to learn. More precisely, this means that the tools and methods for learning that take place in higher education can also be developed through future work [16–21]. However, there is a lack of success in creating commitment and interaction in learning platforms where students and teachers learn together. The students expect teachers to "deliver" the knowledge to them, which often takes form through discussions about formalities around the examination and dissatisfaction with the assessment. In some cases, this may trigger or intensify lacking incentives to pursue one's own learning, and the students fail to understand how digital tools and methods for learning can be used as a facilitator of (a) learning here and now, and (b) for lifelong learning, even after their education is completed, and when working life has begun. Diminishing the boundaries between formal learning and increasing an understanding of lifelong learning improves the likelihood that the student will use the tools learned during education as a lifelong learning tool [22].

Since the introduction of Learning Management Systems (LMS) during the late 1990s, many studies have examined the success factors of using LMS, including various technical and non-technical factors [cf 23, 24]. In IS research, much focus has been on areas such as knowledge management systems and support for knowledge sharing, whereas surrounding communities of IS, for instance, CSCW and HCI have commonly been concerned with evaluations of learning in terms of user behavior, often from cognitive perspectives, with the purpose to inform the design of information systems, such as LMS's. Likewise, in knowledge management studies, learning is often not articulated; instead, the focus is placed on outcomes or effects of learning (efficiency, competitive advantages, cost reductions, etc.) rather than learning per se [20, 25–27].

There are other aspects and tensions of meeting through digital technology that is worth unfolding when talking about the socio-technical arrangement of introducing and using a learning platform where teaching and learning are exchanged. Sennett [28] states that modern society is attempting to destroy the evils of routine by favoring the flexibility of organizations and for workers. Moving the increasing workload of teaching and learning into learning platforms, enables flexibility that is both liberating and constraining. Accordingly, for flexibility to work in modern society, humans would need to have the skillset of trees and to be able to bend and yield but then go back to their original form [28]. However, flexibility also entails providing students with an environment to learn at all hours, which brings us back to the value exchange in such a platform, on the one hand, for the teachers, and on the other hand, for the students. Shifting between the classroom context and the learning platform is not straightforward.

Thus, to survive in a flexible learning environment, there is a growing need for personal preservation and individual sustainability. Knowing how far the teachers can push the students, and knowing how to facilitate a flexible learning community, is something trees seem much better at than humans. This study explores the teachers' role as facilitators and therefore examines the teachers' side of the platform context by focusing on university students' learning from a teacher's perspective. We propose a socio-technical *tool* (i.e. digital teaching and learning material with the focus on facilitating learning between the two) which enables a deeper understanding on how, and for what purposes digital platforms can be used, and how and in what way educational methods can be used and mixed to facilitate the learning exchange. For this, we use the socio-technical approach to information systems, where both social and technical aspects are taken into consideration alongside socio-cultural learning perspectives as a framework.

2.1 A Socio-Technical Perspective

To understand performance in two-sided markets and how the learning exchange happens as a socio-technical process, we will first elaborate on the socio-technical literature in IS research. The socio-technical approach is based on the relationship between the social and technical systems. The social system consists of professionals and their practices, cultures and roles, while the technical system consists of the technologies that support the work processes of the social system. The socio-technical approach is well known in the Scandinavian school of information systems, where early systems development was affected almost equally by social, political, technological and economic factors, with the organization seen as comprised of both social and technical element. Seminal work such as Mumford's sociological studies on socio-technical systems in the UK in the mid-sixties [e.g. 29], influenced Checkland [9], who in turn, influenced Scandinavian research as a response to union concerns aiming for workplace democracy. The ideas of Mumford and Checkland interacted with the political forces in play to form the Scandinavian systems development tradition [e.g. 30, 31].

Historically, the socio-technical approach aimed to overcome the opposition between technological and social determinism. It has in turn been criticized for either favoring the technical or the social [32–34], and for being an instrumental, normative tradition, and the practical impact of the practices involved in socio-technical research has been questioned [e.g. 35–37]. In recent years, the focus of the research done from a socio-technical perspective has shifted. In the early years, the research focused on altering the practices to fit the technical system, whereas today the focus is more on socio-technical design where both the practices involved and the digital artifacts are viewed in an interplay in which both need to be carefully designed and adapted [38]. An inherent ontological distinction between technology and the social has however, been preserved even in recent socio-technical studies, which validate "the viability of a socio-technical approach" [39, p. 385].

Within the socio-technical tradition, there is also a "socio-technical toolbox" [40] consisting of analytical tools that can be used by practitioners and scholars to learn IS as a practice and as a discipline. The toolbox helps to analyze, conceptualize, and understand complex transformation processes within contemporary workplaces. Bednar and Sadok [41] divide the toolbox into eight categories: "change analysis, system structure definition, system purpose, system perspectives, system priorities, desirable system, system action and system for evaluation and engagement" [41, p. 5]. The toolbox is designed to support learning about business system design and has been compared to action research in which practitioners are heavily involved in activities in the workplace to learn and understand the complexity of change in organizations. An important purpose of using the toolbox is to be aware of one's own contextual understanding and simultaneously understand others' by engaging in activities that can enable actors to make sense of the differences. From a socio-technical perspective, a digital tool can be conceptualized as a tool for creating knowledge; for instance, a tool for teachers to enable lifelong learning for students. As described by Treem and Leonardi [42] visibility, persistence over time, and edibility are characteristic affordances of such tools.

A socio-technical approach aligns with a socio-cultural learning perspective discussed below, as both evolved in response to positivist and simplified views of causality (e.g., learning as transfer of knowledge or technology as cause of change). Instead, these perspectives address the emergent dynamics of people interacting with others—including technologies—in a situated context. Thus, suitable to study technology use in complex social practices such as higher education and online learning and teaching.

2.2 A Socio-cultural Perspective

Koschmann [43] elaborates on learning from a socio-cultural perspective and claims that learning takes place in context and that knowledge develops in the interaction with other people. Research and practice interests relate to the use of technology for collaboration and problem-based learning (rather than instructional efficacy, competence or transfer) and a corresponding focus on process rather than outcomes. Similarly, Brown and Adler [44] explain the concept of "social learning" as learning where the understanding of the content and context is socially constructed through conversations about the content and interactions with others about problems or actions. The focus is on how learning occurs rather than on what is learned. Learning is not seen as a characteristic of individuals but of a relationship between those who teach and the world around it. There is a similarity between Brown and Adler's description of social learning and Carmean and Haefner's [45] principles for deeper learning which argue that learning is a result of a meaningful understanding of material and content. This deeper learning occurs when learning is social, active, contextual, engaging and student-owned. Research has shown that to understand, analyze, apply and save information to long-term memory; the learner (e.g. the student) must actively engage in the material. Bates [46] uses experiential learning as an umbrella concept, referring to "learning by doing", as a teaching approach where learning takes place within real contexts.

A transmissive learning perspective is, in contrast to the social learning approach, based on psychological, cognitive, and behavioristic theories, where learning is viewed as something individual, cognitive processes that can be transferred between individuals. Bates [46], emphasizes the importance of mixing different perspectives on learning so that different skills are favored, such as conceptual, practical, personal, and social. For example, students need to learn facts, principles, standard procedures and the like before they can start a well-founded discussion on the subject or before they can begin to solve problems. As such, teachers can apply both transmissive and socio-cultural approaches in their teaching. Traditional classroom lectures and students' own readings are examples of transmissive teaching methods, whereas seminars, workshops and supervision often involve activities of social interaction and thus social learning.

Although our approach to learning is based on a socio-cultural perspective, we see the importance of using transmissive based methods to strengthen a breadth of skills. It is important to see the learning on a course or program from a holistic perspective, where certain perspectives on learning are emphasized in certain parts and some in others. We believe that there is a need for new ways of thinking of learning platforms that provide learning opportunities for individuals to learn how to learn, while at the same time learning how to use the technology, both as students and in professional life.

3 Method

As described in the previous section, we have a socio-technical view, meaning that it is in the interaction between the digital and the technical—in practice—where learning takes place. In addition, our view on learning is based on a constructivist, socio-cultural perspective where the context and the social interaction between people are essential. What triggered our interest in this particular problem is that the reason behind specific methods for teaching in higher education is not always transparent to our students. With teaching methods, we refer to how the teaching is designed based on a view of learning, choice of supportive material, place (physical or online) and how these link to the subject [46]. As teachers, we are often not transparent with our pedagogical motives for the teaching methods and the tools we choose to use, and we often take for granted that the concepts we use are sufficiently accepted for everyone to understand. To elaborate, when we as teachers refer to a seminar, the students do not always understand without guidance what a seminar or a workshop is, what is expected of them as participants, how to prepare if it is mandatory and if so, what participation means.

For that reason, we have developed a tool for teachers to promote a learning spirit that stimulates engagement, interaction, and lifelong learning through the learning platform. This tool is a learning tool, intended to serve as a common learning area, to develop knowledge about, and to create a consensus around, the types of teaching methods used. It is primarily aimed to function as a basis for discussion and learning internally in the teacher's team, but can also be used as a learning object for the students, and an object for teachers to refer to when they talk about different types of teaching with the students. The intention is that the tool or learning object functions as a "buffet" of ideas about learning and technology and how they interact with the subject [TPACK, e.g. 47], which can be put together as one wants based on the circumstances of the teaching. The idea is that it is in fact a dynamic tool that is developed together with all teachers involved over time. The learning tool is created and accessible in the learning platform, Canvas, for all teachers to explore and is presented as a course (see Fig. 1).

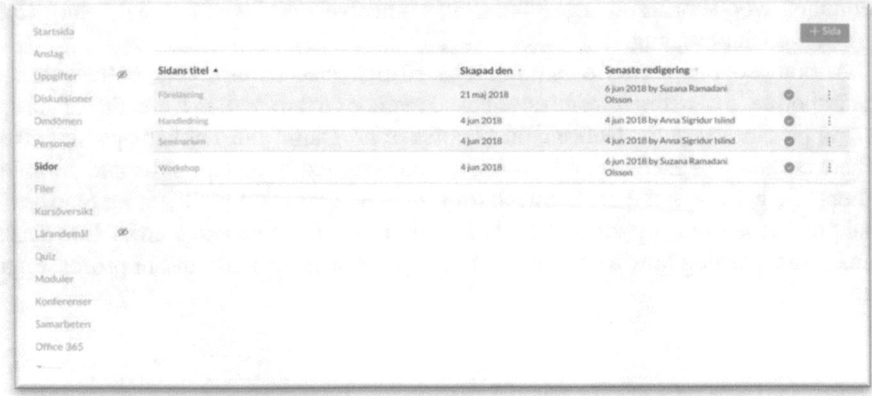

Fig. 1 An overview of the learning tool, embedded within a course in canvas

In this study, we used a qualitative approach and the empirical data consists of semi-structured interviews with 12 university teachers in Informatics at bachelor and masters' levels. The aim was to shed light on their view on how to facilitate learning based on their experience of using different types of teaching methods, as well as learning platforms. The participants were selected using snowball sampling [48]. Nine of the interviewed teachers were male, three were female, and the age ranged from 33 to 64. The interviews were analyzed through content analysis and are elaborated on below.

4 Results

The results are presented as socio-technical snapshots, exemplified with illustrative quotes from the interviews, describing four types of teaching methods frequently used: lectures, seminars, workshops, and supervision. We explain on what pedagogical basis they rest, which digital elements we recommend in connection to the different methods (which was tested through the tool we developed), and how the methods and digital tools can be combined in different ways so that they together contribute to learning.

4.1 Lectures

A traditional lecture where the teacher has the command and instructs the students from a top-down perspective can be understood as a transmissive view of learning where goals and knowledge come from *outside*, in this case, from teacher to student in the form of lecture and instruction [46]. The transmissive view of learning as something internal that can be "transferred" from teacher to student is not the view of learning that primarily governs the teaching today. Nevertheless, it is important to take that perspective and historical view on lectures as a phenomenon into account. While lectures are an important part of higher education, our empirical data shows that moving away from long lectures where the students have a passive role for too long is central.

One teacher that we interviewed reflects on the purpose of lectures. The reflection lands in lectures as an activity for information dissemination aimed to provide all students with the same base of information and that this information can be: "*something that can be recalled, and built on, in following activities on the course*". Three of the teachers like the idea of the 'flipped classroom' where information is published on the learning platform for students to take part in online before meeting with the teacher and other students offline. Through the interviews, there is a distinction between information and communication where 'information' is dedicated to the lecture and 'communication' to other types of teaching methods such as seminars, online discussions, workshops and supervision: "*I try to separate it more like 'ordinary information' about how to do something or you describe something, it can be videos, it can be texts, reading instructions for books. And then you have a part when you 'communicate' in different ways, interact […] That is why I like the idea of flipped classroom because you can reuse the information, the part of teaching that is the same for all students, and spend more time [to] get to know the student and adjust the information in the best way.*"

There is also a discussion present in eight of the interviews regarding the concept of 'lecture' as a teaching method that is often used for recorded presentations that the teachers publish on the learning platform. One teacher emphasizes the importance of distinguishing between recorded presentations which are in the form of a monolog and a recording "*when you put a camera in the room where there is an interaction between the teacher and the audience*", which are something different than lectures as social activities. It gives the wrong impression to talk about lectures in the offline context, as one teacher explains, referring to the difference between recorded lectures as the creation of course material and video presentations of specific topics, which means to "*leave the lecture form and move on to the presentation form.*" Another teacher is skeptical of recorded material for a different reason. That teacher thinks that it is risky to use the word *recorded lecture* for what that teacher sees as a video presentation because the campus lecture involves so much more than a recorded material does: *Recording the lectures gives some students a false sense of being able to skip the lecture […] but when they listen to a recorded lecture, they are missing the context around it, so then they might get more confused than knowledgeable.*

Two methods that can be used to engage students during lectures are *response tools* (e.g. a quiz or mentometer) and *active learning*. These are based on presenting the problem area, using some response tool to collect the students' answers to the question posed; and then ask the students to work in pairs with the same issue, discuss the area, reconcile and improve and finally redo the test. The session should be concluded with a discussion about the answers. The time for these exercises should be short, only a few minutes. In this way, response tools can be a support for, for example, exploring where the students are in relation to the goals they are expected to achieve at the end of the course or education, but that the technology is too much in focus. Response tools and lectures can thus be combined in different ways, depending on the purpose.

As expressed by one of the teachers: "*an experienced teacher notices when the audience's attention is lost, for example, by observing in what way the students use the laptop while the teacher is talking.*" By enabling questions to be asked, the teacher can also choose to deepen some aspects of what is taught when he/she realize that the students do not understand, i.e. engage them in active learning. One teacher emphasizes the importance of being able to move between the different teaching methods and to be perceptive to the particular needs of a unique group and individual students. To dynamically "*switch between different types of teaching*" is a required skill, s/he claims.

4.2 Seminars

A seminar in a higher education context is a meeting either face-to-face or online where students and teachers participate actively. The teachers' role is to be responsible for the implementation of the seminar by acting as a moderator and educator to get everyone to participate and that participation should lead to in-depth knowledge. Unlike the lecture, the seminar is an opportunity for reflection, ventilation of knowledge, and co-creation of new knowledge [46]. One way is to let students conduct seminars independently, to solve problems and use knowledge from previous learning opportunities and make a synthesis that they report back in class, receive criticism, comments, and guidance on how the work can be improved. Another form is that the teacher provides questions to be discussed in the group together with the teacher, to deepen previous knowledge or understanding of specific literature. A third way is to form small groups or conversations with individual students. The students present their work, and the teacher asks in-depth questions. The advantage of small groups or one-on-one meetings is that they can be adapted to the person's ability, knowledge, and personality.

The teachers problematized the size of the groups entering higher education today as an increasingly pressing issue where teachers do not enough time with each of the students: "*You may notice that there are some students who dominate the seminars, who take all questions and then the rest is very quiet, and then you also know these particular students might be silent in a large group but are perhaps better suited for talking in very small groups or individually.*" Also, some students are better at expressing themselves in text, making the online seminar more fitting for those. Motivation is an important factor in learning, which was also apparent through the interviews. The smaller the groups, the more intimate and specialized conversations can be formed. It is, therefore, necessary to find ways that fit these conditions in increasingly large groups. Although online discussions are seen as gateways to serve more students in a shorter time, creating online seminar discussions proves more difficult than on campus: "*The discussions were completely dead in Canvas [the learning platform]. But then a Discord was started and the students started talking there instead. They had seminars without us. It [Discord] is a good tool and forum that is more informative, but it is not an official tool for us. What I have done is that I have appointed some "spies" [some of the students] who report what is happening on Discord. We have to pick up feelings of dissatisfaction [with the course] that we otherwise have no idea about.*"

Digital seminars in the form of threaded online forums are a way to visualize a conversation in a way that makes it easy for the participants in the conversation to follow the conversation by inserting posts with each other in the order they are made. The main idea with the seminars is to offer a diversity that allows the students to talk both in text and in speech, meet on campus and online. It is not always the same students who are most active in the digital forums and face-to-face seminars: "*…also a way to give students who may not talk in class, the opportunity to speak.*" Another valuable aspect of the online seminar brought up in the interviews is that it gives the students a massive written dialogue to use as reading material for further tasks or examination: "*they can copy formulations and reuse materials they have used in the seminar, which can both enhance learning but also entail plagiarism issues if they use material from others.*" As discussed in one of the interviews, plagiarism of discussions is often not seen as an issue by the students but can, in some cases, become a problem. Disadvantages with the online seminar are that it is more challenging to keep track of the group and make sure that everyone is talking. It is quite stressful to move between the groups, and because reading posts demand a lot of attention, the people behind the posts become less visible. In all interviews, there are both pros and cons to online versus offline and the integration of both and evaluating each situation is seen as the way forward. The option of the online seminar was therefore incorporated with a recommendation to use it in an offline context to enrich that setting and create a socio-technical learning experience.

4.3 Workshops

Some of the teachers frequently use workshops as a teaching method. That entails applying "learning by doing" through workshops based on a mix of case methodology and project-based learning. One describes it as "*especially great in subjects where it is difficult to crystallize exactly right from wrong, where there are grey zones, and where different solutions can be identified as possible solutions to the problem.*" Workshops are often being held in full class to jointly review the themes for the workshop, with the purpose of applying the techniques and methods later. Contrary to the intention of the workshop, a teacher points out that: "*experiences from these workshops are that students did not take an active part and contribute to the work. Commonly there are only a few students who talk; the rest of the class is entirely passive.*" The new design discussed in the form of the workshop is to divide the class into smaller groups and use a tool that facilitates a digital message board, for example, the Padlet. All groups document their thoughts and results simultaneously online, which means that they can see how other groups think about an idea or a problem. This was developed as a part of the learning tool and incorporated into the offline workshop in order to better enrichen the workshop as a socio-technical teaching method.

The workshop format allows students to participate in and shape the course, both implicitly and explicitly, but it also allows the teacher, as one participant commented, to be sensitive and adjust the different forms of teaching depending on what might suit this group: "*How that combination of information and discussion, how it looks, it depends on topic and it depends on the group. Sometimes I may have said six weeks before I meet the students that we will have a seminar but then when the course has started and you get to know each other, I'm like - let's have a workshop instead.[…] I know many people who like the course to be fixed and ready from the beginning but I like when my courses are more dynamic and when I involve the students.*"

Active learning as a teaching method can help increase variation in teaching, which in turn can contribute to the students' in-depth learning. By using different digital tools, a collaboration between the students can be facilitated, and the creation of the collective knowledge, which takes place in the interaction with others, is promoted. The digital tool is here a tool for creating knowledge and for teachers to be able to adapt their participation to the different groups. The challenge, as expressed by some of the teachers, was not that the interest in getting involved is low. Instead, the groups are too big for the students to feel safe to participate in the activities, and that the teaching methods not invite the student to take place and be involved: "*By working in small groups, it is easier to involve all the participants in the group to take place, to cooperate with each other*". The participants raised the issue of smaller groups taking more time which led to the discussion of an online workshop tool, which could enable some participants to partake online, and others offline. However, this particular part was what most participants were skeptical about (mixing online offline in a workshop format). They agreed on that helping the students understand what workshops entailed before they entered would help tremendously. That led to the development of informational support included in the learning tool that would help students learn about workshops, on beforehand, with the hope of making them more efficient.

4.4 Supervision

Supervision can be conducted in different ways and arise from different purposes. Supervision can be asynchronous or synchronous and can take place both in a physical meeting offline as well as online. It can be done individually and in groups, depending on the purpose. Individual supervision tends to be more focused on the student's success, while group supervision usually becomes more general [46]. The primary purpose of supervision is to help the students move forward in their knowledge process.

When discussing supervision and how learning occurs, one teacher highlights: "*supervision, just as a lecture, is a highly social activity.*" This teacher makes a distinction between the teaching material (e.g. slides, books and papers discussed in supervision) and the social aspects of meeting face-to-face: "*Well the material is supposed to create the foundation, the structure, arouse thoughts and then I [the teacher] should be able to concretize, exemplify and elaborate on that. And not least, what is the biggest thing about supervision, it is the contact with the person there. Because both the supervision is not one-way communication, it is interactive, yeah, it is an interactive process.*"

Supervision may include digital components that support the process. One simple example is conducting supervision through forums that are used as part of online courses in different programs. Forums often function as a tool for getting messages to more than one at the same time, like a bulletin board. That means that it enables: "*a possibility to digitalize an analog work process that previously took place in the classroom.*" A sub-purpose of a forum can be to archive what previous students have done, which can contribute to the learning of the new students. Two teachers in the interviews highlight that supervision can be done via text, for example, in the form of comments on students writing supported by different types of digital services. For instance, via Google Docs, which is a digital text editing service. The same applies to PowerPoint slides, which can also be edited and shared with classmates and teachers for input through supervision. Another way to conduct supervision is via Zoom, Skype, and Adobe Connect. There, the supervision becomes synchronous, and the students meet the teacher in a virtual room through video and audio-based tools. However, in the interviews, it was apparent that during one-on-one supervision, the teachers preferred to see the student, and they also preferred offline context for that type of supervision. However, the teachers were positive towards mixing, depending on the need at the time. As one teacher said: "*Switching between the digital and the social, that is where the magic happens. To be able to make sense of what happens on [the discussion forum] or during supervision, you need the context of what happens in the classroom or during a face-to-face meeting, to get a deeper understanding of it all.*"

Consequently, supervision can include course-specific components, such as programming or academic writing, which can be seen as an object to interact around during supervision but whether it occurs online or offline is negotiable. What all guidance has in common, regardless of form and content, is the desire to help the student further in the knowledge process, a drive that became very clear during the interviews. What was also seen from the interviews is that in order to get asynchronous supervision in digital forums, teachers need to adapt their communication method and tonality. Forums can be used as a communication tool and act as peer-to-peer support students between. What can be more difficult to achieve is an equal dialogue between students and teachers, where tonality and communication patterns can be of greater importance. It can often be perceived as the teacher interrupts and provide answers during such setup and thus, the discussion stops. Although these types of solutions are traditional video-meeting tools, they can be used in different ways, and the teaching practice can be adapted accordingly. In line with that, the learning tool included zoom as an option to conduct supervision in cases where digitally mediated supervision was seen fit.

5 Discussion

The types of teaching methods: lectures, seminars, workshops, and supervision can be understood as activities constituted by a variety of socio-technical interactions. The goal of these interactions is to enable learning. Through the literature on two-sided markets, transactions are seen as an exchange, which entails monetary value. However, supported by the findings of this paper, we argue that in a learning platform, there is the value exchange of learning which can be seen as a transaction in a two-sided market. The two sides of the market are the teachers and the students, and the market is the learning platform with a range of support included in the platform. In the following section we (1) elaborate on the notion of learning as a transaction between the two actors 'teachers' and 'students' and (2) use a socio-technical alongside a socio-cultural learning perspective to shed light on how the transactions occur in practice, hence how social and technical elements of the transactions are used and combined by teachers and students. We end with a reflection on the competences and strategies needed to utilize technology in a way that helps the participants (teachers and students) enhance learning.

5.1 Learning as a Transaction in a Two-Sided Market

In this paper, we illustrate an understanding of the socio-technical interplay between the learning platform and the learning in the classroom. As a part of that, we want to shed light on performance in relation to digital platforms. McKenzie [49] identifies three types of performance in contemporary culture—organizational performance, technological performance and cultural performance—and talks about the social dimension of technology and how projected technologies are more social than technological. Introducing technology as a facilitator for learning (and understanding the socio-technical process of doing so) involves different types of performance. From a teacher's point of view, the development and design of how the learning is facilitated through a learning platform have to do with organizational performance. However, as our results show, technology use requires technological performance both from the teachers' and from the students' side. It is well known from IS discussions that technology cannot be placed in a setting without consequences. It triggers cultural changes, meaning that this way of teaching and learning also touches upon cultural performances. The cultural changes happen both for the teachers and for the students, as visible through the findings of this paper, where the teachers draw from their experience of shifting between online and offline and the cultural aspects of each.

Seeing a learning management system or a learning platform as a two-sided market, even though it does not entail a business transaction, might be seen as somewhat controversial. Traditionally, a two-sided market facilitates exchange between consumers that have not been in transactions before and enables interaction because the interaction takes place by way of the platform [1, 50]. The lens of the two-sided market has been growing since the early 2000s and has been referred to as two-sided markets, multi-sided markets, and multi-sided platforms in the literature [50, 51]. Here we do not refer to a market as a market where economic exchange takes place but as an exchange of specific service. We see learning (where there are teachers on the one side and students on the other side) as an exchange of knowledge and see that as a transaction in a two-sided market.

By viewing learning as a transaction in a two-sided market, we make the epistemological assumption that learning is a social activity and a relationship between teachers and students, facilitated by digital tools. To unpack this relationship and the role of the actors and the technology, we argue that a socio-technical lens is useful. It helps us to distinguish between social and technical elements in the different types of teaching meanwhile supporting us with an understanding of the relevance of both for learning. The four types of teaching methods: lectures, seminars, workshops, and supervision, can be viewed as assemblages of social and technical elements. The included elements are not fixed or predefined, but we argue that both social and technological elements do need to be present and they need to interplay for learning to be enhanced. Our findings illustrate how the different types of teaching and learning transactions involve different levels of interaction. In the following, we exemplify and discuss the socio-technical character of these interactions.

5.2 Strategies for Flexibility and the Importance of Context

Although learning platforms used for teaching and learning in higher education are relatively easy to use, it requires competence to use them in a way that can potentially support the learning process, instead of hindering it [46]. This has become increasingly apperent during the shift to online learning during the pandemic of covid-19. In this paper, we have identified and described various socio-technical aspects of relevance for teaching and learning. In the following, we reflect on the findings in the two distinct themes of context and flexibility. A summary of the types of teaching, corresponding digital tools, and socio-technical interactions identified in the material is provided in Table 1.

Taking the context seriously. As for the context in which the teaching is conducted, it is important to note that future students will be raised with digital technology for fun and leisure, but they do not per se know how to use it in an effective and professional manner to support their learning. The use of digital tools in private differ from

Table 1 Summary of types of teaching, digital tools, and socio-technical themes

Teaching method	Types of technologies	Socio-technical themes
Lectures: *transmissive learning, active learning*	Quiz, mentometers, response tools	Adaptation of technology to support the purpose one is looking for [37]
Lectures: *transmissive learning, active learning*	Quiz, mentometers, response tools	Adaptation of technology to support the purpose one is looking for [37]
Seminars: *Social learning, moderation, questions, investigative tasks*	Online Collaborative Learning (OCL), threaded forums	Use of technology for collaboration and problem-based learning and instruction as enacted practice [43]
Workshops: *Experiential learning, referring to "learning by doing."*	Digital message board	Use of technology that affords visibility, persistence over time and edibility [42]

competent actions in a professional context. Although there is an increasing focus on digital competence, it will take time before knowledge and methods for digital competence are achieved at all levels. How future students can work with digital technology for learning will probably vary widely between groups and individuals. The pedagogic challenge that comes with the use of various tools, which the future student feels comfortable with, can also be an asset. As teachers, we may be allowed to let go of the control of deciding on the tools and instead deciding on the teaching content. This may, however, disadvantage students who are less well versed in professional digital behavior. A key challenge is to not leave the student with this task since the role of the teacher includes support in navigating the digital tools and the task's learning objectives. A way to deal with these challenges is to evaluate which tools the students use and how they learn with them, to take advantage of their knowledge and make the teaching more relevant.

With the knowledge of the experiences the new students have of how to deal with problems and learn (e.g. moving image instead of text, fast communication, one-time learning, flexibility, other views of authorities, etc.), we believe the teaching needs to be adapted accordingly. For example, it needs to add value to the students, that is something other than a lecture on YouTube. We believe that this added value is about working in practice with problems and issues in workshops and seminars. It can be challenging to do online in an established learning environment like the university. We also think the teaching role is about seeing the students, thus creating a relationship with them so that the teacher can catch those who do not hang around and stimulate those who are at the forefront a little extra. A personal relationship with the teacher gives the student added value to come to school and confidence in the teaching. The actual packaging of knowledge and learning becomes essential so that education can contribute with unique benefits that are difficult to achieve on your own or outside the university.

Flexibility and individualization. Flexibility to adapt to the knowledge and engagement level of the students is a vital skill as a teacher. That can be done by sensing the mode of the students in the classroom and how they engage with the subject being taught. Being flexible is a more difficult task online when the teacher cannot pick up subtle social expressions from the students. Because the tools we use are also used privately, the new technology comes with expectations from the students on what it can be used for. We can see increased individualization and expectation of flexibility and that one wants to do as one wants rather than follow a collective mass. This expectation can be used positively to work with inclusion, for example, students with special needs. It will then be important to focus on what competencies we want students to achieve. In the system development program, we have recently worked on this flexibility and individualization challenge as we have a student who is blind. We have been reviewing how we write the course objectives in relation to what we want to assess. We have discovered that we sometimes write in the syllabus how we will assess a specific course target and we sometimes write in which way, i.e. we specify a specific digital tool one must use in the examination. When a blind student becomes our student, it challenges our view of the form of examination, and we need to think about alternative methods for assessment and what skills we should assess, rather than on the type of technology we use. The tools we deal with on our "buffet", however, are primarily aimed at supporting the teaching practice, rather than supporting the students' competence in absorbing practical knowledge, which is part of taking the degree on our programs. However, all the tools, in the form of use we advocate, have a dual-use because the student is an end-user, as well as the teacher. In the use of digital tools and design of courses, it is important to keep in mind that the students are influenced by our way of using digital tools, although teaching practice is also an important aspect. Adapting the use of these tools to the situation fits in with Suchman and Trigg's [52] argument that the most successful digital tools are those which "co-evolve with practice."

Hence, by viewing the different types of teaching through a socio-technical lens, we see how social interaction and technology in the classroom can interplay to improve learning. The teacher-student relationship is of mutual character. The teacher depends on being close to the students to sense their presence or absence, and the students need nearness to the teacher and other students to engage in course activities. A recorded campus lecture, for instance, is difficult for a student to make sense of without attending fully, as questions, jokes, facial and bodily expressions are lost in the recording.

To sum up, the pedagogical conviction can be described as a constructivist approach where a socio-cultural perspective is crucial. Underpinning this is the assumption that learning occurs in social contexts and that it is impossible not to learn. Our findings illustrate some of the ways digital tools can be used to support this type of learning. For example, using quizzes during lectures, using threaded forums online to practice online conversations, and using digital message boards to collaborate and share knowledge between groups during a workshop. We argue that more flexible approaches to learning and teaching are crucial to prepare students for the digital workplace of the future. Modern work has long been characterized by flexibility and pressure to perform [28, 49], accentuated by the digitalization of professions [53] and the expansion of platforms into everyday life [54]. Furthermore, it is evident that IS has broadened beyond IT and computerization and is increasingly relevant and integrated into almost all aspects of workplaces and society. Finally, our findings highlight the importance of increased transparency for students to utilize the given learning opportunities. From the two-sided market perspective, this benefit both the teachers and the students, as students that are prepared will likely be able to focus on the course-related topics, problems, and questions rather than on formalities and requirements for examinations. From a socio-technical and socio-cultural perspective, we believe that if we succeed in getting the students to understand that the teaching moments are interwoven with the subject and aiming for lifelong learning (not just taking place in a formal context on a course), we can motivate students to get involved and come to campus and participate actively to a greater extent.

6 Conclusion

In this paper, we have addressed the need to develop a better understanding of why and for what purposes digital tools and educational methods are used in higher education, and how they can contribute to lifelong learning. For this purpose, we developed a learning object—a learning tool—consisting of ideas about pedagogy, technology, tools, and how they interact with the subject being taught. The socio-technical and socio-cultural perspectives as a framework for understanding technology and learning in practice helped to shed light on some of the challenges and tensions associated with teaching and using learning platforms and the digital tools embedded in these systems.

In conclusion, a digital tool to support teaching should not be seen as static, but as a dynamic and continuously changing tool, characterized by the interplay between the change of technology and in teaching methods. From a socio-cultural perspective on teaching and learning, the socio-technical interplay involves valuable transactions of learning between two sides of a platform—between students and teachers. It is of vital relevance for teachers, and professionals in general, to see this transaction and put it in foreground when negotiating technological and social aspects of teaching and learning.

References

1. Islind, A. S. (2018). *Platformization: Co-designing digital platforms in practice*. University West.
2. Baskerville, R. (2011). Individual information systems as a research arena. *European Journal of Information Systems, 20,* 251–254.

3. Bødker, S., Lyle, P., & Saad-Sulonen, J. (2017). Untangling the mess of technological artifacts: investigating community artifact ecologies. In *Proceedings of the 8th International Conference on Communities and Technologies* (pp. 246–255). ACM.
4. de Reuver, M., Sørensen, C., & Basole, R. C. (2018). The digital platform: A research agenda. *Journal of Information Technology, 33,* 124–135.
5. Wiberg, M., Ishii, H., Dourish, P., Vallgårda, A., Kerridge, T., et al. (2013). Materiality matters—Experience materials. *Interactions, 20,* 54–57.
6. Islind, A. S., Lindroth, T., Lundin, J., & Steineck, G. (2019). Co-designing a digital platform with boundary objects: Bringing together heterogeneous users in healthcare. *Health and Technology, 9,* 425–438.
7. Norström, L., Arghavan Shahlaei, C., Johansson, L.-O., Islind, A. S., & Lundh Snis, U. (2019). New logics of ethics in the age of digital platforms: Design fictions of autonomous cars. In *Proceedings of the 17th European Conference on Computer-Supported Cooperative Work-Demos and Posters.* European Society for Socially Embedded Technologies (EUSSET).
8. Islind, A. S., Lindroth, T., Snis, U. L., & Sørensen, C. (2016). Co-creation and fine-tuning of boundary resources in small-scale platformization. In Scandinavian conference on information systems (pp. 149–162). Berlin: Springer.
9. Checkland, P. (1981). *Systems thinking, systems practice.* Chichester: Wiley.
10. Mumford, E. (2006). The story of socio-technical design: Reflections on its successes, failures and potential. *Information Systems Journal, 16,* 317–342.
11. Mumford, E., Hirschheim, R., Fitzgerald, G., & Wood-Harper, A. (1985). *Research methods in information systems.* North-Holland Publishing Co.
12. Wynn, E., & Vallo Hult, H. (2019). Qualitative and critical research in information systems and human-computer interaction: Divergent and convergent paths. *Foundations and Trends® in Information Systems, 3,* 1–227.
13. Hanseth, O., & Lyytinen, K. (2010). Design theory for dynamic complexity in information infrastructures: The case of building internet. *Journal of Information Technology, 25,* 1–19.
14. Islind, A. S., Snis, U. L., Lindroth, T., Lundin, J., Cerna, K., & Steineck, G. (2019). The virtual clinic: Two-sided affordances in consultation practice. *Computer Supported Cooperative Work (CSCW), 28,* 435–468.
15. Islind, A. S., & Lundh Snis, U. (2018). From co-design to co-care: Designing a collaborative practice in care. *Systems, Signs and Actions, 11,* 1–24.
16. Billett, S. (2014). Mimetic learning in and for work. In *Mimetic Learning at Work* (pp. 1–21). Berlin: Springer.
17. Islind, A. S., & Lundh Snis, U. (2017). Learning in home care: A digital artifact as a designated boundary object-in-use. *Journal of Workplace Learning, 29,* 577–587.
18. Norström, L., Islind, A.S., & Vallo Hult, H. (2017). Balancing the social media seesaw in public sector: A sociomaterial perspective. In *RIS Selected Papers of the Information Systems Research Seminar in Scandinavia.* Tapir Akademisk Forlag
19. Vallo Hult, H., Hansson, A., Svensson, L., & Gellerstedt, M. (2019). Flipped healthcare for better or worse. *Health Informatics Journal, 25,* 587–597.
20. Vallo Hult, H., Islind, A. S., & Norström, L. (2018). Tuning professionalism in the public sector. In *AIS SIGPRAG pre-ICIS workshop on "Practice-based Design and Innovation of Digital Artifacts".* San Franciso, CA, USA.
21. Islind, A. S. (2014). The "PantryApp": Design experiences from a user-focused innovation project about mobile services for senior citizens. In International working conference on transfer and diffusion of IT (pp. 359–362). Berlin: Springer.
22. Gellerstedt, M., Johansson, K., & Winman, T. (2015). Work integrated learning: A marriage between academia and working life. *Journal of Systemics, Cybernetics and Informatics, 13,* 38–46.
23. Al-Busaidi, K. A. (2012). Learners' perspective on critical factors to LMS success in blended learning: An empirical investigation. *CAIS, 30,* 11–34.
24. Amrou, S., Semmann, M., & Böhmann, T. (2013). Managing for transfer of training: Directions for the evolution of learning management systems. Chicago, Illinois, USA: AMCIS.

25. Vallo Hult, H., Islind, A. S., Johansson, L.-O., & Lundh Snis, U. (2017). Towards learning with digital artifacts. In *IFIP WG 8.6 Working Conference on the Diffusion and Adoption of Information Technology,* Guimares, Portugal. IFIP.
26. Islind, A. S., Lundh Snis, U., & Pries-Heje, J. (2017). Learning at the digital boundaries. In *IFIP WG 8.6 Working Conference on the Diffusion and Adoption of Information Technology,* Guimares, Portugal (pp. 1–4). IFIP.
27. Alavi, M., & Leidner, D. E. (2001). Knowledge management and knowledge management systems: Conceptual foundations and research issues. *MIS Quarterly, 25,* 107–136.
28. Sennett, R. (1998). *The corrosion of character: The personal consequences of work in the new capitalism.* New York: W.W. Norton.
29. Mumford, E., & Henshall, D. (1978). *Participative approach to computer systems design: A case study of the introduction of a new computer system.* Halsted Press.
30. Bjorn-Andersen, N., & Eason, K. (1980). Myths and realities of information systems contributing to organizational rationality. *Human Choice and Computers, 2,* 97–109.
31. Hedberg, B. (1978). *Using computerized information system to design better organizations and jobs.* Swedish Center for Working Life.
32. Cecez-Kecmanovic, D., Galliers, R. D., Henfridsson, O., Newell, S., & Vidgen, R. (2014). The sociomaterialty of information systems: Current status, future directions. *MIS Quarterly, 38,* 809–830.
33. Leonardi, P. M., Nardi, B. A., & Kallinikos, J. (2012). *Materiality and organizing : Social interaction in a technological world.* Oxford: Oxford University Press.
34. Orlikowski, W. J. (2009). The sociomateriality of organisational life: Considering technology in management research. *Cambridge Journal of Economics, 34,* 125–141.
35. Bjerknes, G., & Bratteteig, T. (1995). User participation and democracy: A discussion of Scandinavian research on system development. *Scandinavian Journal of Information Systems, 7,* 1.
36. Kyng, M. (1994). Collective resources meets puritanism. *Scandinavian Journal of Information Systems, 6,* 5.
37. Leonardi, P. (2012). Materiality, sociomateriality, and socio-technical systems: What do these terms mean? How are they different? Do we need them? In P. Leonardi, B. Nardi, & J. Kallinikos (Eds.), *Materiality and organizing: Social interaction in a technological world* (pp. 25–48). Oxford: Oxford University Press.
38. Leonardi, P. M., & Barley, S. R. (2010). What's under construction here? Social action, materiality, and power in constructivist studies of technology and organizing. *The Academy of Management Annals, 4,* 1–51.
39. Robey, D., Anderson, C., & Raymond, B. (2013). Information technology, materiality, and organizational change: A professional Odyssey. *Journal of the Association of Information Systems, 14,* 379–398.
40. Bednar, P., Sadok, M., & Shiderova, V. (2014). *Socio-technical toolbox for business analysis in practice* (pp. 219–227). Springer International Publishing.
41. Bednar, P., & Sadok, M. (2016). *Bridging the gap between theory and practice: Socio-technical toolbox* (pp. 51–62). Springer International Publishing.
42. Treem, J. W., & Leonardi, P. M. (2013). Social media use in organizations: Exploring the affordances of visibility, editability, persistence, and association. *Annals of the International Communication Association, 36,* 143–189.
43. Koschmann, T. D. (1996). *CSCL: Theory and practice of an emerging paradigm.* Hillsdale, NJ, US: Lawrence Erlbaum.
44. Brown, J. S., & Adler, R. P. (2008). Minds on fire: Open education, the long tail, and learning 2.0. *Educause Review, 43.*
45. Carmean, C., & Haefner, J. (2002). Mind over matter: Transforming course management systems into effective learning environments. *EDUCAUSE Review, 37,* 26.
46. Bates, A. W. (2015). *Teaching in a digital age.* Vancouver BC: Tony Bates Associates Ltd.
47. Willermark, S. (2018). Digital Didaktisk Design: Att utveckla undervisning i och för en digitaliserad skola.[Digital didactical design: To develop teaching in and for a digitalised school]. Dissertation. Trollhättan: University West.

48. Bryman, A. (2016). *Social research methods*. Oxford: Oxford university press.
49. McKenzie, J. (2001). *Perform or else from discipline to performance*. London: Routledge.
50. Gawer, A. (2014). Bridging differing perspectives on technological platforms: Toward an integrative framework. *Research Policy, 43,* 1239–1249.
51. Rochet, J. C., & Tirole, J. (2006). Two-sided markets: A progress report. *The RAND Journal of Economics, 37,* 645–667.
52. Suchman, L. A., & Trigg, R. H. (1992). Understanding practice: Video as a medium for reflection and design. Design at work (pp. 65–90). L. Erlbaum Associates Inc.
53. Susskind, R. E., & Susskind, D. (2015). *The future of the professions: How technology will transform the work of human experts*. USA: Oxford University Press.
54. Hult, H. V., Islind, A. S., Master Östlund, C., Holmgren, D., & Wekell, P. (2020). Sociotechnical Co-design with General Pediatricians: Ripple Effects through Collaboration in Action.

The Preferred Learning Styles of Generation Z: Do They Differ from the Ones of Previous Generations?

Beatrice Manzoni, Leonardo Caporarello, Federica Cirulli, and Federico Magni

Abstract A new generation, named Generation Z (born after 1996), is currently in education and it will soon approach the job market. Knowing how they engage in learning is critical to design effective learning experiences both in academia and at work. However, being the newest generation, it is also the least studied one, especially in academic research. With this paper we aim to explore Gen Zers' preferred learning styles and to compare them with the ones of previous generations. We collected data from 870 Italian MSc students and Executive Education participants to assess their learning styles using Kolb's learning style inventory. We found that Gen Zers have higher preferences towards the assimilating learning style (combining abstract conceptualization and reflective observation), while Baby Boomers and Gen X prefer the accommodating style (combining active experimentation and concrete experience). There results conflict with the common stereotypes—mainly based on qualitative evidence—about the youngest generation, which see them as a generation that needs to engage in a highly informal, interactive and experience-based learning. Implications for theory and practice follow.

Keywords Gen Z · Gamers · iGen · Digital natives · Generations · Learning styles · Learning · Experiential learning

B. Manzoni (✉) · L. Caporarello
SDA Bocconi School of Management, Bocconi University, 20136 Milan, Italy
e-mail: beatrice.manzoni@unibocconi.it

L. Caporarello · F. Cirulli
BUILT, Bocconi University, 20136 Milan, Italy

F. Magni
Hong Kong University of Science and Technology, Clear Water Bay, Hong Kong, China

C. Metallo et al. (eds.), *Digital Transformation and Human Behavior*, Lecture Notes in Information Systems and Organisation 37,
https://doi.org/10.1007/978-3-030-47539-0_5

1 Introduction

Generation Z, Generation 2020, iGen, Gamers and Digital Natives are different labels for the same individuals belonging to the newest generation. The bulk of Gen Zers are now going through education and will soon enter the job market. They are the Gen Z because they come after the Millennials, who were labelled Gen Y; the Gen 2020 because this is the year around which many of them will graduate from college; the iGen because Internet always existed for them [1], the Gamers because they grew up playing videogames [2], and the Digital Natives because they were born in a world already heavily reliant on technology [3].

In all these definitions there is a common factor, namely the pervasive presence of technology and internet. Gen Z individuals "grew up with cell phones, had an Instagram page before they started high school, and do not remember a time before the Internet" [1]. Technology in its broad sense affects every area of Gen Zers' life and makes their life experiences different from those of their predecessors, including how they learn (e.g. [4]). Thanks to technology, learning has become more personalized, flexible and adaptive to individual learning needs and preferences [5], and the learning experience includes a much wider variety of learning models and methods [6]. These changes are particularly evident in the first generation born into an integrated and globally connected world.

With this study we aim at exploring how Gen Zers approach learning, analyzing in particular their learning styles, which is under-researched in scientific inquiry [7]. We rely on Kolb's learning styles inventory and experiential learning model [8, 9]. We compare the Gen Z's learning styles with the ones of previous generations.

This inquiry is of interest both for research and practice. From a practice point of view, there are authors and professionals claiming that education is not equipped to meet the needs of this new cohort of learners [10]. As far as scientific research is concerned, there have been very few academic studies on the newest generations, a surprising fact given that generational differences are the subject of countless articles in the popular domain and the management of young workforce is often seen as a critical issue by managers [11].

In the following sections, first we describe the characteristics of Gen Zers, in particular with regard to the impact of technology and internet on how they learn, and we review Kolb's learning styles and its appropriateness in this setting. Secondly, we present our research methods and sample. Results, discussion and conclusions are drawn in the last part of the paper, suggesting that Gen Zers are much less active experience-led than we think. Finally, implications for instructors and organizations are discussed.

2 The Influence of Technology, Internet and Gaming on Gen Zers' Approach to Learning

Research on generational differences suggests that individuals belonging to different generational cohorts tend to exhibit differences both in general life domains and in the workplace in factors such as personality traits, personal values and work values. This means that individuals belonging to a given generation tend to have their own, shared belief about what is important to them in general and at work, and this belief somewhat differs from that of individuals belonging to different generational cohorts. Generational differences affect disparate factors, including work-related attitudes—such as organizational commitment, work-life balance preferences, teamwork orientation, career patters, leadership behaviors and preferences [11, 12]—and technology use patterns and learning characteristics [13].

Generational differences exist because individuals from the same generation share birth years and thus experience significant life events at the same time, especially in the formative years of adolescence and young adulthood [14]. These events affect the development of generational identities, which in turn impact individuals' responses in a rage of life situations.

Among the different generations, Gen Z is the least studied one in higher education, being the one currently in school [15]. Yet Gen Zers will soon approach the job market. It is thus compelling to understand this generation better, because it is the generation that we are educating now and that will represent a significant component of the worldwide workforce in few years [10]. Finding ways to (re)design learning experiences that take into account their needs and preferences, as well as the ones of the labor market, is critical given the dynamicity of the current organizational environment [16].

Individuals belonging to Gen Z are those born approximately from 1996 to 2010. This generation differs in many ways from its predecessors, in particular due to the fact that it is the first generation born into an integrated and globally connected world. Technology and internet influenced their life more than anything else. Gen Zers were born with technology and they have never known a world without internet and smartphones. They cannot thrive without digital resources. They are tech savvy and in constant contact with people via social networks and instant messaging, more than emails and direct contact [1, 3, 17]. Technology is there to facilitate their lives, solve their problems and provide them with relevant information or people [18]. Finally, they grew up with online videogames often preferring the playful virtual world to the real one, and spending a great proportion of their time in parallel gaming realities [2, 19].

Several studies showed that their brain is affected by internet use [20]. They are quick in finding answers to questions in Google and YouTube, but they lack the critical thinking skills to evaluate sources [15]. They have become wired to sophisticated visual imagery [21] and they have difficulties in focusing and analyzing complex information or issues to the extent that they expect information to be delivered in short bursts and they are at risk for attention deficit disorders.

Table 1 The characteristics of Gen Z when they learn

Motivation to learn	Learning is a challenge and an opportunity to develop
Models and methods	Learning best occurs online It has to be self-paced and informal It should include active methods, such as interactive simulations and role plays, and project-based works
Relationships with…	Instructors: they are facilitators of dynamics among students Peers: they are a source of learning through peer learning Technology: it eases learning

Other studies report that the intense use of videogames also affect the brains of these learners reinforcing certain beliefs and working modes. In fact, videogames train people to handle risks and learn from their errors, a skill that is valued in many workplaces [22]. Additionally, videogames create a self-centered universe where the player is the character running the show and manipulating other people and objects to his or her will within certain rules. They teach players that the world is a competitive place, but also that they have to exert individual control over their action, and they reinforce independent problem solving. Furthermore, videogames reinforce players' beliefs about the self, how the world should work, how people relate to one another and, mostly, about the purpose of life in general [2]. Yet, at the same time videogames also contribute to develop teamwork cooperation and the capability to quickly examine, adapt to and interact with new situations [7].

All these factors seem to have profound implications in terms of how Gen Zers engage in learning [23] (see Table 1), and consequently of how instructors and organizations should design learning experiences to be effective for this generation.

Existing research on how Gen Zers engage in learning has focused on different aspects.

Some scholars explored Gen Z's motivation to learn, which seems analogous to the one moving them towards the use of videogames: they look for challenges and tasks because they are used to play increasingly complex games online [24]. Moreover, they see learning as stimulating and as a means to increase their versatility within the workplace, the latter also representing a major driver to learn [25].

Another topic that has been often addressed by scholars is that of learning models, modes and methods that are most effective with Gen Z, and how learning experiences should be designed accordingly [26]. Gen Z's familiarity with technology makes online learning and forms of self-paced learning very well received by individuals belonging to this generation [27]. Gen Z seems intolerant towards formal and structured learning, privileging informal learning and just-in-time learning bits [2, 28]. When they learn, Gen Zers dislike lectures and discussions, whereas they enjoy interactive games, collaborative projects and challenges [15]. They enjoy challenges, because they seem to learn a lot by taking risks in a safe environment and relying on a trial and error approach [2, 29]. "Experience" is a key word for them. Simulated environments or recreated role-play scenarios allow them to enjoy something that is too risky or even physically impossible to achieve in the real world [30, 31].

For Gen Z, learning takes place beyond the boundaries of traditional places and classes [2]. These learners make conscious choices about what learning methods work best for them, these can comprise reading lecture notes online, watching interactive media or digital images, or working in groups [32]. They are naturally inclined to focus on understanding, creating knowledge by adopting discovery methods, active engagement and asking faculty to provide them with a tailored learning experience [33, 34].

Furthermore, other scholars have inquired about who and what do Gen Zers interact with when they are learning, exploring in particular how they relate to instructors, peers and technology. Gen Z uses peer learning, despite the predominant virtual nature of the relationships with others [2, 35]. Instead, they do not seem to take into account the authority from instructors, who are rather seen as facilitators of peer dynamics [2]. Finally, the relationship with technology is by far the strongest one [36, 37], as they did not experience a world without technology. They consider technology as a means to an end rather than as an ultimate objective [38]. For Gen Z, easy-to-use technology is a primary source of information, as it helps organizing their activities and it supports problem solving [15]. Social networks are the main platforms for communication, and keeping online contacts is more important than face to face interactions [39]. In learning, there is a growing trend in Gen Z opting for electronic material and tech-based exercises [40].

Some scholars have also started exploring whether the peculiarities of Gen Zers can be explained in light of their specific preferred learning styles [2, 27, 41]. Yet, so far this topic has not been examined in sufficient depth.

3 Learning Styles

By learning styles, we refer to cognitive, emotional, and physiological features, which are used to recognize how learners understand concepts and interact with the learning environment [42].

Over the years, the existing literature mapped 71 different learning styles models, which translates into hundreds of different learning styles. Curry [43] systematized these theories in a three-layer framework depending on the stability of the style: the most stable ones are the cognitive styles relating to personality, while the least stable ones are environmental and instructional styles. In between these are the information-processing learning styles, which are the most diffusely used in research and practice [44]. Kolb's Learning Style Inventory [8] belongs to the latter category, and it is the most frequently used model in research and practice [45]. In addition, relying on the experiential learning theory, Kolb's model appears to be particularly appropriate to explore Gen Z's learning styles because individuals belonging to this generation seem to learn best when actively involved in experiencing something [46].

According to Kolb, learning is a dynamic process and learners modify their learning style with changing circumstances or "the learning space" [47]. Kolb

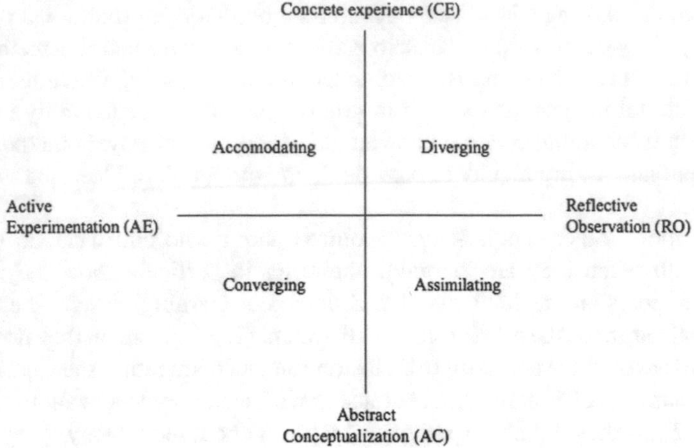

Fig. 1 Kolb's learning styles and experiential learning model

described learning as the students' preferred method of perceiving (grasping experience) and processing (transforming experience) information. The perceiving continuum reveals the extent to which individuals prefer abstractness (abstract conceptualization—AC) over concreteness (concrete experience—CE), while the processing continuum is about action (active experimentation—AE) versus reflection (reflective observation—RO) [9].

Individual learning styles represent a combination of these two independent dimensions, resulting in diverging (CE/RO), assimilating (AC/RO), converging (AC/AE), and accommodating (CE/AE) learning styles (see Fig. 1).

The *accommodating* learning style relies on concrete experience and active experimentation to learn. Individuals who embrace this learning style tend to learn from "hands-on" and challenging new experiences. They tend to act based on instinct, rather than logical analysis. When engaged in problem solving, to get information they rely more on the people around them, rather than on their own technical analyses. In formal learning situations, individuals with this style prefer collaborating with others to complete tasks, define goals, work in the field, and test various approaches.

The *diverging* learning style is based on concrete experience and reflective observation. People with this learning style are very good at looking from various perspectives at concrete situations, which they approach through observation rather than action. They are comfortable in situations that call for brainstorming a broad selection of ideas. In formal learning contexts, they prefer working in groups to gather information, listening with an open mind and receiving personalized feedback.

The *converging* learning style involves using abstract conceptualization and active experimentation. People with this learning style are very adept at finding practical applications for their ideas and theories. They are capable of solving new problems with the solutions to past problems. They would rather deal with technical tasks and issues, rather than interpersonal or social ones. In formal learning situations, they prefer to learn by “first hand”, testing out new ideas, simulations, laboratory procedures and practical applications in general.

The *assimilating* learning styles relies on learning abilities that use abstract conceptualization and reflective observation. People with this style are highly skilled at understanding a wide variety of information and presenting it in a concise, logical way. They are far more focused on ideas and abstract concepts rather than people. In general, people who prefer this style believe that it is more important for a theory to be sound from a logical standpoint rather than valuable from practical one. In formal learning situations, they prefer taking lessons in a classroom setting, doing reading assignments, studying analytical models and having time to thoroughly think things thorough.

We have previously noted that Gen Zers have a liking for challenge and risk-taking in safe contexts. Moreover, they have a preference for applied and uncomplicated information, and they tend to rely on collaboration with their peers. Based on these characteristics of Gen Zers and on their approach to learning, we hypothesize that Gen Zers have higher preferences towards the accommodating learning style than previous generations do, and thus we expect a higher percentage of Gen Zers embracing the accommodating style compared to other generations. Furthermore, we analyze the generational differences in preference towards the four styles in an exploratory fashion.

4 Methods

We collected data from 870 Italian MSc students and participants to executive education at an Italian University in 2018. Out of the 870 participants in our sample (average age 26, 47% females), 68% were Gen Z (born after 1996), 19% Millennials (born 1980–1996) and 13% belonging to generational cohorts born before 1980 (Gen X and Baby Boomers). Students belonging to Gen Z are enrolled in MSc courses in Management and Economics, while the others include participants attending Executive Education courses within the Business School. We decided to merge individuals from Gen X and Baby Boomer because there are fewer of them in the dataset compared to the other generations; moreover, Baby Boomers have almost exited the workforce.

We asked participants to fill in Kolb’s learning style inventory [9], which is constructed in such a way that individuals respond to it as they would respond to a learning situation: it requires them to resolve the tensions between the abstract-concrete and active-reflective orientations. There are eight couples of statements. For each couple respondents pick the one that better represent the way they behave, and they give a score using a Likert scale 1–5 (1 = it represents me a little, 5 = it totally represents me). An example of couple of statements is the following one: “*(a) I am a careful observer of events and people, and I find myself reflecting on what I see and hear from what goes on around me*” *versus* “*(b) I am a decisive and practical problem solver who enjoys putting plans into action.*”

To test our hypothesis, we then performed a One-Way ANOVA and post hoc analyses to test whether there were significant differences in preferred learning styles between Gen Z and previous generations. We further ran a series of binomial logistic regressions to control for the eventual effects of age and tenure on the preferred learning style. In particular, we created dummy variables for each of the four learning styles, with each individual displaying one preferred style based on his/her Learning Style Inventory score. We then split the dataset into three generational cohorts (Gen Z, Gen Y and older generations, including Baby Boomers and Gen X) and ran binomial regressions for each style, introducing first age and then career tenure as predictors. In this way, we were able to check whether age or career tenure had any effect on the likelihood of embracing a learning style within each generation. We decided to perform this analysis to tackle one of the criticisms that is most often moved to generational research, namely that the effects of generational cohort on the outcomes under scrutiny are confounded with age and tenure effects [48, 49], even if previous research found that generational effects exist beyond pure age and period effects (e.g. [48]).

5 Results

The results are reported in Tables 2 and 3. Despite the predominantly qualitative evidence from existing research suggesting Gen Zers' preferences for active experimentation and concrete experience when compared with their predecessors, we found no support for our hypothesis. Indeed, we found that Gen X and Baby Boomers are significantly more accommodating than both Gen Z and Gen Y, while there are no differences between the latter two generations. On the contrary, Gen Zers have higher preferences towards the assimilating learning style when compared to individuals belonging to both other generational cohorts. Our results also showed the Gen Z individuals are marginally more converging than individuals from Gen X and Boomers, while the differences between them and Gen Y are not significant. Finally, we noticed that Millennials (Gen Y) have higher preferences towards the diverging

Table 2 Analysis of variance

Variable	Gen Z		Gen Y		Gen X/B		
	%	SD	%	SD	%	SD	F-test
Accommodating	25.34	43.53	31.71	46.68	50.91	50.22	15.17**
Diverging	25.34	43.53	35.98	48.14	25.45	43.76	3.80*
Converging	21.64	41.22	15.24	36.05	12.73	33.48	3.46*
Assimilating	27.68	44.78	17.07	37.74	10.91	31.31	9.80**

Note $n = 870$; *BB* baby boomers

$^{*}p < 0.05$, $^{**}p < 0.01$

Table 3 Tukey's honestly significant different test

Variable	Gen 1	Gen 2	MD	SE	Sig.
Accommodating	Gen Z	Gen X/BB	-0.2557^{**}	0.0467	0.000
		Gen Y	−0.0637	0.0397	0.244
	Gen Y	Gen X/BB	-0.1920^{**}	0.0555	0.002
Diverging	Gen Z	Gen X/BB	−0.0012	0.0461	0.999
		Gen Y	-0.1064^{*}	0.0392	0.019
	Gen Y	Gen X/BB	0.1052	0.0548	0.134
Converging	Gen Z	Gen X/BB	$0.0892^{\dagger}$	0.0409	0.075
		Gen Y	0.0640	0.0347	0.156
	Gen Y	Gen X/BB	0.0252	0.0485	0.862
Assimilating	Gen Z	Gen X/BB	0.1678^{*}	0.0436	0.012
		Gen Y	0.1061^{**}	0.0371	0.000
	Gen Y	Gen X/BB	0.0616	0.0518	0.460

Note $n = 870$; *MD* mean difference; *SE* standard error; *Sig* significance; *BB* baby boomers
$^{\dagger}p < 0.1$, $^{*}p < 0.05$, $^{**}p < 0.01$

learning style than Gen Zers, while there are no differences between either generation and Gen X and Baby Boomers.

These results suggest that Gen Zers' learning is activated when abstract conceptualization and reflection observation come into play. They seem to need theories and concepts much more than the mainstream stereotype suggests, and they tend to prefer information that is logical, valid, and well thought through. On the contrary the most senior generations (Baby Boomers and Gen X) rely on concrete experience and active experimentation, as they are more accommodating than both Gen Z and Millennials (Gen Y). The latter tend to combine elements of the older generations (specifically the orientation towards concrete experience) and of the youngest one (the orientation towards reflective observation), showing more diverging tendencies than the other generations, especially than Gen Z.

Either as far as the binomial regression that we ran to control for age and tenure effects are concerned, in none of the 12 regression analyses (four styles by three generations) did we find that age or career tenure predicted any of the styles. These results confirm our claim that the generational cohort is an adequate unit of analysis and that generation effects exist beyond age and tenure effects, as also suggested by previous studies [48, 49].

6 Discussion and Conclusions

In this paper we examined Gen Zers' preferred learning styles, in comparison with the ones of individuals from previous generations. We found significant differences between Gen Zers and individuals belonging to the previous generations, even if results differ from what we could have expected from existing academic and practical evidence.

Gen Zers has a higher preference for abstract conceptualization and reflection observation than individuals from previous generations, as Gen Zers showed a significantly stronger preference for an assimilating learning style than the others. In order to activate their learning, they need theories that are logically sound, and they need time to think things through. We can infer that instructors should make an effort to provide them with a sound theoretical and predetermined framework to analyze, interpret and deal with reality. Gen Zers learn better step by step, digesting small and frequent bits of theories and concepts. The more they receive theory in an already structured and logical way, the better it is, despite the common belief that they that they enjoy playing an active role, facing challenges and experimenting. They do like being active, but this is not how their learning process gets started. To engage in an effective relationship with this population, instructors can probably provide small bits of theoretical models and offer examples of their applications, adopting more a deductive rather than an inductive approach. The challenge is to frame theoretical frameworks in such a way that they are accessible. In order to so, instructors could for example adopt interactive methods for collaborative visualization and cross-community knowledge sharing. In fact, visualization typically facilitates information sharing and complex problem solving [41, 50].

On the contrary, the oldest generations—Baby Boomers and Gen X—have a higher preference for concrete experience and active experimentation. They learn best when they can rely on hands-on experience and play an active role in terms of experimenting and facing new challenges. The challenge for instructors is to make their professional experience a key component of the learning process [51].

When different generations learn together in formal occasions (in class) or informal ones (on the job everyday), differences in terms of learning styles represent an opportunity, as well as a challenge. They are an opportunity because individuals train themselves to appreciate and value differences by interacting with diverse people. They are also a challenge, because they need to be accommodated, especially when people have to collaborate and solve problems as a team.

From a research point of view, we provide an empirical test of Gen Zers' learning styles, based on Kolb's model. We also highlight differences in learning style preferences among Gen Z, Millennials (Gen Y) and individuals from the previous generations (Gen X and Baby Boomers).

From a practice point of view, we offer instructors the provocative suggestion to start being more deductive and theory driven when teaching the youngest generation.

This work has some limitations that offer inspiration for future research: the dataset is limited to Italian people in terms of nationality and to students/participants who are enrolled in management and economics courses. Nationality and field of studies influence preferred learning styles [9]. We also call for research on how gender and personality types impact learning styles. Finally, this research belongs to generational research which is often criticised for confounding generational, age and tenure effects. Therefore, more research questions can be tackled with the appropriate rigour with, for instance, longitudinal studies on Gen Zers over the years, to track whether their learning style evolves with age and work experience, or with studies comparing different generations at the same point of their life (e.g. when they enter the job market).

References

1. Twenge, J. M. (2017). *iGen: Why today's super-connected kids are growing up less rebellious, more tolerant, less happy—and completely unprepared for adulthood (and what this means for the rest of us)*. New York: Unabridged.
2. Carstens, A., & Beck, J. (2005). Get ready for the gamer generation. *TechTrends, 49*(3), 22–25.
3. Thompson, P. (2013). The digital natives as learners: Technology use patterns and approaches to learning. *Computers & Education, 65,* 12–33.
4. Seemiller, C., & Grace, M. (2017). Generation Z: Educating and engaging the next generation of students. *About Campus Enriching the Student Learning, 22*(3), 21–26.
5. Jones, V., Jo, J., & Martin, P. (2007). Future schools and how technology can be used to support millennial and generation-Z students. In C. H. Kim (eds.), *Proceedings of 1st International Conference of Ubiquitous Information Technology*, Dubai.
6. Caporarello, L., Giovanazzi, A., & Manzoni, B. (2019). (E)Learning and what else? Looking back to move forwards. In: A. Lazazzara, R. Nacamulli, C. Rossignoli, & S. Za (eds.), *Organizing for digital innovation. Lecture Notes in information systems and organisation* (Vol. 27). Springer, Cham.
7. Spires, H.A. (2008). 21st century skills and serious games: Preparing the N generation. In L. A. Annetta (eds.), *Serious educational games* (pp. 13–23). Sense Publishing, Rotterdam.
8. Kolb, D. A. (1984). *Experiential learning: Experience as the source of learning and development*. Englewood Cliffs, N.J.: Prentice-Hall.
9. Kolb, A. Y., & Kolb, D. A. (2013). The Kolb Learning Style Inventory 4.0: A comprehensive guide to the theory, psychometrics, research on validity and educational applications. Hay Resources Direct, Boston.
10. Oblinger, D., & Oblinger, J. (2004). The next generation of educational engagement. *Journal of Interactive Media in Education, 8,* 1–18.
11. Lyons, S., & Kuron, L. (2014). Generational differences in the workplace: A review of the evidence and directions for future research. *Journal of Organizational Behavior, 35*(S1), 139-S157.
12. Magni, F., & Manzoni, B. (2019). L'enfasi sui Millennial ci fa trascurare gli altri. Harvard Business Review Italia, April, pp. 8–11 (2019).
13. Lai, K. W., & Hong, K. S. (2015). Technology use and learning characteristics of students in higher education: Do generational differences exist? *British Journal of Educational Technology, 46*(4), 725–738.
14. Kupperschmidt, B. R. (2000). Multigenerational employees: Strategies for effective management. *The Health Care Manager, 19,* 65–76.
15. Rothman, D. A. (2016). Tsunami of learners called generation Z. *Maryland Public Safety Online Journal, 1*(1). https://www.mdle.net/Journal/A_Tsunami_of_Learners_Called_Generation_Z.pdf. Last accessed 15 May 2019.
16. Gerber, S., & Scott, L. (2011). Gamers and gaming context: Relationships to critical thinking. *British Journal of Educational Technology, 42*(5), 842–849.
17. Rothman, D. A. (2016). Tsunami of learners called generation Z. *Maryland Public Safety Online Journal, 1*(1). https://www.mdle.net/Journal/A_Tsunami_of_Learners_Called_Generation_Z.pdf. Last accessed 16 May 2019.
18. Gerber, S., Scott, L., Clements, D. H., & Sarama, J. (2005). Instructor influence on reasoned argument in discussion boards. *Educational Technology Research & Development, 53*(2), 25–39.

19. Beck, C. J., & Wade, M. (2004). *Got game: How the gamer generation is reshaping business forever*. Boston MA: Harvard Business School Press.
20. Greydanus, D. E., & Greydanus, M. M. (2012). Internet use, misuse, and addiction in adolescents: Current issues and challenges. *International Journal of Adolescent Medicine and Health, 24*(4), 283–289.
21. Palmer, E. (2011). *Visual learning styles among digital natives*, Department of Computer Graphics Technology Degree Theses. Paper 2.
22. Colbert, A., Yee, N., & George, G. (2016). The digital workforce and the workplace of the future. *Academy of Management Journal, 59*(3), 731–739.
23. Annetta, L. A., Minogue, J., Holmes, S. Y., & Cheng, M. T. (2009). Investigating the impact of video games on high school students' engagement and learning about genetics. *Computers & Education, 53,* 74–85.
24. Gee, J. P. (2003). *What video games have to teach us about learning and literacy*. New York: Palgrave/Macmillan.
25. West Midland Family Center. (Cartographer). (2015). Generational Differences Chart. https://www.wmfc.org/uploads/GenerationalDifferencesChart.pdf. Last accessed 04 2019.
26. Igel, C., & Urquhart, V. (2012). Generation Z meet cooperative learning. *Middle School Journal, 43*(4), 16–21.
27. Hendel-Giller, R., Hollenbach, C., Marshall, D., Oughton, K., Pickthorn, T., Schilling, M., & Versiglia, G. (2010). The neuroscience of learning: A new paradigm for corporate education. The Martiz Institute White Paper (pp. 1–19).
28. Karl, M. (2007). *Gadgets, games, and gizmos for learning: Tools and techniques for transferring know how from boomers to gamers*. San Francisco: Pfeiffer.
29. Levine, J. (2006). Gaming and libraries: Intersection of services. *Library Technology Reports, 42*(5), 10–17.
30. Corti, K. (2006). Games-based Learning; a serious business application. *Informe De Pixel Learning, 36*(4), 1–20.
31. Peciuliauskiene, P. (2014). E-learning and motivation for learning physics at school: the case of generations Y and Z. In *DIVAI 2014: 10th International Scientific Conference on Distance Learning in Applied Informatics* (pp. 441–451). Štúrovo, Slovakia
32. Barnes, K., Marateo, R. C., & Ferris, S. P.(2007). Teaching and learning with the net generation. *Innovate: Journal of Online Education, 3*(4).
33. Williams, J., & Chinn, S. J. (2009). Using web 2.0 to support the active learning experience. *Journal of Information Systems Education, 20*(2), 165–174.
34. Sarkar, N., Ford. W., & Manzo, C. (2017). Engaging digital natives through social learning. *Systemics, Cybernetics and Informatics, 15*(2).
35. Bencsik, A., Horváth-Csikós, G., & Juhász, T. (2016). Y and Z generations at workplaces. *Journal of Competitiveness, 8*(3), 90–106.
36. Wolfson, N. E., Cavanagh, T. M., & Kraiger, K. (2014). Older adults and technology based instruction: Optimizing learning outcomes and transfer. *Academy of Management Learning & Education, 13,* 26–44.
37. Reeves, T. C. (2006). Do generational differences matter in instructional design? https://itforum.coe.uga.edu/Paper104/ReevesITForumJan08.pdf. Last accessed 15 May 2019.
38. Koh, C. (2015). Understanding and facilitating learning for the net generation and twenty-first-century learners through motivation, leadership and curriculum design. In C. Koh (ed.), *Motivation, Leadership and Curriculum Design: Engaging The Net Generation and 21st Century Learners* (pp. 1–10). Springer Science+Business Media, Singapore.
39. Csobanka, Z. E. (2016). The Z Generation. *Acta Technologica Dubnicae, 6*(2), 63–76.
40. Cilliers, E. J. (2017). The challenge of teaching Generation Z. *People: International Journal of Social Sciences, 3*(1), 188–198.
41. Panahandeh, E., Khoshkhoonejad, A., Mansourzadeh, N., & Heidari, F. (2015). On the relationship between Iranian EFL learners' multiple intelligences and their learning styles. *Theory and Practice in Language Studies, 5*(4), 784–791. https://doi.org/10.17507/tpls.0504.14. Last accessed 13 May 2019.

42. Logan, K., &Thomas, P. (2002). Learning styles in distance education students learning to program. In *Proceedings of 14th Workshop of the Psychology of Programming Interest Group*, Brunel University, pp. 29–44.
43. Curry, L. (1983). *An organization of learning styles theory and constructs.* Montreal, Canada: Paper presented at The American Educational Research Association.
44. Passarelli, A. M., & Kolb, D. A. (2012). Using experiential learning theory to promote student learning and development in programs of education abroad. In M. Vande Berg, R. M. Paige, & K. Hemming Lou (eds.), *Student learning abroad: What our students are learning, what they are not, and what we can do about it* (pp. 137–161). Stylus Publishing, Sterling, VA.
45. Pashler, H., McDaniel, M., Rohrer, D., & Bjork, R. (2009). Learning styles: Concepts and evidence. *Psychological Science in the Public Interest, 9,* 105–119.
46. Brown, J. (2000). Growing up digital: How the web changes work. *Education, and the Ways People Learn, Change, 52*(2), 11–20.
47. Felder, R. M. (1996). Matters of style. *ASEE Prism, 6,* 18–23.
48. Twenge, J. M. (2010). A review of the empirical evidence on generational differences in work attitudes. *Journal of Business and Psychology, 25*(2), 201–210.
49. Keyes, K. M., Utz, R. L., Robinson, W., & Li, G. (2010). What is a cohort effect? Comparison of three statistical methods for modeling cohort effects in obesity prevalence in the United States, 1971–2006. *Social Science & Medicine, 70*(7), 1100–1108.
50. Keller, T., & Tergan, S. O. (2005). Visualizing knowledge and information: An introduction. In S. O. Tergan, T. Keller, (eds.), *Knowledge and information visualization—searching for synergies, LNCS* (Vol. 3426). Springer, Berlin.
51. Jurenka, R., Starеček, A., Vraňaková, N., & Caganova, D. (2018). The learning styles of the generation group Z and their influence on learning results in the learning process, pp. 251–260. https://doi.org/10.1109/ICETA.2018.8572186. Last accessed 01 May 2019.

Is This What You Want? Looking for the Appropriate Digital Skills Set

Gianluca Prezioso, Federica Ceci, and Stefano Za

Abstract Digital technology is the heart of the modern economy. Digital skills are then the reference point for many firms and workers. This means that employees should have skills to face change and at the same time have excellent technical preparation. Innovation and competitiveness of organizations are guided by today's skills, the so-called twenty-first century digital skills (DS). In this paper we analyze the DS related to the digital transformation in an Italian firm operating in the manufacturing sector, observing that DS are not adequately distributed among the firm departments. In particular, the desiderata (job descriptions) seem often not aligned with the expectations of the managers (interviews).

Keywords Digital skills · Digital transformation · Digitization · Industry 4.0

1 Introduction

Recent technological innovations in information and communication technologies (ICT) are triggering a new paradigm shift in manufacturing and production: the so-called "4.0 industry" is emerging [1, 2]. Several reports highlight how digital skills are now the reference point for many firms and workers. Some highlight how the acquisition of adequate digital skills is transformed into job opportunities [3] others instead analyze the importance of carrying out certain activities to learn or improve digital skills [4] or how to prepare employees for the digital transformation [5]. From a scholarly viewpoint, evidence regarding the need for qualified human

G. Prezioso (✉) · F. Ceci · S. Za
"G. D'Annunzio, University of Chieti-Pescara, Viale Pindaro, n. 42, 65127 Pescara, Italy
e-mail: gianluca.prezioso@unich.it

F. Ceci
e-mail: f.ceci@unich.it

S. Za
e-mail: stefano.za@unich.it

C. Metallo et al. (eds.), *Digital Transformation and Human Behavior*, Lecture Notes in Information Systems and Organisation 37,
https://doi.org/10.1007/978-3-030-47539-0_6

capital in literature is extensive [6–8]. Already in 2007, Bartel et al. [9] noticed that any investment in ICT coincides with the increase in requirements in the skills of operators, with particular reference to technical skills and problem solving. This is also established through statistical evidence from Mohnen and Roller [10] studies where the single most important innovation obstacle in a wide range of countries and industries was lack of skills.

Therefore, today more than ever, firms are looking for highly skilled workers who can adapt to the changing needs of work and at the same time be able to deal with increasingly interactive and complex tasks. This means that employees must have skills to face change and at the same time have excellent technical preparation [11, 12]. Innovation and competitiveness of organizations are guided by today's skills, the so-called twenty-first century digital skills (DS) [13].

In this paper we analyse the DS related to the digital transformation in an Italian firm operating in the manufacturing sector. The aim of this work is to investigate if DS of a manufacturing firm are in line or not with DS defined from the theory and what are the reasons. We adopted DS classification, elaborated from Ester van Laar et al. [13], in order to compare this, with DS required from the desiderata (job description) and from manager's expectations (interview). We offer a taxonomy that organizations can relate to, in order to obtain a flawless digital transformation: this implies a reinterpretation of the employee skills to fill the gap created by the digital transformation. In the contemporary global economy where the rate of change and the influence of technology are high, employees need to develop DS to cope this change [13]. However, firms can fail in defining which skills to develop and often the perception of the manager is not transformed into operating activities by the Human Resource (HR) department. Therefore, through a case study, we want to respond to the following research question: Exploring the DS's perception across different department in a Manufacturing firm, how are DS distributed in a every department? How can we explain the different perceptions of DS, if present, among departments? Based on past studies [13], we build upon a taxonomy of DS and we explore the diffusion of each digital skill in different departments: we integrated the theoretical understanding with the empirical results, testing how (and if) skills are diffused and perceived in a real case.

The paper follows a well-defined structure: in the next section we report a literature review of the main contributions in the field. In Sect. 3 we explain the research method used to collect empirical evidence. In Sect. 4 we summarize data analysis and the empirical evidence to offer a tentative taxonomy of the DS managed by an Italian manufacturing firm. Section 5 analyses the empirical evidence and identify similarities and differences between practice and theory. In the Sect. 6 we find the conclusion where we discuss the implications of our findings, the limitations of the work and suggest a tentative avenue for future research analysis.

2 Literature Review

Digital technology is the heart of the modern economy as it has added value and granted significant growth opportunities for firms that have implemented ICTs [14].

Firms differ between each other's mainly for the skills and capabilities acquired over time [15, 16]. This leads firms to support workers who spend their time day by day updating their skills and knowledge. In a rapidly evolving knowledge economy, innovation begins with people and is decisive only when human capital is recognized as a draining force of the same innovation [17–20]. What largely influences the demand for skills and employment is precisely the technological change. Dachs and Peters [21] observed employment growth, accompanied by a change in workers' skills. In fact, greater competences and education are required in employees when new technologies are used [22] and with these competences they have a relative benefit in the implementation of new technologies [23–26]. During the early 1990s, a polarization of the labor market began to be observed, on the one hand the demand for workers with average qualifications decreased compared to the low-skilled [27–29], on the other the technological change still favored highly qualified workers. Lowering the price of ICT capital combined with advances in computing power, developments in robotics and artificial intelligence have led to the replacement of standardized jobs with automated processes [30]. During the twentieth century, scholars began to talk about complementarity of technological skills [5, 31–33] leading to the formulation of skill-oriented technological change. It's also true, however, that the continuous increase in the performance of mobile robotics, processing power and machine learning will probably continue to replace workers in the distribution of skills [34–36]. Nowadays, with continuous change, an important factor in innovation are employee skills. This is established through statistical evidence from Mohnen and Roller studies [10] where the single most important innovation obstacle in a wide range of countries and industries was lack of skills. Firms today are looking for highly skilled workers who can adapt to the changing needs of work and at the same time be able to deal with increasingly interactive and complex tasks. This means that employees must have skills to face change and at the same time have excellent technical preparation [11, 12]. Today it is essential to develop DS both for people to obtain a good job and to participate actively in the society in which we live [37] and for organizations for keeping up with developments and innovating products and processes. Several studies including those of Lewin and McNicol [38], supporting the development of twenty-first century skills through ICT. Some of these skills were identified and explored by the studies of Voogt and Roblin [39]. Obviously, the skills we are talking about go beyond the mere knowledge of specific software [11, 40, 41]. An excellent classification of the DS of the twenty-first century, with which we agree, is formulated by Claro et al. [40], they elaborated four macro-classes of skills. However, there are several additional classifications that were realized but to better understand these concepts van Laar et al. [13] differentiate between: technological skills, twenty-first century skills and twenty-first century. Regarding the concept of technological skills, Bawden [42] confirms how the growing importance of computer literacy is linked to the diffusion of information technology that leads to the common use of terms such as information technology (IT) and technology information and communication (ICT). Hatlevik et al. [43] define the technological skills as the set of skills that in most cases are necessary on the one hand to use the Internet, computers, on the other hand for the acquisition of DS of the twenty-first century and they differentiate these Skills in part of the domain and specific knowledge. Ferrari [44] in his research exposes a broad classification of what are digital competences: evaluation and resolution of problems and technical operations, sharing, communication, etc. Talking about the "twenty-first century skills", two are the most important classification realized from the Partnership for the twenty-first century (P21) and from the evaluation and teaching of twenty-first century skills (ATC21S) [13]. The first (P21) differentiate three macro classes of Skills, which are determined by sub-sets of skills; the second (ATC21S) through help of some experts [45] elaborate four macro-classes of Skills, which are determined by sub-sets of skills. The most actual study was realized from E. van Laar et al. [13] where is present a clear classification of the concept of skills needed in a digital environment, identifying what are the digital aspects that should be integrated with the concepts of 21st-century skills. Understanding and studying the differences between these classifications, we decided to take in consideration for our study van Laar et al. [13] classification, that constitute the basis for the development of our taxonomy.

3 Method

This paper applies a case-study methodology [46, 47]. We collected multiple sources of data to establish construct validity [47]. Multiple data sources enabled us to obtain stronger substantiation of constructs by triangulating evidence across cases. Our case study focuses on one firm, that we name "Manufacturing" since we do not have the authorization to disclose the name. Manufacturing realized investment in industry 4.0 and in digitalization from more than 35 years. Manufacturing developed a fully automated warehouse where people and robots work together. This has been possible thanks to relevant investments in robotics, automation, training as well as courses for the employees. Through these investments, Manufacturing was able to become a market leader and to achieve truly incredible production results: what 30 years ago was produced in a time frame of a year, is now produced in a single day. Manufacturing is a multinational firm presents in 18 countries all over the world: Argentina, Brazil, China, Colombia, France, Germany, India, Indonesia, Ireland, Italy, Mexico, United Kingdom, Czech Republic, Russia, Spain, United States, Switzerland and Thailand. The data has been collected the Italian site where we spend 8 months. Manufacturing is composed by 11 departments, as is possible to observe in Table 2, each of which has different objectives, roles and tasks. The increasing number of specialized personnel hired by this firm as well as the continue investments in R&D in the recent years, convinced us to choose this Manufacturing as our case study. In the firm are present different employees' position as is possible to observe in

Table 1. Manufacturing invests 7% (Company's Annual Report, 2018) of its profits in R&D with the aim of increasing production capacity through automation process, robots, employee skills and talent attraction. These costs amounted to $75.3 million, $68.2 million and $66.2 million in 2018, 2017 and 2016, respectively (Company's Annual Report, 2018). The strategy for data collection follows: first, we gathered information from written publication (journal articles, firm internal document, firm annual reports, databases, firms' official websites) in order to obtain background information over the firm and the sector, aiming to get a better understanding of the process of designing and deploying skills. As a second step, we gathered all the job descriptions of the firms. Job descriptions are internal documents that consist in analytical written descriptions of the main characteristics of each organizational position. The job descriptions report includes: name of the position, roles, position in the organization chart, main purposes, relationships with other organizational positions, skills required, and tasks assigned. A job description is the basis of any form of job posting (publication of a job advertisement in a job advertisement portal/Job board) and it aims to present a clear image to candidates, to allow them to decide whether they can/would like to send their own application. Moreover, a job description has a weighting in the subsequent stages of the recruiting process. It is a practical tool used during the job interview to assess the matching (correspondence) between the candidate's profile (Job profile) and the ideal role that line managers have in mind. We analyzed the job description of every single employee to select all DS required from all department and to assign a value for every DS. We decided to adopt a scale from 0 to 5, where 0 represents the absence of consideration regarding a specific skill, 1 low importance, 2 medium–low importance, 3 medium importance, 4 medium–high importance and 5 high importance. Moreover, we decided that the decisional process to assign the score is directly proportional to the position of the employee. This means that the score assigned depends on two factors: (i) the presence or not of the DS in the job description and (ii) the role played by the worker distinguishing between high, medium and low level. We assigned 0 to that DS not present in the job description of the department, 1 when the DS is present in the job description of low level worker (HR generalist, Personnel administration, Master data etc.…), 2 when the DS is present in the job description of medium level worker (Managers) and 3 when the DS is present in the job description of high level worker (Leader, Head, Director of department etc.…).

This means that the maximum score assigned for every department is 5. Thirdly, we collected data from open-ended interviews that served as our principal source of data. We interviewed all the representatives from all departments to ensure that we obtained multiple perspectives. In total, we carried out 37 interviews, which included 35 face-to-face interviews and 2 Skype interviews. The interviews followed a semi-structured protocol and they were conducted on-site in Italy between October 2018 and March 2019. The length of the interviews was between 30 and 75 min and consisted of questions about specific topics related to employees' DS. Table 1 reports the interview details. To perform the interview, we followed an explorative questionnaire. The questionnaire is divided into three parts. The first part asks for a description of educational background and previous works. The second part is related

Table 1 Interviews details

	Position	Date	Time	Department	Length
1	Senior manufacturing manager & technical division manager	11/01/2019	15:00 p.m	Operations	40 min
2	Director, corporate human capital management process	16/01/2019	14:00 p.m	Human capital management system	25 min
3	Quality manager & environmental manager	23/01/2019	14:30 p.m	Quality and sustainability	33 min
4	Product/process leader	21/01/2019	11:00 a.m	R&D	30 min
5	Engineering manager	16/01/2019	12:30 a.m	Engineering/industrialization	60 min
6	Project manager	14/01/2019	15:30 p.m	Engineering/industrialization	35 min
7	Designer engineering DPTM—assembly machines and mould	14/01/2019	16:05 p.m	Engineering/industrialization	35 min
8	Manager, mould engineering	17/01/2019	9:00 a.m	Engineering/industrialization	50 min
9	SR. MRG, delivery management	29/01/2019	16:00 p.m	Information system	40 min
10	Automation manager	17/01/2019	14:00 p.m	Engineering/industrialization	75 min
11	Assembly engineering manager	16/01/2019	14:30 p.m	Engineering/industrialization	45 min
12	Master data	21/01/2019	11:30 a.m	Engineering/industrialization	35 min
13	Master data	21/01/2019	10:00 a.m	Engineering/industrialization	40 min
14	Business' process management analyst	21/01/2019	16:30 p.m	Operations	35 min
15	Vice president operation excellence—BPM & strategic projects	17/01/2019	10:30 a.m	Operations	45 min
16	Manufacturing director	24/01/2019	14:30 p.m	Manufacturing	45 min
17	Director, sales controlling	28/01/2019	15:00 p.m	Finance	30 min
18	Supply chain director	17/01/2019	15:30 p.m	Supply chain	50 min

(continued)

Table 1 (continued)

	Position	Date	Time	Department	Length
19	Head accounting	24/01/2019	15:00 p.m	Finance	30 min
20	Accounting and tax manager	25/01/2019	12:00 a.m	Finance	45 min
21	Credit manager	23/01/2019	16:00 p.m	Finance	45 min
22	Treasury Dpt. accounting	28/01/2019	10:30 a.m	Finance	35 min
23	Assembly production manager	28/01/2019	11:45 a.m	Manufacturing	50 min
24	Quality assurance director	22/01/2019	15:00 p.m	Quality and sustainability	40 min
25	Environmental, health and safety leader	21/01/2019	9:15 a.m	Quality and sustainability	30 min
26	Delivery manager, IS innovation	21/01/2019	17:00 p.m	Information system	60 min
27	Product designer expert center	21/01/2019	15:30 p.m	R&D	45 min
28	Assembly supervisor, production planning	22/01/2019	11:00 a.m	Manufacturing	60 min
29	Personnel administration	28/01/2019	15:00 p.m	Human resources	25 min
30	Director, talent management	28/01/2019	14:30 p.m	Human resources	30 min
31	Human resources manager	12/02/2019	14:00 p.m	Human resources	30 min
32	Human resources generalist	14/01/2019	14:45 p.m	Human resources	40 min
33	HR dirctor	23/01/2019	11:00 a.m	Human resources	23 min
34	Product line manager, marketing	12/02/2019	11:30 a.m	Marketing	45 min
35	Innovation manager expert center	13/02/2019	9:45 a.m	Research and development	45 min
36	prototype shop manager	12/02/2019	15:00 a.m	Research and development	50 min
37	Vice president, IS delivery management	13/02/2019	9:00 a.m	Information system	50 min

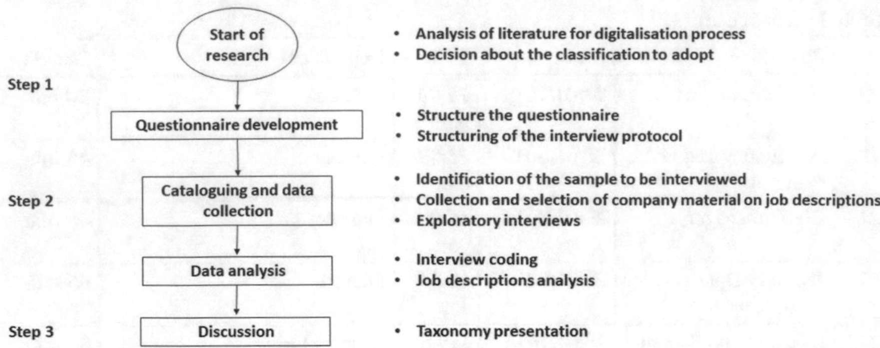

Picture 1 Method steps

to: digitalization process realized by the firm related to employee skills, the necessity to improve some skills or not and what strategies the firm needs to complete for the digitalization process. The third part ask for a description of the most important DS needed for the digitalization process. The responses received during the interviews reflect the particular point of view of the respondents [48] (Picture 1).

Sample selection was carried out in order to ensure theoretical replicability, that is, the selected case study could be reproduced either with results like those of the original framework or with contrasting results but for predictable reasons [47]. We fully transcribed every detail during the interview in order to preserve the veracity of the conversations and interview reports were submitted to interviewees for verification. In this case, as for the job descriptions, we assigned a score from 0 to 5 on that declared in the interviews about DS needed and taking in consideration the position of the interviewees (high, medium or low). The questionnaire is available upon request. In developing the questionnaire, we followed the taxonomy provided by Ester van Laar et al. [13]. Ester van Laar et al. identified twelve types of DS: technical, information management, communication, collaboration, creativity, critical thinking, problem solving, ethical awareness, cultural awareness, flexibility, self-direction and lifelong learning [13]. For each skill, we investigated the level of standardization/customization, the type of professionalism required for the activities, the problems and the critical features. We decided to adopt Ester van Laar et al. taxonomy instead of other taxonomies of prior research because this the most current classification present in the literature and it's a systematic literature review where is present the most important literature about DS of the last 20 years.[13]. Moreover, this is the first study that sufficiently define the digital aspect integrated with 21st Century skills and it examines the relationship between these two concepts.

4 Data Analysis

Table 2 shows the taxonomy arising from the data. The first column reports the DS as they are reported by literature contributions [13]. We used this taxonomy as a starting point for our analysis. A definition of each of the 12 DS follows: (1) Technical: refers to skills to know, use (mobile) devices and applications to navigate and maintain orientation so as to accomplish practical tasks [49, 50], (2)Information management: refers to use ICT efficiently to search, select, organize information to make informed decisions about the most suitable sources of information for a given task [51, 52], (3) Communication: refers to use ICT to transmit information to others, being sure that the message is clearly expressed [40, 53], (4) Collaboration: refers to use ICT to exchange information in a team work, to develop a social network, take decisions and negotiate agreements in respect of others in order to achieve common goal [54, 55], (5) Creativity: refers to the use of ICT to create new ideas, or use familiar ideas in a new way and transform such ideas into a new product, service or process within a particular domain [56, 57], (6) Critical thinking: refers to the use of ICT to make informed decisions and judgements about communications and information received using sufficient evidence and reflective reasoning to support the claims [58, 59], (7) Problem solving: refers to the use of ICT to find a solution to a problem through cognitive process and understand in combination with the use of knowledge [60, 61], (8) Ethical awareness: refers to the ability to use ICT in a socially responsible manner, demonstrating knowledge and awareness of the legal and ethical aspects [40, 62], (9) Cultural awareness, refers to respect other cultures when using ICT and showing cultural understanding for different cultures [47, 63], (10) Flexibility: refers to the capacity to adapt one's behavior, attitude or thinking, to changing ICT environments [4, 64], (11) Self-direction: refers to the ability to appraise your own progress when using ICT through means of fixed targets [26, 37], (12) Lifelong learning refers to the use of ICT for the constant exploration of new opportunities, when these can be integrated into an environment to continuously improve one's skills [65, 66].

We structured Table 2 dividing the data according to the source: interviews and job description. The first source refers to the evidence collected from job descriptions. The second source refer to the evidences collected thought the interviews. Each source gives us information about the distribution and the importance of the DS in the different department, and in some cases the different perception of the same skills by each source. The process through we realize Table 2 is organized in 2 steps. Fist, in the analysis of job descriptions, we focused on the presence of DS in every different department in relationship with the position that the employee has. The higher is the position and the presence of DS in the job descriptions and the higher is the score assigned. Second, in the analysis of interviews we focused on the employees' awareness about DS in relationship with employees' position. Also, in this case, the higher the position, the higher the score assigned to the DS declared during

Table 2 The consideration of each digital skill in the job description and by the interviewees

Source		Job description										
Departments	Twenty-first century digital skills	Manufacturing	Engineering and industrialization	Supply chain	HR	Quality assurance and sustainability	Marketing	IS—information system	Finance	HCMS—human capital management	Operations	R&D
Technical		5	5	0	0	3	5	5	4	5	5	5
Information management		0	0	0	5	5	0	5	0	5	5	0
Communication		5	3	5	3	4	5	5	3	4	3	3
Collaboration		5	3	5	5	5	5	4	3	3	3	0
Creativity		0	0	0	0	0	5	0	0	0	0	0
Critical thinking		0	0	0	0	0	0	0	0	5	0	0
Problem solving		0	0	3	0	0	5	4	0	5	3	3
Ethical awareness		0	0	0	0	0	0	5	0	0	0	0
Cultural awareness		3	3	3	0	3	5	4	3	3	3	3
Flexibility		5	0	5	3	5	5	5	0	0	5	3

(continued)

Table 2 (continued)

Source		Job description										
Departments	Twenty-first century digital skills	Manufacturing	Engineering and industrialization	Supply chain	HR	Quality assurance and sustainability	Marketing	IS—information system	Finance	HCMS—human capital management	Operations	R&D
Self-direction		0	3	0	0	3	3	4	0	3	0	3
Lifelong learning		0	0	0	2	0	4	0	3	0	0	0
Source		Interview										
Departments	Twenty-first century digital skills	Manufacturing	Engineering and industrialization	Supply chain	HR	Quality assurance and sustainability	Marketing	IS—information system	Finance	HCMS—human capital management	Operations	R&D
Technical		5	5	5	5	4	5	3	5	5	5	5
Information management		4	4	0	0	3	5	4	4	5	4	3
Communication		5	5	5	5	5	5	5	5	5	5	5
Collaboration		5	5	0	3	5	5	5	5	5	5	5
Creativity		3	5	5	0	4	0	1	4	0	0	2
Critical thinking		1	1	0	0	3	0	0	1	0	2	4
Problem solving		5	5	5	5	5	0	5	5	0	5	5
Ethical awareness		1	0	0	0	0	0	0	0	0	0	0
Cultural awareness		4	1	0	4	0	0	1	1	0	2	1
Flexibility		4	5	0	2	3	5	3	2	0	2	5
Self-direction		4	1	0	0	0	0	1	1	0	5	1
Lifelong learning		4	4	2	1	3	5	5	5	5	0	1

the interview. Integrating the results obtained from interviews and employee's job description, we concluded that DS are not equally distributed in each department. We found match and mismatch between job descriptions and interviews, that are described in the next section.

5 Discussion

Analyzing Table 2 it is possible to observe how DS are not adequately distributed among the firm departments. Comparing the information concerning job description and interview, the desiderata (job description) seem to not be aligned with the expectations of the managers (interview). Moreover, such misalignment differs among the departments. One of the reasons could derive from a techno-centric business point of view, combined with a lack of awareness of the ongoing digitization process by employees. Another reason could be the fact that many interviewees do not mention some skills because they are considered them taken for granted. We seek to summarize the information arranged in Table 2 in the following six main discussion points.

1. It is possible to recognize how some DS are medium–high or high relevant in the job descriptions and at the same time are not taken into consideration in the interviews. A couple of examples are (i) "information management" skill for the HR department, and (ii) "collaboration and flexibility" skill for the Supply Chain department.
2. On the other hand, some DS are not mentioned in the job descriptions and at the same time are medium–high or high relevant for the interviews. For instance, some of these skills are "technical" and "creativity" skills for the Supply Chain department.
3. There are also some DS with high relevance in both job description and interviews. Some examples are "communication" skill for the Supply Chain department as well as technical, communication, collaboration and flexibility skills for the Manufacturing department.
4. On the contrary, some DS are absent in both job description and interviews for specific department, such as "information management", "critical thinking", "ethical awareness" and "self-direction" skills for the Supply Chain department.
5. There are some DS almost completely neglected in the job description, independently by the department (a sort of "zero row"), such as "creativity" and "critical thinking".
6. There are some DS almost completely ignored by each interviewee, independently by the department, such as "ethical awareness".

This preliminary analysis lead to the following conclusions:

a set of DS are regularly relevant for all departments, specifically: technical, communication and collaboration skills. This set of skills has been very popular both in literature and in practice from decades [67] and therefore their development is considered fundamental in every department. In fact, as shown in Table 2, these skills have the highest score in both job descriptions and interviews. This highlights as functional managers and HR managers perceive the same level of importance of this set of skills. Moreover, concerning the job description section, some DS are less relevant for all departments, such as creativity, critical thinking, ethical awareness and self-direction. Particularly, in the job descriptions section, "creativity" is important only for marketing department, "critical thinking" only for HCMS department, "ethical awareness" is relevant only for information system department and "self-direction" is medium relevant only for few departments. Whereas, considering the interviews, these skills have low level of relevance, few interviewees recognize these skills as important and the majority did not mention those skills at all, probably because they think that are not relevant. Finally, there is a set of DS with a highest mismatch between job descriptions and interviews, specifically: problem solving, critical thinking, lifelong learning and cultural awareness. One possible reason could be related to the fact that some skills are better known than others. In fact, analyzing the literature, critical thinking, cultural awareness and life-long learning are mentioned recently respect to technical, communication or collaboration, that have a higher presence in the literature over the years [67].

The data suggest us that awareness of managers is in line with the theory for some skills and not in line for other skills. We realized that these differences between job descriptions and interviews, i.e. between the managers of the various departments and the person responsible for updating the job descriptions derive from the employees' awareness. In fact, as can be seen from Table 2, the IS department that is immersed in the digital process every day, is the one that is closest to the DS classification resulting from the theory or is the one with a wider awareness of the subject. Our results suggest that the adoption of certain skills compared to others is related to the awareness of managers. The awareness of manager can be linked with the concept of absorptive capacity, as introduced by Cohen and Levinthal [68]. The more managers are connected and informed about digital processes, the greater the awareness they have on the subject resulting in a better alignment between theory and practice [68]. Manufacturing should conduct basic research not only to obtain specific results but to increase the absorptive capacity that is linked to the general background knowledge and the employees' awareness. This allows the firm to quickly exploit the useful scientific and technological knowledge, to apply it daily both for the digitization process and for the exploitation of innovations, but also to respond promptly to changes dictated by the market [68]. Only a deep understanding, a wide awareness and a strong absorptive capacity, will allow the firm to adopt the right skills, make them its own and put them into play during the process of digitization.

6 Conclusion, Limitations and Future Work

6.1 Conclusion

In this paper we analyze an Italian firm located in the manufacturing sector. In particular, the aim of this work is to investigate DS related to the digital transformation, understand if DS's firm are in line or not with DS defined from the theory and what are the reasons. We decided to adopt Ester van Laar et al. [13] classification to compare this with DS obtained from job description and from interview. We realize a taxonomy that firms can use to obtain a successful digital transformation, increase their absorptive capacity and the employees' awareness. Specifically, we explore the DS's perception across different department of the firm, how DS are distributed, and what are the reasons of the different perception. Integrating results derived from interview and job description we concluded that DS are not in line with the theory.

7 Observations, Limitations and Avenues for Further Research

This study is relevant for practitioners because results illustrate what are the most relevant DS across every department therefore department managers and human resources can integrate missing skills with training as well as update the job description in a proper way, in order to reflect the real need of the firm. Moreover, adding these skills in the firm's job description can help recruiter to improve personnel selection. On the other hand, understanding the real need of the firm can allow HR department to realize an appropriate workforce planning in order to cover every possible gap in employees DS and allocate the right person in the right place. Another suggestion that this study offer to employers and HR managers follows the identification of the DS for every department allow recruiters to acquire the most talented candidates as employees in order to remove them from the competition with other firms, realize and balance workforce team, and to retain those already acquired.

Due to its exploratory nature, this study is subject to some limitations. The first limitation refers to the small sample size, we analyzed a single firm located in one country. For this reason, it may be difficult to generalize these findings to the manufacturing industry or to other industries and countries. The second limitation comes from its cross-sectional nature rather than a longitudinal one, in fact this research offers a static view of the phenomenon, and it does not consider the possible cyclical variation of DS.

Future research can refer to these limitations in order to further explore the issue of DS. Moreover, with our research we want to give an input to researchers in order that they can investigate with future research the DS. They can take in consideration a different business sector in order to understand if some sector pay attention to DS more than others or if job descriptions have a different structure in a different business. Could be useful in future understand if any correlation exists between job description and manager's awareness in order to obtain DS that are in line with the theory. Another aspect that can stimulate future research is the size of the sample or the size of the firm, could be useful understand if big firms have more awareness about DS to adopt than small and medium enterprises and what are the DS that they apply in every department. Future research could study what are the most important DS in firms with different nationality, if the culture affects the adoption of some DS respect others and what is the relation between them. Furthermore, there is another aspect that is fundamental to study in future, namely, the relationship between the adoption of the DS and the age of the employees.

References

1. Posada, J., et al. (2015). Visual computing as a key enabling technology for I4.0. *35*(2), 26–40. https://doi.org/10.1109/MCG.2015.45.
2. Posada, J., et al. (2015). Visual computing as a key enabling technology for Industrie 4.0 and industrial internet. *IEEE Computer Graphics and Applications, 35*(2), 26–40. https://doi.org/10.1109/MCG.2015.45.
3. Curtarelli, M., et al. (2016). ICT for work: Digital skills in the workplace|Digital Single Market. https://doi.org/10.2759/498467.
4. Osman, K., et al. (2009). Standard setting: Inserting domain of the 21st century thinking skills into the existing science curriculum in Malaysia. *Procedia—Social and Behavioral Sciences.* https://doi.org/10.1016/j.sbspro.2009.01.454.
5. Katz, L. F., & Goldin, C. (1996). The origins of technology-skill complementarity. https://doi.org/10.2139/ssrn.1537
6. Bartel, A. P., & Sicherman, N. (2002). Technological change and the skill acquisition of young workers. *Journal of Labor Economics*. https://doi.org/10.1086/209904
7. Greenhalgh, C., & Mavrotas, G. (1996). Job training, new technology and labour turnover. *British Journal of Industrial Relations*. https://doi.org/10.1111/j.1467-8543.1996.tb00474.x
8. Lillard, L. A., & Tan, H. W. (2012). Private sector training: Who gets it and what are its effects? *Research in Labor Economics*. https://doi.org/10.1108/S0147-9121(2012)0000035035
9. Bartel, A., et al. (2007). How does information technology affect productivity? Plant-level comparisons of product innovation, process improvement, and worker skills. *The Quarterly Journal of Economics, 122*(4), 1721–1758. https://doi.org/10.1162/qjec.2007.122.4.1721
10. Mohnen, P., & Röller, L. H. (2005). Complementarities in innovation policy. *European Economic Review*. https://doi.org/10.1016/j.euroecorev.2003.12.003
11. Ahmad, M., et al. (2013). Assessing ICT competencies among postgraduate students based on the 21st century ICT competency model. *Asian Social Science*. https://doi.org/10.5539/ass.v9n16p32
12. Carnevale, A. P., & Smith, N. (2013). Workplace basics: The skills employees need and employers want. *Human Resource Development International*. https://doi.org/10.1080/13678868.2013.821267
13. van Laar, E., et al. (2017). The relation between 21st-century skills and digital skills: A systematic literature review. *Computers in Human Behavior, 72*, 577–588. https://doi.org/10.1016/j.chb.2017.03.010.
14. Mitrovic, Z. (2010). Positioning e-skills within an organisation: An information systems management viewpoint. *SA Journal of Information Management*. https://doi.org/10.4102/sajim.v12i1.427

15. Nelson, R. R., & Winter, S. (1982). *An evolutionary theory of economic change*. Cambridge, Massachusetts: Harvard University Press.
16. Penrose, E. T. (1959). *The theory of the growth of the firm*. Oxford: Basil Blackwell.
17. Anderson, R. E. (2008). Implications of the information and knowledge society for education. In *International handbook of information technology in primary and secondary education*. https://doi.org/10.1007/978-0-387-73315-9_1.
18. Kefela, G. T. (2010). Knowledge-based economy and society has become a vital commodity to countries. *International NGO Journal*.
19. Lanvin, B., & Králik, M. (2009). E-Skills : Who made that big dent in my flat world ?* Growing worldwide demand for E-skills. *Information Technologies & International Development*.
20. Lanvin, B., & Passman, P. S. (2008). Building E-skills for the information age. The Global Information Technology Report.
21. Dachs, B., & Peters, B. (2014). Innovation, employment growth, and foreign ownership of firms: A European perspective. *Research Policy*. https://doi.org/10.1016/j.respol.2013.08.001
22. Doms, M., et al. (2002). Workers, wages, and technology. *The Quarterly Journal of Economics*. https://doi.org/10.1162/003355397555181
23. Bartel, A. P., & Lichtenberg, F. R. (2006). The comparative advantage of educated workers in implementing new technology. *Review of Economics and Statistics*. https://doi.org/10.2307/1937894
24. Cooley, T. F., et al. (1997). The replacement problem. *Journal of Monetary Economics*. https://doi.org/10.1016/S0304-3932(97)00055-X
25. Phelps, E. S. (2014). Investment in humans, technological diffusion, and economic growth. In *Studies in Macroeconomic Theory*. https://doi.org/10.1016/b978-0-12-554002-5.50015-7.
26. Welch, F. (2002). Education in production. *Journal of Political Economy*. https://doi.org/10.1086/259599
27. Autor, D. H., et al. (2006). The costs of wrongful-discharge laws. *Review of Economics and Statistics*. https://doi.org/10.1162/rest.88.2.211
28. Goos, M., & Manning, A. (2007). Lousy and lovely jobs: The rising polarization of work in Britain. *Review of Economics and Statistics*. https://doi.org/10.1162/rest.89.1.118
29. Spitz-Oener, A. (2006). Technical change, job tasks, and rising educational demands: Looking outside the wage structure. *Journal of Labor Economics*. https://doi.org/10.1086/499972
30. Castro Silva, H., & Lima, F. (2017). Technology, employment and skills: A look into job duration. *Research Policy*. https://doi.org/10.1016/j.respol.2017.07.007
31. Autor, D. H., et al. (1998). Computing inequality: Have computers changed the labor market? *The Quarterly Journal of Economics, 113*(4), 1169–1213. https://doi.org/10.1162/003355398555874
32. Berman, E., et al. (2006). Changes in the demand for skilled labor within U. S. manufacturing: Evidence from the annual survey of manufactures. *The Quarterly Journal of Economics*. https://doi.org/10.2307/2118467.
33. Bound, J., & Johnson, G. (1995). What are the causes of rising wage inequality in the United States? Federal Reserve Bank of New York.
34. Autor, D. H., et al. (2015). Untangling trade and technology: Evidence from local labour markets. *The Economic Journal*. https://doi.org/10.1111/ecoj.12245
35. Brynjolfsson, B. E., & Mcafee, A. (2011). Why workers are losing the war against machines. *The Atlantic*.
36. Frey, C. B., & Osborne, M. A. (2017). The future of employment: How susceptible are jobs to computerisation? *Technological Forecasting and Social*. https://doi.org/10.1016/j.techfore.2016.08.019
37. Ananiadou, K., & Claro, M. (2010). 21st century skills and competences for new millennium learners in OECD countries. https://doi.org/10.1787/218525261154.
38. Lewin, C., & McNicol, S. (2015). The impact and potential of iTEC: Evidence from large-scale validation in school classrooms. In *Re-engineering the Uptake of ICT in Schools* (pp. 163–186). Springer International Publishing. https://doi.org/10.1007/978-3-319-19366-3_9.

39. Voogt, J., & Roblin, N. P. (2012). A comparative analysis of international frameworks for 21st century competences: Implications for national curriculum policies. *Journal of Curriculum Studies*. https://doi.org/10.1080/00220272.2012.668938
40. Claro, M., et al. (2012). Assessment of 21st century ICT skills in Chile: Test design and results from high school level students. *Computers & Education*. https://doi.org/10.1016/j.compedu.2012.04.004
41. Eshet-Alkalai, Y. (2004). Digital literacy : A conceptual framework for survival skills in the digital era. *Journal of Educational Multimedia and Hypermedia*.
42. Bawden, D. (2008). Digital literacies: Concepts, policies and practices. *Names*. https://doi.org/10.1093/elt/ccr077
43. Hatlevik, O. E., et al. (2015). Predictors of digital competene in 7th grade: A multilevel analysis. *Journal of Computer Assisted Learning*. https://doi.org/10.1111/jcal.12065
44. Ferrari, A. (2012). Digital competence in practice : An analysis of frameworks. https://doi.org/10.1007/978-3-642-33263-0.
45. Binkley, M., et al. (2012). Defining twenty-first century skills. In *Assessment and teaching of 21st century skills* (pp. 17–66). Netherlands, Dordrecht: Springer. https://doi.org/10.1007/978-94-007-2324-5_2.
46. Eisenhardt, K. M. (1989). Building theories from case study research. *Academy of Management Review*. https://doi.org/10.5465/amr.1989.4308385
47. Yang, J., et al. (2014). Strategies for smooth and effective cross-cultural online collaborative learning. *Educational Technology & Society*.
48. Albuam, G., & Oppenheim, A. N. (2006). Questionnaire design, interviewing and attitude measurement. *Journal of Marketing Research*. https://doi.org/10.2307/3172892
49. van Deursen, A. J. A. M., & van Dijk, J. A. G. M. (2010). Measuring internet skills. *International Journal of Human-Computer Interaction*. https://doi.org/10.1080/10447318.2010.496338
50. Ng, W. (2012). Can we teach digital natives digital literacy? *Computers & Education*. https://doi.org/10.1016/j.compedu.2012.04.016
51. Ahmad, M., et al. (2016). The application of 21st century ICT literacy model among teacher trainees. *Turkish Online Journal of Educational Technology*.
52. Snow, E., & Katz, I. R. (2009). Using cognitive interviews to validate an interpretive argument for the ETS iSkills™ assessment. *Communications in Information Literacy*.
53. Siddiq, F., et al. (2016). Teachers' emphasis on developing students' digital information and communication skills (TEDDICS): A new construct in 21st century education. *Computers & Education*. https://doi.org/10.1016/j.compedu.2015.10.006
54. Choy, D., et al. (2016). Singapore primary and secondary students' motivated approaches for learning: A validation study. *Learning and Individual Differences*. https://doi.org/10.1016/j.lindif.2015.11.019
55. Helsper, E. J., & Eynon, R. (2013). Distinct skill pathways to digital engagement. *European Journal of Communication*. https://doi.org/10.1177/0267323113499113
56. Hinrichsen, J., & Coombs, A. (2013). The five resources of critical digital literacy: A framework for curriculum integration. *Research in Learning Technology*. https://doi.org/10.3402/rlt.v21.21334
57. Mengual-Andrés, S., et al. (2016). Delphi study for the design and validation of a questionnaire about digital competences in higher education. *International Journal of Educational Technology in Higher Education*. https://doi.org/10.1186/s41239-016-0009-y
58. Greene, J. A., et al. (2014). Measuring critical components of digital literacy and their relationships with learning. *Computers & Education*. https://doi.org/10.1016/j.compedu.2014.03.008
59. Lee, H., et al. (2016). Cooperation begins: Encouraging critical thinking skills through cooperative reciprocity using a mobile learning game. *Computers & Education*. https://doi.org/10.1016/j.compedu.2016.03.006
60. Greiff, S., et al. (2013). Computer-based assessment of complex problem solving: Concept, implementation, and application. *Educational Technology Research and Development*. https://doi.org/10.1007/s11423-013-9301-x

61. Scherer, R., & Gustafsson, J. E. (2015). The relations among openness, perseverance, and performance in creative problem solving: A substantive-methodological approach. *Thinking Skills and Creativity*. https://doi.org/10.1016/j.tsc.2015.04.004
62. Janssen, J., et al. (2013). Experts' views on digital competence: Commonalities and differences. *Computers & Education*. https://doi.org/10.1016/j.compedu.2013.06.008
63. Young, J. A. (2015). Assessing new media literacies in social work education: The development and validation of a comprehensive assessment instrument. *Journal of Technology in Human Services*. https://doi.org/10.1080/15228835.2014.998577
64. Anderman, E. M., et al. (2012). The challenges of teaching and learning about science in the twenty-first century: Exploring the abilities and constraints of adolescent learners. *Studies in Science Education*. https://doi.org/10.1080/03057267.2012.655038
65. Chai, C. S., et al. (2015). Assessing multidimensional students' perceptions of twenty-first-century learning practices. *Asia Pacific Education Review*. https://doi.org/10.1007/s12564-015-9379-4
66. Uzunboylu, H., & Hursen, C. (2011). Lifelong learning competence scale (LLLCS): The study of validity and reliability. *Hacettepe University Journal of Education*.
67. Benson, A. D., et al. (2002). The use of technology in the digital workplace: A framework for human resource development. *Advances in Developing Human Resources*. https://doi.org/10.1177/152342202237518
68. Cohen, W. M., & Levinthal, D. A. (1990). Absorptive capacity: A new perspective on learning and innovation. *Administrative Science Quarterly*. https://doi.org/10.2307/2393553
69. Brynjolfsson, E., & Mcafee, A. (2014). The digitization of just about everything. *The second machine age: Work, progress, and prosperity in a time of brilliant technologies*.
70. Dahl, A., et al. (2011). Building an innovation community. *Research Technology Management*. https://doi.org/10.5437/08956308x5405006
71. Ferrari, A. (2012). 21st century learning for 21st century skills. Berlin: Springer. https://doi.org/10.1007/978-3-642-33263-0.
72. Holt, L., & Brockett, R. G. (2012). Self direction and factors influencing technology use: Examining the relationships for the 21st century workplace. *Computers in Human Behavior*. https://doi.org/10.1016/j.chb.2012.06.011
73. Levy, F., & Murnane, R. J. (2015). The new division of labor. https://doi.org/10.1515/9781400845927
74. Quieng, M. C., et al. (2015). 21st century-based soft skills: Spotlight on non-cognitive skills in a cognitive-laden dentistry program. *European Journal of Contemporary Education*. https://doi.org/10.13187/ejced.2015.11.72.
75. Yin, R. K. (2003). *Applications of case study research*. https://doi.org/10.1097/FCH.0b013e31822dda9e
76. Yin, R. K. (1994). Applied social research methods series.

The Role of Digital Competencies and Creativity for Job Crafting in Public Administration

Filomena Buonocore, Rocco Agrifoglio, and Davide de Gennaro

Abstract Over recent years, the way public workers perform and interpret the own work has radically changed. Among these changes, what seems to have had a decisive impact is the advent of information and communication technologies. The informatization, digitalization, and computerization of procedures and jobs has made learning and the use of digital competencies necessary to face constant change and to take advantage of it. Digital competencies consist in knowing how to use the information society technologies for work, leisure, and communication with confidence and a critical spirit. So, those who manage to develop basic skills in information and communication technologies can juggle in this changing scenario. In this ongoing study, we hypothesize a relationship between digital competencies and job crafting. We hypothesize that civil servants developing this type of competencies can act proactively on their work by modifying its contents, relationships, and cognitive perception if they are creative. Implications are discussed.

Keywords Digital competencies · Job crafting · Creativity

1 Introduction: The New Digital Scenario

Almost half of the jobs currently being done by people in the world can be automated when technologies have spread on a global scale. According to a report released in 2016 by the World Economic Forum, *The Future of Jobs and Skills Report* [1], in the time frame that reaches 2020, 2 new millions of jobs will be created in the world but at the same time 7 will disappear, with a negative balance—therefore—of over 5 million jobs. As a result, the required skills and abilities for employers and employees will constantly change.

F. Buonocore · R. Agrifoglio
University "Parthenope" of Naples, Naples, Italy

D. de Gennaro (✉)
University of Salerno, Fisciano, Italy
e-mail: ddegennaro@unisa.it

C. Metallo et al. (eds.), *Digital Transformation and Human Behavior*, Lecture Notes in Information Systems and Organisation 37,
https://doi.org/10.1007/978-3-030-47539-0_7

Numerous studies in the literature show that the contribution of technology makes work easier and more satisfying [2–4]: through innovative methods such as the smart working in the company or the technological rethinking of classic activities to be carried out, corporate well-being increases [5]. Indeed, companies are called to build a reality where time is used better and people work and feel better.

This is the end point of a path where digital is an enabling factor, although the human factor always remains at the center [6, 7]. In fact, the digital must support and not crush the workers, helping them to improve performance and live their work in a more pleasant way.

In the light of these considerations, the need to train, cultivate, and constantly update digital skills and competencies emerges. "Digital competencies" initially referred to the ability to know how to use the technologies of the information society with confidence and critical spirit, but with the growing affirmation of the digital transformation it has acquired a broader and more articulated meaning [8, 9]. Digital competencies are a vast set of technological skills that allow people to identify, evaluate, use, share, and create content using information technology and the Internet. They can range from basic skills such as knowing how to use a computer to more specific and advanced skills such as code building or the development of software systems for artificial intelligence [10]. Since the world of technology is constantly evolving, even digital competencies are constantly changing and are destined to rapidly change over the years.

A first definition of digital competence has been proposed in 2006 by the European Parliament in a document indicating the eight key competencies for lifelong learning. Here it is: "Digital competence involves the confident and critical use of information Society technology (IST) for work, leisure, learning, and communication. It is underpinned by basic skills in ICT: the use of computers to retrieve, access, store, produce, present, and exchange information, and to communicate and participate in collaborative networks via the Internet". To actualize the concept of digital competencies it must be taken into account that today ICT is increasingly present in all professions and that digital competencies are strongly affected by technological developments. Therefore, it is no longer a question of a phenomenon that concerns only IT management or technology companies, but a reality that pervades all business sectors and functions [11, 12].

The perspective appears to be clear: ICT spreads within our society, so digital competencies have become essential for all individuals; more in detail, the ICT spreads especially within the work environment, for which most jobs require these new skills [13, 14].

If these considerations are true for the private sector, it is also true that this awareness has not yet established itself in the public sector in all countries [15–17]; digital competencies for public administration are essential for the process of modernization of the country at all levels, so they should be a priority in the training system for public employees [18–20]. Today, those responsible for guiding the public administration are called upon to act as propulsion centers for change and must be able to understand which the priorities are to be addressed, to reason about the feasibility of the projects, and to assess whether a solution is organizationally feasible.

A more efficient and effective public sector at the service of citizens can be obtained if there is a greater propensity to change and innovation, with the ability to deliver and manage digital services and the will to spread greater knowledge of emerging digital issues in the public administration (PA) (e.g., digital citizenship, e-government, open government, etc.) [21–25].

This study proposes to investigate the dynamics related to digital competencies and worker behavior through a study in the Italian public sector.

We hypothesize that public workers who have acquired and can manage digital competencies behave like job crafters, and consequently they work better and produce better. Job crafting is defined as the possibility, by workers, to shape and redefine their job through physical, relational, and cognitive modifications. In practice, employees proactively modify the way they see their work, the form or number of activities, and the social interactions with others. Our assumption is that public workers who have digital competencies will act proactively to change the characteristics of their work, then generating greater well-being and satisfaction at work and better performance for the public sector as a whole, and that this relationship is moderated by creativity. This study may offer interesting implications since the studies on the antecedents of job crafting are few in literature [26], all the more with reference to the public and digital sectors [27]. Implications for theory and practice will be discussed.

2 Theory and Hypotheses

In recent years, digital competence (or digital literacy) has become a key term in the policy-related and managerial literature. Most research has stressed the concept of digital competence for exploring what kind of skills and understanding people should have in the knowledge society [8, 9, 28].

Contrary to what happens in common language, the terms skills and competencies are not synonyms, but they have a different meaning. In this regard, the OECD [29] remarked that "a competence is more than just knowledge and skills. It involves the ability to meet complex demands, by drawing on and mobilizing psychosocial resources (including skills and attitudes) in a particular context" (p. 4). Thus, digital competence consists of not only digital skills but also social and emotional aspects for using and understanding digital device [8]. According to the European Commission definition, "digital competence involves the confident and critical use of Information Society Technology (IST) for work, leisure, learning, and communication. It is underpinned by basic skills in ICT: the use of computers to retrieve, access, store, produce, present, and exchange information, and to communicate and participate in collaborative networks via the Internet". Building upon digital competence stream, Martin [30] stated "digital Literacy is the awareness, attitude and ability of individuals to appropriately use digital tools and facilities to identify, access, manage, integrate, evaluate, analyse and synthesize digital resources, construct new knowledge, create media expressions, and communicate with others, in the context of specific life situations, in order to enable constructive social action; and to reflect upon this process"

(p. 135). In this regard, digital literacy is more than technology knowledge, but it also refers to individual ability to create meanings and communicate effectively with others through digital tools [28].

Digital literacy is a set of technical-procedural, cognitive, and socio-emotional skills that enables people to perform tasks effectively in a digital environment [31]. In contrast with new literacies paradigm that focuses on social practices shaped by emerging technologies, digital literacy emphasizes individual's learning with digital technologies. In this regard, digitally literate should be able to adapt to new ICTs quickly and pick up easily new semiotic language for communication as they arise [28]. Eshet-Alkalai [32] suggested that digital literacy consists of five types of literacies: (i) photo-visual literacy (learning-to-read from visuals); (ii) reproduction literacy (the art of creative duplication); (iii) branching literacy (the ability to create mental models, concept maps and other forms of abstract representations in hypermedial environments); (iv) information literacy (critical thinking and the ability to search, locate and assess Web-based information effectively); and (v) socio-emotional literacy (the emotional and social aspects of online socializing and collaborating).

Building upon Eshet-Alkalai [32] framework, Ng [28] proposed a research model on digital literacy that focuses on three dimensions, such as technical, cognitive, and social-emotional. The first dimension refers to those technical and operational skills possessed by an individual with new and emerging technologies usage for learning and in everyday activities. The second dimension of digital literacy, instead, is related to the individual ability to think critically in the search, evaluate and create cycle of handling digital information. Finally, the last dimension refers to people ability to use web 2.0 technologies for communicating, socializing and learning. Central to as technical, cognitive, and social-emotional dimensions is critical literacy which, as the Tasmanian Department of Education website stated [28], involves "ways of looking at written, visual, spoken, multimedia and performance texts to question and challenge the attitudes, values and beliefs that lie beneath the surface".

Based on the digital competencies scenario represented, we hypothesize that these skills, if possessed by individuals, determine an increase in job crafting behaviors.

Job crafting captures "the physical and cognitive changes individuals make in the task or relational boundaries of their work" [33, p. 179]. It consists of three proactive individual behaviors that enable workers to manipulate their jobs to fit more their natural inclinations: (i) physically altering the task boundaries to incorporate one or more additional tasks in one's job, (ii) enhancing the social environment at work by investing in high–quality relationships with co–workers, supervisors, customers, and so forth, and (iii) working on the cognitive nature of the job by mentally reframing it in more positive terms.

Individuals implement job crafting behaviors when tasks or duties are not well specified [33]. By taking advantage of this "lack of norms", individuals can get the best work performance and motivation in the moment they succeed in modifying the characteristics of their job based on their personal characteristics. Thanks to these behaviors and these modifications, individuals are able to change the organizational routines [34] by altering the way of working of individuals and workgroups.

Job crafting is an activity that employees spontaneously undertake to meet their needs and preferences in the workplace [35]. It's a behavior that requires an adaptation to the challenges and to the constraints imposed by an employer [36] and it represents a strategic advantage for employees and for the organization as a whole, although it will be shown that these changes are not always in line with the organizational goals and needs [37].

When employees mobilize resources through job crafting behaviors, they can create a work environment that meets their needs and that is more in line with their abilities [38]. This means that job performance will be better: happy employees are indeed more sensitive to take the opportunities in their working environment, they engage more often in relationships with their colleagues, and finally they are more optimistic and more confident and these attributes enable better results for the organization. These are actions undertaken from a bottom–up approach that generates greater work engagement and higher performance [39], and that employers should recognize in order to guide workers behavior towards positive actions [40].

In recent years, this definition has been refined and detailed in a new perspective: job crafting represents the modifications in the characteristics on the physical, organizational, and social aspects of the job, in order to balance job demands and job resources (JD-R model) [40, 41]. In practice, the JD-R model assumes that each job position has its own particular characteristics, and these characteristics can be classified into job demands and job resources: job strain develops, regardless of the type of job, when some job demands are high and when some job resources are limited [42].

Job crafting literature examined personality characteristics, work characteristics, and demographics as antecedents of job crafting; common antecedents studied in this approach are proactive personality [41], general self-efficacy [43], work engagement [44], job performance [41, 45], and job satisfaction [46].

Some authors have also dealt with issues related to ICT, such as the use of technology or other information systems to change the processes of work [47], to maintain increased flexibility [48], or to perform one's own tasks in more innovative ways [49]; nevertheless, they did not define any specific technology-related crafting forms and the contributions on the subject are scarce [27]. Similarly, in our knowledge also studies in the public sector are scarce, except for a few examples [50–52].

The objective of this study is therefore to improve the research on job crafting by analyzing a possible antecedent in digital competencies and a little studied context namely the public sector. It is possible that the civil servants who are endowed with digital skills modify their work to make it more in line and fixed with their personal characteristics, thus acting as a job crafters.

Accordingly, we propose the following:

Hp1(a): Digital competencies are positively related to job crafting.

The relationship just presented, however, could not be linear, or at least not only. It is possible that some demographic characteristics may change one's perception of oneself and the behaviors that arise from it. Therefore, the hypothesis of this study is that creativity at work moderates the previously hypothesized relationship between digital competencies and job crafting.

Creativity is more than a social outcome, marked by certain kinds of behavior and having utilitarian value. Being creative at work does not only mean proposing new ideas but also, and above all, giving life to constructive comparisons and promoting innovation, even risking not being appreciated for one's creative thinking [53].

Creative thinking in the workplace allows people to solve everyday problems, to choose the most effective strategies for action [54]. Individuals' creativity is the brick with which organizational innovation can be built [55]. Today, entrepreneurship and innovation are linked to creative ability: the success of a company depends, in large part, on the initiative of creative entrepreneurs who know how to realize innovative ideas by identifying the resources and seizing the opportunities of the area in which they operate, assuming the responsibility of risking investing in their own project [56].

Creativity at work is indeed a resource. The World Economic Forum [1], in presenting a portrait of how work will change by 2020, placed creativity at the third place among the 10 skills considered fundamental in performing jobs. It seems paradoxical that in a hyper-technological and robotic world what will really make the difference will still be the person; on the contrary, to bring value it will be necessary to get the best from technology without being overwhelmed. In fact, as complexity increases, minds will be able to arrive at a useful and innovative synthesis of the myriad of processes, equipment, and data. Creativity needs a concrete application, otherwise it remains an abstract concept impossible to handle. In the case of the 4th industrial revolution, the world of work already needs professionals who are able to combine creative thinking and high technology in different but increasingly connected sectors: robotics, materials science, biotechnology, transport, artificial intelligence, big data, and so on [57, 58].

Based on the above, it is possible that creative personalities can lead to job crafting behaviors for employees who have digital competencies at their disposal (Fig. 1).

In fact, job crafting is based on extra-role behaviors [59] such as creativity, since workers literally "invent" new types of jobs. Accordingly, we propose the following:

Hp1(B): Creativity at work moderates the hypothesized relationship between digital competencies and job crafting (Hp1(a)).

3 Method

Data for the study will be collected through an association of Italian public administrations that is the ANCI (National Association of Italian Municipalities); 7041 Municipalities are members of this association, representing 90% of the whole population.

A pilot study will be conducted to understand more deeply how the civil servants react to the constantly changing digital scenario to maintain up their motivation at work. In particular, our focus will be on public employees, since job crafting is implemented in the case of prescribed jobs [60] and we assume that even individuals

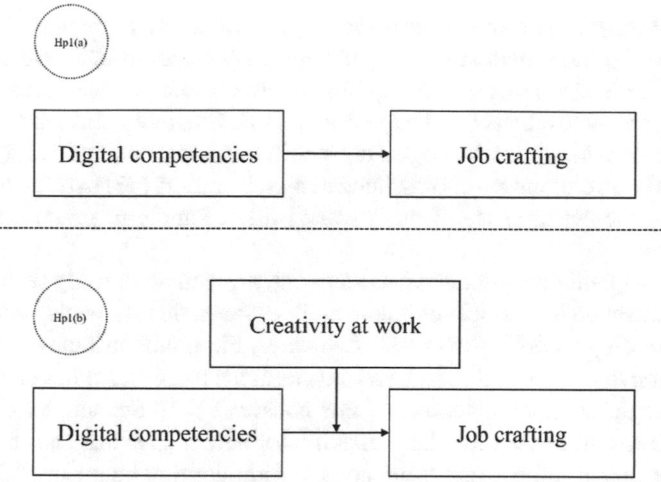

Fig. 1 The hypothesized moderation relationship (Hp1(a) and Hp1(b))

who do not hold senior positions can ensure significant changes in the way the work is done.

Following Gioia method for qualitative analysis [61], this study's approach will depend on a generic research question, i.e. "we want to explore the behaviors that civil servants undertake in response to digital changes occurring to their profession to maintain their motivation at work". The interviews will be administered as informal conversations within which it is possible to range over all the topics that concern the predictors of working behaviors of individuals. Interviews will be later analysed using an online software for qualitative data analysis, Dedoose (SocioCultural Research Consultants), useful to classify the responses in relevant first-order codes/terms and second-order concepts/themes.

Subsequently, a quantitative study will be designed to test the relationships emerged in the pilot study, hopefully the relationships between digital competencies, creativity, and job crafting. To minimize potential bias related to common method variance, data will be collected in two waves with a time gap between surveys of six months.

4 Expected Results

The expected results of this study concern the contribution that creativity may offer to the relationship between digital competencies and job crafting. Creative employees who have basic or in-depth knowledge of technological subjects may be in fact able and stimulated to actively modify the boundaries of tasks, relationships, and cognitions, radically changing the structure of their work.

In accordance with the literature on the subject, this study starts from the assumption that creativity contributes to actively change one's work through job crafting [59]. It is indeed a creative process that requires individual and personal predispositions to generate productive behavioral expressions [43]. Creativity and job crafting find fertile ground in the new technologies present in the world of work: work processes are constantly revolutionized and challenged by job crafters [47] in order to maintain flexibility in the performance of one's work [48] or simply to propose innovative methods [49].

Through a qualitative pilot and a subsequently quantitative study with questionnaires administered to a sample of Italian civil servants, this study may contribute to the literature on job crafting in at least two ways. First, it contributes in improving knowledge on the antecedents of job crafting, as at the moment studies on the subject are less than those on the outcomes of this construct [62]. Second, another contribution concerns the answer to scholars asking for new studies that can shed light on the implications of information technology for job crafting behaviors [27, 63, 64]. Indeed, the rapid technological changes will make work practices quite different from those we are used to studying (for example the subtle difference between work and nonwork, or the virtual and alternative work environments) [65] and studying these relationships can be very timely and interesting. Indeed, it is possible that the results of this study suggest individuals modify the tasks of their work (for example, by adding or reducing activities thanks to the help of new technologies), their relational boundaries (for example, by creating stronger working relationships even with colleagues physically distant from the place where one works), and their cognitive perception (through the modified perception of one's work thanks to computer technology). These changes would only be possible in the presence of digital competencies, and the implications could be boundless. Theoretical and practical implications will be discussed.

References

1. WEF (World Economic Forum). (2016). The future of jobs and skills report. World Economic Forum Ed., Cologny.
2. Davis, F. D. (1989). Perceived usefulness, perceived ease of use, and user acceptance of information technology. *MIS Quarterly, 13*(3), 319–340. https://doi.org/10.2307/249008
3. Krishnaveni, R., & Meenakumari, J. (2010). Usage of ICT for information administration in higher education institutions–a study. *International Journal of Environmental Science and Development, 1*(3), 282–286.
4. Stephens, K. K. (2007). The successive use of information and communication technologies at work. *Communication Theory, 17*(4), 486–507. https://doi.org/10.1111/j.1468-2885.2007.00308.x
5. Davenport, T. H. (2011). Rethinking knowledge work: A strategic approach. *McKinsey Quarterly, 1*(11), 88–99.
6. Jasperson, J. S., Carter, P. E., & Zmud, R. W. (2005). A comprehensive conceptualization of post-adoptive behaviors associated with information technology enabled work systems. *MIS Quarterly, 29*(3), 525–557.

7. Katz, R. (2004). *The human side of managing technological innovation: A collection of readings* (Vol. 2). New York: Oxford University Press.
8. Ilomäki, L., Kantosalo, A., & Lakkala, M. (2011). What is digital competence? In *Linked portal: European schoolnet (EUN)* (pp. 1–12). Brussels
9. Ilomäki, L., Paavola, S., Lakkala, M., & Kantosalo, A. (2016). Digital competence–an emergent boundary concept for policy and educational research. *Education and Information Technologies, 21*(3), 655–679. https://doi.org/10.1007/s10639-014-9346-4
10. Janssen, J., Stoyanov, S., Ferrari, A., Punie, Y., Pannekeet, K., & Sloep, P. (2013). Experts' views on digital competence: Commonalities and differences. *Computers & Education, 68,* 473–481. https://doi.org/10.1016/j.compedu.2013.06.008
11. Alam, S. S., & Noor, M. K. M. (2009). ICT adoption in small and medium enterprises: An empirical evidence of service sectors in Malaysia. *International Journal of Business and Management, 4*(2), 112–125. 10.1.1.652.6803.
12. Cumps, B., Viaene, S., Dedene, G., & Vandenbulcke, J. (2006). An empirical study on business/ICT alignment in European organisations. In *Proceedings of the 39th Annual Hawaii International Conference on System Sciences* (pp. 195a–195a). Kauia, HI, USA: IEEE. https://doi.org/10.1109/HICSS.2006.53.
13. Adler, P. (1986). New technologies, new skills. *California Management Review, 29*(1), 9–28. https://doi.org/10.2307/41165224
14. Lawler, E. E., III. (1994). From job-based to competency-based organizations. *Journal of Organizational Behavior, 15*(1), 3–15. https://doi.org/10.1002/job.4030150103
15. Aurigi, A. (2006). New technologies, same dilemmas: Policy and design issues for the augmented city. *Journal of Urban Technology, 13*(3), 5–28. https://doi.org/10.1080/10630730601145989
16. Demczuk, A., & Pawłowska, A. (2006). Progress toward e-government in Poland: Issues and dilemmas. *Information Polity, 11*(3–4), 229–240. https://doi.org/10.3233/IP-2006-0104
17. Lasio, R. (2014). Il patrimonio culturale digitale verso Horizon 2020. *DigItalia, 2,* 215–219.
18. Asgarkhani, M. (2005). Digital government and its effectiveness in public management reform: A local government perspective. *Public Management Review, 7*(3), 465–487. https://doi.org/10.1080/14719030500181227
19. Weerakkody, V., & Reddick, C. G. (2012). *Public sector transformation through e-government: Experiences from Europe and North America.* Abingdon-on-Thames (UK): Routledge.
20. West, D. M. (2005). *Digital government: Technology and public sector performance.* Princeton: Princeton University Press.
21. Carter, L., & Bélanger, F. (2005). The utilization of e-government services: Citizen trust, innovation and acceptance factors. *Information Systems Journal, 15*(1), 5–25. https://doi.org/10.1111/j.1365-2575.2005.00183.x
22. Chun, S., Shulman, S., Sandoval, R., & Hovy, E. (2010). Government 2.0: Making connections between citizens, data and government. *Information Polity, 15*(1–2), 1–9. https://doi.org/10.3233/IP-2010-0205.
23. Linders, D. (2012). From e-government to we-government: Defining a typology for citizen coproduction in the age of social media. *Government Information Quarterly, 29*(4), 446–454. https://doi.org/10.1016/j.giq.2012.06.003
24. Nam, T. (2012). Citizens' attitudes toward open government and government 2.0. *International Review of Administrative Sciences, 78*(2), 346–368. https://doi.org/10.1177/0020852312438783.
25. Scholl, H. J. (2003). E-government: a special case of ICT-enabled business process change. In *36th Annual Hawaii International Conference on System Sciences* (p. 12). IEEE. https://doi.org/10.1109/HICSS.2003.1174309.
26. Buonocore, F., de Gennaro, D., Russo, M., & Salvatore, D. (2020). Cognitive job crafting: A possible response to increasing job insecurity and declining professional prestige. *Human Resource Management Journal*, 1–16. https://doi.org/10.1111/1748-8583.12270.
27. Lazazzara, A., Tims, M., & de Gennaro, D. (2019). The process of reinventing a job: A meta–synthesis of qualitative job crafting research. *Journal of Vocational Behavior*. https://doi.org/10.1016/j.jvb.2019.01.001

28. Ng, W. (2012). Can we teach digital natives digital literacy? *Computers & Education, 59*(3), 1065–1078. https://doi.org/10.1016/j.compedu.2012.04.016
29. OECD. (2005). The OECD Program Definition and Selection of Competencies. The definition and selection of key competencies. Executive summary.
30. Martin, A. (2005). DigEuLit—a European framework for digital literacy: A progress report. *Journal of ELiteracy, 2,* 130–136. 10.1.1.469.1923
31. Aviram, R., & Eshet-Alkalai, Y. (2006). Towards a theory of digital literacy: Three scenarios for the next steps. *European Journal of Open Distance E-Learning, 9*(1).
32. Eshet-Alkali, Y., & Amichai-Hamburger, Y. (2004). Experiments in digital literacy. *CyberPsychology & Behavior, 7*(4), 421–429. https://doi.org/10.1089/cpb.2004.7.421
33. Wrzesniewski, A., & Dutton, J. E. (2001). Crafting a job: Revisioning employees as active crafters of their work. *Academy of Management Review, 26*(2), 179–201. https://doi.org/10.5465/amr.2001.4378011
34. Leana, C., Appelbaum, E., & Shevchuk, I. (2009). Work process and quality of care in early childhood education: The role of job crafting. *Academy of Management Journal, 52*(6), 1169–1192. https://doi.org/10.5465/AMJ.2009.47084651
35. Kira, M., van Eijnatten, F. M., & Balkin, D. B. (2010). Crafting sustainable work: Development of personal resources. *Journal of Organizational Change Management, 23*(5), 616–632. https://doi.org/10.1108/09534811011071315
36. Berg, J. M., Wrzesniewski, A., & Dutton, J. E. (2010). Perceiving and responding to challenges in job crafting at different ranks: When proactivity requires adaptivity. *Journal of Organizational Behavior, 31*(2–3), 158–186. https://doi.org/10.1002/job.645
37. Van den Heuvel, M., Demerouti, E., Bakker, A. B., & Schaufeli, W. B. (2010). Personal resources and work engagement in the face of change. Contemporary occupational health psychology. In: *Global perspectives on research and practice* (pp. 124–150). https://doi.org/10.1002/9780470661550.
38. Tims, M., & Bakker, A. B. (2010). Job crafting: Towards a new model of individual job redesign. *SA Journal of Industrial Psychology, 36*(2), 1–9.
39. Tims, M., Bakker, A. B., & Derks, D. (2013). The impact of job crafting on job demands, job resources, and well-being. *Journal of Occupational Health Psychology, 18*(2), 230–240. https://doi.org/10.1037/a0032141
40. Petrou, P., Demerouti, E., Peeters, M. C., Schaufeli, W. B., & Hetland, J. (2012). Crafting a job on a daily basis: Contextual correlates and the link to work engagement. *Journal of Organizational Behavior, 33*(8), 1120–1141. https://doi.org/10.1002/job.1783
41. Bakker, A. B., Tims, M., & Derks, D. (2012). Proactive personality and job performance: The role of job crafting and work engagement. *Human Relations, 65*(10), 1359–1378. https://doi.org/10.1177/0018726712453471
42. Crawford, E. R., LePine, J. A., & Rich, B. L. (2010). Linking job demands and resources to employee engagement and burnout: A theoretical extension and meta-analytic test. *Journal of Applied Psychology, 95,* 834–848. https://doi.org/10.1037/2Fa0019364
43. Rudolph, C. W., Katz, I. M., Lavigne, K. N., & Zacher, H. (2017). Job crafting: A meta-analysis of relationships with individual differences, job characteristics, and work outcomes. *Journal of Vocational Behavior, 102,* 112–138. https://doi.org/10.1016/j.jvb.2017.05.008
44. Lichtenthaler, P. W., & Fischbach, A. (2018). Leadership, job crafting, and employee health and performance. *Leadership & Organization Development Journal, 39*(5), 620–632. https://doi.org/10.1108/LODJ-07-2017-0191
45. Gordon, H. J., Demerouti, E., Le Blanc, P. M., & Bipp, T. (2015). Job crafting and performance of Dutch and American health care professionals. *Journal of Personnel Psychology, 14,* 192–202. https://doi.org/10.1027/1866-5888/a000138
46. De Beer, L. T., Tims, M., & Bakker, A. B. (2016). Job crafting and its impact on work engagement and job satisfaction in mining and manufacturing. *South African Journal of Economic and Management Sciences, 19*(3), 400–412. https://doi.org/10.17159/2222-3436/2016/v19n3a7
47. Bruning, P. F., & Campion, M. A. (2018). A role–resource approach–avoidance model of job crafting: A multimethod integration and extension of job crafting theory. *Academy of Management Journal, 61*(2), 499–522. https://doi.org/10.5465/amj.2015.0604

48. Sturges, J. (2012). Crafting a balance between work and home. *Human Relations, 65*(12), 1539–1559. https://doi.org/10.1177/0018726712457435
49. Grant-Vallone, E. J., & Ensher, E. A. (2017). Re-crafting careers for mid-career faculty: A qualitative study. *Journal of Higher Education Theory and Practice, 17*(5), 10–24. https://doi.org/10.33423/jhetp.v17i5.1533
50. Bakker, A. B. (2015). A job demands–resources approach to public service motivation. *Public Administration Review, 75*(5), 723–732. https://doi.org/10.1111/puar.12388
51. Kim, S. (2012). Does person-organization fit matter in the public-sector? Testing the mediating effect of person-organization fit in the relationship between public service motivation and work attitudes. *Public Administration Review, 72*(6), 830–840. https://doi.org/10.1111/j.1540-6210.2012.02572.x
52. Tuan, L. T. (2018). Behind the influence of job crafting on citizen value co-creation with the public organization: Joint effects of paternalistic leadership and public service motivation. *Public Management Review, 20*(10), 1533–1561. https://doi.org/10.1080/14719037.2018.1430247
53. De Stobbeleir, K. E., Ashford, S. J., & Buyens, D. (2011). Self-regulation of creativity at work: The role of feedback-seeking behavior in creative performance. *Academy of Management Journal, 54*(4), 811–831. https://doi.org/10.5465/AMJ.2011.64870144
54. Amabile, T. M., Barsade, S. G., Mueller, J. S., & Staw, B. M. (2005). Affect and creativity at work. *Administrative Science Quarterly, 50*(3), 367–403. https://doi.org/10.2189/asqu.2005.50.3.367
55. Redmond, M. R., Mumford, M. D., & Teach, R. (1993). Putting creativity to work: Effects of leader behavior on subordinate creativity. *Organizational Behavior and Human Decision Processes, 55*(1), 120–151. https://doi.org/10.1006/obhd.1993.1027
56. Baer, M. (2012). Putting creativity to work: The implementation of creative ideas in organizations. *Academy of Management Journal, 55*(5), 1102–1119. https://doi.org/10.5465/amj.2009.0470
57. Cotet, G. B., Balgiu, B. A., & Zaleschi, V. C. (2017). Assessment procedure for the soft skills requested by Industry 4.0. In: *MATEC Web of Conferences* (p. 07005). EDP Sciences. https://doi.org/10.1051/matecconf/201712107005.
58. Erol, S., Jäger, A., Hold, P., Ott, K., & Sihn, W. (2016). Tangible industry 4.0: A scenario-based approach to learning for the future of production. *Procedia CiRp, 54*, 13–18. https://doi.org/10.1016/j.procir.2016.03.162.
59. Demerouti, E., Bakker, A. B., & Gevers, J. M. (2015). Job crafting and extra-role behavior: The role of work engagement and flourishing. *Journal of Vocational Behavior, 91*, 87–96. https://doi.org/10.1016/j.jvb.2015.09.001
60. Berg, J. M., Dutton, J. E., & Wrzesniewski, A. (2013). Job crafting and meaningful work. In Purpose and meaning in the workplace (pp. 81–104). Washington, DC: American Psychological Association. https://doi.org/10.1111/puar.12388.
61. Gioia, D. A., Corley, K. G., & Hamilton, A. L. (2013). Seeking qualitative rigor in inductive research: Notes on the Gioia methodology. *Organizational Research Methods, 16*(1), 15–31. https://doi.org/10.1177/1094428112452151
62. Niessen, C., Weseler, D., & Kostova, P. (2016). When and why do individuals craft their jobs? The role of individual motivation and work characteristics for job crafting. *Human Relations, 69*(6), 1287–1313. https://doi.org/10.1177/0018726715610642
63. Lee, J. Y., & Lee, Y. (2018). Job crafting and performance: Literature review and implications for human resource development. *Human Resource Development Review, 17*(3), 277–313. https://doi.org/10.1177/1534484318788269
64. Parker, S. K., Morgeson, F. P., & Johns, G. (2017). One hundred years of work design research: Looking back and looking forward. *Journal of Applied Psychology, 102*(3), 403–420. https://doi.org/10.1037/apl0000106
65. Torraco, R. J. (2005). Work design theory: A review and critique with implications for human resource development. *Human Resource Development Quarterly, 16*(1), 85–109. https://doi.org/10.1002/hrdq.1125

Competence Development for Teachers Within a Digital Inter-professional Community

Ann Svensson

Abstract Competence development for teachers is of increasing importance as the use of digital tools poses a challenge to the pedagogical approach within the teaching context in schools. Schools are responsible for ensuring that students are able to use modern technology as tools for searching for knowledge and for communication, as well as for creation and learning. Hence, teachers need to develop their competence in integrating digital technologies into their pedagogical practices. Digital tools function as resources for interaction and collaboration across space and time, and also considerably facilitate inter-professional work and communication. This paper is based on an action-based qualitative study of a Nordic education project that focused on competence development among teachers, and where inter-professional collaboration and the use of digital tools was of great importance. The aim of this paper is to analyze how teachers' competence development with regard to innovative pedagogical skills can be supported in an inter-professional community of practice, using digital technologies. Different pedagogical approaches, curricular contents, digital resources and organizational conditions were produced in the virtual collaboration within this community of practice.

Keywords Competence development · Digital technology · Teachers · Pedagogical practice · Trust

1 Introduction

Digital technologies are increasingly integrated into teaching strategies [1, 2], especially since it is considered an educational demand in the knowledge society [3, 4]. In many countries, schools are responsible for ensuring that students are able to use

A. Svensson (✉)
University West, 461 86 Trollhättan, Sweden
e-mail: ann.svensson@hv.se

C. Metallo et al. (eds.), *Digital Transformation and Human Behavior*, Lecture Notes in Information Systems and Organisation 37, https://doi.org/10.1007/978-3-030-47539-0_8

modern technologies as tools for searching for knowledge and for communication, as well as for creation and learning. However, the implementation of new digital tools in classrooms has caused some uncertainty among teachers [5]. As a result, teachers often find it challenging to integrate digital technologies in their pedagogical practices—some teachers are even reluctant to do so [6]. Still, digital technologies create opportunities for actively developing and improving inter-professional learning and competence development among teachers and related professionals. There are indications that the teachers' own personal learning networks play a key role in developing their pedagogical practices related to digital technology [7]. However, teachers often practice their work without extensive interaction with colleagues. Many practicing teachers perform their work more or less in isolation, without exchanging ideas with other teachers [8]. Digital technology has become a resource for interaction and collaboration across space and time, and also considerably facilitates inter-professional work and learning [9, 10].

According to the constructivist perspective on learning and competence development, collaboration, interaction and communication are required elements in these processes, which means dialogues are considered necessary in order to facilitate sense-making, learning and competence development [11]. Participation is thus an intrinsic part of learning and competence development [12–14]. Communities of practice can be defined as groups consisting of individuals from different professions. In such groups, sharing constitutes a specific practice that has been developed as a result of collaboration over time [14]. Mental models that are shared among individuals within a group allow the group to create a common understanding of different situations. However, further studies are required to identify how online communities of practice influence teachers' learning and reflection [15].

This paper is based on an action-based qualitative study of a Nordic education project that focused on how virtual and digital technology can support the development of teachers' competence and innovative pedagogical skills within the pedagogical practice, in an inter-professional community of practice. Regular teaching cases involving digital technology were developed collaboratively in the project, which involved teachers as well as researchers, IT-pedagogues and IT-technicians. The aim of this paper is to analyze how teachers' competence development in using innovative pedagogical skills can be supported in an inter-professional community of practice, with the help of digital technologies. The paper is outlined as follows; the second section describes the theoretical framework; the third section presents the empirical setting; the fourth section describes the research method; the fifth section presents the results; the sixth section discusses the results, and the seventh and final section presents the conclusions of the paper.

2 Theoretical Framework

2.1 Collaboration in Professional Communities of Practice

Professional practice is especially interesting to study, as professions exhibit specific characteristics compared to other types of occupations [16]. When individuals from different professions collaborate in a virtual environment in order to develop new and innovative pedagogical teaching cases, inter-professional learning will take place, and the professions will, in turn, develop their competence. Moreover, there is also such a thing as a professional hierarchy, whereby some professions are given higher authority than others [17]. In relation to the educational context in this paper, communities of practice consist of groups where different professions are represented, and where a shared practice has developed as a result of collaboration [14]. Mental models that are shared among individuals in such groups allow the group to create a common understanding in different educational situations. This might also result in some redundancy of knowledge, which may influence individuals' capacity to share and integrate knowledge in a positive direction when it comes to learning and competence development in this context. The capacity of a group to share and integrate knowledge determines to which extent new and external information is used in practical work [18]. When people are working together, they simultaneously develop a specific sensemaking [19].

Boundaries related to barriers between professions might emerge when knowledge is shared across professions [20, 21]. Trust between professions is crucial in order to establish efficient knowledge sharing across boundaries [16], as trust works as a foundation for an open atmosphere in a community of practice [22]. Trust also positively influences the willingness of people to share knowledge within communities, which in turn promotes knowledge sharing behavior [23, 24]. People within a group need to trust each other and regard their group members as honest, capable and active in order for the group to be able to achieve its common goals. Furthermore, it is important to create and sustain personal relations between group members. Trust is seen as a foundation for efficient interaction that caters for knowledge sharing within groups. Trust is also necessary in order to enable people to share tacit knowledge and create opportunities for learning and knowledge integration [25]. Hsu and Chang [26] studied IT-mediated communities and found that inter-personal trust is a vital component for encouraging knowledge sharing. If trust exists between people, opportunities for creating knowledge will arise spontaneously, and conceptual understanding may consequently be integrated into practical work [18, 21]. In other words, trust facilitates knowledge sharing within communities of practice. Besides trust, reciprocity is another contextual determining factor for processes related to knowledge sharing among professionals. In addition, there may be personal perceptions of knowledge sharing such as self-efficacy, perceived relative advantage and perceived compatibility [27].

2.2 Knowledge Integration for Competence Development

Abel [28] defines competence as a way to practice a type of knowledge within a specific context. Knowledge resides within individuals in a tacit or explicit form and may be converted from abstract ideas and conceptual dimensions to tangible and structured forms. Knowledge can be created through people and processes, and it can be shared between professionals. Professionals can capture existing knowledge and share it among others in order to reuse and integrate the knowledge [29]. Knowledge integration generally refers to processes where knowledge is flowing between groups and individuals within a work context [30]. Such processes are important aspects of learning and knowledge usage within organizations. Alavi and Tiwana [31] define knowledge integration as a synthesis of individuals' specific knowledge in specific situations. When individuals from different professions collaborate, their specific individual knowledge can be unified, combined and integrated, which may in turn lead to learning within communities of practice [32]. Thus, inter-professional learning and knowledge integration is an end-product of such collaboration [25].

Two aspects can be identified within the constructivist perspective on knowledge integration. The first aspect considers knowledge as a complex and sometimes contradictory phenomenon, where ambiguity of knowledge exists within relations between knowledge on the one hand, and individual experiences and values on the other hand. Knowledge is seen as a subject for reflection in situations and actions. From this perspective, knowledge integration is seen as something that is problematic, efficient and complicated to manage and organize, but knowledge integration is also seen as processes characterized by learning [33, 34]. The second aspect considers knowledge as a collective mind, or a collective intelligence, characterized as a social phenomenon. This aspect also considers differences between combining individuals in groups, compared to having individuals acting within groups. Thus, when collaborating within a community of practice, individuals have access to all sources of knowledge within the distributed and collective system of knowledge [35, 36]. The second aspect also considers individual interactions within a context as a complex system where professionals can develop their competence.

2.3 Digital Technology for Competence Development

Nowadays, professionals often use the Internet for accessing different learning materials. Different types of digital technologies offer different ways of learning and accessing knowledge [37]. The Internet also provides access to learning resources for many different kinds of student activities. However, teachers are not always taking advantage of the ways learning can be supported and transformed through access to information and by new tools available on the Internet. According to Wallace [38] and Wright [39], the Internet could be used to a higher extent in order to support learning among students [4], and it may also be used for supporting and promotion of competence development in the area of innovative pedagogical teaching skills. However, the degree to which these potentials are utilized depends on individual teachers' willingness to collaborate and share knowledge, and their opportunities to do so while developing their competence within their pedagogical practice [15].

Digital technology plays a key role in promoting competence development. Different types of digital tools, asynchronous as well as synchronous, are effective in different ways when it comes to facilitating inter-professional learning and competence development. Designing new learning spaces with innovative use of digital tools within educational contexts is challenging and requires virtual collaboration [40]. Majchrzak et al. [41] have pointed out the affordance of wikis and similar digital tools for promoting knowledge reuse through improved knowledge integration and competence development.

3 The Empirical Setting

This study has been conducted within a cross-border Nordic education project called the GNU-project. Eighteen school classes, in grade 4–9, from 13 secondary schools in Denmark, Norway and Sweden, participated in the project. Students, teachers, principals, IT-pedagogues and IT-technicians at the schools were involved, along with researchers from universities in Denmark, Norway and Sweden. The project ran over three years and included subject areas such as the mother tongue language, mathematics, science and social studies. The researchers came from diverse professional areas such as information systems, pedagogy and linguistics. This paper focuses on the part of the project that involved teaching of mother tongues. This part consisted of two class-matches, where one teacher and one class from each of the three countries formed a class-match. During each semester of the project, one teaching case was created and executed in each class-match. Four Swedish researchers were involved; two with an information systems background and one each from the fields of linguistics and pedagogy. A Swedish IT-pedagogue and an IT-technician also supported one of the teachers. The IT-pedagogue's role was to create opportunities for showing examples of technologies and software programs that the teachers could use in their teaching activities, and provide teachers with pedagogical support. The IT-technician provided technical support and offered different technological devices within the practical teaching context. One principal participated in two teaching cases in Sweden. There were two collaborating researchers from Denmark, Norway and Sweden, respectively.

Information and communication technology facilities and infrastructure differed between schools due to different conditions in different countries and municipalities. Differences between schools regarding how digital tools were applied to the different teaching cases were partly due to varying experience among teachers in using digital tools for teaching.

The central aims of the project were, on the one hand, to support collaborative creation of innovative teaching cases using digital tools and, on the other hand, promote students' Scandinavian inter-comprehension skills. The innovative teaching cases conformed with formal curricula requirements in all three countries. In contrast to regular teaching and learning in schools, the purpose of this project was to promote collaboration within a cross-border setting, focusing on the learning context of teachers and students alike. Both synchronous and asynchronous digital tools were used with the aim to promote communication and collaboration, which was in turn used as a basis for developing, planning, executing and evaluating different teaching cases.

Regular meetings were held with teams of teachers from all three countries, where the researchers could also take part. Furthermore, the researchers had their own synchronous meetings and were also invited to participate in the individual teaching cases. Basecamp was used as the collective platform for the GNU-project, where all project information was shared between participants. Synchronous digital tools, such as Adobe Connect and Skype, were used for most meetings. Asynchronous digital tools, such as wikis, and other digital resources, like Google Drive, were sometimes used to create and structure common teaching material that was produced within the project. Google Docs, for example, was used as an asynchronous tool for collaborative writing of texts, while wiki spaces were used for sharing information about learning goals, curricula, results and assessment criteria. Asynchronous digital tools were also used in the teaching cases and for document agreements, division of work between involved professionals, and for general support for inter-professional learning and competence development. The digital tools also made it possible to create both individual and collaborative spaces for reflections on teaching practice. Moreover, Skype, Adobe Connect, Facebook groups, e-mail, blogs and iPads with Swivl, as well as various video recording programs were used by the students in the teaching cases.

4 Research Method

This paper is based on action research conducted within a cross-border Nordic education project. The study focuses on collaboration in teaching the mother tongue of the three countries involved, i.e.; Danish, Norwegian and Swedish.

Action research considers two different interrelated and interactive domains of practice. Intrinsic research focusing on scientific goals constitutes one domain, whereas the other domain consists of practice where problems are discovered and solved in unstructured situations. Action research offers the possibility to develop valuable solutions to practical problems for people working within the changing and studied context. At the same time, research develops theoretical knowledge that is valuable for the research community. Action research thus produces knowledge for both practical and scientific applications [42]. In this project, teachers and researchers collaborated in their roles as change agents in order to improve the practical outcome. Solutions and actions within the studied teaching practice have been characterized as knowledge discoveries made while performing action research in practice.

During the project, a number of teaching cases were planned and executed, and several meetings took place in order to plan the common teaching cases. Teachers as well as researchers from the three neighboring countries participated in these meetings, which were often held using synchronous digital tools such as Adobe Connect and Skype. Wiki spaces, e-mail and Facebook were also important asynchronous tools for collaboration, in particular for the teachers. Teachers and researchers also sometimes met with IT-pedagogues and principals. The teaching cases were designed in such a way that students from all three countries had to collaborate to complete common tasks. During each teaching case, the researchers visited the schools and had the opportunity to participate, record and take photographs. Teaching cases executed using Adobe Connect were recorded. The researchers interviewed some of the teachers and students, and took notes during the collaborative teaching cases. After each visit, the researchers summarized their observations in detail. The teachers were also asked to evaluate the teaching cases together with their students. The researchers and teachers in each country also had a few physical meetings for planning and evaluation. The teachers and researchers together described the teaching cases in words, where the results of the teaching cases were analyzed.

The practice domain was analyzed using thematic analysis [43]. Thematic analysis is based on a theoretical approach where the specific research question works as the point of departure. The aim was to understand how inter-professional learning was achieved and for what purpose, and which type of digital tools were used for which type of learning. This particular analysis was based on a data set related to inter-professional learning. During the analysis process, the author and the teachers discussed the recorded material and the observations of the teaching cases, several times. Especially one teacher, who conducted many collaborative teaching cases, took part in these discussions in order to identify analytical themes. The discussions aimed at obtaining high validity and rigor of the qualitative study. The qualitative research sought to achieve valid results, in the sense that the research is open for careful scrutiny [44]. The themes were reviewed and refined in order to identify the essence of each theme, with the aim to obtain coherence and internal consistence of the collected data. The following themes were identified as interesting in the context of inter-professional learning and competence development:

- Pedagogical issues
- Curricular content
- Digital resources
- Organizational conditions.

5 Results

5.1 Pedagogical Issues

Teachers from different countries may reflect and think outside their own pedagogical approach and consider their Nordic colleagues' pedagogical methods and use of digital technology. Through collaboration, they can find a common pedagogical approach to different learning processes. One example is the need to discuss in which ways and to what extent students and parents can be informed about the purpose of a particular study area and the related use of digital technology. According to the Swedish general guidelines for teaching, teachers are obliged to clearly state in their planning what content from the subject syllabuses they will bring up, which abilities students will acquire, which approaches and working methods will be used in order to train the students in relation to the general curriculum goals, and which parts of the knowledge requirements will be assessed. Swedish teachers are, in contrast to teachers in Denmark and Norway, required to inform both students and parents about these plans in advance, usually known as local educational planning (LPP). Swedish teachers thus need to be aware of the purpose of using digital technologies in their teaching and how to actually use them.

In the online synchronous planning conferences with teachers from the three countries, the Swedish planning process was discussed. Sometimes the discussions resulted in a common Nordic LPP for a common teaching case, consisting of a small portion of content which the teachers formulated together in collective wiki spaces. Each teaching case was then created in order to clarify how digital tools should be used in practice.

The collaboration also provided opportunities for informal interaction in social media like Twitter and Facebook, where different professional groups exchanged information about the latest pedagogical research and digital tools.

5.2 Curricular Content

At the national level, educators and researchers involved in the project came together one full day per semester to exchange ideas and experiences from the teaching cases. Topics such as the purpose, content, curriculum, techniques, digital tools and practical implementation of the collaboration, were discussed at the meetings. Since different teaching cases were executed in different schools, all teachers and researchers had the opportunity to learn from each other. Teachers, on the one hand, pointed out national steering documents containing curriculum and syllabus that schools must follow. Researchers, on the other hand, pointed out eight key competences that the EU and the OECD have identified as goals that every citizen should strive to acquire in order to succeed in the knowledge society. Educators and researchers agreed that the teaching cases must be firmly anchored in each subject's national curriculum in order to practice the eight key competencies.

Inter-professional collaboration at cross-border level consisted of discussions about experiences from practical teaching situations and, not the least, similarities and differences between national steering documents that schools in each country should comply with in relation to each curriculum. Collective reflection also took place. Synchronous meetings made the collaboration possible. Teachers and researchers from each country gathered in one place and virtually met teachers and researchers from their neighboring countries using the conference system Adobe Connect. These meetings, which were led and organized by the researchers, gave the teachers an opportunity to discuss their practice and develop their competence in using digital technologies within their teaching practice.

Specific collaboration tasks were planned and prepared together by teachers and students at the local schools using digital technologies. This work model was for example employed in a teaching case that involved modern children's literature, where the original book was written in the students' native language. Students and teachers in each country together selected a book that all students in the three participating countries read, analyzed and discussed in a synchronous cross-border collaboration. In the initial phase, many students argued that a specific book of their preference should be selected. At the end of the process, all participants were satisfied with the collaborative choice and knew why the selected book had been chosen, in relation to its context of readers with different mother tongues. The teachers tried different digital tools in order to promote collaboration between the students. Afterwards, the virtual community of professionals discussed different advantages, disadvantages and aspects of the curricula content in question.

Collaborating teachers were able to design their wiki according to their needs within a limited teaching area. When planning educational activities, teachers had to consider curriculum requirements as well as students' learning needs. The content as well as the appropriate pedagogy for the curricula had to be taken into account, and the design had to be adjusted according to the affordances of the wiki. From the teachers' perspective, designing the content within a wiki and aligning it with the pedagogy, posed a challenge. It was possible for each teacher to asynchronously plan the content within a collaborative teaching curriculum community.

5.3 *Digital Resources*

The entire project focused on finding software with different functions suitable for cross-border collaboration. A key factor in selecting software was low cost—preferably no cost at all. This is important as it makes it possible for anyone, regardless of their economic situation, to obtain the software. Other important criteria were that the software should be user-friendly and easy to learn to use. In the work related to choosing software, the researchers and teachers exchanged knowledge and experiences. For example, when the teachers needed a software program with photo, video and audio functions, one of the researchers investigated available products, tested the most suitable ones, and put together simplified user manuals for the chosen products. Information about the proposed software along with the user manuals was sent by e-mail to all teachers and researchers in the collaborative group as preparation for a Skype meeting, at which a collective decision was made regarding which program to use. Surprisingly, the chosen program was not one of those that the researchers or teachers said they preferred before the Skype meeting. This shows that inter-professional knowledge sharing took place during the meeting, which resulted in all teachers and researchers agreeing on the most suitable program.

Most students had their own repertoire of digital tools that they found suitable depending on the different teaching cases and their personal preferences. The inter-professional learning and competence development sometimes used the students' knowledge as a starting point, and this knowledge was then shared with the professionals. When it comes to synchronous communication, the students regarded some digital tools as more relevant and suitable than others. The students often preferred solutions within the spur of the current software, and they seemed to have an unconscious collection of compensating solutions and were able to suggest or start to use other digital tools in an ad-hoc based manner. One example is that the students used the chat function to bridge audio quality problems, and another example is that they used chat programs like Kik and Snapchat with emoticons to convey messages or emotions. Involving students in the planning stage contributed to increasing the digital literacy and integrating knowledge, which in turn enhanced the notion that adequate technology was being used, in the sense that the technology—by means of knowledge of different professions and students, experiences and purposes—matched the curricula, pedagogy and economic limits. The inter-professional sharing and integration of knowledge and experiences, in combination with evaluations and a conscious focus on digital technology in relation to pedagogy and usability, formed the basis for the future planning of teaching cases. This type of inter-professional interaction may lead to greater understanding and acceptance, and hopefully better learning outcomes in individual teaching cases.

5.4 *Organizational Conditions*

School principals have to be involved in planning the teaching. In this way, school leaders have the possibilities to set the prerequisites for collaboration and the required digital tools. This issue is of vital importance both for inter-professional learning and competence development, as well as for the students' learning. Organizational conditions that encourage teachers, IT-pedagogues and IT-technicians to participate in communities of practice, is also important. Inter-professional collaboration is necessary in order to determine what technical equipment and digital tools are appropriate considering economic and practical conditions. Inter-professional collaboration is also of great importance in relation to teaching practice, pedagogy and curricular content. Students were also involved in this collaboration to some extent, and often had more pragmatic views of which digital tools were appropriate in different contexts.

Thus, the premise of the project consisted of a constructive and creative collaboration between all concerned professions in the Nordic schools involved in the project. Unfortunately, the school management was seldom involved at a detailed level and therefore not always aware of the requirements in the project. Principals have a more passive role when it comes to teaching and seldom participate in activities with their students. However, it is important that the management is responsive to needs, for example time for inter-professional meetings and other required resources. Teachers need to collaborate with other professionals in order to develop their competence in using digital technologies in their teaching practice. It is important that principals create conditions that enable teachers to participate in competence development activities together with other teachers and professionals from other fields in a community of practice. In this respect, the project could have benefitted from higher participation of principals in the teaching cases.

6 Discussion

Successful sharing of professional knowledge and experiences requires openness and trust within the collaborating group. Positive relations that build on curiousness, trust and informality are required to strengthen the confidence on both a personal and a professional level [16]. This is emphasized since collaboration within this project was mostly virtual [40]. Inter-professional collaboration should be based on the belief that all parties have something to learn from, and share with, each other. The work in this collaborative project, and the results, were also affected by participants who were less engaged in, or showed less motivation to contribute to, inter-professional learning and knowledge sharing. Inter-professional knowledge sharing and integration requires that all professionals are engaged and personally involved in the project. On top of that, there are conditions for inter-professional learning and competence development that could form a basis for organizational improvements that could further enhance competence development for teachers, improve time management related to the teachers' opportunities to share knowledge with other professionals, and promote discussions about required digital tools and how they could be used. Digital tools need to suit the particular pedagogy that is applied in a particular teaching case in a curriculum [6].

The characteristics of the collaboration depended on the participating individuals and their pedagogical approaches and influences from different countries, as well as the structures of the curricular content in different countries. Hence, it was considered important to create small, innovative teaching cases that did not involve too many pedagogical approaches, curricular contents, digital resources and organizational conditions. Moreover, the perceived professional hierarchy had an impact [16]. Implicitly, both teachers and researchers carry the perception that researchers belong higher up within the professional hierarchy, and thus have higher authority

[17]. Since researchers focus on different research areas, there is the risk that they, consciously or unconsciously, influence the design of the teaching cases. Thus, while communities of practice are considered vital for learning, they may also limit sharing of knowledge across professions [21]. However, knowledge boundaries may emerge in relation to existing barriers between professions [20].

All performed teaching cases were described and documented with regard to their pedagogical approaches, curricular content and the digital resources used, and collected in a common and collective knowledge source. Wikis, that were spontaneously used for that purpose, have also proved to be useful for knowledge integration in organizations [41]. This common and collective knowledge can be shared with other teachers in the same school, or other schools in the Nordic countries. The teaching cases can be used as a basis for planning cross-border teaching within a Nordic settings, or by teachers when planning, alone or together, other teaching cases in the future. Therefore, the aim of the project can be related to the system of collective knowledge as an aspect of knowledge integration [35, 36]. The collaboration and knowledge sharing revealed challenges associated with reaching a system of collective knowledge [35, 36]. Since opportunities do exist for teachers, researchers, principals and other professionals to collaborate in communities of practice within the teaching context, this study also included professionals who usually do not collaborate to a great extent. Knowledge acquired collectively is negotiated and accepted within a community of practice [45]. Professionals sometimes made their own individual decisions within the collective system. By doing so, they participated in the community of practice without contributing to a high degree to the common knowledge integration, learning and competence development that took place. As a result, all individual knowledge was not shared inter-professionally.

There were also challenges related to inter-professional processes of learning and competence development, as knowledge may be considered as ambiguous from different professional perspectives [33, 34]. Knowledge is reflected upon by individuals belonging to different professions in specific situations. Therefore, it can be problematic and inefficient to effectively organize for knowledge integration, learning and competence development for teachers regarding new competence areas, such as using digital technologies pedagogically in the curricula. Professional hierarchies also influenced the learning and competence development, since not only school-related professionals, but also researchers, were included in the community of practice. Teaching cases were executed as long-distance learning projects where students collaborated using digital tools. Knowledge associated with each teaching situation is complex and situated. The perspective on knowledge integration as a learning process is related to contextual activities and social relationships [21]. As a result, it may also be very difficult for principals to organize relevant teaching situations without participating in the teaching cases at all. However, school managers need to create opportunities for teachers to collaborate in order to develop their competence in including digital technologies in their teaching.

7 Conclusions

The aim of this paper was to analyze how teachers' competence development in using digital technologies within their pedagogical practice could be supported in an inter-professional community of practice. Different pedagogical approaches, curricular structures and types of digital resources and organizational conditions required virtual collaboration between the involved professions in order to create innovative cross-border teaching cases in the Nordic setting. This study suggests that trust is an important factor, along with participation, in a community of practice consisting of different professions with knowledge related to digital technologies and teaching. In order to create a facilitating context for inter-professional learning and competence development using various digital tools in a virtual environment, a number of teaching cases were planned and executed. Knowledge within the community of practice was to a large extent made explicit through documentation in a collective system with the support of digital tools. Different professionals within the community of practice contributed to varying degrees to the common knowledge integration, learning and competence development. For those teachers who were engaged in the project to a high degree, it was an opportunity to develop their competence in using digital technologies within their teaching practice in collaboration with other professionals.

References

1. Garrison, D. R., & Anderson, T. (2003). *E-learning in the 21st century: A framework for research and practice*. London: Routledge Falmer.
2. Trust, T., Krutka, D. G., & Carpenter, J. P. (2016). "Together we are better": Professional learning networks for teachers. *Computers & Education, 102,* 15–34.
3. Dede, C. (2000). Emerging influences of information technology on school curriculum. *Journal of Curriculum Studies, 32*(2), 282–303.
4. Tseng, F.-C., & Kuo, F.-Y. (2014). A study of social participation and knowledge sharing in the teachers' online professional community of practice. *Computers & Education, 72,* 37–47.
5. Hew, K. F., & Brush, T. (2007). Integrating technology into K-12 teaching and learning: Current knowledge gaps and recommendations for future research. *Educational Technology Research and Development, 55,* 223–252.
6. Kreijns, K., Van Acker, F., Vermeulen, M., & Van Buuren, H. (2013). What stimulates teachers to integrate ICT in their pedagogical practices? The use of digital learning materials in education. *Computers in Human Behavior, 29*(1), 217–225.
7. Ertmer, P. A., Ottenbreit-Leftwich, A. T., Sadik, O., Sendurur, E., & Sendurur, E. (2012). Teacher beliefs and technology integration practices: A critical relationship. *Computers & Education, 59,* 423–435.
8. Donelly, D. F., & Boniface, S. (2013). Consuming and creating: Early-adopting science teachers' perceptions and use of a wiki to support professional development. *Computers & Education, 68,* 9–20.
9. Alavi, M., & Dufner, D. (2009). Technology-mediated collaborative learning: A research perspective. In S. R. Hiltz & R. Goldman (Eds.), *Learning together online: Research on asynchronous learning networks* (pp. 191–213). Mahwah NJ: Lawrence Erlbaum.

10. Hirschheim, R., Klein, H. K., & Lyytinen, K. (1995). *Information development and data modelling, conceptual and philosophical foundations.* Cambridge: Cambridge University Press.
11. Alavi, M., & Leidner, D. E. (1999). Knowledge management systems: issues, challenges, and benefits. *Communications of the Association of Information Systems, 1*(7).
12. Davies, J., & Graff, M. O. (2005). Performance in E-learning: Online participation and student grades. *British Journal of Educational Technology, 36*(4), 657–663.
13. Hrastinski, S. (2009). A theory of online learning as online participation. *Computers & Education, 52,* 78–82.
14. Wenger, E. (1998). *Communities of practice: Learning meaning and identity.* Cambridge: Cambridge University Press.
15. Macià, M., & Garcìa, I. (2016). Informal online communities and networks as a source of teacher professional development: A review. *Teaching and Teacher Education, 55,* 291–307.
16. Evetts, J. (2006). Introduction: Trust and professionalism: Challenges and occupational changes. *Current Sociology, 54*(4), 515–531.
17. Bourgeault, I. L., Hirschkorn, K., & Sainsaulieu, I. (2011). Relations between professions and organizations: More fully considering the role of the client. *Professions & Professionalism, 1*(1), 67–86.
18. Newell, S., Robertson, M., Scarbrough, H., & Swan, J. (2002). *Managing knowledge work.* Macmillan International Higher Education
19. Weick, K. E. (1995). *Sense making in organizations* (Vol. 3). SAGE.
20. Brown, J. S., & Duguid, P. (2001). Knowledge and organization: A social-practice perspective. *Organization Science, 12*(2), 198–213.
21. Swan, J., Bresnen, M., Newell, S., & Robertson, M. (2007). The object of knowledge: The role of objects in biomedical innovation. *Human Relations, 60*(12), 1809–1837.
22. Hashim, K. F., & Tan, F. B. (2009). The mediating role of trust and commitment on members' continuous knowledge sharing intention: A commitment-trust theory perspective. *International Journal of Information Management, 35,* 145–151.
23. Chen, H-L., Fan, H.-L. & Tsai, C.-C. (2014). The role of community trust and altruism in knowledge sharing: An investigation of a virtual community of teacher professionals. *Educational Technology & Society, 17*(3), 168–179
24. Scott, J. E. (2000). Facilitating interorganizational learning with information technology. *Journal of Management Information Systems, 17*(2), 81–113.
25. Svensson, A. (2012). *Kunskapsintegrering med informationssystem i professionsorienterat arbete.* Doctoral Dissertation, Göteborg University, Göteborg
26. Hsu, M.-H., & Chang, C.-M. (2014). Examining interpersonal trust as a facilitator and uncertainty as an inhibitor of intra-organizational knowledge sharing. *Information Systems Journal, 24,* 119–142.
27. Lin, M.-J.J., Hung, S.-W., & Chen, C.-J. (2009). Fostering the determinants of knowledge sharing in professional virtual communities. *Computers in Human Behavior, 25,* 929–939.
28. Abel, M. H. (2008). Competencies management and learning organizational memory. *Journal of Knowledge Management, 12*(6), 15–30.
29. Kushwaha, P., & Rao, M. K. (2015). Integrative role of KM infrastructure and KM strategy to enhance individual competence: Conceptualizing knowledge process enablement. *Vine, 45*(3), 376–396.
30. Maaninen-Olsson, E., Wismén, M., & Carlsson, S. A. (2008). Permanent and temporary work practices: Knowledge integration and the meaning of boundary activities. *Knowledge Management Research & Practice, 6*(4), 260–273.
31. Alavi, M., & Tiwana, A. (2002). Knowledge integration in virtual teams: The potential role of KMS. *Journal of the American Society for Information Science & Technology, 53*(12), 1029–1037.
32. Mohannak, K. (2012). Organisational knowledge integration: Towards a conceptual framework. In L. Uden, F. Herrera, J. Perez, & J. Rodriguez (Eds.), *7th international conference on knowledge management in organizations: Service and cloud computing* (pp. 81–92). Spain: Springer-Verlag, Salamanca.

33. Argyris, C., & Schön, D. A. (1996). *Organizational learning II: Theory method and practice.* Reading, MA: Addison Wesley.
34. Tsoukas, H. (1996). The firm as a distributed knowledge system: A constructionist approach. *Strategic Management Journal, 17,* 11–25.
35. Liang, T. Y. (2010). Innovative sustainability and highly intelligent human organisations (CAS): The new management and leadership perspective. *International Journal of Complexity in Leadership and Management, 1*(1), 83–101.
36. Weick, K. E., & Roberts, K. H. (1993). Collective mind in organizations: Heedful interrelating on flight decks. *Administrative Science Quarterly, 28*(3)
37. Kompf, M. (2005). Information and communications technology (ICT) and the seduction of knowledge, teaching, and learning: What lies ahead for education. *Curriculum Inquiry, 35*(2), 213–234.
38. Wallace, R. M. (2004). A framework for understanding teaching with the internet. *American Educational Research Journal, 41*(2), 447–488.
39. Wright, N. (2015, July–September) Vignettes of pedagogical practices with iPads: Reinforcing pedagogy, not transforming it. *International Journal of Online Pedagogy and Course Design, 5*(3), 62–73.
40. Sutherland, R., & Fischer, F. (2014). Future learning spaces: Design, collaboration, knowledge, assessment, teachers, technology and the radical past. *Technology, pedagogy and education, Special Issue: Designing physical and digital learning spaces for the future, 23*(1), 1–5.
41. Majchrzak A., Wagner, C., & Yates, D. (2013, June). The impact of shaping on knowledge reuse for organizational improvement with Wikis. *MIS Quarterly, 37*(2), 455–467.
42. Chiasson, M., Germonprez, M., & Mathiassen, L. (2008). Pluralist action research: A review of the information systems literature. *Information Systems Journal, 19,* 31–54.
43. Braun, V., & Clarke, V. (2006). Using thematic analysis in psychology. *Qualitative Research in Psychology, 3*(2), 77–101.
44. Vaismoradi, M., Turunen, H., & Bondas, T. (2013). Content analysis and thematic analysis: Implications for conducting a qualitative descriptive study. *Nursing and Health Sciences, 15,* 398–405.
45. Cook, S., & Brown, J. S. (1999, July–August). Bridging epistemologies: The generative dance between organizational knowledge and organizational knowing. *Organization Science, 10*(4), 381–400.

Digital Technology and Individual Behaviour

Exploring the Effects of Social Value on Social Network Dependence

Stefano Za, Federica Ceci, Francesca Masciarelli, and Lea Iaia

Abstract In a world where around 3.5 billions of the entire population are active social media users, the individual usage behavior of social network sites and related aspects should require further investigation. Specifically, this paper focuses on the social network dependence, considering the utilitarian and goal-oriented facet rather than the psychological one, usually referred as addiction. It combines an analysis of personal cultural values with Media System Dependency theory, investigating the role of social axioms in affecting the social network dependence. Using a large dataset composed by 622 observations, we developed and validated a research model to shed new light on the investigation of dependence phenomena in the context of social network sites, exploring the role of individual beliefs.

Keywords Social network dependence · Social axioms · IS usage behavior · Individual beliefs

1 Introduction

Research on social media is increasingly growing since the social media landscape is characterized by rapid changes and existing social media platforms are expanded with new interactive functions or simply replaced by new platforms [22]. Currently, in a world where approximately the 57% (around 4.4 billions) of the entire population

S. Za (✉) · F. Ceci · F. Masciarelli · L. Iaia
University of Chieti-Pescara, Pescara, Italy
e-mail: stefano.za@unich.it

F. Ceci
e-mail: federica.ceci@unich.it

F. Masciarelli
e-mail: francesca.masciarelli@unich.it

L. Iaia
e-mail: lea.iaia@unich.it

C. Metallo et al. (eds.), *Digital Transformation and Human Behavior*, Lecture Notes in Information Systems and Organisation 37,
https://doi.org/10.1007/978-3-030-47539-0_9

is on internet, the 45% (around 3.5 billions) are active social media users and the 42% (around 3.2 billions) are mobile social media users [28]. In this scenario, the IT dependency phenomenon appears to be particularly salient in the social media context [40]. This research study builds on the stream of IS research that has investigated the role played by IT dependency in influencing individuals' reasoned IT usage decisions [63, 70]. However, in line with the core assumptions of Media System Dependency (MSD) theory, this research argues that technology dependency has an unexplored facet that is utilitarian, rational, and goal-oriented in nature [16]. In line with this reasoning, this study aims to explore the antecedents of individual IS usage behavior in terms of social media dependencies (SMDs), focusing on the utilitarian, rational, and goal-oriented IS usage, investigating the social network site (SNS) dependency. In this way, we seek to complement IS studies conceiving dependency as an addiction causing obsessive–compulsive behavior [22, 67, 70], in particular those focus on SNS addiction [59].

Hence, we posit that to accomplish the necessary progress in the field of social media, it is vital to understand the individual antecedents of SMDs. Extant research on SMDs is underestimating the role of culture in explain individual behavior with few notable exceptions. Tsai and Men [69] analyzed the role of individualism and collectivism [68] to examine motivations and antecedents that contribute to American and Chinese users' engagement with brand SNS pages. Despite the value of this contribution, this study explores the role of culture on SMDs focusing on national cultural differences.

Differently from previous work, we contribute to this stream of literature analyzing the effects of individual culture on SMDs. Specifically, we analyze the role of social axioms, which are conceived as individual's general beliefs about the world [43]. The paper is structured as follows: in the next section we provide the theoretical background. This is followed by the presentation of the proposed model and hypotheses. Then, we present research methodology, data analysis and results. The paper wraps-up with discussion and conclusion including recommendations for future research.

2 Literature Review and Theoretical Underpinnings

2.1 Social Axioms

Attempts to predict individual's behavior based on a person's value priorities has always been of a great interest for researchers [13]. Traditionally, values are frequently deployed to account for cross-cultural differences in behavior [62]. Drawing upon research on expectancy–value theory, Leung et al. [41] have proposed a set of five cultural dimensions, i.e. social axioms, identifying beliefs about the world in which each individual lives and works. Social axioms may be described as individual assessments and beliefs about the social context constraining and influencing individuals' behavioral choices. These beliefs about the world may predict an individual's actions [13]

Individual's general beliefs about the world [26, 41] provide a different type of general orientation that may be predictive of values [26]. Individual's beliefs vary across a *continuum* [26], but some beliefs are general, and may be viewed as generalized expectations [56]. These general beliefs about the world, or social axioms, are likely related to social behaviors across geographical contexts, and time [41]. The locus of control represents a proper example. A general belief about the causes of events has been related to how individuals make sense of their personal failures or successes [25, 65]. Also, individuals usually face situations in which they apply their knowledge about the world in general for making decisions about how to behave [41]. This knowledge may be construed as the personal representation that individuals develop over their life experiences about the social context defining their actions in the world. Therefore, adding general beliefs to trans-situational values would increase the predictive power of values with respect to behavior.

Drawing on qualitative research and on literature on beliefs, Leung et al. [41] developed a social axiom survey. Using this survey, they identified the following five factors of beliefs: (i) *reward for application* is the position that an investment of human resources will lead to positive outcomes (e.g. 'Hard working people will achieve more in the end'); (ii) *social cynicism* is a negative assessment of social events and human nature (e.g. 'Kind-hearted people usually suffer losses'); (iii) *social complexity* is the view that there are multiple solutions to social issues, and that the result of events is indeterminate (e.g. 'One has to deal with matters according to the specific circumstances'); (iv) *fate control* is to the general belief that external forces affect social events (e.g. 'Fate determines one's successes and failures'), and finally (v) *spirituality* is the view that spiritual forces influence the human world (e.g. 'Religious people are more likely to maintain moral standards'). These five dimensions and their defining items have been identified in 40 countries.

Social axioms have been studied in relation with a number of different variables, such social beliefs [57], learning [12], moral development [18], and behavioral intentions [20]. However, many literatures remain silent about the role of social axiom in explaining IS usage-related behaviors. Indeed, looking for contributions on the main IS journals and conferences, in very few cases social axioms literature is taken into consideration, and, in these papers, it is used combined with other references for justifying the availability of value-based frameworks for measuring different culture dimensions and values [2, 49]. The current study aims to explore if and how social axioms influence significantly individual IS behavior in terms of SMD.

2.2 Social Media and Social Network Site

Since their introduction, social media provide a two-sided communication channel that has changed the social interactions of people around the world [29]. Social media can be defined as "a group of Internet-based technologies that allows users to easily create, edit, evaluate and/or link to content or other creators of content" [33]. They are socio-technical information platform [75] and encompass social networking sites, blogs, microblogs and websites dedicated to the content sharing [39]. The increasing propagation and widespread adoption of social media among individuals and businesses attracted researchers to examine both their social and technical factors [73], and the motivation behind their use [55]. They emphasizes the interplay between contextual conditions and architectural elements to determine the outcome of social media strategies [36, 64]. All forms of online interactions, improved by social media usage, share the same purpose: make people´s mobilization, discussion, and decision making possible in virtual communities settings [3, 10, 48]. Through social media activities, individuals and members of social groups with common interests are involved in exchanging information, collaborating and building a relationship [21]. Such activities engage in a variety of areas, business strategy [8], healthcare services [64] and political participation [23] among the others.

In management literature, especially in marketing, scholars investigate how social media can generate benefits for the brands through the involvement of customers and stakeholders, in terms of cooperation on common activities [35, 58]; in fact, social media offer firms several tools to engage consumers in online activities [36]. At the same time, social media provide community members with a platform for information sharing, collaboration and collective actions, thanks to their ability to create new ways of connecting people [72], and on engaging them in cross-organizational collective action [79].

On the basis of how social media shape and enable specific social interactions, they can be classified in several categories, taking into account the level (low, medium, high) of the social presence/media richness (based on social presence and media richness theories) and the self-presentation/self-disclosure (social processes), as two key elements of social media [33]. Among these categories, social networking sites belong to one of them. This class of social media emphasizes the capability to create, foster and sustain connections among users, focusing on the relationships and on sharing information among friends or group members [33].

In literature "social networking site" and "social network site" are used often interchangeably [14]. Boyd and Ellison [14] seek to differentiate the two terms, since the former considers, as main purpose, the ability to create and develop connections, whereas in the latter the "networking" ability is not the (only) primary practice, since users like also to articulate and disclose their social networks to the others, even including "latent ties" [27] derived from offline relationships. For the purpose of this research, we focus on "social network site" (SNSs). Specifically SNSs can be defined as web-based services through which people can [14] (p. 211): "(1) construct a public or semi-public profile within a bounded system, (2) articulate a list of other users with whom they share a connection, and (3) view and traverse their list of connections and those made by others within the system".

Several studies focus on the term "addiction" as particular emotion-related psychological state causing behaviors such as obsessive–compulsive in the use of SNSs, investigating the positive and negative effects on various dependent variables (such as: continuance intention to use). In this paper, we would like to explore an alternative concept of "dependence", focused more on the utilitarian, rational, and goal-oriented usage of SNSs, further described in the following section.

2.3 Media Systems Dependency

During the past two decades, the growing number of cases of Internet and video-game related behavioral disorders made scientists aware of the negative effect of technology dependency—IT addiction [16], often recognized as a clinical disorder [37]. Early research contributions, especially in cyberpsychology, started to investigate issues concerning technology dependency [9, 50, 77]. In the last decades, IS research has explored technology dependency, mainly focusing on IT addiction, in a variety of contexts such as online auctions [70], online games [78], social networking sites [71], online social network [67], or smartphones [15, 40]. Specifically concerning the social media, often in literature the term "dependency" is used to describe the problematic use of social media (psychological state), instead the term "addiction" is used more for describing the resulting behavior [74]. Alternatively, in line with the core assumptions of Media System Dependency (MSD) theory [7], we use the term "dependency" referring to the utilitarian, rational, and goal-oriented usage of social media [16].

In the past, MSD theory has been used to investigate dependency relationships through mass communication channels such as television [24, 51, 61], radio and newspapers [45, 46]. From the beginning of the twenty-first century, some studies have revisited MSD in relation to the use of the Internet [31, 44, 47, 52]. More recently, it has been used to investigate dependency relationships with IT healthcare services [38], mobile technology [66], IS work performance [19] and ubiquitous media systems [16]. MSD defines dependency as a "relation between individuals' goals and the extent to which these goals are contingent upon the resources of the media system [in which] those resources have the capacities to create and gather, process and disseminate information" [6]. Hence, dependency relations are goal-oriented, while the scope and intensity of the goals directly impact the strength of the dependency relationships between the user and the media [4, 32].

Individual Media Dependency (IMD) derives from MSD and provides concrete means to assess individual-level dependency relations with regard to a specific media [24, 45]. In line with use and gratification research [34], IMD assumes that the extent to which a media is capable of fulfilling a person's needs and expectations, will stimulate dependency relations with the media per se which, in turn, impacts on usage patterns and media selection [24, 45].

In the same manner, considering SNS as a specific media, dependency relation between a person and a SNS develops proportionally to the extent it is able to fulfill person's needs and expectations. In line with IMD theory, this contribution defines social network dependency as *the extent to which an individual's capacity to reach his or her objectives depends on the use of SNS* [5, 6, 24].

According to IMD theory, there are six levels of dependency relations between an individual and a media system [1, 6, 24]. These levels can be represented as the product of three distinct goals: *understanding*, *orientation*, and *play*; and two different goal targets: *personal* and *social*. *Understanding* refers to the need of individuals to gain a basic understanding of themselves and to understand their social environment (including the perception of everyone's role in society). *Orientation* relates to the need one has to make behavioral decisions and to have guidance for interacting well with other people. *Play* pertains to the capacity of the media to provide an individual the mechanisms for relaxing and releasing stress when he or she is alone or accompanied by others.

3 Hypotheses Development

In line with the definition of the three distinctive goals of the IMD, individuals can use social networks to: (i) gain a basic understanding (perception) of themselves and the social environment (including the roles played by others); (ii) make behavioral decisions and interact with other people; (ii) relax and release stress, alone or together with others [16]. Each social axiom has a different potential to affect a range of human perceptions, attitudes, and behaviors and therefore will discuss their impact separately. We decided to focus on 4 out of 5 social axioms excluding religiosity because this construct is highly debated in the literature of individual culture and values: the conceptualization of religiosity and spirituality is still blurred and confused. Moreover, we believe that religiosity is independent by the analyzed scenario. In the remaining of the section we will briefly discuss the four social axioms and derive hypothesis for each of them.

Reward for Applications is the position of those individuals who believe that an investment of human resources will lead to positive outcomes. Such individuals present an internal locus of control [17] and low hedonistic tendencies [42]: individuals with high values in reward for application achieve personal success through work rather than on pleasure-seeking activities [76]. The use of social networks allows individuals to increase performance at work and specific activities carried out during social networks usage (i.e. social understanding, action orientation). This would suggest that people demonstrating a strong reward for application tendencies rely on social network for performing several work activities. Therefore, we propose:

H1 Reward for Application has a positive impact on Social Network Dependency

Social Cynicism is a negative assessment of human nature and social events (e.g. 'Kind-hearted people usually suffer losses'). Previous literature has related social cynicism with low interpersonal trust [60], highlighting that this correlation derives from the belief that the other will exploit you if the opportunity arises [13]. Therefore, social cynicism is related to the first one goal of the IMD, which consists in gaining a basic understanding of themselves and the social environment (including the roles played by the others). Thus, we propose the following second hypothesis:

H2 Social Cynicism has a positive impact on Social Network Dependency

Social Complexity indicates user's perception on the level of individual behavior variability and the amount of influences involved in determining social outcomes [43]. Hence, it seems reasonable to argue that individual perceiving a high level of social complexity relies on social networks in order to collect more information about the environment and to support his or her decision-making process. Consequently, the following third hypothesis was derived:

H3 Social Complexity has a positive impact on Social Network Dependency

Fate Control includes items concerning the belief that the life events are predetermined. Although people cannot influence events, they have the opportunity to impact on the connected outcomes, as fate control combines locus of control, predictability, and fatedness [41]. In this sense, fate control, being subject to knowledgeable forms of human agency, motivates people to behave differently with the aim to predict and alter the relevant outcomes in their life, and often represents a way to face problems [41, 43]. The belief that exists a way to influence these out-comes could stimulate individuals to reach information on social networks, in order to gain a higher fate control. Hence, the last proposed hypothesis was:

H4 Fate Control has a positive impact on Social Network Dependency

On the basis of the derived hypothesis which emphasize the relation between social axioms and SND, excluding "spirituality" for the above mentioned reasons, the model 1 represented in Fig. 1 aims to evaluate how social axioms impact on SND.

Moreover, with the aim to further explore the relations among social axioms and SND, we propose a second model (Model 2) in which SND is decomposed in the six IMD components, investigating the effects of the four social axioms on each one of them. The IMD components are the product of three distinct goals: *understanding*, *orientation*, and *play*; and two different goal targets: *personal* and *social*. We reported

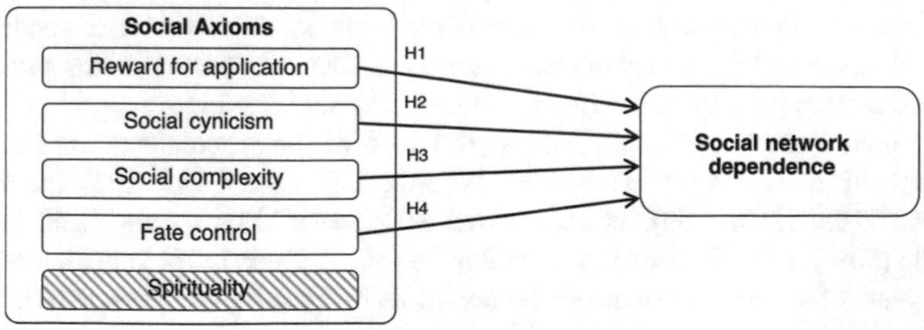

Fig. 1 Model 1

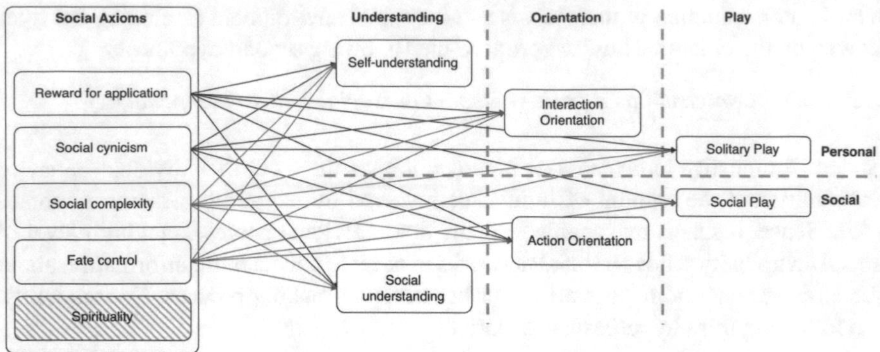

Fig. 2 Model 2

in the previous paragraph a definition of such levels. Figure 2 shows the possible relations. According to IMD theory, there are six levels of dependency relations between an individual and a media system [1, 6, 24] and therefore Model 2 reports 24 possible relations among the variables. We do not develop specific hypothesis for each of those relations because of the lack of previous contributions that could help us in formulating coherent hypothesis. Nonetheless, it is important to start exploring the micro determinants of SND unpacking SND in its constituents: this will shed further light and pave the road for future research.

4 Method

4.1 Data Collection

Data collection was conducted in March 2019 among students enrolled in BA and Master course in Management and Political Sciences. Researchers communicated a link to a Google Form during class hours and the questionnaire was self-administered by the students. Time required for the completion of the questionnaire was 15 min. We collected a total of 622 complete responses. The questionnaire was structured in 3 sections as follows: the first section collected information about age, gender, use of social media and frequency of usage. Section 2 focused on SMD items and lastly, the third section referred to the items related to the social axioms.

The main descriptive results follow: the 43% of the respondents are less then 19 years old (n = 266), while the 47% are between 20 and 24 (n = 295), the 8% are between 25 and 29 (n = 52), the 2% are over 30 (n = 9); 313 respondents declared to be male (50%), and 309 declared to be female (50%). Descriptive statistics relevant to the years of usage of the main social networks in the sample are reported in Table 1. Interestingly, a high percentage of interviewees does not have a Twitter account (n = 447; 72%) or a LinkedIn account (n = 443; 71%). The majority of Facebook

Table 1 Descriptive statistics relative to social networks usage

		No account	Year(s) since first registration					
			1	2	3	4	5	6+
Facebook	Freq	37	9	25	86	178	195	92
	%	*5.95*	*1.45*	*4.02*	*13.83*	*28.62*	*31.35*	*14.79*
	% cum	*5.95*	*7.40*	*11.41*	*25.24*	*53.86*	*85.21*	
Twitter	Freq	447	49	24	56	34	8	4
	%	*71.86*	*7.88*	*3.86*	*9*	*5.47*	*1.29*	*0.64*
	% cum	*71.86*	*79.74*	*83.6*	*92.6*	*98.07*	*99.36*	
Instagram	Freq	30	50	121	282	111	19	9
	%	*4.82*	*8.04*	*19.45*	*45.34*	*17.85*	*3.05*	*1.45*
	% cum	*4.82*	*12.86*	*32.32*	*77.65*	*95.5*	*98.55*	
LinkedIn	Freq	443	108	40	19	7	2	3
	%	*71.22*	*17.36*	*6.43*	*3.05*	*1.13*	*0.32*	*0.48*
	% cum	*71.22*	*88.59*	*95.02*	*98.07*	*99.2*	*99.52*	
YouTube	Freq	242	51	45	90	83	55	56
	%	*38.91*	*8.2*	*7.23*	*14.47*	*13.34*	*8.84*	*9*
	% cum	*38.91*	*47.11*	*54.34*	*68.81*	*82.15*	*91*	

users registered their account 4 or 5 years ago (4 years: n = 178; 28%; 5 years n = 195; 31%) while the majority of Instagram users registered their account 2 or 3 years ago (2 years: n = 121; 19%; 3 years n = 282; 45%).

4.2 Operationalization of the Constructs

SMD was measured through the most commonly used media dependency scale [5, 6, 24]. The set of items were adapted to the context of the research. Social axioms has been measured using the items provided by the literature [41, 43]. Details of the items used in the survey are available upon request. Since data were collected in Italy, the items initially were written in English and subsequently translated in Italian. Back-translation was applied to check the accuracy of the translation and changes were made if inaccuracies were revealed [11]. The assessments were based on a five-point scale. To increase the response rate, we guaranteed confidentiality and confirmed that that data would be used only for academic purposes. Finally, an online questionnaire was created using the Google Forms tool and a pre-test was carried out to ensure clarity.

4.3 Data Analysis Procedure

Our research strategy followed a two-step approach. We firstly analyzed the impact of the 4 social axioms selected on SND as a whole (Fig. 1—Model 1) and we then unpacked the construct into its 6 elements, namely: Action Orientation, Interaction Orientation, Solitary Play, Social Play, Self-Understanding, Social Understanding. This represents the second step of our research strategy and it is aimed to explore deeper the impact of social axioms on the different components of the constructs object of the analysis, as reported in Model 2 (Fig. 2).

We used Partial Least Squares (SmartPLS v.3.2.1) [54] to estimate our model. PLS estimates latent variables as exact linear combinations of observed measures and, therefore, assumes that all measured variance is useful variance and can be explained. PLS models are analyzed and interpreted in two stages: (i) assessment and reliability of the measurement model; and (ii) testing the structural model [30]. We assessed the adequacy of the measurement model by examining individual item reliabilities, and convergent and discriminant validity. Table 2 reports the internal consistency values for the constructs and the correlation matrix between constructs, with the diagonal indicating the square root of the average variance extracted. Since the questionnaire is based on self-reported measures, we tested for common method variance (CMV) using Harman's single factor test [53]. Results (available upon request) showed no evidence of CMV.

4.4 Results

Since PLS does not try to minimize residual item covariance, there is no summary statistic to measure the overall model fit as in the case of structural equation modelling (SEM) techniques. The sign and significance of the path coefficients are used to assess nomological validity. A bootstrapping "sampling with replacement" method was used to assess the statistical significance of the parameter estimates. Standard errors were computed on the basis of 500 bootstrapping runs. Table 3 presents the results of the structural model for the Model 1 (Fig. 1) and Table 4 presents the results for the Model 2 (Fig. 2).

Results reported in Table 3 indicate that Fate Control ($\beta = 0.196\ p < 0.05$) and Reward for Applications ($\beta = 0.149\ p < 0.01$), are positively related to SND, which supports hypotheses 1 and 2.

Table 4 reports the results for Model 2, that goes deeper into the analysis of the constituents of the SND. Results partially confirm the insights obtained from Model 1 but also shed further lights on how the different components of SND interacts and are differently influenced by the social axioms. More specifically, Fate Control exerts a positive relation with Social Understanding ($\beta = 0.139\ p < 0.05$), Solitary Play ($\beta = 0.099\ p < 0.05$), Social Play ($\beta = 0.159\ p < 0.05$), Interaction Orientation ($\beta = 0.129\ p < 0.05$) and Action Orientation ($\beta = 0.220\ p < 0.05$). Similarly, and in line

Table 2 Construct-level measurement statistics and correlation of constructs

		Cronbach's alpha	1	2	3	4	5	6	7	8	9	10	11
1	Fate control	0.89	**0.82**										
2	Reward for application	0.81	0.43	**0.72**									
3	Social complexity	0.78	0.49	0.61	**0.21**								
4	Social cynicism	0.68	0.64	0.51	0.63	**0.20**							
5	Action orientation	0.82	0.21	0.07	−0.04	0.11	**0.73**						
6	Interaction orientation	0.89	0.21	0.04	−0.14	0.18	0.60	**0.89**					
7	Solitary play	0.58	0.17	0.28	0.20	0.16	0.30	0.34	**0.25**				
8	Social play	0.80	0.25	−0.04	−0.25	0.24	0.40	0.52	0.31	**0.28**			
9	Self-understanding	0.69	0.26	−0.02	−0.24	0.24	0.46	0.63	0.24	0.63	**0.61**		
10	Social understanding	0.80	0.15	0.27	0.21	0.08	0.38	0.28	0.43	0.16	0.17	**0.71**	
11	SND	0.90	0.29	0.26	0.23	0.24	–	–	–	–	–	–	**0.36**

Diagonal elements in bold are average variance extracted [30]

Table 3 Model 1: standardized PLS coefficients

Dependent variable	Independent variable	Standardized coefficient[a]	
Fate control	Social network dependence	0.196	**
Reward for application	Social network dependence	0.149	***
Social complexity	Social network dependence	0.035	
Social cynicism	Social network dependence	0.020	

[a]*Significant at the 0.10 level. **Significant at the 0.05 level. ***Significant at the 0.01 level

Table 4 Model 2: standardized PLS coefficients

Dependent variable	Independent variable	Standardized coefficient[a]	
Fate control	Social understanding	0.139	**
	Self-understanding	0.175	
	Solitary play	0.099	**
	Social play	0.159	**
	Interaction orientation	0.129	**
	Action orientation	0.220	***
Reward for application	Social understanding	0.206	**
	Self-understanding	−0.014	
	Solitary play	0.177	**
	Social play	−0.044	
	Interaction orientation	0.036	
	Action orientation	0.046	
Social complexity	Social understanding	0.111	
	Self-understanding	−0.223	
	Solitary play	0.115	
	Social play	−0.215	
	Interaction orientation	−0.153	
	Action orientation	−0.049	
Social cynicism	Social understanding	−0.086	
	Self-understanding	0.136	**
	Solitary play	0.036	
	Social play	0.155	**
	Interaction orientation	0.090	
	Action orientation	−0.044	

[a]*Significant at the 0.10 level. **Significant at the 0.05 level. ***Significant at the 0.01 level

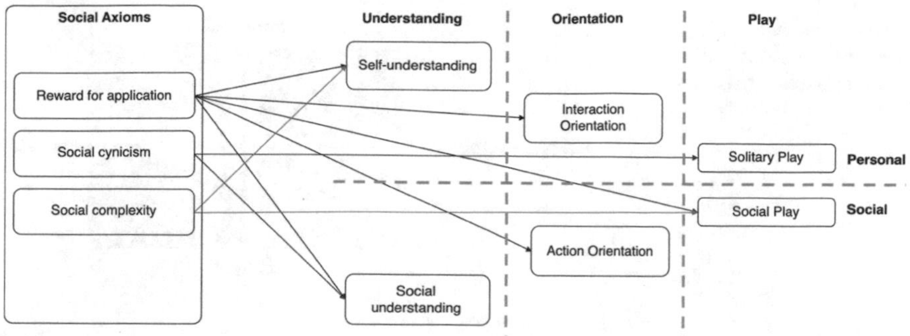

Fig. 3 Results of PLS analysis of model 2

with Model 1, also Reward for Application has a positive relation with the following components of SND: Social Understanding ($\beta = 0.206$ $p < 0.05$) and Solitary Play ($\beta = 0.177$ $p < 0.05$). Additionally, and differently from Model 1, Model 2 reports a significant relation between Social Cynicism and the following components: Social Understanding ($\beta = 0.136$ $p < 0.05$) and Social Play ($\beta = 0.155$ $p < 0.05$). Results are graphically represented in Fig. 3. While Model 1 gives us a general understanding of the impact of social axioms on SND, Model 2 offers interesting insights that shed new lights on the complex phenomenon of SND. A brief discussion of the results is provided in the following section.

5 Discussion and Conclusions

This paper focus on SND, considering the utilitarian and goal-oriented facet rather than the psychological one, usually referred as addiction. Often, in IS literature, the concept of IS usage dependency (and addiction) is studied as variable influencing the individuals' IS usage decisions [15, 16]. Alternatively, considering the dependency as a dependent variable, this study explores whether and how individual believes can affect the SND. For this aim, we build upon the contribution provided by Leung et al.: people generally make decisions concerning how to behave on the basis of their believes and knowledge about the world, built on their life experiences [41]. With their study, Leung et al. defined five factors of beliefs, namely social axioms [41]. Summarizing, this paper combines social axiom construct [41] with MSD theory [4], and investigates the role of individual beliefs in affecting SND. A research model was developed and validated, shading some new light on the investigation of dependence phenomena in the context of SNSs, exploring the role of individual antecedents. As theoretical implication, this paper contributes to the IS body of knowledge by increasing the number of application of MSD in IS context, as well as fostering, in addition, the application of social axioms [41] in the IS field.

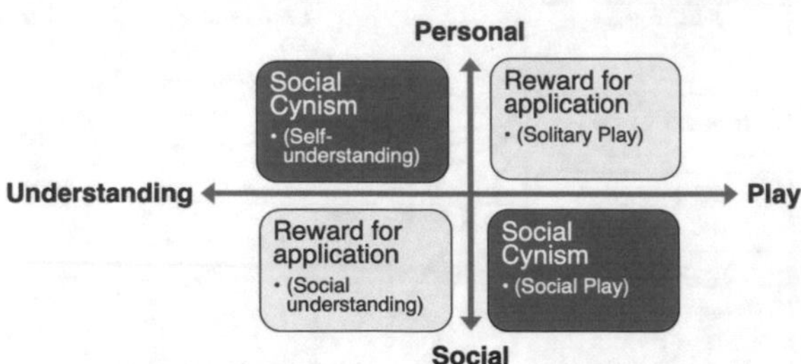

Fig. 4 The intertwining effect of two social axioms on two specific goals of the SND

Results concerning Model 1 show as Fate Control and Reward for Applications have a positive effect on SND, drawing two main implications: (i) individuals focused more on work rather than on pleasure-seeking activities [76], feel dependent by the use of SNSs in order to increase performance at work and carried out specific activities; (ii) people feeling they cannot influence events but have the opportunity to impact on the connected outcomes [43], perceive themselves particularly dependent by the social network usage in order to reach information for gaining a higher fate control. Model 2 introduces new details, considering the impact of each social axiom on the six components of SMD (3 goals and 2 goal targets). In particular, the positive impact of *Fate Control* is confirmed on five out of six components of SND, whereas *Reward for application* positively affects only 2 of them: *Solitary Play* and *Social Understanding*.

Moreover, a new relation arises: *Social Cynicism* affects positively *Social Play* and *Self-understanding*. It is interesting to note the similarity as well as the differences between the impact of the last two social axioms. Both of them have a positive impact on *understanding* and *play* goals of the SND, but for the first one Social Cynicism is focused on *personal* goal targets and Reward for Applications on the *social* one, whereas for the second goal the relation is diametrically opposed. From a theoretical point of view, this result highlights a sort of intertwining effect of the two social axioms on two specific goals of the SND, as described in Fig. 4. It suggests that people perceiving a low interpersonal trust [60] and the presence of opportunistic behaviors [13] usually feel dependent by the use of SNSs for relaxing and releasing stress together with other people and for collecting information about themselves. Moreover people focused more on work rather than on pleasure-seeking activities [76], feel dependent by the use of SNSs in order to understand the social environment and at the same time for relaxing and releasing stress when they are alone.

Undoubtedly, this research project has some limitations. It is important to acknowledge that this study focused mainly on one specific class of users—people between 20 and 29 years old. Moreover, the sample is composed only by Italian people. Investigating the stability of the results with a more representative population (such as enlarging the possible values for age and nationality) using SNSs [28], would help to assess the extent to which the results can be generalized. We hope that the advances made in this paper will stimulate further reflections about how individual beliefs can influence the dependency perception of SNSs, with specific attention to its micro determinants. Moreover, it could be interesting to revise existing body of knowledge in IS research combining the social axioms and dependence into previous IS usage-related model.

References

1. Alcañiz, E. B., et al. (2006). Dependency in consumer media relations: An application to the case of teleshopping. *Journal of Consumer Behaviour, 5*(5), 397–410.
2. Ali, M. et al. (2009). The impact of national culture on e-government implementation: A comparison case study. In: Proceedings of the fifteenth Americas conference on information systems, paper 137
3. Arazy, O., et al. (2011). Information quality in Wikipedia: The effects of group composition and task conflict. *Journal of Management Information Systems, 27*(4), 71–98. https://doi.org/10.2753/MIS0742-1222270403
4. Ball-Rokeach, S. J. (1998). A theory of media power and a theory of media use: Different stories, questions, and ways of thinking. *Mass Communication and Society, 1*(1–2), 5–40.
5. Ball-Rokeach, S. J. et al. (1984). The great American values test: Influencing behavior and belief through television.
6. Ball-Rokeach, S. J. (1985). The origins of individual media-system dependency: A sociological framework. *Communication Research, 12*(4), 485–510.
7. Ball-Rokeach, S. J., & DeFleur, M. L. (1976). A dependency model of mass-media effects. *Communication Research, 3*(1), 3–21.
8. Baptista, J., et al. (2016). Social media and the emergence of reflexiveness as a new capability for open strategy. *Long Range Planning*. https://doi.org/10.1016/j.lrp.2016.07.005
9. Beard, K. W., & Wolf, E. M. (2001). Modification in the proposed diagnostic criteria for internet addiction. *Cyberpsychology Behaviour, 4*(3), 377–383. https://doi.org/10.1089/109493101300210286
10. Bennett, W. L., & Segerberg, A. (2012). The logic of connective action. *Information, Communication Society 15*(5):739–768. https://doi.org/10.1080/1369118X.2012.670661.
11. Bensaou, M., & Venkatraman, N. (1995). Configurations of interorganizational relationships: A comparison. *Management Science, 41*(9), 1471–1492.
12. Bernardo, A. B. I. (2009). Exploring the links between social axioms and the epistemological beliefs about learning held by Filipino students. In *Psychological Aspects of Social Axioms* (pp. 163–175). Springer.
13. Bond, M. H., et al. (2004). Culture-level dimensions of social axioms and their correlates across 41 cultures. *Journal of Cross-Cultural Psychology, 35*(5), 548–570.
14. Boyd, D. M., & Ellison, N. B. (2007). Social network sites: Definition, history, and scholarship. *Journal of Computer-Mediated Communication, 13*(1), 210–230. https://doi.org/10.1111/j.1083-6101.2007.00393.x
15. Carillo, K. et al. (2014). An investigation of the role of dependency in predicting continuance intention to use ubiquitous media systems: Combining a media system perspective with expectation-confirmation theories. In: Proceedings of the twenty second European conference on information systems (ECIS2014) (pp. 1–17). Tel Aviv, Israel.
16. Carillo, K., et al. (2017). The role of media dependency in predicting continuance intention to use ubiquitous media systems. *Information and Management, 54*(3), 317–335. https://doi.org/10.1016/j.im.2016.09.002
17. Chen, S. X., et al. (2006). Going beyond self-esteem to predict life satisfaction: The Chinese case. *Asian Journal of Social Psychology, 9*(1), 24–35.
18. Comunian, A. L. (2009). Social axioms in Italian culture: Relationships with locus of control and moral development. In *Psychological aspects of social axioms* (pp. 269–282). Springer.

19. Deng, Y., & Chang, K. T. T. (2013). Task-technology fit for low-literate consumers: Implications for IS innovations in the developing regions. In *Thirty Fourth International Conference on Information Systems* (pp. 1–11). Milan, Italy.
20. Dincă, M., Iliescu, D. (2009). Linking social axioms with behavioral indicators and personality in Romania. In *Psychological aspects of social axioms* (pp. 145–162). Springer.
21. Edosomwan, S., et al. (2011). The history of social media and its impact on business. *Journal of Applied Management and entrepreneurship, 16*(3), 79–91.
22. van den Eijnden, R. J. J. M., et al. (2016). The social media disorder scale. *Computers in Human Behavior, 61,* 478–487. https://doi.org/10.1016/j.chb.2016.03.038
23. Federici, T., et al. (2015). 'Gentlemen, all aboard!' ICT and party politics: Reflections from a mass-eParticipation experience. *Government Information Quarterly, 32*(3), 287–298. https://doi.org/10.1016/j.giq.2015.04.009
24. GRANT, A. E. et al. (1991). Television shopping: A media system dependency perspective. *Communication Research 18*(6):773–798 https://doi.org/10.1177/009365091018006004.
25. Gupta, A. et al. (2018). Dispositional sources of managerial discretion: CEO ideology, CEO personality, and firm strategies. *Administrative Science Quarterly* 0001839218793128.
26. Hahn, R. A. (1973). Understanding beliefs: An essay on the methodology of the statement and analysis of belief systems. *Current Anthropology, 14*(3), 207–229.
27. Haythornthwaite, C. (2005). Social networks and internet connectivity effects. *Information, Community & Society, 8*(2), 125–147. https://doi.org/10.1080/13691180500146185
28. Hootsuite: Digital 2019. (2019).
29. Hornung, O. et al. (2018). When emotions go social–understanding the role of emotional intelligence in social network use. In *Proceedings of Twenty-Sixth European Conference on Information Systems*, paper 40.
30. Hulland, J. (1999). Use of partial least squares (PLS) in strategic management research: A review of four recent studies. *Strategic Management Journal, 20*(2), 195–204.
31. Jung, J.-Y., et al. (2001). Internet connectedness and inequality: Beyond the "Divide." *Communication Research, 28*(4), 507–535.
32. Jung, J.-Y., et al. (2012). The dynamic relationship between East Asian adolescents' use of the internet and their use of other media. *New Media & Society, 14*(6), 969–986.
33. Kaplan, A. M., & Haenlein, M. (2010). Users of the world, unite! The Challenges and Opportunities of Social Media. *Business Horizons, 53,* 59–68. https://doi.org/10.1016/j.bushor.2009.09.003
34. Katz, E., et al. (1973). Uses and gratifications research. *Public Opinion Quarterly, 37*(4), 509–523.
35. Keller, K. L. (2009). Building strong brands in a modern marketing communications environment. *Journal of Marketing Communications, 15*(2–3), 139–155. https://doi.org/10.1080/13527260902757530
36. Kietzmann, J. H., et al. (2011). Social media? Get serious! Understanding the functional building blocks of social media. *Business Horizons, 54*(3), 241–251. https://doi.org/10.1016/j.bushor.2011.01.005
37. King, D. L., et al. (2012). Clinical interventions for technology-based problems: Excessive internet and video game use. *Journal of Cognitive Psychotherapy, 26*(1), 43–56. https://doi.org/10.1891/0889-8391.26.1.43
38. Lakshmi, K. B., & Rajaram, M. (2012). Impact of information technology reliance and innovativeness on rural healthcare services: Study of Dindigul district in Tamilnadu, India. *Telemedicine and e-Health, 18*(5), 360–370.
39. Lam, S. Y., et al. (2004). Customer value, satisfaction, loyalty, and switching costs: An illustration from a business-to-business service context. *Journal of the Academy of Marketing Science, 32*(3), 293–311. https://doi.org/10.1177/0092070304263330
40. Lapointe, L. et al. (2013). Is smartphone usage truly smart? A qualitative investigation of IT addictive behaviors. In *Proceedings of the Annual Hawaii International Conference on System Sciences* (pp. 1063–1072). https://doi.org/10.1109/HICSS.2013.367.

41. Leung, K., et al. (2002). Social axioms: The search for universal dimensions of general beliefs about how the world functions. *Journal of Cross-Cultural Psychology, 33,* 286–302.
42. Leung, K., et al. (2007). Social axioms and values: A cross-cultural examination. *European Journal of Personality: Published for the European Association of Personality Psychology, 21*(2), 91–111.
43. Leung, K., & Bond, M. H. (2004). Social axioms: A model for social beliefs in multicultural perspective
44. Leung, L. (2009). Effects of internet connectedness and information literacy on quality of life. *Social Indicators Research, 98*(2), 273–290.
45. Loges, W. E. (1994). Canaries in the coal mine: Perceptions of threat and media system dependency relations. *Communication Research, 21*(1), 5–23.
46. Loges, W. E., & Ball-Rokeach, S. J. (1993). Dependency Relations and newspaper readership. *Journalism & Mass Communication Quarterly, 70*(3), 602–614.
47. Lyu, J. C. (2012). How young Chinese depend on the media during public health crises? A comparative perspective. *Public Relations Review, 38*(5), 799–806.
48. Majchrzak, A., et al. (2013). The contradictory influence of social media affordances on online communal knowledge sharing. *Journal of Computer-Mediated Communication, 19*(1), 38–55. https://doi.org/10.1111/jcc4.12030
49. Miller, S. et al. (2006). National culture influences on European ERP adoption. In Proceedings of the fourteenth European conference on information systems, paper 100.
50. Ng, B. D., & Wiemer-Hastings, P. (2005). Addiction to the internet and online gaming. *Cyberpsychology Behavior, 8*(2), 110–113. https://doi.org/10.1089/cpb.2005.8.110
51. Nossek, H., & Adoni, H. (1996). The social implications of cable television: Restructuring connections with self and social groups. *International Journal of Public Opinion Research, 8*(1), 51–69.
52. Patwardhan, P., & Yang, J. (2003). Internet dependency relations and online consumer behavior: A media system dependency theory perspective on why people shop, chat, and read news online. *Journal of Interactive Advertising, 3*(2), 57–69.
53. Podsakoff, P., et al. (2003). CommonMethod biases in behavioural research: A critical review of the literature and recommended remedies. *Journal of Applied Psychology, 88*(5), 879–903.
54. Ringle, C. M. et al. (2015). SmartPLS 3. https://www.smartpls.com.
55. Rishika, R., et al. (2013). The effect of customers' social media participation on customer visit frequency and profitability: An empirical investigation. *Information Systems Research, 24*(1), 108–127. https://doi.org/10.1287/isre.1120.0460
56. Rotter, J. B. (1966). Generalized expectancies for internal versus external control of reinforcement. *Psychological Monographs: General and Applied, 80*(1):1.
57. Safdar, S., et al. (2006). Social axioms in Iran and Canada: Intercultural contact, coping and adjustment. *Asian Journal of Social Psychology, 9*(2), 123–131.
58. Schau, H. J., et al. (2009). How Brand Community Practices Create Value. *Journal of Marketing, 73*(5), 30–51. https://doi.org/10.1509/jmkg.73.5.30
59. Serenko, A., & Turel, O. (2015). Integrating technology addiction and use: An empirical investigation of Facebook users. *AIS Transactions on Replication Research 1*, June, 1–18. https://doi.org/10.17705/1atrr.00002.
60. Singelis, T. M., et al. (2003). Convergent validation of the social axioms survey. *Personality and Individual Differences, 34*(2), 269–282.
61. Skumanich, S., & Kintsfather, D. (1998). Individual media dependency relations within television shopping programming a causal model reviewed and revised. *Communication Research, 25*(2), 200–219.
62. Smith, P. B., & Bond, M. H. (2003). Honoring culture scientifically when doing social psychology. *Sage Handbook of Social Psychology*, 43–61.
63. Sorensen, C. (2011). *Enterprise mobility: Tiny technology with global impact on work*. Palgrave Macmillan.
64. Spagnoletti, P., et al. (2015). Design for social media engagement: Insights from elderly care assistance. *The Journal of Strategic Information Systems, 24*(2), 128–145. https://doi.org/10.1016/j.jsis.2015.04.002

65. Spector, P. E. (1982). Behavior in organizations as a function of employee's locus of control. *Psychological Bulletin, 91*(3):482.
66. Stafford, T. F. et al. (2010). Exploring dimensions of mobile information technology dependence. In *ICIS 2010 Proceedings*.
67. Thadani, D. R., Cheung, C. M. K. (2011). Exploring the role of online social network dependency in habit formation. In *International Conference on Information Systems 2011*, ICIS 2011, pp 3446–3461.
68. Triandis, H. C. (1995). Individualism and collectivism (Boulder, CO: Westview). Kirschner, B. E. (2009), Fam. Scale Furth. Converg. Validity Explor. Sch. Psychol. (p. 113).
69. Tsai, W.-H.S., & Men, L. R. (2017). Consumer engagement with brands on social network sites: A cross-cultural comparison of China and the USA. *Journal of Marketing Communications, 23*(1), 2–21.
70. Turel, O., et al. (2011). Integrating technology addiction and use: An empirical investigation of online auction users. *MIS Quarterly, 35*(4), 1043–1061.
71. Turel, O., & Serenko, A. (2012). The benefits and dangers of enjoyment with social networking websites. *European Journal of Information Systems, 21*(5), 512–528. https://doi.org/10.1057/ejis.2012.1
72. Vaast, E., & Kaganer, E. (2013). Social media affordances and governance in the workplace: An examination of organizational policies. *Journal of Computer-Mediated Communication, 19*(1), 78–101. https://doi.org/10.1111/jcc4.12032
73. Wan, J., et al. (2017). How attachment influences users' willingness to donate to content creators in social media: A socio-technical systems perspective. *Information & Management, 54*(7), 837–850. https://doi.org/10.1016/j.im.2016.12.007
74. Wang, C., et al. (2015). A theory of social media dependence: Evidence from microblog users. *Decision Support Systems, 69,* 40–49. https://doi.org/10.1016/j.dss.2014.11.002
75. Wang, T. et al. (2013). Understanding user acceptance of micro-blog services in China using the extended motivational model. PACIS 2013 Proc. Paper 214, Paper 217.
76. West, B., et al. (2014). Building employee relationships through corporate social responsibility: The moderating role of social cynicism and reward for application. *Group & Organization Management, 40*(3), 295–322. https://doi.org/10.1177/1059601114560062
77. Whang, L.S.-M., et al. (2003). Internet over-users' psychological profiles: A behavior sampling analysis on internet addiction. *Cyberpsychology & Behavior, 6*(2), 143–150. https://doi.org/10.1089/109493103321640338
78. Xu, Z., et al. (2012). Online game addiction among adolescents: Motivation and prevention factors. *European Journal of Information Systems, 21*(3), 321–340. https://doi.org/10.1057/ejis.2011.56
79. Zheng, Y., & Yu, A. (2016). Affordances of social media in collective action: The case of free lunch for children in China. *Information Systems Journal, 26*(3), 289–313. https://doi.org/10.1111/isj.12096

Motives Behind DDoS Attacks

Scott Traer and Peter Bednar

Abstract Behind everything we do in our daily lives there is a reason for doing it. This paper looks into the motives behind DDoS attacks as a form of cyberattack along with attacker personas. This paper also investigates DDoS attacks technically and it is suggested that there is a need for a socio-technical approach to these attacks to investigate why they occur and the reasoning the attacker(s) could have for launching these attacks. This paper finds several motives behind DDoS attacks and discusses the profiles that attackers can be sorted into. Also discussed are the motives that attacker profiles can have for launching DDoS attacks. Although mitigation techniques are in place to control the damage a DDoS attack can cause to a company, if the motives can be addressed first, these attacks could be prevented. With the use of case studies, visualisations and tables, the motives behind DDoS attacks and attacker personas are presented.

Keywords Socio-technical · DDoS attacks · Cyberattacks · Motives · Profiles

1 Introduction

It is often said that "everything happens for a reason" and this is true within the field of cyberattacks. Behind every DDoS (Distributed Denial of Service) attack (a form of cyberattack) there is an attacker with a motive for launching the attack. This paper aims to cover and discuss a selection of these motives. Some companies do have security measures in place to mitigate the chance of an attack or mitigate the damage of a cyberattack, including a DDoS attack. However in some cases if the motive can

S. Traer (✉)
University of Portsmouth, Portsmouth, UK
e-mail: Scott.Traer@myport.ac.uk

P. Bednar
Lund University, Lund, Sweden
e-mail: Peter.bednar@port.ac.uk

C. Metallo et al. (eds.), *Digital Transformation and Human Behavior*, Lecture Notes in Information Systems and Organisation 37,
https://doi.org/10.1007/978-3-030-47539-0_10

be addressed it could be possible to prevent a cyberattack being launched in the first place.

A DoS (Denial of Service) attack involves an attacker forcing a machine or network resource to become unavailable in order to prevent intended users from being able to access it. An example of a DoS attack is discussed later on in this paper in "Table 3. Accident Case Studies". DDoS attacks, unlike DoS attacks, often involve multiple machines flooding a network forcing it to become inaccessible. DDoS attacks have been defined in a variety of different ways with each definition either providing additional details to a previous definition or using different terminology. A selection of definitions from sources include:

- Uses a network of machines usually compromised by malware and under the control of a host to funnel traffic towards a target, flooding the system and henceforth disrupting resources and access [1].
- An attempt to exhaust the resources available to a network, application or service so that genuine users cannot gain access [2].
- An attack that occurs when legitimate users are unable to access information systems, devices, or other network resources due to the actions of a malicious cyber threat actor [3].

In some cases malware is spread from machine to machine compromising machines as it spreads. This then allows a host to create a "botnet" which allows the compromised machines to be controlled. Commands can be used to perform malicious acts such as download files, upload documents and DDoS an address provided by the host.

This paper discusses motives behind DDoS attacks as a form of cyberattack and presents several motives that can be connected specifically to DDoS attacks. This paper also discusses attacker personas and profiles and the motives that attackers in a category may have. It can be argued that there is a need for tools supporting assessment of risks and that cover stakeholders' point of views [4]. Motives and personas can be used to support the assessment of cyberattack risks. Behind a cyberattack can be a singular motive, such as revenge, or several motives, such as in order to gain an advantage in business and as an act of revenge against a previous employer.

Companies have measures in place to defend against cyberattacks, including DDoS attacks and can mitigate the consequences. In some cases these defence mechanisms are not as good as they could be. It is reported that "cyberattacks in 2016 alone cost UK businesses as much as £30bn" [5] and therefore it can be suggested that research into other aspects of cyberattacks need to be researched, including the social side. The analysis of hacker communities and the way they behave may lead to possible motives behind launching cyberattacks. This can be used to potentially prevent attacks being launched in the first place, taking the focus away from mitigating the consequences of cyberattacks.

This paper firstly addresses some background knowledge in order to address what motives are, what motives can be linked to DDoS attacks and some case studies to back up these claims. This paper then progresses to motives behind DDoS attacks. The author details case studies and extracts the motives and discusses the attacker's reasoning for launching the cyberattack. Case studies are used to highlight different motives that an attacker could potentially have for launching cyberattacks. Following this is a discussion piece where motives are discussed within the context of DDoS attacks. Four tables (smokescreen, revenge, accident and cyberwarfare) are included to present case studies linked to DDoS attacks and the motives behind them. This will discuss the overlap between cyberattack motives and DDoS attack motives. The paper also discusses motives that could be argued are only connected to DDoS attacks. Attacker personas and profiles are then discussed with reference to an informal paper as well as security companies and discusses their categorisation of attackers and the motives that these attacker categories have.

2 Background

A motive can be defined as the reason why something is done or the reason for doing something. Motives can be seen in daily life and are used often without even knowing it. One motive for going to school is to learn, one motive for learning to drive is to get somewhere quicker. Motives behind cyberattacks and specifically DDoS attacks can be complex and sometimes unknown to a victim and investigators. Findings from research into this field suggest that motives can be anything from revenge, to protest, to financial gain. There can be more than one motive behind an attack. An interesting feature of cyberattacks is, much like crime in general, financial gain appears to take the largest share percentage for motives behind cyberattacks every year.

The company Verizon Enterprise released a 2018 security incident report with the finding that 78% of security breaches were for financial gain [6]. Other motives included revenge, for fun, protest, cyberwarfare and by accident. Although a DDoS attack does not breach a system and data, including personal information, is left untouched. This means data is not then used for blackmail or sold for profit. However it can be suggested that some DDoS attacks were also launched with a motive of financial gain. Research and findings suggest, a large amount of profit exists embedded inside the dark web, with DDoS-For-Hire services and DDoS tools being sold for a price online [7]. These attackers can be placed into a group called "Vendors". Password brute forcing and DDoS-For-Hire services are claimed to accumulate more than $100,000 a year [8]. Two individuals fitting the "vendor profile" go by the names AppleJ4cks and M3ow. They founded a company named vDOS, an Attack-For-Hire site and reportedly made $600,000 in its first two years of operating before it's demise in late 2016 [9]. With vendors being just one categorisation of cyber attackers, it can be argued that other categories can also be determined. Attackers could then be sorted into these categories.

In 2013 Hilbert wrote in the Network Security journal that cybercrime could be broken into four categories, including cybercrime, cyber-espionage, cyber-warfare and cyber-activism [10]. He discusses cyber-warfare and the intention being "to disable or destroy systems" and discusses other reasons for attacks including a disgruntled employee who wishes to destroy a former company and groups who wish to "make a mark on the world stage". In 2011, Hjortdal discussed that there are other reasons why cyber-warfare and cyber-espionage is felt necessary. Key reasons being to deter other states by infiltrating their critical infrastructure, to gain knowledge through espionage and to make economic gains where technological progress has been made [11]. Cybercrime happens multiple times a day all over the world and will continue to do so due to the financial gain that can be made and the relative ease with which these crimes can be carried out [10]. Hollier discussed cybercrime and mentioned personal factors such as financial gain can be viewed as a motivation for both crime and cybercrime [12]. The motives behind attacks can be viewed as a subjective matter and therefore further research into why cyberattacks occur is needed.

It is suggested that there is "a need for increased research on who is involved in hacking and their motivations" [13]. Further research into cyberattack motivations benefits companies. It is reported that "cyberattacks in 2016 alone cost UK businesses as much as £30bn" [5] and it being claimed that North Korea's cyber war attacks have seen financial costs of around $805 million for South Korea [14]. Cyberattacks, including DDoS attacks, do not exclusively target large companies and organisations but small companies can also be targeted "causing them to lose millions of money and billions of data" [15]. Costs include compensation to clients and improvements to the information system's security. If motives are researched further, signs can be developed and once spotted, dealt with accordingly. The same can be done with attacker personas. If personas can be created and sorted into types then measures can be put in place in order to mitigate the consequences of an attack or prevent the attack. In order for this to be effective, research into cyberattack motives need to be conducted fully and discussed.

As discussed, financial gain is one of the largest motives behind cyberattacks and this includes attacks from ransomware. When discussing crime Hollier states that the rational choice approach to crime suggests that "law-violating" behaviours occur when a person has assessed their personal and situational factors and then decide to risk breaking the law [12]. Personal factors included financial gain, revenge and entertainment. Situational factors included "how well a target is protected and the efficiency of the local police force". Hollier goes onto state that if a person decided that the reward outweighed the risk then it is likely that they would commit the crime. Therefore if an attacker decides that the risk of launching a cyberattack is outweighed by the profit or financial gain, they may decide to launch the attack.

Members of hacker groups such as Lulzsec and LulzRaft often state they hack "just for fun" and although the attacks can often be harmful it is not for personal gain but rather mostly for ego and competition [16]. It can be seen as an "intellectual challenge". An example of this was the unauthorised access of Vevo's YouTube account by two french citizens (one by the name of "Prosox") who went on to deface popular youtube videos by changing thumbnails and captions of the videos. On "Prosox's" twitter page, he wrote "the whole hack was just for fun. Don't judge me, I love YouTube" [17].

Research suggested that launching cyberattacks and particularly DDoS attacks with the motive of protest seems to be popular within hacker communities such as the hacktivist group Anonymous. In 2014, Martin Gottesfeld launched a series of cyberattacks on a Boston children's hospital on behalf of Anonymous. He claimed he did it in order to protest the treatment of a teenager in a high-profile custody dispute. The dispute was between a young girl's parents and the Boston children's hospital who believed the parents were interfering with the girls treatment. The young girl was taken into state custody [18]. These hacktivist group members feel strongly about issues that occur and are motivated to launch cyberattacks as a means of protest. Due to its effectiveness and sometimes ease of use, an attacker is motivated to use a DDoS attack in order to protest against a company and disrupt the website and services.

Cyberattacks are also launched due to cyberwarfare. Motives behind these can include protest, revenge and to display a cyber weapon. Nations can be motivated to launch cyberattacks, including DDoS attacks, against other nations in retaliation for physical events, to damage critical infrastructure and to show cyber dominance. It can also be suggested that motives for these attacks can be to weaken the country's defences, prove cyber capability or simply to "poke the bear".

Not all cyberattacks can be placed into the category of "cybercrime". Penetration testing is "essentially a controlled form of hacking in which the 'attackers' operate on your behalf to find the sorts of weaknesses that criminals exploit" [19]. When this occurs, a "pen tester" is employed by a company to effectively launch a cyberattack on their system in order to test the security of the system. Once this is done a report is created and vulnerabilities can be patched by the company. The motive taken from these instances can be defined as "employed to do so".

It must be accepted that accidents do happen. An employee might move an executable or delete a file, or change a single digit on a piece of software that overloads the system. The employee of a company is often seen as the weakest link in the security chain [20] and in 2013 Symantec released a report stating that in 2012, two thirds of data breaches were caused by human and system errors [21] (Fig. 1).

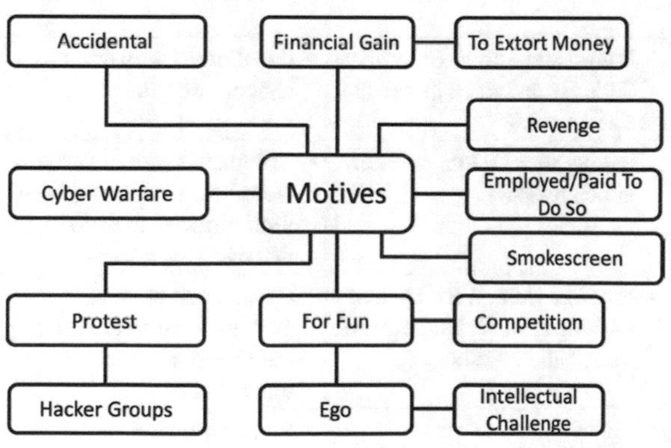

Fig. 1 Motives behind cyberattacks overview

3 Discussion: Motives Behind DDoS Attacks

Several of the motives behind cyberattacks can also be specific to DDoS attacks. For example, attackers use DDoS attacks in order to protest a company or organisation. In some cases these attacks prevent users from seeing the content of the company's webpage. Research found that attackers sometimes launch DDoS attacks as a means of distraction. "Basically a DDoS attack is not being used to take anything down but to distract and confuse the IT staff in a company" whilst attackers infiltrate a system on a different layer [9]. Examples of these can be seen in Table 1 where an attacker(s) has been motivated to use a DDoS attack as a smokescreen or distraction.

Cyberattacks can be used as a form of revenge or anger and DDoS attacks are no exception [25]. Ghandi et al. also discuss the timings of revenge attacks and the occurrence of revenge attacks on anniversaries of events such as a Burmese Web site that came under attack on the anniversary of 2010 failed uprising against the Burmese junta. Table 2 shows three case studies where an attacker has been motivated to use a DDoS attack as a means of revenge.

Table 1 Smokescreen case studies [22–24]

Knox County election night cyberattack was smokescreen for another attack Whetstone, T 2018	Carphone Warehouse hackers 'used traffic bombardment smokescreen' Williams, C 2015	The Great Sony PSN Hack Philips, T (2016) 2011
• Attack did not affect election results	• 2.4 million people affected by hack	• Attack began with the group Anonymous launching a DDoS Attack
• DDoS on election commission website	• Hackers stole personal and banking details	• 77m user's personal details accessed
• Used as a smokescreen	• "Sophisticated attack"	• Sony soon admitted an "external intrusion"
• Sword and Shield Enterprise Security dissected attack at $250 an hour	• DDoS used to distract as hackers went in	• Hack estimated a cost of at least £105m
• 6 days after DDoS, another attack realised	• Companies online systems were being swamped with junk traffic in the run up to discovery of breach	• Everyone wanting to change their passwords caused the server to crash once more
• Hackers were in the system looking around. No personal information stolen	• Caused just enough problems without rendering the network completely inaccessible	• At one point Sony faced 55 class action lawsuits
• DDoS "wasn't overly impressive but background attack was more sophisticated"	• Realised DDoS smokescreens were becoming more popular	• Anonymous not happy about treatment of George Hotz

Table 2 Revenge case studies [26–28]

Man Gets 15 Years for DDoS Revenge Campaign Muncaster, P 2018	NCA targeted by Lizard Squad in apparent DDoS revenge attack Hall, K 2015	WoW player sentenced to a year in federal prison for crashing Blizzard servers Jeffrey, C 2018
• New Mexico man sentenced to 15 years in prison	• DDoS performed as "apparent" act of revenge as NCA were cracking down on users of Lizard Squad	• Romanian World of Warcraft player sentenced to a year in prison
• Launched DDoS attack against former employers and business competitors	• NCA responded stating they are an attractive target	• Conducted a series of DDoS attacks again WoW servers
• He attacked companies who chose not to hire him	• No security breach	• He would often have arguments with other players on game
• Launched attacks from own computer via DDoS-as-a service offerings, on roughly three dozen targets	• Caused*a* temporary inconvenience	• When he didn't get his own way he would go offline and DDoS the server so that his friends also couldn't play
• Used IP anonymization, crypto currency to pay for "DDoS-for- hire" fake emails and HDD encryption and cleaning tools	• Lizard Squad mocked NCA on twitter	• Had to pay a fine to Blizzard for disruption to their servers
• Case highlighted ease of DDoS	• NCA had measures in place meaning site is generally up and running within 30 minutes but can sometimes take a bit longer	• Although the DDoS attack seemed harmless, it cost the company

As discussed earlier, accidents do happen when it comes to data breaches and cyberattack and this also applies to DDoS attacks. Rather than a motive behind DDoS attacks this is more of a DDoS cause. There would be an unknown motive behind an accidental DDoS attack as the "attacker" or an investigator would be unaware of his/her actions and consequences. However accidents are still a reason and a cause for why DDoS attacks occur. Table 3 shows three case studies where accidents occur and have caused a DDoS attack.

Another motive discussed earlier and shared between cyberattacks and specifically DDoS attacks is cyberwarfare. Arguably the first major newform of warfare since the development of nuclear weapons and intercontinental missiles [32], cyber warfare has become the norm across many nations with nation-state sponsoring and damage to critical infrastructure playing a key role. Nations can be motivated to launch DDoS attacks by unfair treatment, as a mean of defence and as a way to protest. Table 4 shows three case studies where nations and hacker groups have been motivated to engage in cyberwarfare.

Table 3 Accident case studies [29–31]

This is how one man accidentally destroyed the internet 30 years ago Shackelford, S (2018) 1988	Apple's iOS 10.3 fixes flaw used in accidental DDoS attack on 911 call system Campbell, M 2017	Breitbart News' FBI file details how site accidentally DDoS'd itself Morisy, M (2017) 2016
• The Morris worm	• Apples accidental flaw allowed code to be written that caused target iPhones to continually dial 911 emergency call centres	• Breitbart News site noticed a large amount of traffic straining its servers
• Robert Morris wanted to know how big the internet was	• The code went live and Arizona Police Departments received more than 100 hang-up calls within a few minutes	• Two days later it sent an email to the FBI requesting assistance with the source of the IP addresses
• Created a program to spread to computers and send a ping back to a server	• Calls were traced to a twitter link that when clicked activated the 911 call	• They wanted to know if the IP addresses were known to identify the criminal
• Mitigation was not good enough	• Code could also be used to trigger pop-ups and open emails.	• The FBI investigated and it was concluded that once the network traffic had been excluded it was traffic coming from a malfunctioning ad network
• Program began to clog up the internet by both copying itself to new machines and sending those pings back	• Desai was hoping to collect a bug bounty from Apple	• It essentially DDoS'd itself
• The server recording the pings became flooded and all connections to it became blocked		
• Didn't mean to start a DDoS attack		

With every motive discussed, there is an attacker who possesses the motive to launch the attack. These attackers can have similar traits that link them to one another and the motive for launching these attack. With this information, profiles and personas are expected to exist in order to group together attackers and provide motives for each category rather than each individual attacker.

In an informal paper written by Jack Krupansky, he defines persona as a type of person who has a type of role and uses "worker role, consumer role, or management role" as examples of this [36]. Later on in his paper, Krupansky labels "the people responsible for making cybersecurity necessary" as Offensive Threat Actors (Fig. 2).

The persona, offensive threat actor (OTA), is used as an umbrella term to cover several different types of hacker or attacker including state, amateur, and sociopolitical hackers. Krupansky also gives some motives for these type of attackers that

Table 4 Cyberwarfare case studies [33–35]

Massive DDoS Attack Shut Down Several Pro-ISIS Websites Sultan, O 2016	US Blames North Korea for Series of DDoS Attacks Conger, K 2017	Russia accused of unleashing cyberwar to disable Estonia Traynor, I 2007
• Attacker(s) went by the handle "Mons"	• US Department of Homeland Security and FBI issue bulletin linking North Korea to series of DDoS attacks to US businesses and critical infrastructure since 2009	• Estonia sparked a row with Russia after it wanted to move a memorial to the Soviet Red Army to a position of less prominence in Tallinn
• Conducted a series of DDoS attacks against several ISIS websites shutting them down	• Malware found that was used by North Korean Government to launch DDoS attacks	• Riots broke out in Tallinn and Estonia was hit by major cyber attacks
• It was to protest against the sudden increase of terrorist attacks	• Targeted the media, aerospace, financial and critical infrastructure sectors	• DDoS attacks took down online services of Estonian banks, media outlets and government bodies
• DDoS attacks varied from 50 Gbps to 460 Gbps	• Only an accusation but both departments have "teeth" when it comes to blaming North Korea	• Journalists were unable to upload articles to be printed Estonian learnt and set up more cyber defence mechanisms
• "This war needs to be fought on many fronts, and we try to cover one of them"		
• Sites were spreading violent content and terrorist ideology		
• Some sites restored and others listed for sale		

agree with motives discussed earlier in Sect. 3. In this group are whistleblowers. A whistleblower is a worker who reports a certain type of wrongdoing. Usually something seen at work but not always. Any report must be in the public interest [37]. In this case, one famous OTA is Edward Snowden. A whistleblower and previous NSA contractor. Snowden leaked documents containing the NSA's programs and capabilities that were being used to monitor and record personal communications in both the US and abroad [38].

One profile that appears consistently within literature, from companies such as InfoSecurity and Zonefox, is the Insider Threat profile. "Insider threats can be detrimental to your organization, its data, and its brand reputation" [39]. This profile has a lack of predictability or structure and can occur anytime and when it is least expected. One of the only ways to prevent it is to observe behavioural changes that the insider displays [40]. An insider threat profile can have several motives including to gain an

Fig. 2 Visualisation of Krupansky's OTA Persona

advantage in a new job, in order to prove or make a point, and as a "harmless" joke on a fellow employee.

Not all attacks are criminal and "security researchers" do have to be taken into consideration. Bugcrowd, a company that connects organisations to trusted security researchers, believe that these attackers can be profiled and sort them into five main types. They also provide a description of what motivates these sort of white hat hackers. Knowledge seekers are motivated by fun and enjoy the challenge whilst full timers hack in order to provide themselves with a primary income. Hobbyists hack as a hobby and spend their expendable income on cyber tools, virtuosos seek difficult to find bugs and enjoy a difficult challenge and protectors are primarily motivated to hack in order to make the internet a safer place [41].

Profiles are a subjective topic and companies and individuals create them based on their needs. This may be to prevent a future attack, secure themselves in order to mitigate the consequences of an attack, and as a way to recruit new employees who may have the qualities of an attacker but can be beneficial to a company.

4 Conclusion

This paper looked into the motives behind cyberattacks and provided a section based on DDoS attacks. Findings show attackers and the large range of motives that they can have for launching cyberattacks. The motives ranged from individuals out for revenge, to nation states engaged in cyberwarfare. This paper discussed the motives that attackers have and found that these attackers could be, and in some cases have been, sorted into types and these types could have their own set of motives. For example, the insider threat profile could have several motives including to gain an advantage in a new job, as an attack of revenge, to make a point/be noticed and as a joke on a colleague. Financial gain was also discussed as one of the main motives for cyberattacks and this was found to be true in the case of DDoS attacks as well. The claim that AppleJ4cks' vDoS site made $600,000 in it's first two years shows the financial gain motive. It must be considered that the person visiting and purchasing a DDoS attack from a DDoS-For-Hire site may have another motive, such as revenge or protest but fundamentally the attacker hired is attacking for monetary gain.

In future developments the research presented in this paper could be extended beyond DDoS attacks to look at other specific cyberattacks such as ransomware, worms, or phishing individually and the motives that they share with other attacks as well as motives that are exclusive to the specific attack. A new selection of attacker profiles could be developed and then attackers sorted into these profiles. This would provide evidence to back up the profiles and provide a justification as to why they were created. These profiles could then be used in order to predict future "offenders" and their motives and potentially be used as a method to mitigate the chances of a cyberattack occurring. This could lead to a universally accepted collection of profiles.

This paper's findings suggest that profiles and the motives that they possess are subjective and are developed based upon the companies needs. Bugcrowd is interested in white hat hackers and the personas that they could create to cover these attackers and the motives that they possess, whilst other companies such as ZoneFox focus on cyberattack damage from within a company and mitigating the chances of this threat.

Research conducted whilst writing this paper showed that there are still cases where motives behind the cyberattack are completely unknown and may stay that way as the attacker cannot be traced, is unwilling to discusses their reasoning, or the company has no interest in investigating why the cyberattack occurred. In many of these cases only assumptions about motives can be made but there will not be possible to know the real motive.

References

1. Fruhlinger, J. (2018). *What is a cyber attack? Recent examples show disturbing trends*. Retrieved from https://www.csoonline.com/article/3237324/what-is-a-cyber-attack-recent-examples-show-disturbing-trends.html
2. Netscout. (n.d). *What is DDoS?* Retrieved from https://www.netscout.com/what-is-ddos
3. CISA. (n.d). *Understanding denial-of-service attacks*. Retrieved from https://www.us-cert.gov/ncas/tips/ST04-015
4. Sadok, M., Katos, V., & Bednar, P. (2014). Developing contextual understanding of information security risks. *Conference: Human Aspects of Information Security & Assurance (HAISA 2014)*. Retrieved from https://www.researchgate.net/publication/263939773_Developing_Contextual_Understanding_of_Information_Security_Risks
5. Russell, G. (2017). Feature: Resisting the persistent threat of cyber-attacks. *Computer Fraud & Security,* 7–11. https://doi.org/10.1016/S1361-3723(17)30107-0
6. Verizon. (2018). *2018 Data breach investigations report*. Retrieved from https://enterprise.verizon.com/resources/reports/DBIR_2018_Report_execsummary.pdf
7. Makrushin, D. (2017). *The cost of launching a DDoS attack*. Retrieved from https://securelist.com/the-cost-of-launching-a-ddos-attack/77784/

8. Radware. (2017). *Anatomy of a hacker: Profiles, motivations & tools of the trade*. Retrieved from https://security.radware.com/WorkArea/DownloadAsset.aspx?id=1396
9. Mansfield-Devine, S. (2016). DDoS goes mainstream: How headline-grabbing attacks could make this threat an organisation's biggest nightmare. *Network Security,* (11), 7–13. https://doi.org/10.1016/S1353-4858(16)30104-0
10. Hilbert, E. (2013). Feature: Living with cybercrime. *Network Security,* 15–17. https://doi.org/10.1016/S1353-4858(13)70126-0
11. Hjortdal, M. (2011). China's use of cyber warfare: Espionage meets strategic deterrence. *Journal of Strategic Security*, *4*(2), 1. Retrieved from https://search.ebscohost.com/login.aspx?direct=true&db=edsjsr&AN=edsjsr.26463924&site=eds-live
12. Hollier, R. (n.d). *Criminology: Why do people commit crimes?* Retrieved from https://www.thelawproject.com.au/blog/criminology-and-why-do-people-commit-crimes
13. Thackray, H., McAlaney, J., Dogan, H., Taylor, J., & Richardson, C. (2016). *Social psychology: An under-used tool in cybersecurity*. British HCI 2016 Conference Fusion. https://doi.org/10.14236/ewic/HCI2016.64
14. Mehan, J. (2014). *Cyberwar, cyberterror, cybercrime & cyberactivism. Chapter 2.* IT Governance Publishing. Retrieved from https://www.jstor.org/stable/j.ctt7zsxqq.7
15. Sibi Chakkaravarthy, S., Sangeetha, D., Venkata Rathnam, M., Srinithi, K., & Vaidehi, V. (2018). Futuristic cyber-attacks. *International Journal of Knowledge Based Intelligent Engineering Systems, 22*(3), 195–204. https://doi.org/10.3233/KES-180384
16. Oliveira, M. (2011 Updated 2018). *Hacking group says they do it for the 'lulz'*. Retrieved from https://www.theglobeandmail.com/technology/tech-news/hacking-group-says-they-do-it-for-the-lulz/article556865/
17. Dellinger, A. J. (2018). *French teens arrested for hacking Vevo, defacing Despacito music video*. Retrieved from https://gizmodo.com/french-teens-arrested-for-hacking-vevo-defacing-despac-1826348217
18. Raymond, N. (2019). *Massachusetts man gets 10 years in prison for hospital cyberattack*. Retrieved from https://www.reuters.com/article/us-massachusetts-cyber/massachusetts-man-gets-10-years-in-prison-for-hospital-cyberattack-idUSKCN1P42J8
19. IT Governance. (n.d.). *Penetration testing*. Retrieved from https://www.itgovernance.co.uk/penetration-testing
20. Boulton, C. (2017). *Humans are the weakest cybersecurity link*. Retrieved from https://www.cio.com/article/3191088/humans-are-still-the-weakest-cybersecurity-link.html
21. Ponemon & Symantec. (2013). *Ponemon and Symantec find most data breaches caused by human and system errors*. Retrieved from https://www.symantec.com/about/newsroom/press-releases/2013/symantec_0605_01
22. Whetstone, T. (2018). *Knox county election night cyberattack was smokescreen for another attack*. Retrieved from https://eu.knoxnews.com/story/news/local/2018/05/17/knox-county-election-cyberattack-smokescreen-another-attack/620921002/
23. Williams, C. (2015). *Carphone warehouse hackers 'used traffic bombardment smokescreen'*. Retrieved from https://www.telegraph.co.uk/finance/newsbysector/epic/cpw/11794521/Carphone-Warehouse-hackers-used-traffic-bombardment-smokescreen.html
24. Phillips, T. (2011). *The great Sony PSN Hack*. Retrieved from https://www.eurogamer.net/articles/2016-04-26-sony-admitted-the-great-psn-hack-five-years-ago-today
25. Ghandi, R, & Sharma, A. (2011). Dimensions of cyber-attacks: Cultural, social, economic, and political. *IEEE Technology and Society Magazine* (1), 28. https://doi.org/10.1109/MTS.2011.940293
26. Muncaster, P. (2018). Man gets 15 years for DDoS revenge campaign. Retrieved from https://www.infosecurity-magazine.com/news/man-gets-15-years-for-ddos-revenge/
27. Hall, K. (2015). NCA targeted by Lizard Squad in apparent DDoS revenge attack. Retrieved from https://www.theregister.co.uk/2015/09/01/nca_targeted_by_lizard_squad/
28. Jeffrey, C. (2018). WoW player sentenced to a year in federal prison for crashing Blizzard servers. Retrieved from https://www.techspot.com/news/74517-wow-player-sentenced-year-federal-prison-crashing-blizzard.html

29. Shackelford, S. (2018). *This is how one man accidentally destroyed the internet 30 years ago.* Retrieved from https://www.inverse.com/article/50422-worlds-first-cyberattack-happened-30-years-ago-robert-tappan-morris
30. Campbell, M. (2017). *Apple's iOS 10.3 fixes flaw used in accidental DDoS attack on 911 call system.* Retrieved from https://appleinsider.com/articles/17/03/30/apples-ios-103-fixes-flaw-used-in-accidental-ddos-attack-on-911-call-system
31. Morisy, M. (2017). *Breitbart News' FBI file details how site accidentally DDoS'd itself.* Retrieved from https://www.muckrock.com/news/archives/2017/sep/19/breitbart-fbi-file-details-how-site-ddos/
32. Dipert, R. (2010). The ethics of cyberwarfare. *Journal of Military Ethics, 9*(4), 384–410. https://doi.org/10.1080/15027570.2010.536404
33. Sultan, O. (2016). *Massive DDoS attack shut down several pro-ISIS websites.* Retrieved from https://www.hackread.com/ddos-attack-on-pro-isis-websites/
34. Conger, K. (2017). *US blames North Korea for series of DDoS Attacks.* Retrieved from https://gizmodo.com/us-blames-north-korea-for-series-of-ddos-attacks-1796070321
35. Traynor, I. (2007). *Russia accused of unleashing cyberwar to disable Estonia.* Retrieved from https://www.theguardian.com/world/2007/may/17/topstories3.russia
36. Krupansky, J. (2018). *Cybersecurity personas, use cases, and access patterns.* Retrieved from https://medium.com/@jackkrupansky/cybersecurity-personas-use-cases-and-access-patterns-41fb8c9894ad
37. Gov.uk. (n.d.). *Whistleblowing for employees.* Retrieved from https://www.gov.uk/whistleblowing
38. The Courage Foundation. (n.d). *Who is Edward Snowden and what did he do?* Retrieved from https://www.edwardsnowden.com/frequently-asked-questions/
39. ZoneFox. (n.d). *Insider threat profiles.* Retrieved from https://www.zonefox.com/download-insider-threat-profiles/
40. Bell, A. J. C., Rogers, M. B., & Pearce, J. M. (2019). The insider threat: Behavioral indicators and factors influencing likelihood of intervention. *International Journal of Critical Infrastructure Protection, 24,* 166–176. https://doi.org/10.1016/j.ijcip.2018.12.001
41. Bugcrowd. (2017). *Inside the mind of a hacker.* Retrieved from https://www.bugcrowd.com/inside-the-mind-of-a-hacker-2-0/

How Do Employees Learn Security Behavior? An Integrated Perspective on Social Learning and Rational Decision Making

Adriana Niechoy, Kristin Masuch, and Simon Trang

Abstract The information security has become one of the most important topics in the modern information technology of companies. It influences the way companies work and the exchange of information between them. Information security policies are one of the most important instruments for compliance with information security (ISC). It is particularly important that the defined rules are adhered to. In order to explain human behaviour with regard to ISC, this paper uses the established theory of Social Learning Theory (SLT) and Rational Choice Theory (RCT). However, they are rarely used to explain the ISC. This article aims to combine behavioral and IS research to better understand ISC. We provide an overview and description of the effects of SLT and RCT on ISC through a PLS analysis. The results of this study show that SLT has an influence on RCT and therefore the ISC can be explained by the two theories used.

Keywords Information security policy compliance (ISPC) · Social learning theory (SLT) · Rational choice theory (RCT)

1 Introduction

Along with digital transformation, information security has cemented itself as a significant con-juncture within the business world. Due to the growing tendency to handle all processes digitally and to store information in cloud platforms, the question of a suitable information security strategy is gaining in importance [25, 27]. However, as is the case with many aspects of information technology (IT), information security is not tangibly understood for everyone. Nevertheless, it is a construct which is based on the cooperation of every part of a business, especially since new technological developments have a significant influence on people outside the organization. In everyday life raise the question of how they are to be securely managed.

A. Niechoy · K. Masuch (✉) · S. Trang
Georg-August-University Goettingen, Platz der Goettinger Sieben 5, 37073 Goettinen, Germany
e-mail: kristin.masuch@wiwi.uni-goettingen.de

C. Metallo et al. (eds.), *Digital Transformation and Human Behavior*, Lecture Notes in Information Systems and Organisation 37,
https://doi.org/10.1007/978-3-030-47539-0_11

Current research is searching for solutions that will guarantee information security, while simultaneously avoiding losses to its overall efficiency [17]. An important motivator for the economy is still the use of private smartphones, tablets, and laptops at work, steadily adding to the growing trend of bring your own device (BYOD) [12]. At this instant, the employee, who also plays an essential role in the implementation of information security policies, acts as the link between various devices [9]. In most cases, an employee's individual decision determines whether a data breach or security incident may occur. Besides this, there are also technical weak points in the information security policy of a company which directly cause security gaps [16, 22]. Recent studies have shown that data breaches caused or facilitated by employees cost companies billions of dollars [8, 29], and since 2017, over 500 breaches have been. Characterizing specific incidents into categories clearly demonstrate that more than 65% of these are caused by accidental disclosures [28]. Again, the purpose of new technologies is to support a person's daily challenges and facilitate his or her work. Yet, this also blurs the boundaries between one's private life and work [32]. Routines that were developed at one time to simplify different situations in life should likewise have the same capacity to be used in all circumstances accordingly. By using technical tools, sensitive information is either processed, or new sensitive data is therein created. The processing or creation of sensitive data, or research results worthy of protection, should be accompanied by a balanced information security strategy. Meanwhile, the information security policy (ISP) has long been an agenda for businesses. However, experience exhibits how compliance with the ISP is not yet intensely anchored via the behavior of employees [16]. To manage this challenge, increased influence and control is needed for implementing stricter ISPs. One applicable solution is to educate users and analyze their behavior to establish long term information security sensitization [11, 25]. The area of information security does not exclusively refer to the business con-text, with even public institutions like universities or town halls facing the challenge of a well elaborated and initiated ISP.

This paper strives to find out how individuals learn and acquire information security behavior and consequently how they implement it. Since the understanding of information security and compliant behavior is mandatory for everyone, it can therein be educational to analyze behavior patterns as they occur [8]. Therefore, the theory of social learning is used for this purpose. The findings can provide information on how individuals learn from the behavior of others associated with them. In a later phase, the "learned" behavior is defined by a reinforcement transfer by authorities [1, 5]. Based on this idea, information on ISP compliance can be better distributed in the future [18]. Further-more, another focus of this paper will be on the constructs of Rational Choice Theory. This theory examines decisions made by individuals using rational indicators [26, 34]. In the context of this paper the following research questions (RQ) are addressed:

RQ1: How do social group influence and reinforcement shape an individual's process of rational decision making in the context of information security behavior?

RQ2: How do rational choices influence information security behavior?

The following chapter provides an overview of information security, Social Learning Theory, and Rational Choice Theory. Subsequently, the research model of the empirical studies is described. Moreover, the hypotheses on the structural equation model (SEM) and the research design are described in detail below. The fourth chapter gives an insight into the methodology, while the results of the studies are described in the fifth chapter. Finally, a discussion and a summary of the results conclude this paper.

2 Theoretical Framework

2.1 State of the Art Information Security

Information security affects businesses in almost all areas, with one example being the implementation of new computer firewalls or software. Threats or security gaps lurk everywhere, including when hiring of a new employee or upgrading equipment [17, 20, 33]. Nowadays, every business has a defined security policy, with the information security policy being regulated. The inside security policy terms refer to maintaining the internal data from, for instance, hacker or malware attempts [25], while the outside security policy terms protect the business and its business partners. The research field of information security continues to increase, in part due to unsatisfactory solutions yet to be found, of which could cover all problem areas adequately. In most cases, studies on the analysis of the causes of information security breaches depict employees as the main perpetrators [17]. Reasons with this depiction are e.g. the lack of accuracy in the execution of the ISP, the ignorance of the specifications, as well as resistance against ISP in general [29]. Therefore, most research questions relate to the improvement of employee compliance towards the companies' ISPs [33]. Latest research has displayed enhanced knowledge about ISP, demonstrating a better attitude towards ISP [29]. Furthermore, various\methods established from the fields of behavioral psychology and social theories are implemented to increase employee awareness. Likewise, psychological aspects often play a role in behavior formation [23]. One example of a theory that relates to behavioral education is the theory of social learning [3]. In reference to information security, this theory to be combined incrementally enough [18]. Due to its structure, the Social Learning Theory offers possibilities to explain how people adopt behavior patterns and eventually reuse them in their later behavior [1, 5]. By breaking down behavior patterns, new insights can be found and used to create adept training measures. Another intriguing aspect of information security comprehension is the analysis of information security gap emergences. Since the main reason for violations is an already ISP informed employee of the company, it can be assumed that subjective decisions are made in accordance with ISP compliance, or therein lacking. Current literature on behavior oriented theories examine the Rational Choice Theory, often incorporated into research models to explore the rationality of behavior [13]. For this research paper, a model is developed that includes: the intention to comply with ISP, rational decision in a violation situation, and analysis of previously acquired behavior patterns. In the next chapters, the characters and components of Social Learning Theory and Rational Choice Theory will be presented.

2.2 *Social Learning Theory*

The theory of social learning was primarily developed by two different authors: Akers (1979) applied social learning for the first time as a unique theory, as previously social learning was only a part of the social structure theory. Additionally, in 1964 Bandura and Walters had defined the different items and features of the theory, being differential association, imitation, definition, and differential reinforcement. Together with these applications, the combined theory has its origins in behavioral research and is frequently used in the field of criminology, while criminal traits can also be identified in the area of information security. This connects Social Learning Theory (SLT) and information security. Thus, the awareness of information security is particularly made aware to the public through criminal incidents such as data theft or whistleblowing. Previous studies, which investigate behavior and other variables, present a basis for the hypothesis that behavior can be managed in the context of social learning. Through this application and by focusing on behavioral education at a young age, upcoming influencing structures can be pointed out [3, 18]. Henceforth, the SLT is divided into four different phases: The first step is to establish a learning environment. Often, the division into different groups is applied, all with an emotional connection to the subject and familiar with the theme of the interview. This stage is called differential association and forms the basis of the theory. Received attitudes and values from others are taken up by the subject and are subsequently imitated in the imitation phase [1, 7]. During the second step, imitation, the subject independently forms definitions of his or her behavior, which can be drawn upon in later situations. Experiences gained by applying certain behavioral patterns are stored by the individual. Therefore, the person decides independently if these behavioral patterns will be reapplied for future situations, or if they will be rejected, with this step being titled definition. The last phase of SLT is differential reinforcement. In this state, the learned and implemented behavior itself can be regulated by the outside world, since the reactions of third parties influence certain behavior, hence achieving reaction through positive or negative feedback. That means the applied behavior is either followed by a sanction or confirmation [1, 5, 23, 31].

The SLT allows us to explain behavior within specific groups. Furthermore, SLT can be used to investigate different reinforcement measures of behavior. We use this feature of SLT in our study to find out how people are influenced by others as they acquire new behavioral patterns related to their information security behavior.

2.3 *Rational Choice Theory*

The Rational Choice Theory (RCT) originates from the microeconomic theories [8, 10, 13] and therefore formally does not belong in the scope of behavioral theories, such as the theory of social learning. In many research projects, however, the RCT has been linked to behavioral research. Thus, it is difficult to give a clear definition of RCT, as many different aspects can be integrated into the framework of the theory [13]. It can be additionally noted that RCT relies on the means with which individuals choose to achieve their intended goal [13, 26]. As a result, the aim is to use RCT to analyze decisions that motivate respondents in maximizing their expected benefits as homogeneously as possible throughout particular scenarios [10, 13, 34]. However, the assessment of the expected utility depends on the individual evaluation of the influencing factors. The expected utility can be calculated by balancing benefits and costs of choices [8, 34]. A relativization of the influencing factors is difficult to implement through their subjective evaluations. Externalization of the triggering factors can be achieved by numerical representation of these factors. In this way, the rationality of the decision can be, in parts, better understood externally. Studies in this field have already analyzed that individuals, after measuring all factors, do not choose the best alternative choice, but rather the most satisfying one [34]. A decision balanced over all costs and benefits is consistent with preferences of an individual and therefore rational [8]. Another reoccurring problem is the level of consideration. The alternation between decisions at the micro level and individual actions in decision making is often blurred. If incentive systems are created, they likewise considered in the decision making process, disassembling the rationality of this decision [10]. Moreover, Coleman and Fararo (1992) previously pointed out that the theory of rational choice is best combined with theories that better analyze the field of social questions. In our research design, this role is adopted by the theory of social learning. With the guidance of the SLT, the social influencing factors of the decisions are covered, while these social factors have an influence on the personal evaluation of the decision. One contrasting challenge of RCT is to evaluate the costs and benefits in a measurable or transparent manner for the respondent. If this is not guaranteed, the personal effects of the action cannot be assessed as efficient or inefficient by the concerned persons and the decision is not based on rationality [10].

3 Research Model

Inspired by current research in information security, we chose a two-stage research model. The focus of our study was to discover how employees build their information security behavior to develop future measures in improving the sensitization of employees and prevent misconduct. The research model is presented in Fig. 1.

It is based on the Rational Choice Theory and the other the Social Learning Theory, both from the field of decision-making. RCT deals with the question of how

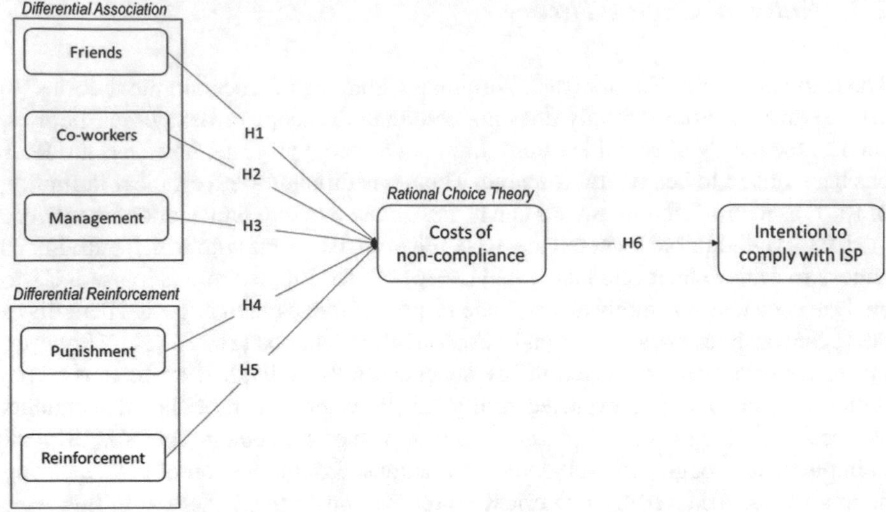

Fig. 1 Research model with hypotheses

benefit-cost calculations are used to make decisions [8, 24], while the theory of social learning describes historical influences that unconsciously influence an individual in his or her actions. In this research design, we use the RCT to show how the theory of rational choice has an influence on a subject's final decision. Linked to the SLT, it should be clarified whether the rationality of a decision is influenced by social groups or differential reinforcement of the SLT.

3.1 Aspects of Social Learning Theory

As already mentioned in Sect. 2.2, only some aspects of SLT are used in this research model, as a reference to the entire theory would over-extend the scope of the present research work. For the investigated research model two aspects of SLT are used: Social influencing groups, as part of the item Differential Association, as well as punishment and reinforcement as variables of the item Differential Reinforcement.

To specify, social influencing groups are one of the defining characteristics of the SLT. In connection with the idea of the costs of your actions, the theory of social learning successfully paves the way for "moral detriments" [2]. The variable of social influence explains behavior that is monitored by other people [23]. These people define peer groups, who have an influence on individuals during different periods of his or her life. As young adults, the group of friends is the most important reference group, while later on, co-workers and managers become a more important influencing factor regarding work-related issues. Thus, the influential peer groups change throughout a person's lifetime and its different stages. Behavioral patterns are adopted as the result of the peer group that is most likely to influence the individual. Correspondingly, the initial hypotheses in our research model are the influence between the social influencing groups and our assessment of the costs of non-compliance with ISP:

Hypothesis 1: Friends influence the evaluation of the costs of ISP non-compliance.
Hypothesis 2: Co-workers influence the evaluation of the costs of ISP non-compliance.
Hypothesis 3: Management influences the evaluation of the costs of ISP non-compliance.

Differential Reinforcement is the second variable of the SLT involving the aforementioned reinforcement of behavior patterns already in use. Either positive reinforcements such as rewards, advantages or recognition can be used or negative feedback such as punishment, negative recognition or consequences is given. In our research model, both manners are investigated. The following hypotheses are modeled:

Hypothesis 4: Sanctions influence the evaluation of the cost of ISP non-compliance.
Hypothesis 5: Advantages influence the evaluation of the cost of ISP non-compliance.

3.2 Aspects of Rational Choice Theory

The purpose of this research model is to understand which part is inherently represented by the demand to optimize the costs of making a decision. In order to address this question, the RCT deals with the balancing of actions and their expected results [10]. It consists of three constructs which analyze the expected costs of an activity, the expected benefits of an activity and the costs of no activity whatsoever. After weighing all alternatives, that the option which represents the most satisfactory solution is decided upon [13], ensuring that the benefit is at its maximum, the costs minimized and the highest expected benefit for the decision maker still [10]. Only one aspect of the RCT is used in the research model in order to expand the scope of the present research work. For the investigated research model, the aspect of the cost of non-compliance is likewise used. The construct of non-compliance related costs is described by the costs which can occur if the prescribed course of action is not followed. Additionally, the expected disadvantages of a violation are queried. If a decision for a security breach is made, the personal disadvantages are therein calculated, while simultaneously being shaped by what taken place contrary to that of the benefits of compliance, such as intrinsic costs, sanctions and the vulnerability of resources [8]. Thus, the following hypothesis is developed:

Hypothesis 6: The costs of non-compliance influence the intention to comply with ISP.

4 Research Design

4.1 Experimental Design

The research model is implemented with a scenario-based questionnaire. The aim is to find out how people behave in the case of a security breach and which factors lead to their decision. A total of 276 questionnaires were submitted. 215 answers could be used for the evaluation. To measure ISP compliance recent research suggests two different approaches: the first approach is the scenario-based measurement, while the second approach is the behaviorally anchored approach. Both methods have advantages and disadvantages [25, 33], whereas for the following study, we employed the scenario-based approach in order to show the participants a scenario before answering the questions, within which they can place themselves easily into the situation of an ISP breach [21]. Thereafter, questions regarding their individual opinion about their behavior and attitudes follow, with the attitudes of the participants being checked by the item of the RCT. The presented scenarios are orchestrated in two separate ways through items of the SLT. Thus, the constructs of social influence of "close" peer groups and the reinforcement of behavior are equally covered. Furthermore, according to the research design, single components or combinations of the components from the SLT can likewise be used. To implement our research method, we use adaptations of the component called Differential Association. The Differential Association represents the adoption of values and attitudes of others through interactions [7, 23]. Therefore, we have derived the indicator of social influence, which describes interaction partners through specified peer groups. The second manipulation was the indicator of the Differential Reinforcement items, punishments, and reinforcements. The aim was to give the participants an impression of which experience has already been gained with ISP breaches. Thus, four possibilities were distinguished, while either sanctions or rewards were received with either high or low intended impact. As mentioned before, the scenario was followed by questions regarding the individual assessment of the costs for not complying with the ISP of the business. Based on the RCT items of these constructs, an answer as to whether or not individuals will act rationally when deciding to commit a security breach can be pursued. The indicators of SLT should establish a relationship between related peer-groups and measure the influence the subsequent group attitudes and their effect on the decisions of the individual. Another important goal pursued is the linkage between two theories in the research model towards identifying the behavioral pattern of ISP Compliance. On the one hand, the SLT is used to analyze influencing factors and learning environments [1], while at the same time the RCT, which does not officially depict behavior patterns, but provides insight into the decision-making process [13].

4.2 Operationalization

The survey began with a scenario, which described a new employee from the hiring process to an IT security breach. A total of 24 different plot structures were used in the questionnaire. In each subsequent interview, one single scenario was allocated to the participants. The scenarios were hence manipulated on two different levels: On the one hand, an indication was made about either friends, co-workers or management personnel, which reflects how this group assesses ISP, embodied by the distinction implied between “ISP is relevant” and “ISP is negligible”. On the other hand, the second indication describes previous experiences with ISP breaches. A total of two groups were distinguished, the first of which with sanctions. A differentiation between high treatment and low treatment was made, while in the second group, positive reinforcement of behavior was applied. As in the first group, a differentiation was made within high and low treatments. Subsequent to the scenario, various questions were posed to interviewees. A total of six blocks were asked, as well as various demographical data, which are presented in the following: The first block contained four questions, which asked for an evaluation of the presented behavior. A 6-point Likert scale was used for possible answers. All the questions were formulated to apply with a “agree or disagree” scale, where 1 means “strongly disagree” and 6 means “strongly agree”. There are different opinions in the literature as to whether an odd or even scale makes more sense. Whereas for this research model, we have deliberately chosen an even scale, so that our test persons do not have the possibility to decide for a neutral statement. Since many questions ask for the opinion that refers to the discrete scenario, it was important to us that the answers point in a clear direction. Questions in Block II refer to the understanding of the scenario. The purpose of these questions was to check whether respondents had read the scenario carefully enough. The questions were specifically tailored to the group of people addressed in the scenario. In addition to the 6-point Likert scale, the answering option “Not specified” was added, in order to give respondents the opportunity to indicate if the scenario was unable to mention the topic at all. Moreover, Block III asked two questions about the personal behavioral intention in the case of the described scenario. The two behavioral possibilities, “I behave in the same way/act differently”, were formulated. The Blocks IV–VI referred to the items of the RCT and asked with four questions each concerning the benefits of compliance, costs of compliance and costs of non-compliance the attitudes of the test persons, while these questions could likewise be answered with a 6-point Likert scale. Subsequently, personal data of the test persons was also collected, ranging from age, gender, educational graduation, number of professional years and the field of work. On top of that, a block of questions was asked with regard to how IT competence is assessed and how often sensitive data is used at the workplace. The questions in sections block IV (BoC) and block V (CoC) and the personal data were used as control variables in the analysis of the SEM.

5 Results

5.1 Sample Characteristics and Scenario Check

Within the sample, 52% of the participants were under 25 years of age and also displayed an amount of work experience of 51% in total less than 3 years. This matches with our research design. Because it is more likely that behavior patterns will change at a younger age. Furthermore, a large part of the sample has already achieved a university degree, from which it can be concluded that participants are working full-time. Nearly 80% of the participants indicated that they use IT at their job, from which over 51% strongly agreed. The data on BoC, CoC and the demographic data additionally serve as control variables for the SEM. The control variables were checked with the Smart PLS software and are represented along with the rest of our SEM variables in Table 1 and Fig. 2. When analyzing the scenario manipulations, it can be concluded that the treatments of the management group were best understood in comparison to the other groups. Considering the mean values of each scenario, we can see that the low treatment that affected the management was the least understood. The directions intended to increase ISP compliance were not perceived. Thus, the scenarios that had a low treatment were rated as more beneficial than those with high treatment.

5.2 Measurement Model

Before testing our structural model, we run tests to check the quality of our reflective constructs. First, we examined the convergent validity, which is defined by two different values. The composite reliability (CR) which describes how well the associated items are suitable to measure the latent variable. The acceptable range of values for exploratory research is above 0.6 [4]. In addition, it is recommended to generate the AVE values at least up to a limit of 0.5, so that the influence of the error is less than the variance [19]. As shown in Table 1 all inter-construct correlations have values for CR which are higher than 0.6, as well as values for the AVE which are higher than 0.5.

Secondly, we examined the discriminant validity. An index to this quality factor follows the Fornell-Larcker-Criteria, which is the square root of the AVE [14]. In Table 1, all relevant values of these scores are pictured in blue frames. To confirm the discriminant validity, all square rooted AVE of this model have to be higher than the latent variable correlation values of this construct. Additionally, another value to verify the discriminant validity is the cross-loadings. The PLS-indicators load much higher on their hypothesized factor than on other factors (i.e. own loadings are higher than cross-loadings). The loadings of our items (Appendix A) indicate that the discriminant validity is confirmed.

Table 1 Inter-construct correlations, CR, AVE

Constructs	CR	AVE	INT	BoC	CoC	ConC	G_F	G_C	G_M	Pun	Rein	Aff	Age	Gen	Grad	Indu	WE
INT	0.924	0.801	0.895	0	0	0	0	0	0	0	0	0	0	0	0	0	0
BoC	0.854	0.594	0.473	0.771	0	0	0	0	0	0	0	0	0	0	0	0	0
CoC	0.789	0.556	−0.392	−0.435	0.746	0	0	0	0	0	0	0	0	0	0	0	0
ConC	0.933	0.776	0.461	0.450	−0.232	0.881	0	0	0	0	0	0	0	0	0	0	0
G_F	n.a.	1	−0.003	0.024	−0.006	0.077	n.a.	0	0	0	0	0	0	0	0	0	0
G_C	n.a.	1	0.126	0.080	−0.029	0.222	−0.211	n.a.	0	0	0	0	0	0	0	0	0
G_M	n.a.	1	0.065	0.026	0.074	0.112	−0.184	−0.193	n.a.	0	0	0	0	0	0	0	0
Pun	n.a.	1	−0.086	−0.011	−0.005	0.040	−0.059	0.034	−0.055	n.a.	0	0	0	0	0	0	0
Rein	n.a.	1	0.019	−0.004	0.005	−0.105	0.028	0.006	0.007	−0.335	n.a.	0	0	0	0	0	0
Aff	0.918	0.789	0.039	−0.066	0.004	−0.094	0.100	−0.036	0.074	0.068	−0.022	0.888	0	0	0	0	0
Age	n.a.	n.a.	0.128	0.083	0.029	0.155	0.025	0.114	−0.057	−0.050	0.030	0.001	n.a.	0	0	0	0
Gen	n.a.	n.a.	0.074	0.025	0.045	0.123	0.060	0.048	−0.002	−0.131	0.111	−0.017	0.568	n.a.	0	0	0
Grad	n.a.	n.a.	0.047	0.009	−0.010	−0.033	−0.091	−0.032	−0.046	0.089	0.002	0.135	0.068	−0.066	n.a.	0	0
Indu	n.a.	n.a.	0.097	0.130	−0.067	0.109	0.090	−0.067	0.025	0.009	−0.044	0.161	0.067	0.038	0.227	n.a.	0
WE	n.a.	n.a.	0.011	0.084	−0.031	0.169	0.090	0.069	−0.008	−0.008	−0.094	0.065	0.204	0.030	0.046	0.185	n.a.

Note INT—Intention to comply with ISP, BoC—Benefit of Compliance, CoC—Cost of Compliance, ConC—Cost of non-Compliance, G_F—Friends, G_C—Co-workers, G_M—Management, Pun—Punishment, Rein—Reinforcement, Aff—Affinity, Gen—Gender, Grad—Graduation, Indu—Industry, WE—Work-Experience

5.3 Structural Model

The analysis of the research model was performed using the partial least squares (PLS) method of the Smart PLS 2.0 software. The results of the estimation are presented in Fig. 2. To assess the structural model, a bootstrapping procedure operating with 8500 subsamples was used to estimate the statistical significance. In PLS estimation, the primary indicators of model fit are the R^2 values of the dependent constructs [15]. The R^2 value of 0.3602 of Intention to comply with ISP indicates that the examined costs of ISP-non-Compliance explain about 36% of the variance of Intention to comply with the ISP. Furthermore, the examined category explains

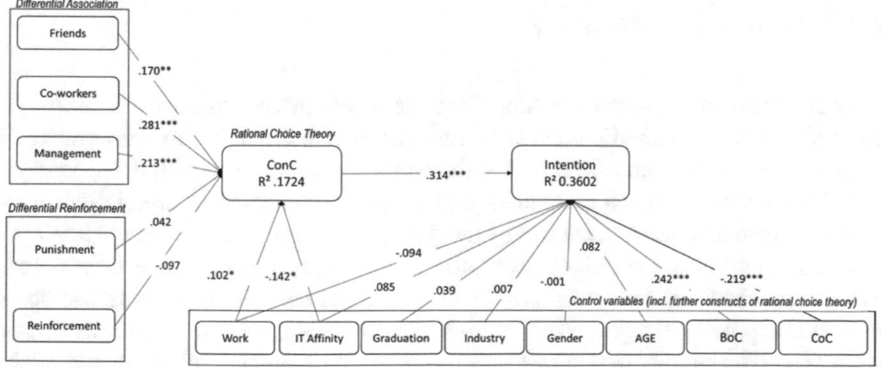

Fig. 2 SEM with R2 and path coefficients (*Note* *significant at 0.1; **significant at 0.05; ***significant at 0.01)

17.24% of the Costs of non-Compliance. The hypotheses which revealed to be significant are the different social influencing groups (friends, co-workers, and management) on the Costs of non-compliance with ISP. The only hypothesis that is not significant is the Differential Reinforcement on the Costs of non-compliance with ISP. In addition, it should be noted that the control variables Cost and Benefits of compliance are significant with Cost of non-compliance and Work and IT Affinity are significant with ISP.

With the presented research concern, we have attempted to discern whether social groups and punishments or reinforcement of behavior influence our rational decision making. We investigated 5 groups that we related to RCT. A total of 6 hypotheses were formed which represent the individual dependencies. All three hypotheses of the social influencing groups were confirmed: H1, H2, and H3. These examined the influence between Friends (H1 0.170**), Co-workers (H2 0.281***), and Management (H3 0.213***) on the Costs of non-compliance. Besides social groups, the influence of experiences was also investigated for whether Punishment for misconduct or Reinforcement of behavior, such as rewards or other incentives, each have an influence on the rational choice (H4 and H5). However, neither of the two hypotheses could be confirmed with our sample. Furthermore, we investigated to what extent the assessment of Costs of non-compliance has an influence on the Intention to comply with ISP. The hypothesis was confirmed with the highest level of significance (H6 0.314***). Furthermore, the cost of non-compliance, which describes the costs that can occur if the prescribed course of action, is divergent from our findings [8]. The aim of the RCT is to locate the person's most satisfying alternative [34]. It can therefore be confirmed that the lower the cost of a non-compliant action, the more one chooses this alternative.

6 Discussion

6.1 Summary of Findings

To examine the first research question (How do social group influence and reinforcement shape an individual's process of rational decision making in the context of information security behavior?), we analyzed the impact of Differential Association and Reinforcement on costs of non-compliance. Our results show that Differential Association in this case represented by the groups of friends, employees and management has a significant positive impact no matter which social group is considered. Thus, the attitudes of the social groups influence the behavioral patterns, the costs of non-compliance are perceived as high, the attitude carries over just as if they were perceived as low. In contrast, differential reinforcement, neither as a punishment nor as a reinforcement, has a significant effect on rational choice indicators. This suggests that differential reinforcements do not lead to a significantly increased cost of non-compliance. To answer our second research question (How do rational choices influence information security behavior?), we researched the construct of Cost of ISP non-compliance of RCT. Our survey has shown that the construct has a significant positive impact on information security behavior. This can confirm that the costs of non-compliant influence the intention to behave compliantly, suggesting that the higher the costs of non-compliant behavior is perceived, the more likely it is that employees will have the intention to behave compliant.

6.2 Contribution

This paper provides a contribution to research by linking the aspects of two theories together. Although most of the known literature tries to explain ISP behavior with different theories, most are only considered side by side and not directly connected to each other [21, 30]. Using the items of SLT, a relationship between a behavior-oriented theory and RCT was established and applied to a behavior-oriented question. This allowed us to confirm that, although the RCT does not provide a focus for the explanation of behavior, it remains still suitable for the evaluation of actions. For the practical implications of this paper, we generally recommend considering the specific characteristics of our positively linked relationship between SLT and RCT as part of understanding employee behavior. However, no clear results have been obtained yet, while there is still potential for further research to identify indicators that encourage employees to behave compliantly. The resulting measures for training programs help companies to subsequently protect their information and thereby protecting their employees as well.

6.3 Limitation and Future Research Directions

A chronological approach is used to identify the limitations associated with the development of the research model. All scenarios were manipulated on two levels, with an attempt to achieve a treatment with a high impact on the reader and a lower treatment being applied. The results of the manipulation checks show that the manipulations were not formulated clearly enough, due to the difference between the high and low scenarios not fully considered. Another vulnerability of the survey's conception relates to the design of the manipulations. In four scenarios, each which refers to the management low level of ISP, the management group was not explicitly mentioned. As a result, the respondents attached less importance to the statement of the scenario reflected in the mean value (5.282) of the manipulation check. From the RCT, only the aspect of cost of non-compliance assessments was effectively approached. By further inquiries, this aspect can be analyzed on a deeper level. For instance, it is possible to analyze what is considered to be the cost of non-compliance with the ISP. In addition, the impact of benefits and costs of compliance on ISP could be examined, and due to the small research framework, this analysis was not carried out in the study. The survey data was collected online and primarily aimed at students at German universities. Therefore, the group of participants is characterized by young students, which does not exclude a distortion of the data. During the data evaluation with Smart PLS, the suitable sample size for the bootstrapping was searched. Since the computer capacity is limited, no sample larger than 8500 was allowed, although the values of the T-statistics varied.

6.4 Conclusion

With the present research study, we attempted to make a further contribution to the analysis of the participation of employees in the protection of information security. We were able to show that there is a connection between decision-making and social influence groups. Nonetheless, the analysis of items that motivate or discourage us to behave appropriately needs to be further elaborated in additional studies, thereby important aspects for training measures can be derived. In this way, companies retain control over what can be done to protect themselves from data loss. In addition, investigating how the results change when the study is conducted in a different cultural context could yield interesting results. This information is particularly noteworthy for organizations that operate globally and employ people with different cultural backgrounds. In summary, training measures need to consider this aspect in order to maximize the effect upon employee capabilities with respect to information security.

References

1. Akers, R. L. (1979). Social learning and deviant behavior: A specific test of a general theory. *American Sociological Review, 44*(4), 636–655.
2. Akers, R. L. (1990). Rational choice, deterrence, and social learning theory in criminology: The path not taken. *Journal of Criminal Law and Criminology, 83*(3), 653–676.
3. Akers, R. L. (1998). *Social learning and social structure: A general theory of crime and deviance*. Boston: Northeastern Univ. Press.
4. Bagozzi, R. P., & Yi, Y. (1988). On the evaluation of structural equation models. *Journal of the Academy of Marketing Science, 16*(1), 74–94.
5. Bandura, A. (1977). *Social learning theory, Prentice-Hall series in social learning theory*. New Jersey: Prentice-Hall, Englewood Cliffs.
6. Bandura, A., & Walters, R. H. (1964). *Social learning and personality development*. New York [u.a.]: Holt, Rinehart and Winston, Inc.
7. Brauer, J. R. (2009). Testing social learning theory using reinforcement's residue: A multilevel analysis of self-reported theft and marijuana use in the national youth survey. *Criminology, 47*(3), 929–970.
8. Bulgurcu, B., Cavusoglu, H., & Benbasat, I. (2010). Information security policy compliance: An empirical study of rationality-based beliefs and information security awareness. *MIS Quarterly, 34*(3), 523–548.
9. Cheng, L., Li, Y., Li, W., Holm, E., & Zhai, Q. (2013). Understanding the violation of IS security policy in organizations: An integrated model based on social control and deterrence theory. *Computers & Security, 39*, 447–459.

10. Coleman, J. S., & Fararo, T. J. (1992). *Rational choice theory: Advocacy and critique*. Newbury Park/London/New Delhi: Sage Publications.
11. D'Arcy, J., & Herath, T. (2011). A review and analysis of deterrence theory in the IS security literature: Making sense of the disparate findings. *European Journal of Information Systems, 20*(6), 643–658.
12. Disterer, G., & Kleiner, C. (2013). BYOD bring your own device. *Procedia Technology, 9*, 43–53.
13. Eriksson, L. (2011). *Rational choice theory: Potential and limits, political analysis*. Basingstoke: Palgrave Macmillan.
14. Fornell, C., & Larcker, D. F. (1981). Evaluating structural equation models with unobservable variables and measurement error. *Journal of Marketing Research*, 39–55.
15. Hair, J. F., Sarstedt, M., Ringle, C. M., & Mena, J. A. (2012). An assessment of the use of partial least squares structural equation modeling in marketing research. *Journal of the Academy of Marketing Science, 40*(3).
16. Herath, T., & Rao, H. R. (2009a). Encouraging information security behaviors in organizations: Role of penalties, pressures and perceived effectiveness. *Decision Support Systems, 47*(2), 154–165.
17. Herath, T., & Rao, H. R. (2009b). Protection motivation and deterrence: A framework for security policy compliance in organisations. *European Journal of Information Systems, 18*(2), 106–125.
18. Higgins, G. E., Fell, B. D., & Wilson, A. L. (2007). Low self-control and social learning in under-standing students' intentions to pirate movies in the United States. *Social Science Computer Review, 25*(3), 339–357.
19. Homburg, C., & Baumgartner, H. (1995). Beurteilung von Kausalmodellen: Bestandsaufnahme und Anwendungsempfehlung. *Marketing: Zeitschrift für Forschung und Praxis*, 162–176.
20. Ifinedo, P. (2014). Information systems security policy compliance: An empirical study of the effects of socialisation, influence, and cognition. *Information & Management, 51*, 69–79.
21. Johnston, A. C. (2016). Dispositional and situational factors: Influences on information security policy violations. *European Journal of Information Systems, 25*, 231–251.
22. Kim, S. H., Yang, K. H., & Park, S. (2014). An integrative behavioral model of information security policy compliance. *The Scientific World Journal, 2014*, 463870.
23. Lowry, P. B., Zhang, J., Wang, C., & Siponen, M. (2016). Why do adults engage in cyberbullying on social media? An integration of online disinhibition and deindividuation effects with the social structure and social learning model. *Information Systems Research, 27*(4), 962–986.
24. McCarthy, B. (2002). New economics of sociological criminology. *Annual Review of Sociology, 28*(1), 417–442.
25. Moody, G. D., Siponen, M., & Pahnila, S. (2018). Toward a unified model of information security policy compliance. *MIS Quarterly, 42*(1), 285–311.
26. Paternoster, R., & Pogarsky, G. (2009). Rational choice, agency and thoughtfully reflective decision making: The short and long-term consequences of making good choices. *Journal of Quantitative Criminology, 25*(2), 103–127.
27. Pereira, T., Barreto, L., & Amaral, A. (2017). Network and information security challenges within Industry 4.0 paradigm. *Procedia Manufacturing, 13*, 1253–1260.
28. Privacy Rights Clearinghouse. A Chronology of Data Breaches. https://www.priva-cyright.org/data-breaches.htm. Last accessed September 17, 2018.
29. Safa, N. S., Solms, R., & Furnell, S. (2016). Information security policy compliance model in organizations. *Computers & Security, 56*, 70–82.
30. Siponen, M., & Vance, A. (2010). Neutralization: New insights into the problem of employee information systems security policy violations. *MIS Quarterly, 34*(3), 487.
31. Skinner, W. F., & Fream, A. M. (1997). A social learning theory analysis of computer crime among college students. *Journal of Research in Crime and Delinquency, 34*(4), 495–518.
32. Terpitz, K., & Louven, S. (2011). *Eine generation sucht Wege aus dem stress*. https://www.handelsblatt.com/unternehmen/beruf-und-buero/buero-special/immer-auf-standby-eine-generation-sucht-wege-aus-dem-stress/v_detail_tab_print/4675790. Last accessed September 17, 2018.

33. Trang, S. (2018). When does deterrence work? A moderation meta-analysis of employees' information security policy behavior. In *International Conference on Information Systems (ICIS)*, 29.
34. Wolf, D. (2005). Ökonomische Sicht(en) auf das Handeln: Ein Vergleich der Akteursmodelle in ausgewählten Rational-Choice-Konzeptionen, Zugl.: Witten/Herdecke, Univ., Diss, Institutionelle und evolutorische Ökonomik. Marburg: Metropolis-Verlag.

Digital Emancipation: Are We Becoming Prisoners of Our Own Device?

Ariana Polyviou, Nancy Pouloudi, Katerina Pramatari, and Gurpreet Dhillon

Abstract Contemporary information systems in combination with high-speed internet, liberate individuals as they set them free from time, place and device restrictions of their everyday life. As a result, they blur the boundaries between work, social and personal life contexts. In this paper we introduce the concept of digital emancipation to refer to the notion of freedom experienced by individuals due the wide use of contemporary information systems. We argue that digital emancipation may have both a positive and a negative impact in each context as the individual may be at the same time be digitally emancipated, but also bound to the technology and its capabilities or limitations. We draw on existing literature to provide indications that digital emancipation is associated to both positive and negative experiences within each context and highlight that tensions between these mixed experiences exists. Building on this analysis, we then set the ground and motivates the need for an integrated theoretical framework for understanding the balancing effort of the digitally emancipated individual.

Keywords Digital emancipation · Contemporary IS · Work-life · Social-life · Personal-life · Tensions

A. Polyviou (✉)
University of Nicosia, Nicosia, Cyprus
e-mail: polyviou.a@unic.ac.cy

N. Pouloudi · K. Pramatari
Athens University of Economics and Business, Athens, Greece

G. Dhillon
University of North Carolina, Greensboro, USA

C. Metallo et al. (eds.), *Digital Transformation and Human Behavior*, Lecture Notes in Information Systems and Organisation 37,
https://doi.org/10.1007/978-3-030-47539-0_12

1 Introduction

The more widespread, ubiquitous and sophisticated information technologies become, the greater are the opportunities and challenges that they present for their users. Contemporary information systems (IS), such as cloud computing, wearables, smart home devices, RFID tags, smartphones, in combination with the wide deployment of high-speed Internet promise convenience, speed and enhanced user experience. As such IS become increasingly omnipresent, intelligent and interconnected, individuals become liberated from time, space and device constraints. Blikstein [4] describes an experiment in a low income community in São Paulo, Brazil and concludes that "use of expressive technologies could be a powerful agent of emancipation". The word emancipation encapsulates this notion of freedom, but also extends it; it also assumes empowerment to do things and implies the users' willingness to reach a better state or status, in this case by exploiting an enabling digital technology. We therefore propose the use of the term *digital emancipation* to define this IS-enabled state where individuals are set free from time, place and device restrictions in the different contexts (personal, social or work) of their everyday life. We argue for this broad definition, because it will enable us to theorize about the new state of affairs of IS use. In particular, we are interested in the tensions created by the positive implications of digital emancipation, its negative implications and the way in which these tensions span different contexts of use.

In the past, physical and time boundaries or technological limitations made it difficult for individuals to operate persistently within more than one context at a time. Such boundaries become increasingly blurred, offering IS users notable choices and benefits. A single device such as a smart phone may, for example, simultaneously support work flexibility, health monitoring, enhanced communication and so on. At the same time, digital emancipation may also have a negative impact on the individual such as a pressure to be 'always on', leading to information overload, lack of work-life balance, anxiety and so on. The individual is therefore called to appreciate, evaluate and choose among the opportunities and restrictions of digital emancipation across different contexts (Fig. 1).

In each context, digital emancipation can have both a positive and a negative impact, whereby the individual may be at the same time digitally emancipated, but also bound to the technology and its capabilities or limitations. This state may create tensions for the individual. For example, in the work context, the individual can work remotely, while 'on the move'. This makes the worker more flexible, and potentially more productive, but may create the expectation to be 'always on', at the expense of other work activities. In the social context, people are brought together through social media, but their communication patterns may change as they develop habits of texting short messages or communicate with physically remote friends while ignoring friends who are physically close. In the personal context, digital emancipation affects both utilitarian and hedonic technology use. For example, wearable technologies may enhance an individual's personal health by encouraging healthy habits such as walking, but may simultaneously create stress if the desired number of steps per day

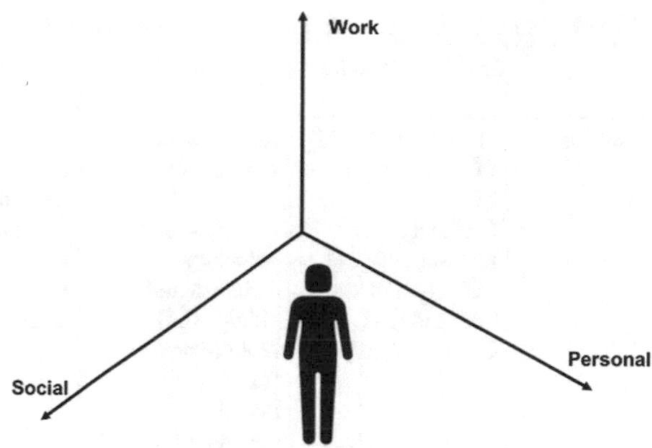

Fig. 1 Contextual dimensions of digital emancipation

is not reached. Similarly, online gaming may offer entertainment, but may also lead to addictive behavior.

2 Literature Review

Such benefits and limitations have been studied in the extant literature, through a set of related concepts and constructs (see Table 1 for indicative examples). This literature presents a valuable mosaic of in-depth studies, each typically focusing on a particular IS phenomenon (e.g., telework) or on a particular technology or platform (e.g., mobile devices, cloud computing, social media, wearables, virtual worlds). As a result, these studies concentrate on IS adoption or use in one context, with some exceptions that focus on boundaries, presenting tensions across the work and personal/family context, as in the case of work-life balance studies (e.g. [1, 21]), or studies of portable devices [15, 17].

By introducing the concept of digital emancipation in this paper, we provide the basis for an integrated framework for positioning this research work, and for bringing to the fore the tensions that digital emancipation entails. This is depicted in Table 1 with examples of the positive and negative impact of digital emancipation, both within and across contexts, and the resulting tensions. While this table can serve as a mapping device for relevant research work, it is not intended to provide an exhaustive account of relevant issues. Its value rather lies in serving as a sensitizing device for considering the broader impact of digital emancipation. This is important, because as technology use intensifies so do the tensions triggered by digital emancipation.

Digital emancipation, by definition, acknowledges that the boundaries between work, social and personal contexts of use are blurred, as it enables the individual to co-exist in more than one context at a time (e.g., replying to an email while being out with friends, checking number of steps on wearable while at work). When contexts merge, as a result of digital emancipation, its positive and negative impact

Table 1 Indicative impact of digital emancipation in diverse contexts and across contexts

	In the work context	In the social context	In the personal context	Across contexts
Positive	Flexibility [11, 21] Job autonomy [1, 21] Creativity [2, 6] Productivity [21] Reduction of work overload [21] Collaboration [7]	Enhanced social support [15] Increased participation in voluntary activities and politics [20] Making new friends [16] Social contagiousness [3]	Enjoyment [8] Health monitoring [9, 10] More motivated [3] Enhanced exercise habits [3]	Improved work-life balance [11] Enhanced exercise habits [3]
Negative	Work exhaustion [1] Job stress [20]	Inattention [13] Communication with family members [14] Comparison to others [3]	Stress [19] Depression [19] Poor sleep [5]	Work-family conflict [3] Work-life conflict [21] Autonomy paradox [15] Internet paradox [12]
Indicative tensions	Job autonomy versus work exhaustion Flexibility versus job stress	Social contagiousness versus comparison to others	Enjoyness versus stress	Better monitoring of employees versus privacy

may be redefined (last column of Table 1). Benefits in one context may have multiplying effects for other contexts (e.g., increased connectivity and flexibility across all contexts; improved work-life balance) or may have constraining effects and present new tensions (e.g., enhanced health habits but). By creating new tensions across contexts, digital emancipation signifies the emergence of a new overarching, unified context where the distinction among work, social and personal spaces become less relevant. With reference to Fig. 1, the individual has to navigate this novel integrated space where work, social and personal life represent dimensions rather than distinct spaces, as they did in the past. Digital emancipation provides a vocabulary that enables a discussion about this novel space, focusing on the individual rather than a specific technology.

3 Building a Framework of Digital Emancipation

As digital emancipation fosters the creation of tensions within and between contexts, it increases the pressure experienced by the individual. To be able to reduce the pressure felt, the individual strives to find a balance between the positive and the

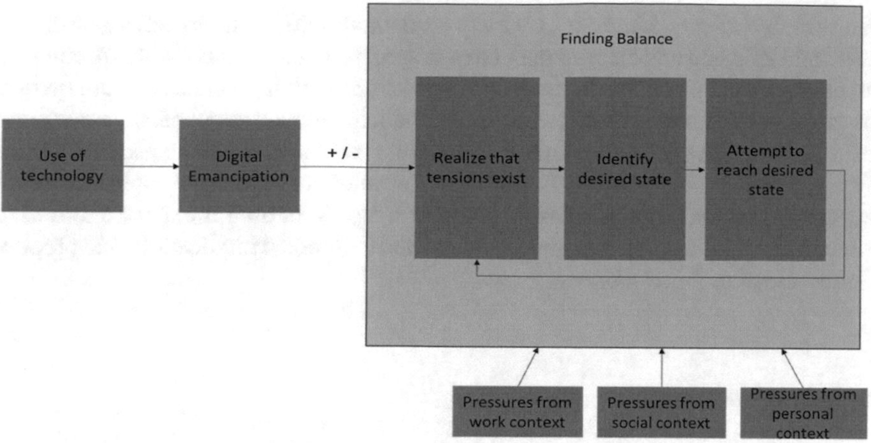

Fig. 2 The ongoing balancing act for the digitally emancipated individual

negative impacts of digital emancipation. Achieving a sense of balance is tough, because multiple tensions need to be managed, and temporary, because new tensions arise. The first step in this ongoing process, is realizing that tensions exist. For the digitally emancipated individuals, tensions may not be obvious as they are already immersed in this complex context and take some of these pressures for granted. Once the tensions are realized however, the individual can identify a desired state, where the positive impacts of digital emancipation are maximized and the negative impacts are minimized, and then attempt to reach that desired state (for example, by managing expectations or putting limitations or boundaries to the use of certain technologies). However, while attempting to reach the desired state, the individual may become conscious of additional tensions, or additional pressures from work, social or personal contexts may arise. Such pressures may be expectations from both the family/social and the work context to be increasingly flexible, increasingly available, or increasingly productive. There may also be pressures from one's self (personal context) (e.g., psychological pressure to appear to have achieved a balance, or a personal need to appear as successful and happy to others). This balancing act of positive and negative implications of digital emancipation can therefore be depicted as a continuous process (Fig. 2).

4 Theorizing and Validating Digital Emancipation

Widely-cited theories from disciplines such as organizational studies, sociology and psychology inform which pressures are experienced in each context and why they come about. Drawing on such theories, we aim to inform the development of the proposed theoretical framework and extensively reflect on the existence of tensions in the various contexts. Moreover, a variety of methods will be employed to gain empirical validation and enhance our understanding of the phenomenon. More specifically, an ethnographic study and focus group discussions with individuals that are divided in groups based on the degree of digital emancipation across contexts are used to explore potential positive and negative impacts and the mechanism used for identifying and addressing tensions. Following this exploratory phase, a Delphi study with experts in this matter (e.g. editorial board of a top IS journal) is expected to further validate the findings, identify their practical and theoretical implications and propose future research directions.

5 Conclusion

It is noteworthy that while the pertinent literature studies the various contexts in isolation, we argue that we need a more holistic understanding of technology-enabled impact and use the concept of digital emancipation to explore this broader picture. Moreover, the role of technology in this discussion is central [18]. However, it is no longer a single, specific type of technology or platform that we need to study, but rather a constellation of devices and IS applications that lead to digital emancipation. The central role of technology signals an opportunity for the IS field to set the future research agenda in this area for other disciplines that provide relevant theoretical insights. We thus anticipate that the theoretical framework to be proposed in the extended version of this paper may be used to better explain the impact of technology on individuals with important implications for psychology, sociology and organizational behavior.

Acknowledgements Nancy Pouloudi and Katerina Pramatari acknowledge the financial support of the Research Center of Athens University of Economics and Business.

References

1. Ahuja, M. K., Chudoba, K. M., Kacmar, C. J., McKnight, D. H., & George, J. F. (2007). ICT road warriors: Balancing work-family conflict, job autonomy, and work overload to mitigate turnover intentions. *MIS Quarterly, 31*(1), 1–18.
2. Amabile, T. M., Conti, R., Coon, H., Lazenby, J., & Herron, M. (1996). Assessing the work environment for creativity. *Academy of Management Journal, 39*(5), 1154–1184.
3. Aral, S., & Nicolaides, C. (2017). Exercise contagion in a global social network. *Nature Communications, 8,* 14753.
4. Blikstein, P. (2018). *Travels in Troy with Freire.* Rotterdam, Netherlands: Sense.
5. Calamaro, C. J., Mason, T. A. B., & Ratcliffe, S. J. (2009). Adolescents living the 24/7 lifestyle: Effects of caffeine and technology on sleep duration and daytime functioning. *Pediatrics, 123*(6), 1005–1010.

6. Chamakiotis, P., Dekoninck, E. A., & Panteli, N. (2013). Factors influencing creativity in virtual design teams: An interplay between technology, teams and individuals. *Creativity & Innovation Management, 22*(3), 265–279.
7. Chamakiotis, P., & Panteli, N. (2017). Leading the creative process: The case of virtual product design. *New Technology, Work & Employment, 32*(1), 28–42.
8. Dwyer, R., Kushlev, K., & Dunn, E. (2018). Smartphone use undermines enjoyment of face-to-face social interactions. *Journal of Experimental Social Psychology, 78*(3), 233–239.
9. Fisch, M. J., Chung, A. E., & Accordino, M. K. (2016). Using technology to improve cancer care: Social media, wearables, and electronic health records. *American Society of Clinical Oncology Educational Book, 36,* 200–208.
10. Hawn, C. (2009). Take two aspirin and tweet me in the morning: How Twitter, Facebook, and other social media are reshaping health care. *Health Affairs, 28*(2), 361–368.
11. Hilbrecht, M., Shaw, S. M., Johnson, L. C., & Andrey, J. (2008). 'I'm Home for the Kids': Contradictory implications for work-life balance of teleworking mothers. *Gender, Work & Organization, 15*(5), 454–476.
12. Kraut, R., Patterson, M., Lundmark, V., Kiesler, S., Mukophadhyay, T., & Scherlis, W. (1998). Internet paradox. A social technology that reduces social involvement and psychological well-being? *American Psychologist, 53*(9), 1017–1031.
13. Kushlev, K., Proulx, J., & Dunn, E. (2016). Silence your phones: Smartphone notifications increase inattention and hyperactivity symptoms. In *Proceedings of the 2016 CHI Conference on Human Factors in Computing Systems (CHI '16)* (pp. 1011–1020). New York, NY, USA: ACM.
14. Kushlev, K., Proulx, J., & Dunn, E. (2017). Digitally connected, socially disconnected: The effects of relying on technology rather than other people. *Computers in Human Behavior, 76*(3), 68–74.
15. Mazmanian, M., Orlikowski, W. J., & Yates, J. (2013). The autonomy paradox: The implications of mobile email devices for knowledge professionals. *Organization Science, 24*(5), 1–21.
16. Morahan-Martin, J., & Phyllis, S. (2003). Loneliness and social uses of the internet. *Applied Psychology Journal, 19*(6), 659–671.
17. Prasopoulou, E., Pouloudi, A., & Panteli, N. (2006). Enacting new temporal boundaries: The role of mobile phones. *European Journal of Information Systems, 15*(3), 277–284.
18. Searls, D. (2014). Time for digital emancipation. *Harvard Education Blog*. Posted on 17 July 2014. Retrieved on November 14, 2018. Available at https://blogs.harvard.edu/doc/2014/07/27/time-for-digital-emancipation/.
19. Thomée, S., Eklöf, M., Gustafsson, E., Nilsson, R., & Hagberg, M. (2007). Prevalence of perceived stress, symptoms of depression and sleep disturbances in relation to information and communication technology (ICT) use among young adults. An explorative prospective study. *Computers in Human Behavior*, *23*(1), 1300–1321.
20. Wellman, B., Haase, A. Q., Witte, J., & Hampton, K. (2001). Does the internet increase, decrease, or supplement social capital? Social networks, participation, and community commitment. *American Behavioral Scientist, 45*(3), 436–455.
21. Yun, H., Kettinger, W. J., & Lee, C. C. (2012). A new open door: The smartphone's impact on work-to-life conflict, stress, and resistance. *International Journal of Electronic Commerce, 16*(4), 121–152.

Customer Experience Formation in Online Shopping: Investigating the Causes of Positive and Negative Emotions During a Visit to an Online Store

Tiina Kemppainen, Markus Makkonen, and Lauri Frank

Abstract This study explores customer experience formation in an online shopping context by investigating the causes of customers' positive and negative emotions during their visit to an online store. Survey data collected from 1786 Finnish online customers was used to identify individuals who experienced strong positive (N = 138) or negative emotions (N = 215) during their visit. The causes of negative and positive emotions were studied by analyzing customers' open-ended, written explanations attributed to their emotions. Attribution theory is utilized to explain how individuals make sense of their emotions. The findings show that customers offer various explanations for the emotions evoked during a visit to an online store. Three main themes were identified with respect to the causes of such emotions and related to: (1) the online store, (2) the socio-material environment, and, (3) the customer her/himself. Customers generally blame the online store for negative emotions, whereas positive emotions are mostly associated with oneself and one's success as a consumer. Both negative and positive emotions are to some extent explained by the sociomaterial environment. The findings demonstrate the complexity of customer experience formation. Further investigation of the topic is therefore warranted.

Keywords Customer experience · E-commerce · Online consumption · Emotions · Attribution theory

T. Kemppainen (✉)
Faculty of Information Technology & School of Business and Economics, University of Jyväskylä, Jyväskylä, Finland
e-mail: tiina.j.kemppainen@jyu.fi

M. Makkonen · L. Frank
Faculty of Information Technology, University of Jyväskylä, Jyväskylä, Finland

C. Metallo et al. (eds.), *Digital Transformation and Human Behavior*, Lecture Notes in Information Systems and Organisation 37,
https://doi.org/10.1007/978-3-030-47539-0_13

1 Introduction

The importance of customer experience as a component of a company's competitive advantage is widely acknowledged among academics and practitioners, as today's consumers have unprecedented power and a variety of means whereby such power can be exerted. Due to technological advances, customers are no longer constrained by shopping time or place, and consumption choices are guided by peer-reviews available through social media. It is easy for customers to change their service provider (such as an online store) if the service fails to meet customer's expectations. In an online environment, an alternative service is merely one click away. The importance of customer experience is therefore especially emphasized when providing online services for consumers.

A vast number of studies have analyzed the influence of customer experience on customer behavior in online [1–4] and offline [5–8] contexts. As such, previous research has demonstrated the consequences of positive and negative customer experiences and how such experiences affect a company's performance. The literature notes that a positive customer experience which meets or exceeds customer's demands and expectations leads to greater customer satisfaction, long-lasting relationships and loyalty, and in doing so, creates a competitive advantage for a company and boosts its revenue [9, 10]. In comparison, negative customer experiences weaken the company's competitive position. Negative customer experiences (which fail to meet customer expectations) lead to loss of sales and entail extra costs, for example, through customer service demands. Previous research posits that negative experiences negatively influence customer loyalty [11], word-of-mouth and complaining behaviors [12], repurchase intentions [13], and customer attitudes toward the company [14]. Negative customer experiences are also frequently communicated to other customers [15].

The purpose of this paper is to advance the understanding of how positive and negative customer experiences are created in an online shopping context during a visit to an online store. Since previous studies in the online consumption context have for the most part focused on human-to-computer interactions [16] and examined customer experience through technical and company standpoints, this study makes use of a contrasting perspective and investigates customer experience formation with an open-ended approach as depicted by customers themselves and in their own words. Investigating customer experience formation through the lens of a customer provides important knowledge for service providers and academics, as it depicts how customers make sense of services and what they find truly meaningful for themselves in a given context. This study contributes to the existing literature consisting of a small number of studies [1, 17] that have focused on the customer perspective in an online shopping context.

The study was conducted using survey data collected from 1786 Finnish online store customers. As researchers have suggested that customers engage in affective and cognitive processing during their consumption activities and customer experience construction [2, 18], an initial step in this study involved the identification of customers who felt strong negative or positive emotions during their visit to an online store. An analysis of how customers explained their emotions cognitively was carried out by investigating the open-ended, written descriptions attributed to their emotions. In the qualitative analysis, we utilize Attribution theory [19, 20], which is concerned with how people explain the causes of events and behaviors they encounter in daily life. This provided a useful lens with which to frame how individuals make sense of online services and their emotions.

This study includes five sections. Section 2 discusses the theoretical background of the study including online customer experience and Attribution theory. Section 3 presents the methodological choices for the empirical study, and Sect. 4 presents the empirical findings. Section 5 discusses study contributions and managerial implications.

2 Theoretical Background

2.1 Customer Experience

Various marketing and information systems studies have contributed to our understanding of customer experience by investigating an individual's experiences in a variety of contexts. Individual experiences of online environments have been researched by making use of several concepts in marketing, including the online customer experience, online customer service experience, and the online shopping experience [1, 3, 21, 22]. Information systems research typically employs the user experience concept, highlighting the usability of different services and products [23]. While these marketing and information systems studies are very much intertwined and customer experience and user experience concepts refer to the same essential idea (how individuals perceive different services or products provided by a company), these concepts usually have different scopes. The user experience is generally understood as a customer or user's use experience with a specific product, such as a website, app, or software. Customer experience, on the other hand, is a more flexible concept with a wider scope, it can encompass, for instance, end-to-end customer interactions with a company or its offerings and can include many channels and touchpoints. This study makes use of the customer experience concept, as our aim is to understand customer experience formation with an open-ended approach, including customers' experience of the online store interface, and, in addition, the other important factors contributing to customer experience beyond the store interface.

Customer experience is usually characterized and studied as either a process or an outcome. As customer experience is widely recognized as consisting of a customer's internal and subjective response (outcome) to any interaction with a company, many studies have either measured the quality of customer experience (outcome) or the kind of interaction (process) between online service providers and customers that lead to a certain experience [24–28]. In the online context, the focus of customer experience studies has been on human-to-computer interactions [16] and the study of what type of operating environment an enterprise should create for individuals so as to make their experience as pleasant as possible. A vast amount of research has examined the features of a high-quality e-commerce platform and how different service attributes affect the online customer experience within a business-to-consumer context [2, 29, 30]. An extensive amount of research has been conducted over the years which aimed to find the best ways to design user-friendly online systems and interfaces [31–33] to guide the development and execution of online services or systems [34, 35]. The literature outlines numerous variables which a company can make use of to influence the customer experience in online environments, such as ease of use, website aesthetics, customization, interactivity, engagement, and enjoyment [36].

However, while customer experience studies have focused on measuring the service elements' effect on experience, the other contributors to customer experience outside the company's interface have attracted less attention. Researchers [2] have argued that the customer experience involves much more than customers' reactions to service stimuli and that the lack of understanding regarding the other contributors to customer experience is a shortcoming in online customer experience studies; this issue has been the subject of limited investigations [17, 22]. A greater focus on the customer perspective and the mechanisms through which customers process and interpret company offerings has been called for [37, 38]. For example, from the customer's point of view, visiting an online store is more complicated than merely the interaction between the service provider and the customer [39]. It involves elements that are not visible to the company, such as a background, purpose, and goal of the online store visit. The visit also includes a device outside the online store, as well as the physical conditions in which the device is used. Customers use and interpret online environments differently and construct their experiences in unique ways. Customer experience is always internal, subjective, and event- and context-specific [40]. Hence, the analysis of customer experience should go beyond the immediate service delivery system and consider how customers create value in their own context [41].

To advance the understanding of customer experience from a customer's perspective, this study examines how customers depict the causes of their positive and negative emotions during an online store visit. We suggest that when customers construct their customer experience, understood as a mental mark comprising of different meanings, emotions and cognitive explanations given to emotions during the service encounter define the nature of the customer experience. In this study, the customer experience is understood as an outcome of a customer's visit to an online store, including all the meanings created by the individual during the visit. For instance, negative thoughts that occur during a store visit are likely to direct the customer experience towards a negative perception, while positive thoughts are likely to do the opposite. It is therefore of importance to understand what kind of cognitive processing [2, 18] customers engage in during the construction of their customer experience. In this study, we provide insights on how customers make sense of their online store visit by making use of Attribution theory [19, 20] as our theoretical lens.

2.2 Attribution Theory

Individuals are motivated to assign causes to events, actions, and behaviors; people prefer the idea that things happen for a reason rather than being caused randomly. Attribution theory provides explanations on how events and behaviors observed during daily life are explained by individuals. Heider [19] was the first to propose a psychological theory of attribution, and his ideas were extended by Weiner et al. [20, 42, 43], who developed a theoretical framework that has become a major research paradigm of social psychology. Attribution is a cognitive process including the internal (thinking) or external (speaking) activities by which people make judgments; attributes seek to explain what caused a particular behavior or event and who or what is responsible for it [19, 20]. Attributions are made in order to understand and to explain one's experience and to plan future actions. Unlike scientific psychology, which attempts to prove the causes of an individual's behavioral predisposition, naive psychology—as attribution theory has been called—emphasizes people's perceptions of causes. In this study, we regard an attribute as an explanation given by an individual for his/her positive or negative emotions that occur during an online store visit.

Heider [19] divides the attributes into two categories: internal and external. An internal attribute is always related to a person and is external to the situation. In an internal or "dispositional" attribution, individuals assign causality to something within their own control, such as effort or personal factors such as abilities, traits, or emotions. In an external attribution, causality is explained by situational or environmental factors, something that is outside an individual's control. The types of attributes individuals choose to assign to the causes of events affect their motivation and future behaviors [20], therefore, identifying attributes can be useful for companies aiming to better understand their customers' behavior and the reasons for it.

Human attributes are seen to be subject to various distortions. As Jackson [44] explains, people often develop biases or faulty reasoning. This reasoning is either self-enhancing (strengthening an individual's ego) or self-protective, which means that individuals protect their ego by blaming others for their own mistakes. Attributions are often considered to entail two basic errors: the fundamental attribution error and the self-serving bias [45]. The fundamental attribution error means that individuals tend to over-emphasize dispositional or personality-based explanations for behaviors observed in others. In other words, people tend to emphasize the agent's internal characteristics (i.e., "what kind of person that person is") rather than external factors (such as the social and environmental forces that influence the person) when explaining someone else's activities. Individuals also tend to perceive themselves in an overly favorable manner. Self-serving bias involves an individual's tendency to explain positive outcomes such as their own success or other people's positive behavior towards themselves by reference to internal attributions and to blame external attributions for negative outcomes such as their own failures.

Research shows that customers' attributions can have important implications for companies. For instance, attributions are a significant determinant of customer satisfaction, including satisfaction with the service encounter and post-purchase behaviors [46]. Iglesias [46] found that customers who attribute service failure to the company make a less positive evaluation of the overall quality of the service encounter than customers who associate the failure to external causes outside the company. Previous studies have used Attribution theory to study customer experience in the context of tourism. As there are only a few such studies making use of attribution theory in the context of customer experience [44, 47], its application in the context of this study provides a fresh perspective with which to gain insights on a variety of aspects of customer experience in online shopping. As attribution theory is concerned with individuals' sensemaking, it allows for investigations of how customers construct their customer experience through their own lenses, without company-led restrictions. By identifying, categorizing, and defining the distinct elements that contribute positively or negatively to customer experience, this study enables deeper insights into the distinct components that shape customer experience in the online shopping context.

3 Methodology

As the purpose of this study was to examine how customers explain the causes of their positive and negative emotions during a visit to an online store, empirical data were collected via an online survey conducted in co-operation with 18 Finnish online stores between September and December 2018. This survey method was selected as it allowed the respondents to consider their online store visit in a real-life context, both safely and at a place of their choice. The selected approach was determined to be suitable for our research aim as we were able to collect data that describes authentic customer experiences in existing online stores.

The stores included various types of business-to-consumer (B2C) stores selling cosmetics, clothing, music, electronics, groceries, home decorations, and recreation products and accessories. Customers of the online stores were presented with a link to the survey after they had successfully placed an order. In the survey, respondents were first briefly asked about their demographics (including age and gender) as well as their online shopping habits, such as how often they shop online, what they had just purchased and how many times they had previously shopped at the online store in question. Respondents were then asked about the emotions they had experienced during their online store visit. The intensity of different emotions was measured by using a set of ten first-order emotion constructs with 28 specified emotions taken from the hierarchical framework by Laros and Steenkamp [48]. Positive emotions included contentment (contented, confident), peacefulness (calm, peaceful), optimism (optimistic, encouraged, hopeful), joy (happy, pleased, joyful), and excitement (excited, thrilled, attracted). Negative emotions included anger (angry, annoyed, irritated), frustration (frustrated, discontented, disappointed), fear (afraid, nervous, worried), sadness (depressed, sad, guilty) and shame (embarrassed, ashamed, humiliated). The respondents rated these emotions on a scale from one to seven. A value of one indicated that they had not experienced that specific emotion, while a value of seven indicated that they had strongly experienced that specific emotion during their online store visit. In the latter part of the survey, the respondents were asked to describe in their own words their experienced emotions and to explain what caused the strongest positive and negative emotions. The respondents were also given an opportunity to freely comment on the survey itself.

In total, 1803 respondents completed the online survey. However, the survey results of 17 respondents were excluded due to invalid or missing data, resulting in a sample size of 1786 Finnish adult respondents. From these, we identified respondents who experienced strong positive or negative emotions during their online store visit; an emotion that differed by more than two standard deviations from the average value for that emotion was considered a strong emotion. The number of respondents with at least one strong negative emotion was 387, while the number of respondents with at least one positive emotion was 321. We then excluded all respondents who did not also comment on their negative or positive emotions related to the online store visit or whose comments were unclear; the final number therefore included 215 respondents with negative emotions and 138 respondents reporting positive emotions. Out of these, 28 respondents included individuals who had experienced both strong negative and positive emotions. The final sample size was therefore 325 individual respondents. A large proportion of respondents were women and under 40 years of age. Most reported making online purchases at least monthly and were also familiar with the online store they were visiting. Respondents' descriptive statistics are reported in detail in Appendix 1.

We analyzed the written data provided by the 325 respondents in the open-ended section of the survey using NVivo software. The software was used to assess the trustworthiness, rigor, and quality of our findings. It was also useful for coding and organizing data into themes, for finding connections and relationships, to calculate attributions, and to share coding and categorization with the research team. Based on Attribution theory, the respondents' explanations for their emotions were first coded as either internally or externally attributed based on their overall content and most frequent cause. Explanations that included two or more distinct points were split into separate units for analysis. The length of the units ranged from 2 to 429 words. Each unit was coded multiple times before tallying the final counts and categorizations of the negative and positive attributes expressed by the respondents. It is important to note that although the main themes explaining the positive and negative emotions were identified based on attribute counts, this study was based on an interpretive approach. Our principal objective was to make sense of and recognize patterns that contribute to customer experience, rather than quantifying the attributes.

4 Findings

The findings demonstrate the complexity of customer experience formation in an online shopping context; customers have various explanations for their emotions and these explanations are not merely attributed to the online store in question. Three main themes were identified with regards to the customers' reasons for their emotions during online store visits. These included factors related to (1) the online store (external attributes), (2) the sociomaterial environment (external attributes), and (3) the customer themselves (internal attributes). The findings indicate that customers mostly blame the online store they visited for their negative emotions (68% of all negative attributes), whereas positive emotions are attributed mostly to customers themselves (47% of all positive attributes). Both negative and positive emotions are also quite equally attributed to the sociomaterial environment (12% of all positive attributes and 8% of all negative attributes). In this context, the sociomaterial environment is referred to as the "surrounding world" in which the company and customer operate. Figure 1 demonstrates the main themes of the attributes given to positive and negative emotions.

The findings demonstrate that strong negative emotions were more commonly experienced by the participants as compared to strong positive emotions. The main explanations given for the positive and negative emotions are discussed and analyzed in more detail in the following subsections with translated sample quotes.

4.1 *Positive Emotions During an Online Store Visit*

A total of 219 explanations for customers' positive emotions were identified from the data. Positive emotions were explained especially by factors related to the

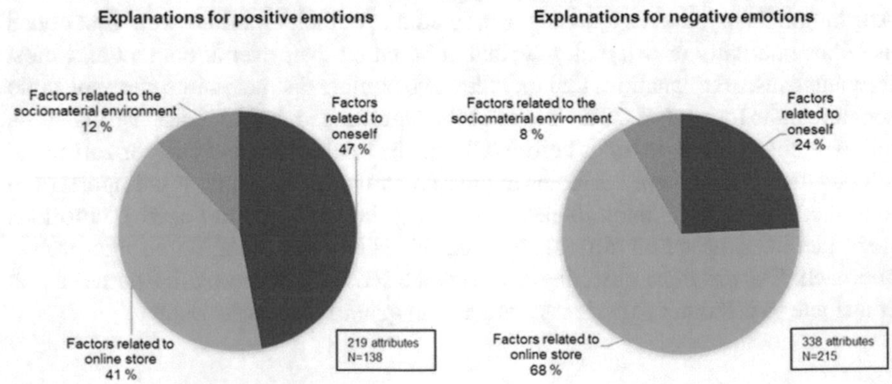

Fig. 1 The main themes of attributes given to positive and negative emotions during an online store visit

customer themselves (47%, 103 attributes) but also often by the features of the online store (41%, 90 attributes). In addition, the sociomaterial environment (12%, 26 attributes) was identified as an important contributor to positive emotions and customer experience.

Oneself. Explanations given to positive emotions highlight the importance of a customer's personal success (i.e., perceiving oneself as a clever and skillful shopper) with respect to the customer experience. Personal success was attributed to one's expertise and efforts as a consumer (51% of self-related attributes). The ability to find and close good deals, succeeding in a "treasure hunt," finding "perfect products for oneself," and saving money with one's findings, caused positive emotions in many respondents.

> I was excited when I found the right products for myself. It caused the most positive emotions. (Female, 24)
>
> I was pleased because I found the product at lower cost than in many other online stores. (Female, 40)

Furthermore, feeling surprised and lucky because of one's finds contributed positively to customer experience; finding something new, neat, and unexpected while visiting an online store was experienced as a positive contributor to one's experience. Trying some new things, such as a new store or a product (13% of self-related attributes) was perceived positively as it was associated with some additional excitement when making a purchase.

> I'm excited about trying some new products. (Female, 42)

In addition to sales and other kinds of "finds," facilitating one's everyday life (11% of self-related attributes), including saving time for "something more important" and "getting something out of the agenda" were typical explanations given for positive emotions. The findings demonstrate that the positive consequences of shopping were linked to the future and the outcomes of the purchase and to how will it make one's life easier in the nearby or distant future.

> I felt joy and the satisfaction of making my life easier when I was able to buy a variety of groceries inexpensively at once, without having to try to drag them by bus with my daily shopping. (Female, 48)

In addition to daily tasks and everyday life necessities, the positive consequences of the purchase for oneself were visualized along with other aspects of life (e.g., how the purchased product will be part of joyful celebrations with one's family).

The online store. The positive emotions associated with an online store were explained for the most part by ease of shopping and trouble-free service (32% of store-related attributes). Positive emotions were often aroused by a "smooth" and "as fast as expected" shopping journey.

> I was pleased with the ease of making a purchase. All the steps went smoothly. (Female, 41)

The product and service range (23% of store-related attributes) and price level (11% of store-related attributes) as well as the store atmosphere (11% of store-related attributes) were also identified as important contributors to customer experience. Providing enough choices for customers was identified as important as many respondents reported an expectation of having a wide range of products and services from which to choose their favorite. Affordable prices and discounts, as well as special offers and services, were attributed as pleasant surprises which supported the purchase decision. Furthermore, as the following comments demonstrate, one's positive emotions were often explained as being the consequence of many different and meaningful issues.

> The range of products. They had cheap prices and the range is so variable that you never knew what new and exciting items to expect at the next page. (Female, 26)
>
> Most pleasing was the breadth of the range and sufficient product information, flexible payment and delivery methods, and the extra service provided for the frying pan I purchased. The provision of this additional service seemed very attentive. (Male, 43)

The store's atmosphere, including the visual design and communication, appeared as a notable contributor to customer experience, as respondents reported that a store with "good vibes" makes them "feel good," with the effect of experiencing positive emotions such as joy and happiness while shopping. "Good vibes" were attributed to "cute products and displays" and to a company's friendly manner when communicating with its customers.

Sociomaterial environment. The findings demonstrate that during a visit to an online store, customers explain their positive emotions in terms of issues related to the sociomaterial environment and by considering the wider context of shopping; i.e., how and where such shopping takes place and what the benefits and consequences of different consumption choices are. With respect to these considerations, the benefits of one's purchase for the environment (including ecological and ethical benefits) were highlighted (73% of sociomaterial environment-related attributes). Many respondents explained that they experienced positive emotions especially as a consequence of the "goodness and eco-friendliness of their purchase." Contributing positively to the environment and the general wellbeing of humankind as a consequence of one's own consumption actions was considered both possible and important (e.g., because of the importance of such things as climate change).

> I feel good that I can slow down climate change by this choice of purchase. (Female, 48)
>
> Purchasing from this store is easy, comfortable, and ethical. (Female, 39)

E-commerce as a service for today's consumers also caused positive emotions (13% of sociomaterial environment-related attributes) among the participants. Rather than being happy with the particular online store they were visiting, these customers explained their positive emotions in terms of all the benefits (such as ease-of-use) that e-commerce generally provides for today's consumers.

> It's wonderful when you can do the shopping from your couch. (Female, 43)

> Enthusiastic about not having to shop in the midst of countless options (at a grocery store). […] Big stores are the worst. A lot of walking, a lot of choices and decision making. (Female, 26)

A few participants also discussed the social aspect of shopping. A positive surprise for one's close friends and family resulting from a purchase (12% of sociomaterial environment-related attributes) was perceived as a positive contributor to one's emotions while visiting an online store.

> I ordered a small gift for my uncle and became very happy about it. I'm thrilled to wait as he gets it and calls me; what his reactions are. (Female, 43)

While purchasing items for oneself caused plenty of positive emotions among the participants, envisioning how one's purchase may offer joy for others seemed to have a positive effect on the customer experience.

4.2 *Negative Emotions During a Visit to an Online Store*

A total of 338 explanations for customers' negative emotions were identified from the data. Whereas the participants credited almost half (47%) of their positive emotions to internal attributes and to themselves, negative emotions were explained especially by factors related to the online store (68%, 228 attributes). "Oneself" was identified as the cause of some negative emotions with 82 attributes (24%). "Sociomaterial" attributes were identified as a contributor to negative emotions with 28 attributes (8%).

The online store. The online store was identified as the main cause of customers' negative emotions during a visit. The negative emotions were mostly attributed to unpleasant surprises and disappointments caused by the store. These included surprises such as "the desired product was not available" (14% of store-related attributes), "there were not enough products to choose from" (7% of store-related attributes), "technical errors" (11% of store-related attributes), and "complications in navigation and managing the order" (10% of store-related attributions) which made the purchase journey complicated and time-consuming. Many respondents reported multiple explanations for their negative emotions, as the following quotes demonstrate:

> Frustration and other negative emotions arose when the website did not work and the selected products did not go to the shopping cart. Also, if the products I searched for were not available and the discounts were low. (Female, 39)

> The site threw me out many times while processing order data and the page was loading really slowly. (Male, 57)

> I was a little worried about the quality of the products and the reliability of the online store. The cost and versatility of the products did not meet my expectations, which was somewhat disappointing. (Male, 37)

The way an online store displays its products, including products categories, filter possibilities, and product information, was important for respondents as they reported plenty of negative emotions (15% of store-related attributes) resulting from a badly presented product range. Poor product displays were thought to complicate a purchase, as a significant effort was required to manage the shopping process. Some participants specified a time-consuming shopping process (5% of store-related attributes) as being the cause of their negative emotions during a visit to an online store.

> I had to put in a lot of effort to find suitable products for myself. It caused frustration. (Female, 70)

Furthermore, pricing (11% of store-related attributes) was identified as an important contributor to the customer experience. Prices that were considered too expensive (together with unclear and misleading pricing) were reported as causes of one's negative emotions. Furthermore, quantity discounts (5% of store-related attributes) aroused negative emotions. "Chasing" the discount limit was considered as something that one could easily end up doing, yet was nevertheless considered stressful and sometimes an impossible mission.

> I couldn't find enough to buy so that I would have reached the 20€ limit (for free delivery). It began to irritate me as I was forced to buy more and did not know whether I will use those products. (Female, 50)

Discounts were indicated as a cause of unnecessary consumption, as discount limits were considered to encourage customers to purchase items which they might not need.

Oneself. The participants also identified themselves and their own actions as the cause of their negative emotions. These negative emotions were mostly attributed to one's consumption habits and to the guilt associated with buying (36% of self-related attributions). In particular, buying unnecessary items and surrendering to one's consumption desires caused disappointment with oneself and hence were experienced negatively.

> Negative emotions were mostly guilt and anxiety because I ordered more than I need. Consuming and collecting stuff (to your home) is distressing. (Female, 29)

> I felt guilty and greedy for getting tempted - I ordered sweets in bulk packages. I wouldn't have bought them from a physical store. (Male, 28)

One's unpleasant financial situation (22% of attributes related to oneself) also caused negative emotions as both a lack of money and "spending money" were reported as "distressing." Overall, consuming seemed to cause mixed emotions for many respondents; shopping induced an inner battle in which the many negative and positive aspects of shopping were considered simultaneously, as the following quote demonstrates.

> Shopping for children's clothes makes me happy, but at the same time it costs and I don't really have money for this hobby. I am perhaps a little hooked on this, and in the midst of a hectic and busy everyday life, I get pleasure from it. But my wallet does not like it at all. I have promised to stop, but online shopping is so easy, and Instagram and Facebook are so full of wonderful children's clothes that I cannot resist them. (Female, 33)

Pondering one's purchasing choices and the different aspects was a cause of stress for the study participants. Negative emotions were reported by some participants, as they were not able to decide whether they were making a good purchase during their visit to an online store (15% of attributes related to the category of oneself).

The sociomaterial environment. Considering the context of consumption and worrying about its environmental effects was a cause of concern among the study participants. Today's environmental problems and the irresponsible actions of people (46% of attributes related to the sociomaterial environment) were reported as a cause of negative emotions while visiting an online store. Today's culture of consumption was found to be troubling due to its harmful consequences for the environment. The act of considering irresponsible and unnecessary consumption caused frustration and anguish among respondents.

> I'm annoyed as there are so many products produced in the world that really do not need to be produced. All kinds of useless trash. (Female, 58)
>
> I became frustrated and annoyed at the fact that stores have to have absurdly large selections available all the time, because then much of it is eventually thrown away when there is no demand. Less would be enough. (Female, 35)

In addition, the purchase environment (such as other participants in the physical space in which the online shopping was being done) was also named as a cause of negative emotions. Family members such as spouses and even dogs were accused of contributing negatively to one's shopping experience by disturbing one's concentration during a visit to an online store or by not contributing enough to the purchase process (29% of attributes related to the sociomaterial environment).

> I felt anger and frustration when I tried to make my spouse participate in the decision making and tell his opinion. (Female, 28)
>
> Negative emotions were caused by the coughing and questioning spouse sitting next to me. (Female, 34)

Furthermore, the purchase context (18% of attributes related to the sociomaterial environment) was also reported as a cause of negative emotions. These negative emotions were explained with feelings of shame and "forced buying." Some respondents reported that they were ashamed to buy from the store they had chosen, and thus experienced negative emotions. Furthermore, shopping for certain products such as groceries were reported as acts of "forced buying," meaning that such mandatory purchases always caused negative emotions.

5 Discussion, Conclusions, and Managerial Implications

The aim of this study was to gain a greater understanding of customer experience formation in the context of online shopping and from the perspective of customers (as described by the customers themselves). As previous research has predominantly examined how different service elements directly affect online customer experience as an outcome [24, 25] and the interaction between service providers and customers has been highlighted [49], the present study contributes to the customer experience literature by investigating customer experience formation more extensively with an open-ended approach and beyond direct customer-company interactions. In other words, this study did not focus on how customers react to different online store characteristics but instead explored what kinds of other issues (in addition to the online store interface) can be meaningful for customers when they are using online services and constructing their customer experience.

Consistent with previous studies, the findings of this investigation highlight the important role of a company with respect to customer experience. As expected based on Attribution Theory and the previous customer experience literature, the respondents in this study attributed most of their negative emotions to the characteristics of an online store. Attribution theory suggests that individuals tend to blame external factors for negative events and issues and this was found to be the case here. As most negative emotions (68%) were caused by unpleasant surprises and disappointments caused by the online store, our findings, consistent with the existing literature [34, 50], highlight the importance of both a well-functioning user interface and carefully selected online store content in making the purchase journey as easy and pleasant as possible for the customer.

When considering their positive emotions, the respondents attributed most of these to "themselves" (47%) (i.e., by making reference to their own efforts and skills). Positive emotions were experienced due to respondents' personal success as a consumer. These findings are consistent with Attribution theory, suggesting that individuals tend to explain positive issues using internal attributions and a self-serving bias and by attributing their success to their own abilities. Previous customer experience studies have reported similar findings. For instance, Jackson et al. [47] showed that tourists were more likely to use internal attributions for positive outcomes and external attributions for negative experiences. Hence, as individuals' reasoning can be rather self-enhancing (and as positive emotions seem to be especially self-emphasized), it is important for online stores and other service providers to find ways that allow customers to perceive themselves as being successful, clever, and skillful shoppers (i.e., to feel good about themselves) during their online encounters. Such methods could entail highlighting the positive outcomes of a purchase and providing customers with an opportunity to find some unexpected "treasures" in an online store.

As a whole, our findings demonstrate the complexity of the customer experience both in terms of when customers construct their customer experiences and the multiple factors that can contribute to it. The findings indicate that the online store environment is not the only influencer to customer experience during a shopping visit. Customers actively consider and evaluate themselves, the surrounding world and other people when using online services and when constructing their customer experience. The customer experience is affected by the elements (such as other people) in the physical space in which the customer is using the online store. On the other hand, the perceived impact of one's purchasing decision on the sociomaterial environment and on other people, can influence the customer experience. Therefore, it can be concluded that by its choice of service design, the online store can influence how customers perceive the store while visiting it. Nevertheless, some of the emotions experienced by a customer cannot be influenced by the company as a customer's thoughts may not be focussed on the actual moment of consumption and the online store interface. Consistent with Trischler et al. [41], our findings indicate that in future studies other factors external to the online store should be more carefully considered when attempting to understand the holistic customer experience.

Finally, the findings demonstrate that customers' emotions during a visit to an online store can be versatile and cannot be inferred, for example, on the basis of the purchase decision. All of the respondents of this study completed the survey after they had successfully placed an order at an online store. Whereas customers who have placed an order may appear as "satisfied and happy" from a company's perspective, the findings of this study demonstrate that it may not be the case; many respondents reported experiencing strong negative emotions during their store visit but ended-up purchasing despite those emotions. Furthermore, some experienced both very strong positive and negative emotions during their visit, which demonstrates that an online store visit can be an emotional rollercoaster. From a managerial perspective, these findings highlight the importance of understanding the entire customer journey during an online store visit and not just the outcome (such as a purchase). Even though the negative emotions experienced during an online store visit may not contribute to the accompanying purchase, they may persist in the mind of a customer and affect future customer behavior (such as the willingness to shop at the store again in the future) [13].

The customer insights gained through this study can be utilized and further investigated in research and practice aiming to more thoroughly understand online shopping behavior and the customer experience therein. As the data for this study was collected from Finnish consumers and because our sample was dominated by women and consumers under 40-years of age, replications of this study in other countries with more balanced demographic samples could provide new insights. In addition, the formation of negative and positive customer experiences in the online context should be studied further with various methods and in diverse service settings. From a managerial perspective in particular, it is important to identify the causes of customers' positive and negative emotions, as they may have an effect on customers' future choices when shopping. Researchers and practitioners are encouraged to study the customer experience beyond that of the company-customer interaction, as well as during the entire customer journey encompassing the prepurchase and postpurchase phases.

Appendix 1: The Descriptive Statistics of the Respondents

	Negative emotions		Positive emotions	
	N = 215	(%)	N = 138	(%)
Gender				
Male	26	12.1	23	16.7
Female	189	87.9	115	83.3
Age				
18–29 years	69	32.1	47	34.1
30–39 years	59	27.4	36	26.1
40–49 years	42	19.5	26	18.8
50–59 years	29	13.5	20	14.5
60–69 years	10	4.7	6	4.3
70–years	6	2.8	3	2.2
On average, how often do you shop online?				
Daily	1	0.5	2	1.4
Weekly	54	25.1	29	21.0
Monthly	111	51.6	69	50.0
Yearly	44	20.5	36	26.1
Less than yearly	5	2.3	2	1.4
How many times have you shopped in this online store?				
Never	76	35.3	45	32.6
1–3 times	83	38.6	47	34.1
4–10 times	41	19.1	33	23.9
Over 10 times	15	7.0	13	9.4

References

1. Izogo, E. E., & Jayawardhena, C. (2018). Online shopping experience in an emerging e-retailing market: Towards a conceptual model. *Journal of Consumer Behaviour, 17*(4), 379–392.
2. Rose, S., Clark, M., Samouel, P., & Hair, N. (2012). Online customer experience in e-retailing: An empirical model of antecedents and outcomes. *Journal of Retailing, 88*(2), 308.
3. Khalifa, M., & Liu, V. (2007). Online consumer retention: Contingent effects of online shopping habit and online shopping experience. *European Journal of Information Systems, 16*(6), 780–792.
4. Bilgihan, A., Kandampully, J., & Zhang, T. (2016). Towards a unified customer experience in online shopping environments: Antecedents and outcomes. *International Journal of Quality and Service Sciences, 8*(1), 102–119.
5. Bitner, M. J. (1992). Servicescapes: The impact of physical surroundings on customers and employees. *The Journal of Marketing*, 57–71.

6. Bravo, R., Martinez, E., & Pina, J. M. (2019). Effects of service experience on customer responses to a hotel chain. *International Journal of Contemporary Hospitality Management, 31*(1), 389–405.
7. Bustamante, J. C., & Rubio, N. (2017). Measuring customer experience in physical retail environments. *Journal of Service Management, 28*(5), 884–913.
8. Lucia-Palacios, L., Pérez-López, R., & Polo-Redondo, Y. (2016). Cognitive, affective and behavioural responses in mall experience: A qualitative approach. *International Journal of Retail & Distribution Management, 44*(1), 4–21.
9. Pappas, I. G., Pateli, A. N., Giannakos, M., & Chrissikopoulos, V. (2014). Moderating effects of online shopping experience on customer satisfaction and repurchase intentions. *International Journal of Retail & Distribution Management, 42*(3), 187–204.
10. Bridges, E., & Florsheim, R. (2008). Hedonic and utilitarian shopping goals: The online experience. *Journal of Business Research, 61*(4), 309–314.
11. Roos, I., Friman, M., & Edvardsson, B. (2009). Emotions and stability in telecom-customer relationships. *Journal of Service Management, 20*(2), 192–208.
12. Stephens, N., & Gwinner, K. P. (1998). Why don't some people complain? A cognitive-emotive process model of consumer complaint behavior. *Journal of the Academy of Marketing Science, 26*(3), 172–189.
13. Grewal, D., Levy, M., & Kumar, V. (2009). Customer experience management in retailing: An organizing framework. *Journal of Retailing, 85*(1), 1–14.
14. Davidow, M. (2003). Organizational responses to customer complaints: What works and what doesn't. *Journal of Service Research, 5*(3), 225–250.
15. Svari, S., Slåtten, T., Svensson, G., & Edvardsson, B. (2011). A SOS construct of negative emotions in customers' service experience (CSE) and service recovery by firms (SRF). *Journal of Services Marketing, 25*(5), 323–335.
16. Lallemand, C., Gronier, G., & Koenig, V. (2015). User experience: A concept without consensus? Exploring practitioners' perspectives through an international survey. *Computers in Human Behavior, 43*, 35–48.
17. Kawaf, F., & Tagg, S. (2017). The construction of online shopping experience: A repertory grid approach. *Computers in Human Behavior, 72*, 222–232.
18. Gentile, C., Spiller, N., & Noci, G. (2007). How to sustain the customer experience: An overview of experience components that co-create value with the customer. *European Management Journal, 25*(5), 395–410.
19. Heider, F. (1958). *The psychology of interpersonal relations*. New York: Wiley.
20. Weiner, B. (1985). An attributional theory of achievement motivation and emotion. *Psychological Review, 92*(4), 548–573.
21. Klaus, P. (2013). The case of Amazon.com: Towards a conceptual framework of online customer service experience (OCSE) using the emerging consensus technique (ECT). *Journal of Services Marketing, 27*(6), 443–457.
22. McLean, G., & Wilson, A. (2016). Evolving the online customer experience … is there a role for online customer support? *Computers in Human Behavior, 60*, 602–610.
23. Hassenzahl, M., & Tractinsky, N. (2006). User experience—A research agenda. *Behaviour & Information Technology, 25*(2), 91–97.
24. Cho, N., & Park, S. (2001). Development of electronic commerce user-consumer satisfaction index (ECUSI) for internet shopping. *Industrial Management & Data Systems, 101*(8), 400–406.
25. Novak, T. P., Hoffman, D. L., & Yung, Y. (2000). Measuring the customer experience in online environments: A structural modeling approach. *Marketing Science, 19*(1), 22–42.
26. Hoffman, D. L., & Novak, T. P. (2009). Flow online: Lessons learned and future prospects. *Journal of Interactive Marketing, 23*(1), 23–34.
27. Constantinides, E. (2004). Influencing the online consumer's behavior: The web experience. *Internet Research, 14*(2), 111–126.
28. McLean, G., & Osei-Frimpong, K. (2017). Examining satisfaction with the experience during a live chat service encounter-implications for website providers. *Computers in Human Behavior, 76*, 494–508.

29. Ozkara, B. Y., Ozmen, M., & Kim, J. W. (2017). Examining the effect of flow experience on online purchase: A novel approach to the flow theory based on hedonic and utilitarian value. *Journal of Retailing and Consumer Services, 37,* 119–131.
30. Skadberg, Y. X., & Kimmel, J. R. (2004). Visitors' flow experience while browsing a web site: Its measurement, contributing factors and consequences. *Computers in Human Behavior, 20*(3), 403–422.
31. Ranganathan, C., & Ganapathy, S. (2002). Key dimensions of business-to-consumer web sites. *Information & Management, 39*(6), 457–465.
32. Lohse, G. L., & Spiller, P. (1999). Internet retail store design: How the user interface influences traffic and sales. *Journal of Computer-Mediated Communication, 5*(2), JCMC522.
33. Lee, Y., & Kozar, K. A. (2009). Designing usable online stores: A landscape preference perspective. *Information & Management, 46*(1), 31–41.
34. Nielsen, J. (1999). *Designing web usability: The practice of simplicity*. New Riders Publishing.
35. Spool, J. M., Scanlon, T., Snyder, C., Schroeder, W., & DeAngelo, T. (1999). *Web site usability: A designer's guide*. Morgan Kaufmann.
36. McLean, G. J. (2017). Investigating the online customer experience—A B2B perspective. *Marketing Intelligence & Planning, 35*(5), 657–672.
37. Heinonen, K., & Strandvik, T. (2018). Reflections on customers' primary role in markets. *European Management Journal, 36*(1), 1–11.
38. McColl-Kennedy, J. R., Zaki, M., Lemon, K. N., Urmetzer, F., & Neely, A. (2019). Gaining customer experience insights that matter. *Journal of Service Research, 22*(1), 8–26.
39. Kemppainen, T., Makkonen, M., & Frank, L. (2019). Exploring online customer experience formation: How do customers explain negative emotions during online shopping encounters? In *32nd Bled eConference Proceedings* (pp. 655–675). University of Maribor Press.
40. Helkkula, A. (2011). Characterising the concept of service experience. *Journal of Service Management, 22*(3), 367–389.
41. Trischler, J., Zehrer, A., & Westman, J. (2018). A designerly way of analyzing the customer experience. *Journal of Services Marketing, 32*(7), 805–819.
42. Weiner, B. (1974). *Achievement motivation and attribution theory*. General Learning Press.
43. Jones, E. E., Kanouse, D. E., Kelley, H. H., Nisbett, R. E., Valins, S., & Weiner, B. (1972). *Attribution: Perceiving the causes of behavior*. Morristown: N. J. General Learning Press.
44. Jackson, M. (2019). Utilizing attribution theory to develop new insights into tourism experiences. *Journal of Hospitality and Tourism Management, 38,* 176–183.
45. Miller, D. T., & Ross, M. (1975). Self-serving biases in the attribution of causality: Fact or fiction? *Psychological Bulletin, 82*(2), 213.
46. Iglesias, V. (2009). The attribution of service failures: Effects on consumer satisfaction. *The Service Industries Journal, 29*(2), 127–141.
47. Jackson, M., White, G. N., & Schmierer, C. L. (1996). Tourism experiences within an attributional framework. *Annals of Tourism Research, 23*(4), 798–810.
48. Laros, F. J., & Steenkamp, J. E. (2005). Emotions in consumer behavior: A hierarchical approach. *Journal of Business Research, 58*(10), 1437–1445.
49. Lemon, K. N., & Verhoef, P. C. (2016). Understanding customer experience throughout the customer journey. *Journal of Marketing, 80*(6), 69–96.
50. Preece, J. (2000). *Online communities: Designing usability and supporting socialbilty*. Wiley.

What Foster People to Purchase Further Smart Devices? A Research Proposal

Stefano Za, Alessandra Lazazzara, Jessie Pallud, and Daniele Agostini

Abstract Drawing on the assemblage theory and the concept of personal digital ecosystem, this study aims to propose a model for investigating the willingness to buy a further smart device in order to increase the number of devices shaping the personal digital ecosystem. This research in progress paper describes the main theoretical underpinnings on which the proposed model is built. The model considers continuance intention (CI) to use smart devices and smart device dependence (SD) as antecedents of the purchase intention (PI). Moreover, it considers the moderating effect of users' satisfaction and the number of smart devices already owned on the relationships between CI and PI, and SD and PI respectively. Finally, the model proposed could further allow to investigate the consequences of technological possession by exploring the motivations leading people to own more smart devices.

Keywords Smart-devices · Continuance intention to use · Purchase intention · Dependency · Assemblage theory

S. Za (✉)
University of Chieti-Pescara, Pescara, Italy
e-mail: stefano.za@unich.it

A. Lazazzara
University of Milan, Milan, Italy
e-mail: alessandra.lazazzara@unimi.it

J. Pallud
EM Strasbourg Business School, Strasbourg, France
e-mail: jessie.pallud@em-strasbourg.eu

D. Agostini
LUISS University, Rome, Italy
e-mail: dagostini@luiss.it

C. Metallo et al. (eds.), *Digital Transformation and Human Behavior*, Lecture Notes in Information Systems and Organisation 37,
https://doi.org/10.1007/978-3-030-47539-0_14

1 Introduction

The Internet of Things concerns the ability of objects to interact with other objects or subjects through the network, be they humans or machines. The communication between connected devices is a crucial element in the Internet of Things (IoT) paradigm, where smart objects are considered among the most relevant components [1]. Particularly, smart devices are rapidly changing the market and our lives, transforming our habits and the way we relate to the world around us [2]. From the business point of view, these new devices represent an attractive market opportunity [3–5]. In 2003 there were about 6.3 billion people and around 500 million connected devices, in other words there were 0.08 devices per person [6, 7]. Market researchers have estimated the amount of devices connected to the Internet in the coming years, forecasting a number of approximately 50 billion by 2020, it means an average of more than six devices per person [6]. In line with these forecasts, a more recent analysis predicted that, excluding smartphones and tablets, IoT devices will be around 20 billion by 2020 [8]. With regard to the value of the IoT market, it has been estimated that it could generate a total of 4 to 11 trillion dollars per year by 2025 [9]. Considering the increasingly relevant role played by the smart objects in the near future, it is even more interesting to investigate which drivers influence consumer purchase intention of smart devices.

For this reason, this study focuses specifically on smart devices taking into consideration the dynamics affecting people in creating their personal digital ecosystem [10, 11]. Using the principles of the assemblage theory [12], the present research aims to propose a model for investigating the willingness to buy further smart devices and, as such, to increase the number of devices shaping personal digital ecosystem by leveraging on IS continuance intention and the social media dependency concepts.

The next section develops the theoretical background, followed by a description of the proposed model. Discussion and conclusion will close the paper.

2 Theoretical Background

This section describes the theoretical underpinning concerning the main variables taken into consideration. The first subsection is related to the purchase intention of an additional smart device, the second one describes IS continuance intention, and the third subsection introduces the role of media system dependence.

2.1 Purchase Intention

This study intends to explore the purchase intention of a new smart device in order to update the personal digital ecosystem. Purchase intention of a further smart device differs from repurchase intention, which is the individual's estimation to rebuy products or services from the same company, based on previous purchasing experiences [13]. Indeed, customer repurchase decision is often based on a general assessment of the service/product and the related provider/supplier on the basis of multiple transaction experiences with the same provider/supplier [14]. Therefore, this is more related to the loyalty towards a specific brand or store rather than to the willingness to buy another product in general [15, 16].

In this study we use the purchase intention as a dependent variable in order to analyze the real intention to buy an additional smart device, which could be different from the ones individuals already own. A recent survey conducted in Italy, with over a thousand of respondents, shows a clear predisposition of consumers to buy a smart device in future: 79% of them were inclined to purchase one, breaking down into 21% in the near future (within a year) and the remaining 58% in the coming years [17]. To the best of our knowledge, what has not been studied yet is whether consumer intention to keep using their own smart device (e.g. their own smartphone) increases their willingness to buy an additional smart product (e.g. a smartwatch or a smart TV). The so-called assemblage theory offers a theoretical underpinning useful to better understand this phenomenon. This theory explains the process by which the identity of a whole, where the whole is more than the mere sum of its parts, emerges from the interactions between its heterogeneous parts [12]. Therefore, an assemblage is an emergent entity with new capabilities deriving from the continuous interactions of its individual components, whether they be humans or devices [18]. This theoretical framework has been applied a lot in the IoT field, and especially in the smart home environment, introducing the concept of assemblage thinking [19]. Hoffman and Novak [19] tried to depict the process of the smart home adoption from the consumer's perspective. Initially, individuals do not purchase a set of devices, but rather they identify a single smart product that they perceive as suitable in satisfying certain needs. Afterwards, they can have the desire to purchase further smart devices. When the number of smart products reaches a critical mass (around five or more), people start to perceive the added value derived by the interactions of these products [19]. Indeed, customers end up realizing that the real value of such objects increases according to the number of devices added over time [20]. This line of thought can be applied to devices such as smartphones or smartwatches. Actually, a smartwatch has limited functionalities. So, by connecting it to a smartphone, people are able to exploit the smart nature of this object, increasing and expanding capabilities of the smartwatch and the smartphone as well. In this scenario the concept of continuance intention to use a smart device could be crucial in order to exploit the potentialities of the personal digital ecosystem. The following further discusses on this.

2.2 IS Continuance Intention

The IS continuance model [21] is one of the most widely acknowledged and empirically validated model for investigating the continuance intention to use an IS after its first adoption [22]. This represents an area of high interest for the IS research community [23]. Several theories focus on the initial acceptance of an information system, such as the Innovation Diffusion theory [24], the Theory of Planned Behavior [25] and the Technology Acceptance Model [26]. Bhattacherjee [21] asserts that the long term survival of a technology depends more on its continued use by its consumers rather than the mere first use.

The theoretical foundations of the IS continuance model are grounded in the *Expectation Confirmation Theory (ECT)*. The ECT is a widely used theory in the consumer behavior literature to investigate consumer satisfaction and post purchase behavior of a brand, a product or marketing services in general [27]. According to Oliver [28], a consumer reaches the repurchase phase after a several steps process. This process will lead eventually to a confirmation evaluation whether the product performances are greater than the expectations or, conversely, to a disconfirmation. Finally, satisfied consumers will be more likely to repurchase the product or service, while those dissatisfied will cease their use.

Among the others, Bhattacherjee [21] associates the dependent variable of the repurchase intention with the continuance intention, so adapting the original model to the information system context. However, the IS continuance model differs from Oliver's ECT one. Each variable belongs to a time frame labeled "t2", that is a post-consumption phase; this because the ex-ante effects are already included in the *confirmation* construct. Furthermore, a substantial difference lies in the form in which the (ex post) expectation of the ECT model is presented, substituted for the *perceived usefulness* construct, defined as the degree to which a person believes that the use of a certain system can improve his or her work performance [26].

Among others, a recent stream of research extends the IS continuance model [22, 29] combining the theory of Media System Dependency [30] with the conceptual model of Bhattacherjee [21]. The concept of *dependency* is described in the next section.

2.3 Media System Dependency

Nowadays individuals are gradually ceasing to perceive their technological devices as individual independent entities, but rather they view them as a set of interconnected devices that progressively occupy a central role in their daily life [31]. This phenomenon seems to suggest that users are becoming more dependent on these devices and therefore on this digital ecosystem [22, 29]. Such artificial environment is defined as a *ubiquitous media system*, that is a complex aggregation of digital artifacts, multi-purpose, multi context, connected to the network, which uses a dynamic set of interconnected devices, providing a fluid access to information through a variety of channels; this allows the user to perform a multitude of tasks and to interact in a smart way within the digital ecosystem [22]. Understanding the role played by media dependency in consumer behavior has only been slightly investigated by researchers. The concept of *media system dependency* differs from *addiction*. While *addiction* refers to a psychological state that causes irrational and obsessive–compulsive behaviors in the use of technology [32], *dependency* consists in a rational phenomenon, oriented to the objectives that individuals intend to achieve, that is a goal-oriented *dependency* [22]. The Media System Dependency (MSD) stream of research defines the dependency as a "relation between individuals' goals and the extent to which these goals are contingent upon the resources of the media system in which those resources have the capacities to create and gather, process and disseminate information" [33]. Thus, goal-oriented dependency and psychological dependency are two distinct constructs. From the MSD derives the more specific theory of the Individual Media Dependency (IMD), which provides a concrete view of an individual's dependency level toward a specific media. Indeed it is stated that the degree to which a media is able to satisfy individuals' needs and expectations will directly affect the dependency relations with that specific media [34]. This means that the level of dependence with regard to a specific media will be given by the extent to which such media is perceived by individuals as particularly useful to pursue their objectives [35]. Therefore, this research is based on this very last assumption, but rather than referring to a media channel, it is intended to study the personal digital ecosystem dependency which can be defined, in line with the IMD theory, as the extent to which an individual's ability to achieve and pursue his or her objectives depends on the use of his or her personal digital ecosystem [22].

In order to make clearer the technology dependency facet defined as goal-oriented dependency, it is worth clarifying a further difference with a more familiar construct in the IS research stream, which is the Task Technology Fit (TTF) theory. Although some overlaps between the MSD and the TTF exist, there are substantial differences that make those two concepts quite distinct. First, since the Task Technology Fit is defined as the extent of the ability of information technology (IT) to support a specific task [36], it seems clear that TTF theory has a "task" or activity focus, which pertains mainly to work settings. The MSD, instead, represents a more encompassing concept as it includes both personal and professional environments. Second, TTF adopts a performance perspective, which is particularly suitable to work contexts (the higher is the task-technology fit, the higher will be employee performance), capturing the task characteristics that only relate to a given job, and not the pursued objective. This represents a key difference because MSD focuses on individual informational needs and goals, a wider perspective that goes beyond work boundaries. Third, TTF is more a device-centric theory as it includes technological characteristics (e.g. ease of use, reliability). MSD considered in this research refers to a collection of interconnected devices that forms the personal digital ecosystem.

In summary, TTF is about matching the capabilities of the technology to the demands of the task [36], while Media Dependency is about matching the informational capabilities of the personal digital ecosystem to the information needs and goals of an individual, including both personal and professional contexts.

3 Research Model and Hypotheses Development

Following the assemblage thinking [19], the perception of a higher value of a personal digital ecosystem should increase proportionally to the number of its interacting components, represented by a set of smart devices. Moreover, according to the IS continuance model [21], the continuance intention is based on the congruence between initial expectations and actual performance (confirmation) of an IS. Focusing on the personal digital ecosystem, if the expectations on its performance are confirmed, users tend to perceive a higher value. In accordance with Chang and Wildt [15], if a product is judged high in value, this judgment is expected to lead to higher purchase intention. Hence, it seems reasonable to argue that individuals having high level of continuance intention to use smart devices will be willing to increase the overall value of the personal digital ecosystem by adding an additional smart-device, according to the assemblage thinking. Consequently, the following hypothesis was derived:

H1: Continuance Intention to Use Smart-Devices Has a Positive Impact on Purchase Intention of a Further Smart-Device.

In this paper we consider the goal-oriented facet of the IT dependency phenomenon, having an influence on usage-related behaviors [22]. It seems reasonable to argue that the rational and goal-oriented facet of dependency could have a distorting effect on the extent to which the system satisfies the utility perceived of the personal digital ecosystem (formed by a set of smart devices) usage. High dependency could thus lead to magnifying positive experiences and minimizing (or omitting) negative ones [22]. Moreover, in accordance with MSD theory, once individuals realize the effectiveness of a media, they tend to explore further benefits from the same media in order to better attain their goals [33, 37]. Hence, individuals who are dependent of smart devices could seek to increase the number of technological components by purchasing a further smart device. As a result, it could be hypothesized that:

H2: Smart-devices dependence has a positive impact on purchase intention of a further smart-device.

The concept of "satisfaction" describes the degree of overall pleasure and gratification perceived by users, resulting from the ability of the product or service to fulfil the their desires, expectations and needs [13]. User's satisfaction usually is strongly associated with the intention to return to the same provider for repurchasing the product or service [13]. Therefore, a high level of satisfaction in using smart-devices should influence the intention to purchase a further smart-device. Moreover, in line with Bhattacherjee's [21] research, satisfaction occurs when the expected benefits are achieved, and the level of satisfaction resulting from usage experiences should have a positive effect on continuance intention [22]. Similarly, satisfaction should reinforce the perception of the goal-oriented dependence. In summary, satisfaction could play the role of a moderator in the relationship between both the continuance intention and smart-devices dependence on the purchase intention of a further smart device. Thus, we propose the two following moderation hypotheses:

H3a. Satisfaction moderates the relationship between continuance intention and purchase intention of a further smart device, so that the relationship is stronger at higher level of satisfaction compared to lower.
H3b. Satisfaction moderates the relationship between smart-devices dependence and purchase intention of a further smart device, so that the relationship is stronger at higher level of satisfaction compared to lower.

Finally, considering the concept of assemblage thinking [19], users start by identifying a single smart device considered suitable in satisfying certain needs. Afterwards, they purchase additional smart devices. When the number of smart products reaches a critical mass (around five or more), people start to perceive the added value derived by the interactions of these multiple products [19], realizing that this value increases according to the number of devices added over time [20]. Therefore, in according with this research stream, we posit the existence of a moderating effect of the number of devices a user already owns on the effect that satisfaction could have on the remaining relationships (three-way interaction). Thus, we propose the following hypotheses:

H4a. The combined effect of number of smart-devices owned and satisfaction on the relationship between continuance intention and purchase intention will be stronger for users with higher level of satisfaction.
H4b. The combined effect of number of smart-devices owned and satisfaction on the relationship between dependence and purchase intention will be stronger for users with higher level of satisfaction.

Figure 1 shows the proposed model.

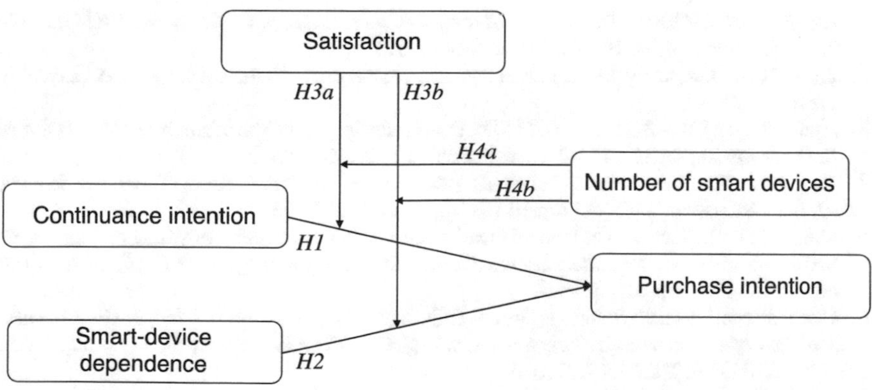

Fig. 1 The proposed research model

4 Discussion and Conclusion

This paper seeks to contribute to the IS stream of research on MSD and digital ecosystems by calling researchers to explore new factors driving purchase intentions of smart devices. In accordance with the assemblage theory principles, individuals tend to create a set of interconnected devices in order to increase their satisfaction [19].

Exploring these dynamics behind the purchase intention of further smart devices, could shed new light of several issues. First, the number of smart devices could play a significant role, thus highlighting the role of smart device possessions. The concept of possessions has been extensively examined in marketing research, especially with a rich literature on material possessions and on the role of possessions as extensions of self [38–42]. Belk [39] defines the extended self as "a superficially and Western metaphor comprising not only that which is seen as "me" (the self), but also that which is seen as "mine" (p. 140). Testing the proposed model, could offer interesting insights to understand what moves users to possess more smart devices, investigating further the consequences of technological possession. More specifically how smart device possession motivates users to purchase more smart devices. At the same time, this desire to possess more smart devices can also represent a new form of technological addiction or a type of compulsive behavior [43]. IS research has already revealed that technologies such as Internet, social networks [44], and smartphones [45] can create dependency. Therefore, future research could explore the consequences of having many smart devices not only from a purchase perspective, but also from social and behavioral perspectives.

References

1. Atzori, L., et al. (2010). The internet of things: A survey. *Computer Networks, 54*(15), 2787–2805. https://doi.org/10.1016/j.comnet.2010.05.010
2. Za, S. (2018). *Internet of things.* Rome: Persone, organizzazioni e società 4.0. LUISS University Press.
3. Allmendinger, G., & Busine, L. H. (2005). Four strategies for the age of smart services. *Harvard Business Review, 83*(10), 131–145. https://doi.org/10.1225/R0510J
4. Ju, J. et al. (2016) Prototyping business models for IoT service. *Procedia Computer Science, 91*, Itqm, 882–890. https://doi.org/10.1016/j.procs.2016.07.106.
5. Shin, J. (2014). New business model creation through the triple helix of young entrepreneurs, SNSs, and smart devices. *International Journal Technology Management, 66*(4), 302. https://doi.org/10.1504/ijtm.2014.064969
6. Cisco Internet Business Solutions Group (IBSG). (2011). *The internet of things—How the next evolution of the internet is changing everything.* CISCO white Pap. April, 1–11. https://doi.org/10.1109/IEEESTD.2007.373646.
7. U.S. Census Bureau. (2018). *World population.*
8. Gartner. (2016). *Forecast: Internet of things—Endpoints and associated services*, Worldwide.
9. McKinsey Global Institute. (2015). The internet of things: Mapping the value beyond the hype. *McKinsey Global Institute, 144*. https://doi.org/10.1007/978-3-319-05029-4_7.

10. Future. Customer. *Customer interaction of the future*, Part 1: Your Personal Digital Ecosystem, https://www.future-customer.com/customer-interaction-of-the-future-part-1-your-personal-digital-ecosystem/, Last Accessed June 01, 2019.
11. Kay, J., & Kummerfeld, B. (2012). Creating personalized systems that people can scrutinize and control. *ACM Transactions on Interactive Intelligent System, 2*(4), 1–42. https://doi.org/10.1145/2395123.2395129
12. De Landa, M. (2011). *Philosophy and simulation: The emergence of synthetic reason.* London: Continuum. Bloomsbury Publishing.
13. Hellier, P. K., et al. (2003). Customer repurchase intention. *European Journal of Marketing, 37*(11/12), 1762–1800. https://doi.org/10.1108/03090560310495456
14. Danaher, P. J., & Mattsson, J. (1998). A comparison of service delivery processes of different complexity. *International Journal of Service Industry, 9*(1), 48–63. https://doi.org/10.1108/09564239810199941
15. Chang, T.-Z., & Wildt, A. R. (1994). Price, product information, and purchase intention: An empirical study. *Journal of the Academy of Marketing Science, 22*(1), 16–27. https://doi.org/10.1177/0092070394221002
16. Dodds, W. B., et al. (1991). Effects of price, BRAND, and store information on buyers' product evaluations. *Journal of Marketing Research, 28*(3), 307–319. https://doi.org/10.1177/002224379102800305
17. Doxa. Accesibile da https://www.statista.com/statistics/681951/willingness-to-purchase-smart-devices-in-italy/.
18. Belk, R. (2014). Digital consumption and the extended self. *Journal of Marketing Management, 30*(11–12), 1101–1118. https://doi.org/10.1080/0267257X.2014.939217
19. Hoffman, D. L., Novak, T. P. (2015). Emergent Experience and the connected consumer in the smart home assemblage and the internet of things. https://doi.org/10.2139/ssrn.2648786.
20. Hoffman, D. L., & Novak, T. P. (2016). How to market the smart home: Focus on emergent experience not use cases. *SSRN Electronic Journal.* https://doi.org/10.2139/ssrn.2840976
21. Bhattacherjee, A. (2001). Understanding information systems continuance: An expectation-confirmation model. *MIS Q., 25*(3), 351–370.
22. Carillo, K., et al. (2017). The role of media dependency in predicting continuance intention to use ubiquitous media systems. *Information & Management, 54*(3), 317–335. https://doi.org/10.1016/j.im.2016.09.002
23. Bagayogo, F. F., et al. (2014). Enhanced use of IT : A new perspective on post-adoption. *Journal of the Association for Information Systems, 15*(7), 361–387.
24. Rogers, E. (1995). *Diffusion of innovations.* Free Press
25. Ajzen, I. (1991). The theory of planned behavior. *Organizational Behavior and Human Decision Processes, 50*(2), 179–211. https://doi.org/10.1016/0749-5978(91)90020-T
26. Davis, F. D. (1989). Perceived usefulness, perceived ease of use, and user acceptance of information technology. *MIS quarterly, 13*(3), 319–340. https://doi.org/10.2307/249008
27. Anderson, E. W., & Sullivan, M. W. (1993). The antecedents and consequences of customer satisfaction for firms. *Marketing Science, 12*(2), 125–143. https://doi.org/10.1287/mksc.12.2.125
28. Oliver, R. L. (1993). Cognitive, Affective, and Attribute Bases of the Satisfaction Response. *Journal of Consumer Research, 20*(3), 418. https://doi.org/10.1086/209358
29. Carillo, K. et al. (2014). An investigation of the role of dependency in predicting continuance intention to use ubiquitous media systems: Combining a media sytem perspective with expectation-confirmation theories. In: *Proceedings of the twenty second European conference on information systems* (ECIS2014) (pp. 1–17). Israel: Tel Aviv.
30. Ball-Rokeach, S. J., & DeFleur, M. L. (1976). A dependency model of mass-media effects. *Communication Research, 3*(1), 3–21.
31. Scheepers, R., & Middleton, C. (2013). Personal ICT ensembles and ubiquitous information systems environments: Key issues and research implications. *Communications of the Association for Information Systems, 33*(1), 381–392.

32. Turel, O., et al. (2011). Integrating technology addiction and use: An empirical investigation of online auction users. *MIS quarterly, 35*(4), 1043–1061.
33. Ball-Rokeach, S. J. (1985). The origins of individual media-system dependency. *Communication Research, 12*(4), 485–510.
34. Grant, A. E., et al. (1991a). Television shopping. *Communication Research, 18*(6), 773–798. https://doi.org/10.1177/009365091018006004
35. Loges, W. E. (1994). Canaries in the coal mine: Perceptions of threat and media system dependency relations. *Communication Research, 21*(1), 5–23.
36. Mark, D. T., & Strong, M. D. (1999). Extending the technology acceptance model with task±technology ®t constructs. *Akademik Araştırmalar ve Çalışmalar Dergisi (AKAD), 36*(49), 161–175. https://doi.org/10.1016/S0378-7206(98)00101-3
37. Grant, A. E., et al. (1991b). Television shopping: A media system dependency perspective. *Communication Research, 18*(6), 773–798.
38. Belk, R. W. (2013). Extended self in a digital world. *Journal of Consumer Research, 40*(3), 477–500. https://doi.org/10.1086/671052
39. Belk, R. W. (1988). Possessions and the Extended Self. *Journal of Consumer Research, 15*(2), 139. https://doi.org/10.1086/209154
40. Schultz, D. E. (2014). Extending the extended self in the digital world. *Journal of Marketing Theory and Practice, 22*(2), 143–146. https://doi.org/10.2753/mtp1069-6679220207
41. Siddiqui, S., & Turley, D. (2006). Extending the self in a virtual world. *Advances in Consumer Research, 33,* 647–648.
42. Wong, P., et al. (2012). Consumption narratives of extended possessions and the extended self. *Journal of Marketing Management, 28*(7–8), 936–954. https://doi.org/10.1080/0267257X.2012.698632
43. Lee, Y., et al. (2014). The dark side of smartphone usage: Psychological traits, compulsive behavior and technostress. *Computers in Human Behavior, 31,* 373–383.
44. Kefi, H., et al. (2016). Comprendre le phénomène de dépendance envers les réseaux sociaux numériques : Les effets de l'habitude et de la surcharge informationnelle dans le cas de Facebook. *French Journal Information Systems, 21*(4), 7–42.
45. Clayton, R. B., et al. (2015). The extended iSelf: The impact of iPhone separation on cognition, emotion, and physiology. *Journal of Computer, 20*(2), 119–135.

Human or Machine? A Study of Anthropomorphism Through an Affordance Lens

Dana Lunberry and Jonathan Liebenau

Abstract Anthropomorphism—the tendency of humans to apply human-like attributes to non-human objects—has received growing attention by scholars across multiple disciplines. With increasing popularity of service and personal robotics and conversational agents, scholars of information systems have begun to shed light on some of the technology features and processes related to anthropomorphism. This study applies a socio-technical approach using affordance theory to examine the relationship between technology and anthropomorphic perceptions among users. Evidence is gathered from an empirical study involving the introduction of interactive voice response (IVR) with savings clients of a savings and loans company in Ghana. The findings highlight four main ways that the IVR technology exhibited human-like qualities within the user-technology interaction (as perceived by users). This paper illustrates how a study on the relationship between technology and anthropomorphism might be conducted through an affordance perspective. It also offers implications for technology development.

Keywords Anthropomorphism · Technology affordances · Interactive voice response · Financial services

1 Introduction

Affordances, or "potentials for action" [1], can be employed as a conceptual tool for examining the link between technology and anthropomorphic perceptions of users. Anthropomorphism refers to the tendencies of humans to apply human-like attributes to non-human objects. Anthropomorphism as a psychological concept is becoming increasingly relevant in the field of information systems (IS) with the rise

D. Lunberry (✉) · J. Liebenau
London School of Economics, London, UK
e-mail: d.d.lunberry@lse.ac.uk

J. Liebenau
e-mail: j.m.liebenau@lse.ac.uk

C. Metallo et al. (eds.), *Digital Transformation and Human Behavior*, Lecture Notes in Information Systems and Organisation 37,
https://doi.org/10.1007/978-3-030-47539-0_15

of human-like robots (often referred to as "humanoids") and conversational agents such as voice assistants and chatbots. As more organizations digitize the customer-institution interface, human-to-human interactions are being replaced by human–computer interactions which use natural learning processing, artificial intelligence, and machine learning to mimic human-to-human communication [2].

Until now, anthropomorphism has largely been studied as psychophysiological processes [3–5] but the literature outside of psychology and behavioral studies is growing and is shedding light on other related processes. In IS and especially the field of robotics, the literature has begun to shed light on the technological processes involved in anthropomorphism and anthropomorphism's implications for technology design and diffusion [6]. Key examples include Tondu [7], Iossifidis et al. [8], Schuetzler et al. [2], Taddeucci et al. [9], and Hashimoto et al. [10]. In 2012, Tondu (p. 612) [7] introduced the term "technical anthropomorphism" to refer to the technological artefact which results from the human–machine mimicking process.

In IS literature, anthropomorphism has been recognized for playing a key role in helping technologies adapt to human society, which in turn helps humans adopt these technologies as users [7, 11]. By developing technologies to mimic human-like attributes, these technologies afford increased familiarity for humans which helps facilitate the user adoption process. This paper builds on the existing IS literature and examines anthropomorphism in the adoption of a new technology by users in the context of financial services in Ghana. Using an empirical study, we employ an affordance lens to examine aspects of the technology and the socio-technical relationships which help facilitate anthropomorphic perceptions among users. In doing so, we shed light on some of the most conceptually important issues of today's digital age which are located at the core of technology design, diffusion and adoption.

We start with the theoretical underpinnings of the research on technology affordances and summarize the existing affordance literature in IS. Next, we describe our research methodology, describing our case study and research methods. We then present our findings, showing how and in what ways IVR exhibited human-like qualities as perceived by users from a socio-technical perspective. Lastly, we discuss the findings and their implications for scholarship and practice. We argue that affordances as a conceptual framework offers an improved understanding of the socio-technical relationship related to anthropomorphic outcomes.

2 Affordances as a Conceptual Framework

Affordance theory originated from James J. Gibson's work [12, 13] in the field of ecological psychology. Gibson conceptualized an affordance as a link between an organism and its environment. "The affordances of the environment are what it offers the animal, what it provides or furnishes, either for good or ill" (p. 127) [13]. Gibson conceptualized affordances as phenomenal in nature and not as physical properties. Affordances are not properties of the organism nor the environment. Instead, they are relational and are situated within an interaction. They are a direct link between perception and action and can be conceptualized as "action possibilities" [13].

The affordance literature in IS has grown substantially in the last decade (i.e., Markus and Silver [14]; Leonardi [15]; Anderson and Robey [16]; Leonardi [17]; Yoo et al. [18]; Majchrzak and Markus [19]; Majchrzak et al. [20]; Robey et al. [21]; Seidel et al. [22]; Volkoff and Strong [23]; Strong et al. [24]). Within IS, the term affordance has become a concept that broadly encapsulates the relationship between technology and its users but no single conceptualization of affordances dominates the literature. While IS scholars tend to agree that the concept of affordances is useful for examining socio-technical phenomena, Stendal et al. [25] highlight the lack of consistency among scholars around whether affordances are intended or emergent, functional or non-functional, and potential or actual.

In addition to IS, various disciplines including psychology and design fields, human–computer interaction (HCI), organizational studies, and communications and media studies have used (and expanded) upon affordance theory, making the conceptualization of affordances suit various research needs and contexts. In communications and media studies, Nagy and Neff [26] have introduced the term "imagined affordances" to underscore the importance of the imagination in affordances, which they state are located somewhere between the technology and human actors amongst expectations, intentions, perceptions, attitudes, and actions. Nagy and Neff [26] argue that *imagined affordances* provide users with agency.

Following Gibson et al. [26], and the work of many other scholars, this research applies affordances as a multi-faceted concept that highlights the critical role of user perception within the socio-technical relationship. User perception is critical to technology development and technology-related outcomes. According to Kardes et al. (p. 100) [27], "understanding perception and how it influences consumers' attention to the environment, their interpretation and comprehension of stimuli, and ultimately their behavior, are essential to developing successful products and marketing messages." Hence, an affordance lens—which focuses on the socio-technical relationship and user perceptions—provides a particularly suitable tool for carrying out research on technology and anthropomorphism.

3 Methodology

3.1 Case Study

This research uses an empirical case involving a pilot project that introduced interactive voice response (IVR) with financial savings clients of a large savings and loans company in Ghana ("ABC Company"). The research examines ways in which the IVR technology exhibited human-like qualities for the user-technology interaction. IVR is a computerized phone system that enables organizations to send pre-recorded voice messages via mobile phone and to receive responses from listeners typically through voice applications or by typed commands on a phone keypad.

The pilot project took place over an 11-month period in 2017–2018 and targeted 46,671 clients of the institution (nearly 10% of the institutions' existing clientele). In total, 23 IVR messages were sent to clients ("users") during the project period, at a rate of one message per week on average. While most messages were focused on the topic of savings, five of the messages contained other content such as information about the project and holiday greetings. The messages that were savings-related gave basic information on savings such as tips on how and when to save, how to develop positive savings habits, and the importance of savings and goalsetting. Some messages provided information about the institutions' savings products, such as types of savings accounts and channels for making savings deposits. The content aimed to associate savings with positive outcomes for people's wellbeing by framing savings as a safety net for times of emergency, a good way to cover familial expenses such as school fees and retirement, and an aid for fulfilling life ambitions.

Some of the messages responded to recent activity in the users' savings accounts. For example, if balances increased, these users received a congratulatory message and were encouraged to continue saving regularly. If balances declined, these users received a message that encouraged them to make small yet regular efforts to increase their balances.

Some of the calls were used to collect information from clients through IVR surveys known as *prompts*. The following provides an example of a prompt:

> Hello valued customer, this is Alice again, from ABC Company. We have noticed that your savings account at ABC Company has stayed at a low balance. Can you tell me why you haven't been saving?
>
> Press 1 if you save somewhere else.
>
> Press 2 if you save at home.
>
> Press 3 if you have no excess money to save.
>
> (A different voice: Once you press 1, 2 or 3, listen again to hear what Alice wants to tell you. Would you like to re-listen to this message? If yes, press 0.)

As illustrated by this example, users were able to interact with the institution through IVR in two main ways. First, users could respond to a message using the keypad on their mobile phone handset. Around 30% of the calls requested a response such as, "press 1 if…, press 2 if…." and every call allowed the user to relisten to the message by pressing 0. The IVR system was limited to typed commands and lacked the voice capability which some other IVR systems offer. The second way users could interact with the institution was by calling the IVR system back using the same number that been used to call them. This elicited a callback feature so that the users would be automatically called by the system, allowing users to hear the IVR messages at no-cost (as opposed to being charged for the cost of sending a call).

Nearly all the messages were scripted as being delivered by the same character with the name "Alice." Throughout the project, the same voice actors were used for the voice recordings so that users receiving the messages would become familiar with the same voice for "Alice." Multiple voice actors were employed since the messages were recorded into four commonly spoken languages in Ghana (English, Ga, Twi, and Dagbani) following a translation process. An audio menu was used during some of the calls to allow listeners to select their preferred language for future calls.

3.2 Methods of Data Collection and Analysis

Data was collected using participant observations and key informant interviews. Participant observations were gathered by the lead researcher who worked alongside the project team for a period of over one year to gain a deep understanding of the IVR system. Observations of the technology artefact, design, and processes were recorded in observation memos throughout the project period. Interviews were conducted at two intervals, mid-project and end-of-project, to collect user perceptions. The interviews were conducted with 154 key informants consisting of 102 users (clients) and 52 branch staff. The methods included staff interviews because staff also listened to the IVR messages and were responsible for collecting client feedback. To ensure proportional representation of various savings and call behaviors, cluster sampling was used to select the users for interviews, while random sampling was used to select the branch staff. The interviews enabled the researchers to collect perceptions related to the IVR calls and to understand if and how users experienced human-like qualities through the IVR system. The interviews were conducted by phone and in the local languages of the informants. The interview responses were translated and recorded in English.

The observation memos and transcribed interviews were analyzed using NVivo software. Thematic analysis following Miles and Huberman [28] was applied to identify human-like factors perceived by users. In total, human-like factors of the technology were identified using 24 unique codes which were descriptive and interpretive in nature (i.e., Alice as memorable, Alice as monitor of past behavior, Alice doesn't listen). Based on patterns among the codes, we categorized these codes into seven meta-codes (such as Alice as caller, Alice as staff member, etc.). These meta-codes were inferential in nature and sought to explain how and in what ways IVR exhibited human-like qualities as perceived by the users. The code hierarchy was established through an iterative process and evolved over time following periods of reflection.

Following this coding process, we applied the analytical tools of pattern matching and explanation building [29] to understand the roles of technology as they related to the codes (the human-like factors). From this analysis, we identified patterns in the relationship between the human-like factors and the technology artefact, design, and processes. Once identified, these patterns helped explain how various affordances of the technology played a role in enabling anthropomorphism as identified in our case.

4 The "Alice Effect" and the Technology Behind It

It is useful to summarize the anthropomorphic perceptions which we found in our dataset before we elaborate on the key technical aspects of our analysis to explain how the IVR technology exhibited human-like qualities for the user-technology interaction.

4.1 Anthropomorphic Perceptions

The IVR system was designed to deliver a series of pre-recorded phone calls from a voice self-identified as "Alice." While the name "Alice" was created by the IVR project team as a fictitious character who delivered the IVR messages, evidence in our data showed that "Alice" was perceived and talked about by both clients and staff as if "Alice" were a real person. Various types of anthropomorphic perceptions of "Alice" were found in the data. We categorized the anthropomorphic perceptions into seven main classifications based on inferred identities being attributed to "Alice," which are: 1. caller, 2. staff member, 3. monitor, 4. conversationalist, 5. talker, 6. instigator of action, and 7. gendered (i.e., mysterious female caller, homewrecker, etc.). Jointly, we call these seven classifications of anthropomorphism the "Alice effect" (Table 1).

4.2 Technical Aspects

The *Alice effect* was made possible by various sociopsychological and physical elements. Within the scope of our study, we focused on the role of technology within the human–machine interaction which gave rise to anthropomorphic perceptions of "Alice." Hence our analysis presents technical explanations for how the "Alice effect" was made possible.

Based on our investigation of the socio-technical relationship between users and the IVR system, we found that the *Alice effect* was enabled through various features and configurations of the technology. Through an analytical interweaving of interview and observational data, we drew connections among various technological aspects and anthropomorphic perceptions of "Alice." By applying affordances as a conceptual lens, we identified several technology affordances which we found to culminate in four main ways that helped explained how the IVR system helped facilitate anthropomorphic perceptions among users. The following table presents a summary of our findings (Table 2).

Capture, Storage and Renderings of Voice Recordings. The IVR system used pre-recorded voice messages which were stored on hundreds of short audio clips. The audio clips could be manipulated and edited by the project team to configure the messages to the intended users (listeners). The IVR technology possessed the

Table 1 The *Alice effect*: classifications of anthropomorphism

Meta-codes and descriptions	Codes	Examples from the data
1. Alice as (Regular) caller *Alice was referred to by clients and staff as the deliverer of the messages. Alice made it easy for people to differentiate the IVR calls from other calls that they may have received from the organization.*	• Message deliverer • Familiar • Recognizable • Memorable Distinct part of the call	• "The client said she didn't remember the message but when I mentioned Alice's name she said she remembered." -Staff • "There were times I didn't pick [up] Alice's call." -Client
2. Alice as (Mysterious) staff member *Clients and staff asked who Alice was and where she was located. Clients came to the branch looking for Alice. Clients and staff would describe the calls as being sent from a staff member and typically from someone based at the head office.*	• Looking for Alice • Who is Alice • Where is Alice • Someone from the head office • A staff member	• "People asked, 'who is Alice?'" —Staff • "I went to the branch looking for Alice. I was told Alice was in the head office." —Client • "There's a teller at Tamale named Alice so the clients thought it was her." —Staff
3. Alice as monitor *Clients talked about Alice as someone who could observe their financial behavior and would check in on them.*	• Monitor of past behavior • Monitor of future behavior	• "Alice said it's been a long time since I visited the bank to deposit savings." –Client • "I have finished paying for the car so now Alice will see me saving more." -Client
4. Alice as conversationalist *Clients talked about Alice as someone who engaged in a conversation with them. Some clients described the conversations as two-way, as if Alice asked them questions (including questions not scripted in the IVR messages).*	• Asks how the client was doing • Greets • Informs • Advises • Joins in a conversation	• "One of my clients…her account was dormant. Her daughter had passed away so she had stopped saving. Alice asked her what is happening, how is her business, said that she should come back."—Staff • "Whenever Alice calls, she greets me." —Client • "He said it < the call > was questions about his business, how he was doing, an advice to him." —Staff

(continued)

Table 1 (continued)

Meta-codes and descriptions	Codes	Examples from the data
5. Alice as talker *According to staff, clients talked about Alice as talking and not listening to them nor engaging in a two-way conversation.*	• Doesn't listen • Client unable to respond	• "The client wanted to know who Alice was and complained that they wanted to talk back. It means they didn't know it was a recording."—Staff • "Clients want to interact with Alice. A common complaint is that she just talks and talks and won't listen." —Staff
6. Alice as instigator of action *According to staff, clients talked about Alice as asking them to do certain actions (save), including actions not scripted in the IVR messages (borrow a loan).*	• Save • Borrow a loan	• "She remembers the calls, that Alice would say you should save" —Staff • "Most of the clients come to the branch saying that Sister Alice said they should come for a loan. It puts us, the officers, under pressure to explain." —Staff
7. Alice as gendered (Mysterious Female Caller/Homewrecker, etc.) *Clients and staff used gendered language (i.e., "she," "her") when speaking about the IVR calls. In some cases, the gendered aspect of Alice generated consequential effects. According to staff, clients mentioned cases of household conflict related to Alice: women confronted their male partner out of curiosity or with the belief that their partner was romantically involved with "Alice."*	• Husband accused of cheating on wife • Wife curious • "Sister Alice"	• "The wife was suspecting him of cheating because someone called Alice has been calling him." —Staff • "One client commented that the wife picked [up] the call and was curious who Alice is." —Staff

Table 2 Summary of technical aspects that contributed to the *Alice effect*

	Underpinning affordances	Embedded human-like elements
Capture, Storage and Renderings of Voice Recordings	Capability to capture and store human voice as audio clips Capacity to integrate and combine audio clips Capacity to rapidly introduce, combine and rearrange audio clips	Human voice messages Tailored messages Two-way conversation format
Mimicry of Human-like Conversation Methods	Capacity to integrate IVR and mobile network operator systems to deliver phone calls Capability to transfer patterns of sound waves from human speech into electronic impulses [30]	Phone calls
Mimicry of Human-like Conversational Elements	Capability to capture, store, and integrate human voice	Prosodic features of human speech (intonation, stress, tone, and rhythm) Gendered
Presentation of Human-like Message Content	Capacity to send calls on a pre-programmed schedule Capacity to pre-program audio responses following customer input Capacity to capture, store, and apply customer call data Capacity to integrate customer savings data from core banking system Capability to solicit customer input and interaction via mobile phone connectivity	Informational, interactive, culturally relevant, and affect-laden message content

capacity to rapidly introduce, combine and rearrange audio clips. The audio clips could be sliced and rearranged to render variations in the sequencing of the audio clips and to develop pre-made voice-loops. The ability to rapidly manipulate the recordings enabled the project team to develop messages in an iterative fashion, while the ability to set pre-made voice-loops enabled clients to re-listen to messages and to select alternative messages from a menu of options. These technology affordances can therefore be summarized as enabling the common human-like elements: human voice messages, tailored messages and the format of a two-way conversation.

Mimicry of Human-like Conversation Methods. For IVR messages to be delivered by phone to users, the technology was integrated with the system of one of the largest mobile network operators in the country. The seamless integration made the IVR calls indistinguishable from human-delivered calls based on the calls' method of delivery. Phone calls are human–machine interactions which rely on telephone systems that transfer patterns of sound waves from human speech into electronic impulses [30]. With over a hundred years in existence, telephony has become readily available and is easily understood [30]. In our case, phone calls were already a familiar medium of human-to-human communication for users hence receiving the IVR messages as a phone call presented a human-like element.

Mimicry of Human-like Conversational Elements. Mimicking human-like conversation was enacted through various conversational elements such as style and approach. The voice recordings contained human patterns of speech. By using voice actors for the recordings instead of machine-generated voice synthesis, the IVR system was able to model human speech without various limitations faced by some text-to-speech systems. For instance, the voice actors naturally conveyed prosodic features of human speech such as intonation, stress, tone, and rhythm. The message scripts included instructions for the voice actors through punctuation (i.e., periods, question and exclamation marks) and special notations (i.e. a " < pause > " to signal when a longer break between sentences was necessary).

Another characteristic of human-like conversation found in the data was the gendered nature of the technology due of the use of a female voice and the named character "Alice." In the interview data, clients and staff referred to the caller as "Alice" and "she" as opposed to "the machine" or "it." This provided additional evidence for the phenomenon of anthropomorphism.

These technology affordances—from the voice recordings and the integration of these recordings—can therefore be summarized as enabling the human-like elements of gender and various prosodic features of human speech.

Presentation of Human-like Message Content. The IVR system also modeled human-like conversation through the message content which was substantively informational, interactive, culturally relevant, and affect-laden.

The IVR messages provided various types of information which by nature would typically be provided to clients by bank staff. Some of the information came as push communications, meaning that the content was programmed to provide information according to a predetermined call schedule. Other information was availed by the users through their interaction with the system. Users could use the keypad of their mobile phone to interact with the system such as by dialing a number that corresponded to a number on a menu. For instance, "Alice" might pose a question such as, "Use your mobile handset to tell us if you have set a savings goal for you or your family. Press 1 if you have a savings goal. Press 2 if you don't have a savings goal and want some help with setting one." Responses from "Alice" could take into consideration user-generated content or other sourced information (i.e., bank account information from the core banking system). This question and answer format might feel familiar and human-like to the user, while the input method for responses might feel unfamiliar and machine-like. It is the familiar elements which help the user adapt to the unfamiliar aspects of the technology [6].

The voice messages were designed to contain cultural and emotional relevancy. Because the IVR messages were typically short—less than 1 minute per message—the language used in each message was carefully selected and often relied on short soundbites commonly known or associated with local knowledge. "Alice" started each call with an introduction and greeting which modeled human phone conversation etiquette. One client commented, "Whenever Alice calls, she greets me." Furthermore, some of the messages contained cultural expressions and idioms which helped convey specific meanings using a concise format.

Additional evidence for anthropomorphism came from user language which attributed "Alice" as having carried out certain actions, such as calling, talking, asking questions, and watching them save. Some clients even reported that "Alice" behaved in ways that went beyond the limitations of the IVR system. For instance, some clients described "Alice" as responding to their individual needs, such as calling to follow-up on specific challenges they faced and to ask questions about their specific businesses. Although such personalized interactions were technically infeasible, these findings suggest that an emotional connection with "Alice" was present in some of the users' experiences of anthropomorphism. "Alice" represented a staff member of ABC company for which human relationships between clients and bank staff had been the norm [30].

5 Discussion and Implications

In addressing our research question on how an IVR technology exhibits human-like qualities within the user-technology interaction, our findings highlight various technical aspects that contributed to anthropomorphism in the case of ABC company. Using an affordance lens, we identified four main ways that the IVR system helped facilitate anthropomorphic perceptions among users. In this section, we consider the significance of anthropomorphism for IS scholarship and practice based on our findings.

5.1 Contributions to the IS Affordance Literature

Anthropomorphism, a phenomenon that has historically involved attributing human-like qualities to a vast array of living and non-living subjects, has become increasingly relevant for IS especially due to the growing popularity of robotics and conversational agents. As more cases of anthropomorphism are situated in socio-technical relationships, the field of IS becomes particularly important for shedding light on the technological processes which underpin anthropomorphism. As demonstrated by our research, an affordance lens enables a rigorous methodological study of various technical aspects which underpin anthropomorphic perceptions. This conceptual lens, as we have shown, offers an improved understanding of the role of technology in anthropomorphism.

The IS affordance literature has focused largely on cognitive perceptions, particularly actor intentions, to explain the relationship between technology and affordance actualization (action). This research expands the ways of theorizing affordance perception by highlighting the roles of imagination and affect (emotion) for triggering affordance actualization. As demonstrated by our research, technology affordances can work together to evoke users' imaginations and emotions, fostering anthropomorphic perceptions and outcomes. Building on the work of Nagy and Neff [26], who underscored the importance of the imagination in affordances, this research highlights how the development of *technical anthropomorphism* [7] occurs within a socio-technical relationship between technologies and user perceptions, imagination, and affect.

5.2 Anthropomorphism's Role in Technology Adoption and Diffusion

Anthropomorphism is important for IS because of the significant role it can play in the adoption and diffusion of technology. According to Pfeuffer et al. [6] and Sims et al. [11], anthropomorphism helps users in their adoption of technology. This is because machines can be designed to provide contextually sensitive and seemingly accurate responses which makes the interactions seem more natural and human-like [6]. As found in our analysis, the IVR system contained human-like components which were familiar to users and helped users in their adoption of IVR as a new communications channel at ABC Company.

Understanding the technical aspects underpinning anthropomorphism is important because it can lead to improved business practices. Anthropomorphic design of technologies can help facilitate ease of use in the user experience by bridging the gap between human familiarity and technological unfamiliarity. The phenomenon of anthropomorphism is situated within the socio-technical relationship and can be co-produced by users and systems managers. Anthropomorphic perceptions, imaginations, and affect among users can be cultivated by systems managers through the configuring and reconfiguring of anthropomorphic design. Through our affordance study, we offer practical implications for identifying and developing anthropomorphic design features which can positively impact technology adoption and diffusion.

5.3 The Anthropomorphic Outcome of Relationship Building

Along with helping users bridge a technical knowledge gap, anthropomorphic design can help bridge relational gaps through human affect. Technology companies such as Apple and Google have found that anthropomorphic design features have helped foster social connections and built trust among users [6]. Evidence was found in our case that the human-like elements of the IVR calls helped build the client-institution relationship. When asked how clients felt about ABC Company after getting the IVR messages, many clients expressed a sense of feeling closer to the organization. One client responded, "Good. I feel well connected. Anytime I saw the call, I will < be > like 'eei my people'." Another client responded, "I realized that you think about your customers and that really touched my heart." Based on our analysis, client-institution relationship building took place directly (i.e., with clients perceiving "Alice" as a person with whom they form a relationship) and indirectly (i.e., with clients prompted by the IVR calls to connect with the institution such as by visiting a bank branch). These findings provide implications for how relational value might be generated, cultivated, or otherwise affected by technology artefacts when these artefacts are configured to embed human-like qualities.

6 Conclusion

Through this case study on anthropomorphism and an enfolding of the literature [31], we have demonstrated how technologies can have consequential outcomes. By decomposing anthropomorphism from an affordance perspective, we have demonstrated how affordance theory can help shed light on the technological processes that underpin anthropomorphism. By bringing to the forefront various technical aspects which helped generate (perceivable) human-like elements, we have provided an improved understanding of the role of technology in anthropomorphism.

This research generates new insights into the utility of affordance theory and expands the IS affordance literature by highlighting the roles of imagination and affect for triggering affordance actualization. It also provides a methodological roadmap for other scholars wishing to investigate the relationship between technology affordances and anthropomorphism. These contributions to the IS affordance literature provide an entry point for the topic of anthropomorphism. It is our hope that future research will uncover many more insights on the relationship between technology affordances and anthropomorphism.

References

1. Pozzi, G., Pigni, F. & Vitari, C. (2014). Affordance theory in the IS discipline: a review and synthesis of the literature. In: *Proceedings twentieth Americas conference on information systems*. Savannah.
2. Schuetzler, R. M., Giboney, J. S., Grimes, G. M., & Nunamaker, J. F. (2018). The influence of conversational agent embodiment and conversational relevance on socially desirable responding. *Decision Support Systems, 114,* 94–102.
3. Freud, S. (1930). *Civilization and its discontents.* Norton.

4. Epley, N., Waytz, A., & Cacioppo, J. (2007). On seeing human: A three- factor theory of anthropomorphism. *Psychological Review, 114*(4), 864–886.
5. Urquiza-Haas, E. G., & Kotrschal, K. (2015). The mind behind anthropomorphic thinking: Attribution of mental states to other species. *Animal Behaviour, 109,* 167–176.
6. Pfeuffer, N., Benlian, A., Gimpel, H., & Hinz, O. (2019). Anthropomorphic information systems. *Business Information Systems Engineering, 61*(4), 523–533.
7. Tondu, B. (2012). Anthropomorphism and service humanoid robots: An ambiguous relationship. *Industrial Robot, 39*(6), 609–618.
8. Iossifidis, I., Theis, C., Grote, C., Faubel, C. & Schoner, G. (2004). Anthropomorphism as a pervasive design concept for a robotic assistant. In *Proceeding IEEE international conference on intelligent robots and systems.* (pp. 3465–3472).
9. Taddeucci, D. et al. (2002). Model and implementation of an anthropomorphic system for sensory-motor perception. In*Proceeding of IEEE international conference on intelligent robots and systems* (pp. 1962–1967).
10. Hashimoto, S. et al. (1997). Humanoid robot-development of an information assistant robot Hadaly. In *Proceedings of IEEE international workshop on robot and human communication* (pp. 106–111).
11. Sims, V. K. et al. (2005). Anthropomorphism of robotic forms: A response to affordances? In *Proceeding of human factors and ergonomics society 49th annual meeting* (pp. 1922–1926).
12. Gibson, J. J. (1977). The theory of affordances. In Shaw R., & Bransford (Eds.), Perceiving, acting, and knowing. Towards an ecological psychology. Hoboken, NJ: Wiley.
13. Gibson, J. J. (1986). *The ecological approach to visual perception.* Psychology Press.
14. Markus, M. L., & Silver, M. S. (2008). A foundation for the study of IT effects: A new look at DeSanctis and poole's concepts of structural features and spirit. *Journal of the Association for Information, 9*(10/11), 609.
15. Leonardi, P. M. (2011). When flexible routines meet flexible technologies: Affordance, constraint, and the imbrication of human and material agencies. *MIS quarterly, 35*(1), 147–167.
16. Anderson, C., & Robey, D. (2017). Affordance potency: Explaining the actualization of technology affordances. *Information and Organization, 27*(2), 100–115.
17. Leonardi, P. M. (2013). When does technology use enable network change in organizations? A comparative study of feature use and shared affordances. *MIS quarterly, 37*(3), 749–775.
18. Yoo, Y., Boland, R. J., Lyytinen, K., & Majchrzak, A. (2012). Organizing for innovation in the digitized world. *Organization Science, 23*(5), 1398–1408.
19. Majchrzak, A. & Markus, M. L. Technology affordances and constraints in management information systems (Mis). In *Encyclopedia of management theory*, 5 Social Science Research Network.
20. Majchrzak, A., Markus, M. L., & Wareham, J. (2016). Designing for digital transformation: Lessons for information systems research from the study of ICT and societal challenges. *Management Information Systems Quarterly, 40*(2), 267–277.
21. Robey, D., Anderson, C., & Raymond, B. (2013). Information technology, materiality, and organizational change: A professional odyssey. *Journal of the Association for Information Systems, 14*(7), 379–398.
22. Seidel, S., Recker, J., & vom Brocke, J. (2013). Sensemaking and sustainable practicing: Functional affordances of information systems in green transformations. *Management Information Systems Quarterly, 37*(4), 1275–1299.
23. Volkoff, O., & Strong, D. M. (2013). Critical realism and affordances: theorizing IT-associated organizational change processes. *MISQ, 37*(3), 819–834.
24. Strong, D., et al. (2014). A theory of organization-EHR affordance actualization. *Journal of the Association for Information Systems, 15*(2), 53–85.
25. Stendal, K., Thapa, D. & Lanamaki, A. (2016). Analyzing the concept of affordances in information systems. In *Proceeding of annual hawaii international conference on system sciences 2016-March* (pp. 5270–5277).
26. Nagy, P., & Neff, G. (2015). Imagined affordance: Reconstructing a keyword for communication theory. *Social Media + Society, 1*(2), 1–9.

27. Kardes, F., Cronley, M. & Cline, T. (2015). Consumer behavior. (Cengage Learning).
28. Miles, M. B. & Huberman, A. M. (1994). Qualitative data analysis: An expanded sourcebook. Sage Publications.
29. Yin, R. K. (2003). *Case study research: Design and methods.* Sage Publications.
30. Liebenau, J., Backhouse, J. (1990). *Understanding information: An introduction.* Palgrave.
31. Eisenhardt, K. M. (1989). Building theories from case study research. *Academy of Management Review, 14*(4), 532–550.

How Perceptions of Work-Life Balance and Technology Use Impact upon Creativity in Collaborative Spaces

Carlotta Cochis, Elisa Mattarelli, Fabiola Bertolotti, Anna Chiara Scapolan, Fabrizio Montanari, and Paula Ungureanu

Abstract This paper unpacks creative processes in collaborative spaces (CS). We focus on how the positive resources related to wellbeing and work-life balance derived from working in CS interplay with the use of collaborative technology in affecting individual creativity. We conducted a survey study with individuals working in 27 different CS in Italy. We propose and find a positive relationship between the perceived level of work-life balance satisfaction and individual creativity. Instead we do not find a significant relationship between the frequency of technology mediated interactions with external actors and individual creativity. Furthermore, the relationship between work-life balance and creativity is negatively moderated by technology mediated interactions with external actors. In other words, an intense use of collaborative technology with actors external to the CS can generate perceptions of overload thus making the impact of work-life balance on creativity not significant. We conclude with theoretical and practical implications.

C. Cochis (✉) · F. Bertolotti · P. Ungureanu
Department of Sciences and Methods for Engineering (DISMI), University of Modena and Reggio Emilia, Via Giovanni Amendola, 2, 42122 Reggio Emilia RE, Italy
e-mail: carlotta.cochis@unimore.it

F. Bertolotti
e-mail: fabiola.bertolotti@unimore.it

P. Ungureanu
e-mail: paula.ungureanu@unimore.it

E. Mattarelli
Department of Management, San Jose State University, One Washington Square, San Jose, CA 95112, USA
e-mail: elisa.mattarelli@sjsu.edu

A. C. Scapolan · F. Montanari
Department of Communication and Economics, University of Modena and Reggio Emilia, Viale Antonio Allegri, 9, 42121 Reggio Emilia RE, Italy
e-mail: annachiara.scapolan@unimore.it

F. Montanari
e-mail: fabrizio.montanari@unimore.it

C. Metallo et al. (eds.), *Digital Transformation and Human Behavior*, Lecture Notes in Information Systems and Organisation 37,
https://doi.org/10.1007/978-3-030-47539-0_16

Keywords Creativity · Collaborative space · Collaborative technology · Work-life balance

1 Introduction

Collaborative spaces (CS), such as incubation spaces, social innovation hubs, fab labs, cultural hubs, co-working spaces, and technology parks bring together different actors to favor interactions and knowledge sharing and therefore stimulate creativity in individuals, groups, and organizations. Despite the increased diffusion of collaborative spaces, few studies have empirically investigated what might sustain or impair their outcomes, especially in relation to creativity and innovation. Most of the literature explores how the physical properties of the space (e.g., light, noise levels, furniture, layout, e.g. [1–3]. impact individual or group creativity (for a relevant discussion see Moultrie [4]). Collaborative spaces are designed and built following the assumption that face-to-face contact has a positive impact on the propensity of individuals with different backgrounds to interact and exchange ideas [5], thus favoring the development of a sense of creative community [6]. Moreover, the creation of a collaborative space within organizations or in public spaces is often associated to smart work strategies intended to favor individual well-being and work-life balance. For instance, smart work centers and co-working spaces are set up to enhance temporal and spatial flexibility of workers. In these collaborative spaces a variety of potential users, including public and private employees, free-lancers, entrepreneurs, small and micro-businesses, operate taking advantage of several technological resources and services [7]. The ensuing work flexibility is expected to foster work-life balance, with positive implications for individual and group outcomes.

However, there is mixed evidence that the positive resources provided by collaborative spaces increase creativity and innovation [4, 8]. For example, the open spaces that often characterize collaborative spaces can also reduce interactions and increase coordination costs [9]. Exemplar collaborative spaces, such as science parks, face difficulties in actually bringing together different parties and creating breakthrough innovations [10, 11].

In addition, the literature on collaborative spaces rarely takes into account the fact that CSs are used by individuals and groups on a temporary, part-time or irregular basis. For instance, inhabitants of co-working spaces do not typically spend their full working time within the space [12]. In other words, individuals work in and out of collaborative spaces and typically make an intensive use of collaborative technology to keep in touch with the different groups and individuals they work with (e.g., [13]). The literature on collaborative technology use and distributed work describes the challenges posed by the lack of proximity (e.g., reduced trust and knowledge sharing, increased conflict and coordination costs [14–16]. An intense use of collaborative technology, and the associated possible over-connectivity, could also affect the relationship between work-life balance and creativity. More recently, a few authors have started to recognize that the investigation of the impact of creative spaces on innovation cannot ignore the role played by collaborative technology use in everyday interactions between knowledge workers within and outside of collaborative spaces [7, 13, 17]. However, it is not clear how on-site experiences and technology mediated interactions interplay in creating affordances and constraints for innovation in collaborative spaces.

The objective of this paper is thus to provide a more nuanced view of creative processes within collaborative spaces by explicitly recognizing the fundamental role of collaborative technology use. In particular, we aim to explore how the positive resources related to wellbeing and work-life balance in collaborative spaces interplay with the use of collaborative technology in affecting individual creativity. In the next sections, we first present our hypotheses on the relationship between work-life balance, technology mediated interactions, and individual creativity in collaborative spaces. Then, we present the survey study we conducted in the collaborative spaces of one of the most industrialized regions in Europe. Finally, we illustrate our preliminary results and discuss their theoretical and practical implications.

2 Hypotheses Development

Figure 1 visually synthesizes the hypotheses that we are going to discuss next.

2.1 *The Effect of Work-Life Balance on Creativity in Collaborative Spaces*

Collaborative spaces are designed to offer flexibility to workers in terms of timing (flextime) and location (flexplace) of work (SHRM Foundation 2001). Flextime refers

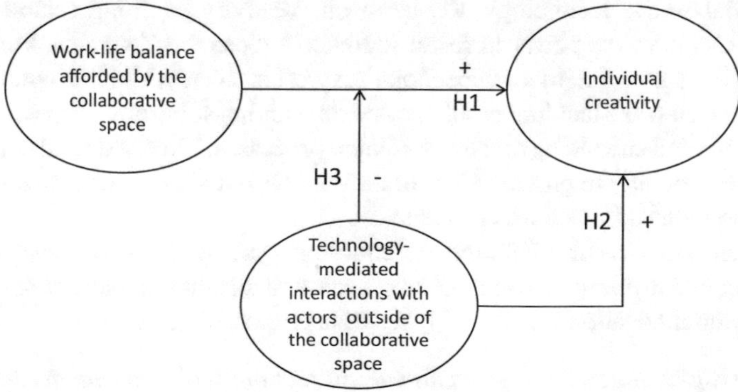

Fig. 1 Hypotheses

to the 'ability of rearranging one's working hours within certain guidelines' (Hill et al. [18], p. 50), while flexplace reflects the degree of control given to workers over where to work [19]. Flextime and flexplace are resources intended to improve individuals' work-life balance (see [20]). Work-life balance refers to situations where individuals are equally satisfied and equally involved in their work and their family role [21]. Perceptions of work-family balance are strengthened by high levels of inter-role facilitation [22] that can be accrued by workers' flexibility in terms of time and space. For instance, the studies of Hammer et al. [23] and Hill and colleagues [18], although not conducted in collaborative spaces, found that the perceived flexibility in terms of time and space was associated to higher levels of work-family balance. Providing CS workers with a positive perception of the ability to manage the interface between work and life domains may lower negative emotions and increase workers' perception of control over their work environment [18, 24–27]. This, in turn, can help individuals to develop more and better ideas. In addition, an increased ability to manage the interface between work and life, thanks to a reduction of stress and perception of overload, has the potential to free individuals' cognitive resources and enhance creativity [28].

We thus hypothesize that the work-life balance experience through the participation in a collaborative space has a positive impact on individual creativity.

H1 The higher the perceived level of work-life balance experience through the CS, the higher the creativity.

2.2 The Effect of Technology Mediated Interactions on Creativity in Collaborative Spaces

While collaborative spaces offer numerous resources and inputs for individuals to develop creative ideas (e.g. [4, 8, 29].), workers do not carry out their tasks only within collaborative spaces and in collaboration with other members of CSs. They also maintain contacts with individuals outside of the collaborative space, making use of collaborative technology. Research on creativity has long established that 'external' ties have the power to foster innovative ideas. For instance, Perry-Smith [30] underlines how external connections may offer to individuals a wide range of ideas to draw on when tackling problems and developing solutions, stimulating divergent thoughts and enhancing creativity-related processes. Thus, external connections are expected not only to provide ideas to individuals but also to enhance and enlarge the way individuals think about problems.

Research on the use of collaborative technology has also shown the positive impact of collaborative technology use in getting access to distant resources that can foster creativity and innovation [15, 31–33]. We thus propose that:

H2 The higher the technology mediated interactions with external actors (outside of the CS), the higher the creativity.

2.3 The Interactive Effect of Work-Life Balance and Technology Mediated Interactions on Creativity in Collaborative Spaces

While collaborative technology is deemed fundamental for the new world of work, it also poses serious challenges for individuals and groups in organizations. Literature on the disruptive effect of technology underlines how collaborative technology increases interruptions and disruptions on individuals' work, burdening them with an increased cognitive load (e.g. [34, 35].). We argue that, if individuals make an intense use of collaborative technology, they will be less able to take advantage of the well-being experience provided by the CS. We base our argument on the fact that a high use of technology may fragment one's attention over multiple resources, tasks and activities, and increase a person's reachability. In relation to the first mechanism, a higher work fragmentation, that has been associated to perceptions of overload [36] can counterbalance the positive effect on creativity coming from a reduced stress and reduced perception of role overload. In addition, the feeling of being always on, engendered by an intense use of collaborative technology, and coupled with the perception of being always available to others' requests, can generate additional perceptions of overload related to the sheer number of requests and the handling of multiple colleagues. Also, this latter mechanism can counterbalance the positive influence on creativity of an enhanced wok life balance provided by the CS. We thus propose that:

H3 The positive relationship between work-life balance and creativity is negatively moderated by technology mediated interactions with external actors.

3 Data and Methods

3.1 Context and Data

Our study is based on data collected thorough a survey sent to individuals working in the collaborative spaces of an industrialized region of Northern Italy. The survey involved all the collaborative spaces located throughout the region, with greater density in larger cities. The survey reached individuals in different types of collaborative spaces, mainly co-working spaces (55% of respondents), business incubators (8%), science parks (20%), and hybrid spaces (17%). Co-working spaces are collaborative spaces that offer a work environment designed to allow users to work in the same way as they do in a traditional office, but shared with other workers, typically professionals, freelancers, or people who travel frequently. Members of co-working spaces work independently but typically share values and have interest in the synergy that can occur when working in contact with other people. In particular, co-working spaces are designed to promote creativity and productivity, thus combining the economic benefits of a shared office with an environment designed to stimulate innovation [7]. Business incubators or business centers are designed to accelerate the development of companies providing a series of resources to support businesses, services, and a network of contacts. Incubators vary in the way they provide their services, their organizational structure, and the type of customers they serve. Science parks are built to support and to promote technological transfer between universities, public organizations and private companies, and often host incubators of university spin-offs. Among the spaces studied, there are spaces that have features common to several types, i.e. hybrid spaces.

We first created a list of all the collaborative spaces of the region by looking at documents and searching on the web. The main keywords used were: “Name of province + collaborative spaces”, “Name of province + incubator”, + “Name of province + innovation hub”, “Name of province + coworking”, “Name of province + creative space". The initial list included 73 spaces. Since some of the spaces of our first list did not seem fully consistent with our definition of collaborative space (e.g. they appeared more as ‘rented office space’ than a co-working space), we called a referent person in those spaces to ask for more information. At the same time, we performed an accurate analysis of their website. As a consequence, we eliminated some of the spaces from our research. Our final list included 66 spaces. We then developed a multi-section questionnaire that explores the individual work-related and social experience within collaborative spaces, focusing on constructs such as work-life balance, face to face interactions, work interactions mediated by technology tools, perceptions of innovation climate, and creativity. The questionnaire was initially created in English and then translated into Italian with a translation–back translation procedure [37].

The survey was submitted to individuals working in all selected collaborative spaces. We got responses from 132 individuals working in 27 collaborative spaces (co-working, scientific park, hybrid, hub, business incubator). The average age of respondents was 37 years (s.d. = 8.9) and the majority of the population sample were males (61%). 67% of the population sample declared themselves “self-employed”. As far as their education is concerned, most of them had a graduate or undergraduate degree (master’s degree 35%, bachelor’s degree 20%), 21% held a high school diploma, 11% had a postgraduate degree master, and 5% had a Ph.D.

3.2 Measures and Analyses

Dependent variable. To measure creativity, we followed Sue-Chan and Hempel’s [38] guidelines and recognized that novelty and usefulness are two components of creativity. Novelty was evaluated asking the degree of agreement on a 7-point Likert scale with the following statements: “I have original ideas”, “I often have a fresh approach to problems”, “I have a unique perspective”, “I generate unprecedented solutions to a problem”, “My solution is often different from traditional ways of doing a task”, “My solution is out-of-the box” [38]. The Cronbach Alpha was 0.89.

Usefulness was evaluated using six items: "I develop solutions focused on the needs of the user, not on the functions of a product", "I produce simple solutions to problems", "I identify opportunities for implementing new products/processes", "I develop adequate plans for the implementation of new ideas", "I integrate multiple perspectives in a constructive manner", "I combine ideas in a constructive manner" [38]. The Cronbach Alpha was 0.85.

Considering that Amabile [39–41], when referring to a product or service, defined creativity as new, appropriate or useful and since most of the studies concerning creativity in organizational field are consistent with the definition of Amabile (e.g. [42, 43].) we studied creativity as a composite measure computed as the average of novelty and usefulness ($\alpha = 0.91$).

Independent variables. We measured the individual experience of work-life balance using the scale of Work-life Balance Satisfaction developed by Valcour [44]. Respondents were asked to express their degree of satisfaction (using a Likert scale, from 1—"very dissatisfied" to 7—"very satisfied") with the following items: "The way you divide your time between work and personal or family life", "The way you divide your attention between work and home", "How well your work-life and your personal or family life fit together", "Your ability to balance the needs of your job with those of your personal or family life", "The opportunity you have to perform your job well and yet be able to perform home-related duties adequately". The Cronbach Alpha was 0.94.

The frequency of work interaction with external actors mediated by technology was collected through a 7-point frequency scale where: 1—"never", 2—"annually or less", 3—"many times per year", 4—"many times per month", 5—"many times per week", 6—"many times per day", 7—"many times per hour", by asking to respondents to answer the following items: "How frequently do you have synchronous, i.e. same time, technology-mediated communication (e.g. phone calls, video conference, instant messaging) with others (e.g., work colleagues or clients who are not members of the CS)?","How frequently do you have asynchronous technology-mediated interactions (e.g. exchange of emails, SMS, voice messages) with others (e.g., work colleagues or clients who are not members of the CS)?". The final variable we used was computed as the mean of the two measures.

Control variables. We used several control variables, i.e. climate for innovation, type of employment, education, gender, and age. The literature on creativity has shown how the climate for innovation promoted in the environment significantly influences the level of creativity of the outputs (e.g. [45, 46].). We, therefore, used the climate for innovation as a control variable. We adapted the scale designed by Scott and Bruce [47] for traditional organizational contexts to the case of a collaborative space and selected 4 meaningful items. In particular the survey asked to report on a 7-point Likert scale the level of agreement with the following statements: "Creativity is encouraged in this CS", "This CS can be described as flexible and continually adapting to change", "This CS is open and responsive to change", "Assistance in developing new ideas is readily available in this CS", "There are adequate resources devoted to innovation in this CS". The Cronbach Alpha was 0.92.

We considered that individuals who are self-employed may be more entrepreneurial and creative. Thus, we controlled for the form of employment with a dummy measure in which 0 = Employed and 1 = Self-Employed. We asked respondents to choose the employment status that best described them from a short list—created with 6 items reflecting the types of employment in Italy—and then merging the six collection items into the two macro categories.

The educational level may impact the ability of individuals to develop new ideas in specialized fields [48]. Thus, the educational level was collected asking to choose one of the following items: 1 secondary school, 2 professional qualification, 3 high school Diploma, 4 bachelor's degree, 5 master's degree, 6 master post degree, 7 Ph.D., 8 others.

We also controlled for gender with a dummy variable (coded 0 = female, 1 = male). Although there is no evidence that gender influences creativity, the literature recognizes that female professionals have sometimes fewer access to resources that can be fundamental to initiate and develop creative ideas [49].

Age may be a proxy of one's experiences. Previous experiences, especially in terms of breadth can be predictors of one's capability to spot new innovative courses of actions. We thus controlled for the age of each respondent, calculated from year of birth (reference year is 2018, when the data collection was completed).

Analyses. The described variables were used to run OLS models. Model 1 and 2 test the direct effects of the control and independent variables on creativity, through a multiple linear regression analysis. In order to test for moderation, we centered our variables. Model 3 tests the role of moderator of the frequency of work interactions with external actors mediated by the use of technologies, through a moderated multiple regression analysis. We used the variance inflation factor (VIF) to rule out issues of multicollinearity. The maximum VIF was 1.14 and the average VIF was 1.10. Therefore, we do not have reasons to suspect that multicollinearity was a problem. We recognize that common method bias may be a problem in our dataset. However, previous studies on individual creativity have extensively tested models where dependent and independent variables came from the same source, since "employees themselves are best suited to report creativity because they are aware of the subtle things they do in their jobs that make them creative" [1, 50, 51].

In addition, we decided to keep self-reported variables considering the particular context of our study. CSs are mostly attended by self-employed professionals and freelancers, and these professions are practiced in multiple and distinct professional fields, for example, computer programming, design, journalism, etc. Given such heterogeneity, it would have been difficult, if not impossible, to identify a common source of external data on individual creativity (for example the number of awards received, or an evaluation provided by a client or another stakeholder).

Also, it would have been difficult, if not impossible, to ask other individuals (e.g. managers, stakeholders) to evaluate the creative performance of our informants, because many of the individuals working in collaborative spaces are freelancers and individual contractors. The managers of the CS do not have specific knowledge in all the occupational fields covered by coworkers, and it is difficult for them to have all the necessary information to judge the creativity of inhabitants of a CS.

We thus followed Ng and Feldman [52], who argue that the presence of individual and/or contextual factors can make the self-assessment of creativity acceptable or more appropriate. According to these authors, using creativity self-assessments is acceptable when the individual's creative changes or performance may not be visible to a third person. To conclude, in agreement with Kaufman [53], although self-assessment is not the best method to collect measures of individual creativity, it is acceptable when the conditions of research make it necessary.

To contain the effect of common method bias, in our questionnaire we separated the independent and dependent variables [54]. To further evaluate the problem, we computed the Harman's single factor test in which all items (measuring latent variables) are loaded into one common factor (Podsakoff et al. 2012). The total variance for a single factor was less than 50% (total variance = 0.32), suggesting that common method bias did not affect your data, hence our results.

4 Results

Table 1 presents a correlation matrix and descriptive statistics for all the measured variables. Not surprisingly for collaborative spaces devoted to innovation, the descriptive statistics show high levels of perceptions of climate for innovation (mean = 5.24, s.d. = 1.39). Above average values were also recorded for the perception of the work-life balance satisfaction level (mean = 4.75, s.d. = 1.33) and for the frequency of work interactions with external actors mediated by technology (mean = 4.91, s.d. = 1.63). In accordance with the hypotheses of our study, creativity is significantly and positively correlated with the level of personal satisfaction about work-life balance, as well as with the climate for innovation. Furthermore, there is also a positive correlation between creativity and frequency of work interaction with external actors mediated by technology.

Table 2 presents the results of the regression analysis. In model 1, only climate for innovation was significantly related to creativity ($\beta = 0.24$; $p < 0.001$). The results of the regression in model 2 show the satisfaction of the individual work-life balance is positively associated to creativity ($\beta = 0.12$; $p < 0.05$), providing support for our first hypothesis, H1: The higher the perceived level of work-life balance experience through the collaborative space, the higher the creativity.

Our second hypothesis pertains to the direct effect of frequency of work interactions with external actors to CS enabled by technology, on creativity. In Model 2 there is not a significant relationship between technology mediated interactions and creativity, suggesting that H2 is not supported.

In model 3 we test the interaction effect between work-life balance experience through the collaborative space and technology mediated interactions with external actors on creativity. Consistently with H3, we find that the moderating effect is negative and significant ($\beta = -0.10$; $p < 0.001$). The plot in Fig. 2 shows that, at low levels of technology mediated interactions with external actors, there is a positive relationship between work-life balance and creativity. However, at high levels of

Table 1 Univariate statistics and pearson correlations among study variables (N = 132)

	Mean	s.d.	Max	Min	1	2	3	4	5	6	7
1. Employed Versus Self- Employed	0.67	0.47	1	0	1.00						
2. Education	4.67	1.40	8	2	0.09	1.00					
3. Gender	0.61	0.49	1	0	−0.01	−0.28**	1.00				
4. Ase	36.65	8.93	59	20	−0.18*	−0.15*	0.01	1.00			
5. Climate for innovation	5.24	1.39	7	1.4	0.21*	−0.06	−0.03	−0.05	1.00		
6. Work life balancc	4.75	1.33	7	1	0.13	−0.09	0.02	0.03	0.20*	1.00	
7. Work interactions (ext.)	4.91	1.63	7	1	−0.08	−0.02	0.01	0.21*	0.19*	0.12	1.00
8. Creativity	5.09	0.91	7	1.58	0.14	−0.11	0.09	0.05	0.38***	0.26**	0.19*

*$p < 0.05$. **$p < 0.01$. ***$p < 0.001$

Table 2 Results of regression analysis

	Model 1			Model 2			Model 3		
	Estimate	Std. Error	*p*-value	Estimate	Std. Error	*p*-value	Estimate	Std. Error	*p*-value
(Intercept)	3.54	0.57	0.00	2.96	0.61	0.00	0.64	0.90	0.48
Employed Versus Self-Employed	0.17	0.16	0.30	0.15	0.16	0.35	0.22	0.16	0.17
Education	−0.04	0.06	0.47	−0.03	0.06	0.54	−0.02	0.05	0.65
Gender	0.16	0.16	0.32	0.15	0.15	0.32	0.19	0.15	0.19
Age	0.01	0.01	0.37	0.00	0.01	0.59	0.01	0.01	0.44
Climate for innovation	0.24^{***}	0.05	0.00	0.20^{***}	0.06	0.00	0.19^{***}	0.05	0.00
Work-life balance				0.12^{*}	0.06	0.04	0.61^{***}	0.16	0.00
Work interactions (ext.)				0.06	0.05	0.19	0.52^{***}	0.14	0.00
Woik-life balance *Work interactions (ext.)							-0.10^{***}	0.03	0.00

$p < 0.001$ '***', $p < 0.01$ '**', $p < 0.05$ '*'.

Table 3 Fit of Regression Models

	Model 1	Model 2	Model 3
Observations	132	132	132
R^2	0.17	0.21	0.28
Adjusted R^2	0.14	0.17	0.23
Residual Std. error	0.85 (df = 126)	0.83 (df = 124)	0.80 (df = 123)
F statistic	5.12 (df = 5; 126)	4.72 (df = 7; 124)	5.90 (df = 8; 123)

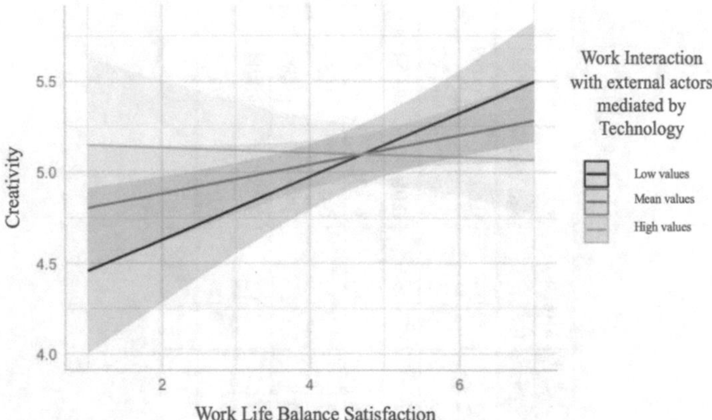

Fig. 2 Plot of interaction effect between technology mediated interactions with external actors and work-life balance on creativity

technology mediated interaction the effect of work-life balance on creativity seems marginal, if not negative.

The frequency of work interactions mediated by collaborative technology was investigated through two separate questions asked to respondents: one referring to synchronous technology interaction work (e.g., via conference calls) and the other related to asynchronous technology interaction work (e.g. through emails). By analyzing the data of the single answers, it is possible to further deepen our analysis. We re-ran models 2 and 3, using synchronous technology mediated interactions with external actors and asynchronous technology mediated interactions with external actors. The results of these four new models replicate the results already discussed of model 2 and model 3 in Table 2, i.e. there is no different effect on the dependent variable if the technologies that mediate the working interaction are synchronous or asynchronous.

5 Discussions and Conclusions

The aim of this paper was to investigate the experience of professionals working in collaborative spaces, such as co-working spaces and innovation labs, created for enhancing individual and group creativity. We wanted to move beyond the common rhetoric that collaborative spaces impact on creativity by increasing individual well-being and by stimulating face to face interactions (e.g., [7, 55]) and recognize the fundamental role played by collaborative technology in such environments. Our study focused on how the positive resources related to work-life balance in collaborative spaces interplay with the use of collaborative technology in affecting individual creativity.

Our survey analysis, conducted in 27 collaborative spaces in a highly industrialized area of Northern Italy, provides support for our theorizing. In particular, we first hypothesized and found that perceptions of work-life balance are positively associated to increased creativity in collaborative spaces. These results are in accordance with previous literature that has linked the implications of a positive interface between work and life domains to individual success in organizations [56]. Most of the literature on work-life balance, however, is based on empirical data collected in traditional work contexts, e.g. large companies, public organizations, small and medium enterprises [57], and often does not take into account the changing nature of the workplace. Research has recently started to address the issue of work-life balance in relation to telework, smart work, and flexible work arrangements (e.g., [58, 59]). Our research contributes to this emerging debate by showing the importance of work-life balance for innovation in non-traditional contexts, in particular in collaborative spaces.

Second, we hypothesized that technology mediated interactions with actors outside of the CS are related to increased creativity. In CSs multiple opportunities are offered to interact face to face with other occupants of the space, e.g. meetings, social events, spatial features. Technology mediated interactions are fundamental to get in, or maintain, interaction with external actors. Such external interactions are instrumental to get new ideas, to access resources, and to be exposed to different points of view. However, contrary to our expectations, our second hypothesis was not supported because we did not find a significant effect for the relationship between the aggregated measure of technology mediated interactions and creativity and the same happened when we distinguished between synchronous and asynchronous technology use.

The role and implications of technology-mediated interactions (both synchronous and asynchronous) are further elucidated by the results of our third hypothesis that shows how the effect of work-life balance on creativity is negatively moderated by the frequency of technology mediated interactions with external actors. Thus, our results point out that the ability to exploit the positive resources developed thanks to the experience in CS (in our case in terms of enhanced work-life balance afforded by increase work flexibility) is contingent to the way individuals make use of other types of resources (in our case collaborative technology). Requests and interactions (both in real time or deferrable), arguably through an increase in the perception of role overload, may reduce the positive implications of the wellbeing offered by a collaborative space to creativity, thus providing a more nuanced understanding of how creative processes play out in new flexible and boundaryless workplaces. These results also contribute to understand the implications of collaborative technology on innovative and creative work in general, and in collaborative spaces in particular. Interestingly, very few organizational scholars have specifically taken into account the role of technology mediated interactions on creativity (see Burkhardt et al. [60] for a meaningful example) and none have considered the diverse effects provided by different types of mediated interactions. We thus contribute to this emerging field.

This work offers practical implications for designers, managers, and workers of collaborative spaces. First, when designing collaborative spaces, architects and designers should consider the sociotechnical nature of a collaborative space. They should design the physical characteristics of the space taking into account (and possibly integrating within their design) the role played by collaborative technology. Managers of collaborative spaces should be aware of the fundamental role played by collaborative technology in fostering innovation results. Even if we know that collaborative spaces allowing spontaneous interactions may favor unexpected forms of knowledge exchanges also between people belonging to different communities [61], space managers should not just focus on fostering face to face interactions within the space, by also offer additional opportunities for interactions with external actors. For instance, they could institute webinars or offer specific platforms that could be accessed both by members of the space as well as by external constituencies. However, in doing so, they should be careful in not overwhelming individuals with technologies that require them to be always 'on'. Finally, workers should recognize that the wellbeing guaranteed by the space may lead to their increased creativity only when they enact certain interaction patterns. Enacting a targeted and 'regulated' use of collaborative technologies with actors outside of the space may be a strategy to get the best out of the flexibility offered by a collaborative space.

This work is not, of course, without limitations. We collected our data in a limited number of spaces and with a limited number of respondents. Although the context of our data collection (a highly industrialized area) is extremely relevant and representative of knowledge intensive contexts, future work should replicate and extend our study in other contexts. The dataset we have used relies on data coming from a single source. Although we have ruled out possible issues related to common method bias, future studies should explore ways to assess creativity outcomes through other sources (expert evaluations, documents, client's evaluations). Although it is not easy to obtain multi-sources for the detection of individual creativity in the context examined, and, as already discussed in the methodology, there is a theoretical motivation for using self-assessment to measure creativity, we believe it is useful to try to integrate the study with additional measures of creativity coming from other sources, such as opinions of clients and supervisors of freelances or peers. As an alternative measure, it could be interesting to develop a new measure of self-assessment of creativity that incorporates assessments from freelances at different points in time.

Our paper has started to explore the different roles played by different technologies on the work experiences of inhabitants of collaborative spaces. We believe more efforts should be put in place to distinguish the different uses and affordances of collaborative technology in collaborative spaces, for instance by distinguishing different type of technology (e.g., social media, instant messaging system), the provider of the technology (e.g., the individual worker, the collaborative space), and the multiple interpretations that different professionals may develop about the use of a technology (e.g., designers, engineers, creative workers).

Another direction for future research could be investigating whether the type of profession may differentially affect creativity processes in the context of CSs. We propose to distinguish professions into macro-categories, for instance technology-oriented professions and non-technology-oriented professions. This way we can create a dummy variable that could act as a control variable for the professional background and test if it plays a direct or moderating role.

Another possible avenue could be to investigate how collaborative spaces can reduce the negative effect of technology in relation to the work-life balance of the individual. Indeed, these spaces can offer physical and mental boundaries to the worker, thanks to which workers could better manage their online status, thus becoming more focused on their task, instead of being continually distracted by the invasiveness of technology.

References

1. Dul, J., Ceylan, C., & Jaspers, F. (2011). Knowledge workers' creativity and the role of the physical work environment. *Human Resource Management, 50,* 715–734.
2. Kristensen, T. (2004). The physical context of creativity. *Creativity and Innovation Management, 13,* 89–96.
3. Haner, U. E. (2005). Spaces for creativity and innovation in two established organizations. *Creativity and Innovation Management, 14,* 288–298.
4. Moultrie, J., Nilsson, M., Dissel, M., Haner, U. E., Janssen, S., & Van Der Lugt, R. (2007). Innovation spaces: Towards a framework for understanding the role of the physical environment in innovation. *Creativity and Innovation Management, 16,* 53–65.
5. Oksanen, K., & Ståhle, P. (2013). Physical environment as a source for innovation: Investigating the attributes of innovative space. *Journal of Knowledge Management, 17,* 815–827.
6. Garrett, L. E., Spreitzer, G. M., & Bacevice, P. A. (2017). Co-constructing a sense of community at work: The emergence of community in coworking spaces. *Organization Studies, 38,* 821–842.
7. Errichiello, L., & Pianese, T. (2018). Smart work centers as "creative workspaces" for remote employees. *CERN IdeaSquare Journal of Experimental Innovation, 2,* 14–21.
8. Vignoli, M., Mattarelli, E., & Mäkinen, S. J. (2018). Experimenting with innovation in creative spaces. *CERN IdeaSquare Journal of Experimental Innovation, 2*(1), 1–2.
9. Pearce, B., & Hinds, P. (2018). How to make sure your people won't hate your new open office plan. *Harvard Business Review.*
10. Skelcher, C., Mathur, N., & Smith, M. (2005). The public governance of collaborative spaces: Discourse, design and democracy. *Public Administration, 83,* 573–596.
11. Ungureanu, P., Bertolotti, F., & Macri, D. (2018). Brokers or platforms? A longitudinal study of how hybrid interorganizational partnerships for regional innovation deal with VUCA environments. *European Journal of Innovation Management, 21,* 636–671.
12. Spinuzzi, C. (2012). Working alone together: Coworking as emergent collaborative activity. *Journal of Business and Technical Communication, 26,* 399–441.

13. Ungureanu, P., Cochis, C., Rodighiero, S., Bertolotti, F., Mattarelli, E., Montanari, F., et al. (2018). Innovating onsite or coordinating online? An exploration of how knowledge practices shape the onsite and online collaboration interplay across the lifecycle of collaborative communities. *CERN IdeaSquare Journal of Experimental Innovation, 2,* 22–29.
14. Crisp, C. B., & Jarvenpaa, S. L. (2013). Swift trust in global virtual teams. *Journal of Personnel Psychology.*
15. Gupta, A., Mattarelli, E., Seshasai, S., & Broschak, J. (2009). Use of collaborative technologies and knowledge sharing in co-located and distributed teams: Towards the 24-h knowledge factory. *The Journal of Strategic Information Systems, 18,* 147–161.
16. Poliandri, V., Mattarelli, E., Bertolotti, F., Tagliaventi, M. R., Grandi, A. (2014). Integrating knowledge through consistency between leadership and technology in distributed teams. In *Academy of management proceedings. academy of management briarcliff manor* (pp. 10510, 15767), NY.
17. Cirella, S., & Yström, A. (2018). Creativity and science parks: More than just a physical platform? *CERN IdeaSquare Journal of Experimental Innovation, 2,* 8–13.
18. Hill, E. J., Hawkins, A. J., Ferris, M., & Weitzman, M. (2001). Finding an extra day a week: The positive influence of perceived job flexibility on work and family life balance. *Family Relations, 50,* 49–58.
19. Shockley, K. M., & Allen, T. D. (2007). When flexibility helps: Another look at the availability of flexible work arrangements and work–family conflict. *Journal of Vocational Behavior, 71,* 479–493.
20. Beauregard, T. A., & Henry, L. C. (2009). Making the link between work-life balance practices and organizational performance. *Human Resource Management Review, 19,* 9–22.
21. Greenhaus, J. H., Collins, K. M., & Shaw, J. D. (2003). The relation between work–family balance and quality of life. *Journal of Vocational Behavior, 63,* 510–531.
22. Frone, M. R. (2003). Work-family balance. *Handbook of Occupational Health Psychology, 7,* 143–162.
23. Hammer, L. B., Allen, E., & Grigsby, T. D. (1997). Work–family conflict in dual-earner couples: Within-individual and crossover effects of work and family. *Journal of Vocational Behavior, 50,* 185–203.
24. Anderson, S. E., Coffey, B. S., & Byerly, R. T. (2002). Formal organizational initiatives and informal workplace practices: Links to work-family conflict and job-related outcomes. *Journal of Management, 28,* 787–810.
25. Kossek, E. E., & Ozeki, C. (1999). Bridging the work-family policy and productivity gap: A literature review. *Community, Work & Family, 2,* 7–32.
26. Saltzstein, A. L., Ting, Y., & Saltzstein, G. H. (2001). Work-family balance and job satisfaction: The impact of family-friendly policies on attitudes of federal government employees. *Public Administration Review, 61,* 452–467.
27. Thomas, L. T., & Ganster, D. C. (1995). Impact of family-supportive work variables on work-family conflict and strain: A control perspective. *Journal of Applied Psychology, 80,* 6.
28. Florida, R., & Goodnight, J. (2005). Managing for creativity. *Harvard Business Review, 83,* 124.
29. Capdevila, I. (2015). Co-working spaces and the localised dynamics of innovation in Barcelona. *International Journal of Innovation Management, 19,* 1540004.
30. Perry-Smith, J. E. (2006). Social yet creative: The role of social relationships in facilitating individual creativity. *Academy of Management Journal, 49,* 85–101.
31. Malhotra, A., Majchrzak, A., Carman, R., & Lott V. (2001). Radical innovation without collocation: A case study at Boeing-Rocketdyne. *MIS quarterly* 229–249.
32. Yoo, Y., Henfridsson, O., & Lyytinen, K. (2010). Research commentary—the new organizing logic of digital innovation: An agenda for information systems research. *Information Systems Research, 21,* 724–735.
33. Standing, C., & Kiniti, S. (2011). How can organizations use wikis for innovation? *Technovation, 31,* 287–295.

34. Speier, C., Valacich, J. S., & Vessey, I. (1999). The influence of task interruption on individual decision making: An information overload perspective. *Decision Sciences, 30,* 337–360.
35. Karr-Wisniewski, P., & Lu, Y. (2010). When more is too much: Operationalizing technology overload and exploring its impact on knowledge worker productivity. *Computers in Human Behavior, 26,* 1061–1072.
36. Zika-Viktorsson, A., Sundström, P., & Engwall, M. (2006). Project overload: An exploratory study of work and management in multi-project settings. *International Journal of Project Management, 24,* 385–394.
37. Brislin, L., & Lonner, W. (1973). *Thorndike Cross Cultural Research Methods.* New York: John Wiley and Sons.
38. Sue-Chan, C., & Hempel, P. S. (2016). The creativity-performance relationship: How rewarding creativity moderates the expression of creativity. *Human Resource Management, 55,* 637–653.
39. Amabile, T. M. (1982). Social psychology of creativity: A consensual assessment technique. *Journal of Personality and Social Psychology, 43,* 997.
40. Amabile, T. M. (1983). The social psychology of creativity: A componential conceptualization. *Journal of Personality and Social Psychology, 45,* 357.
41. Amabile, T. M. (1988). A model of creativity and innovation in organizations. *Research in Organizational Behavior, 10,* 123–167.
42. Zhou, J., & George, J. M. (2001). When job dissatisfaction leads to creativity: Encouraging the expression of voice. *Academy of Management Journal, 44,* 682–696.
43. Oldham, G. R., & Cummings, A. (1996). Employee creativity: Personal and contextual factors at work. *Academy of Management Journal, 39,* 607–634.
44. Valcour, M. (2007). Work-based resources as moderators of the relationship between work hours and satisfaction with work-family balance. *Journal of Applied Psychology, 92,* 1512.
45. West M. A. (1990). The social psychology of innovation in groups.
46. Eisenbeiss, S. A., Van Knippenberg, D., & Boerner, S. (2008). Transformational leadership and team innovation: Integrating team climate principles. *Journal of Applied Psychology, 93,* 1438.
47. Scott, S. G., & Bruce, R. A. (1994). Determinants of innovative behavior: A path model of individual innovation in the workplace. *Academy of Management Journal, 37,* 580–607.
48. Fasko, D. (2001). Education and Creativity. *Creativity Research Journal, 13,* 317–327.
49. Ibarra H. (1992). Homophily and differential returns: Sex differences in network structure and access in an advertising firm. *Administrative Science Quarterly* 422–447.
50. Baer, M. (2012). Putting creativity to work: The implementation of creative ideas in organizations. *Academy of Management Journal, 55,* 1102–1119.
51. Shalley, C. E., Gilson, L. L., & Blum, T. C. (2009). Interactive effects of growth need strength, work context, and job complexity on self-reported creative performance. *Academy of Management Journal, 52,* 489–505.
52. Ng, T. W., & Feldman, D. C. (2012). A comparison of self-ratings and non-self-report measures of employee creativity. *Human Relations, 65,* 1021–1047.
53. Kaufman, J. C. (2019). Self-assessments of creativity: Not ideal, but better than you think. *Psychology of Aesthetics, Creativity, and the Arts, 13,* 187.
54. Podsakoff, P. M., Mackenzie, S. B., Lee, J.-Y., & Podsakoff, N. P. (2003). Common method biases in behavioral research: A critical review of the literature and recommended remedies. *Journal of Applied Psychology, 88,* 879.
55. Khazanchi, S., Sprinkle, T. A., Masterson, S. S., & Tong, N. (2018). A spatial model of work relationships: The relationship-building and relationship-straining effects of workspace design. *Academy of Management Review, 43,* 590–609.
56. Wayne, J. H., Butts, M. M., Casper, W. J., & Allen, T. D. (2017). In search of balance: A conceptual and empirical integration of multiple meanings of work–family balance. *Personnel Psychology, 70,* 167–210.
57. Johari, J., Yean, T. F., & Tjik, Z. Z. I. (2018). Autonomy, workload, work-life balance and job performance among teachers. *International Journal of Educational Management, 32,* 107–120.

58. Hilbrecht, M., Shaw, S. M., Johnson, L. C., & Andrey, J. (2008). 'I'm home for the kids': Contradictory implications for work–life balance of teleworking mothers. *Gender, Work & Organization, 15,* 454–476.
59. Holland, P., & Bardoel, A. (2016). The impact of technology on work in the twenty-first century: Exploring the smart and dark side. In Taylor & Francis.
60. Burkhardt, J.-M., & Lubart, T. (2010). Creativity in the age of emerging technology: Some issues and perspectives in 2010. *Creativity and Innovation Management, 19,* 160–166.
61. Ungureanu, P., & Bertolotti, F. (2018). Building and breaching boundaries at once: An exploration of how management academics and practitioners perform boundary work in executive classrooms. *Academy of Management Learning & Education, 17*(4), 425–452.

Interaction-Context Schema: A Proposed Model to Support Interaction Analysis in Small and Medium Enterprises

Michele Cipriano and Peter Bednar

Abstract Information Systems Interactions are a pivotal point in developing an understanding of a socio-technical system. From this perspective, Information Systems could be defined as the cooperation, coexistence and integration of a socio-technical approach with the social aspect. This research investigates how people communicate in a business and how this is likely to support knowledge sharing practices. Given this, the real-work practices that drive a business emphasise the interactions. This paper proposes an "Interaction-Context" schema, which factors in the interactions sparked by several stakeholders that occurs in different areas of interest of a business. Therefore, a multi-proposal expanded analysis of interactions which seek to attends diverse purposes in different contexts. The schema envisages three categories to classify the interaction. Similarly, there are three contexts which distinguish the orientation. Hence, the interplay between interactions, technology and ICT competencies, which support or develop a business, underpin the Proposed Model "Interaction-Context" schema.

Keywords Interaction analysis · ICT maturity · Organisational excellence · SMEs · Knowledge sharing · Real-work practices

M. Cipriano (✉) · P. Bednar
University of Portsmouth, Hampshire UKJ33, Portsmouth, UK
e-mail: michele.cipriano@unich.it

P. Bednar
e-mail: peter.bednar@port.ac.uk

M. Cipriano
Università degli Studi di Salerno, Fisciano, Italy

P. Bednar
Lund University, Lund, SE, Sweden

C. Metallo et al. (eds.), *Digital Transformation and Human Behavior*, Lecture Notes in Information Systems and Organisation 37,
https://doi.org/10.1007/978-3-030-47539-0_17

1 Introduction

The "*Interaction-Context*" schema presented in this study emphasises a practical proposition useful to analyse interactions in context. The authors have developed the Proposed Model to support analysts as well as researcher to better understand interactions which underpin real-work practices. The schema follows up a fore-runner study which has been a "Pre-Analysis" originated on a large-scale project. This large-scale project involved different stakeholders as well as a research team-group. In addition, approximatively 40 companies and at least three employees for each have constituted the subject of the project. Therefore, 46 trainee junior analysts have collaborated to the data collection (questionnaire) in order to gather information consequentially analysed (Raw-data). After that, this section briefly presents approaches and perspectives which underpin this study.

Digital innovation, analytics, big data and AI, are emerging areas which results from the ubiquity of IT and its relevance to business and society. Consequently, in the same way, information systems are involved in these innovations and progressively developing changes. The authors considered this aspect through the conception of the social-technical continuum, where the diverse nature of relationships between the social and the technical take place, as well as the intertwining of the instrumental and humanistic outcomes [1]. In addition, the proposal accommodates Social Practice Design [2], where innovation and organizational changes are considered in the context of the development of information systems.

The long-term ambition of the authors is to emphasize a multi-proposal perspective of interaction analysis, in order to support knowledge and management in practice. The analysis of the interaction is dependent on the adoption and understanding of socio-technical systems related to the organizations. Indeed, the interactions produced by the stakeholders and different environments involved, define the flow of information which underpin an information system. Given this, the analysis of interactions aims to investigate the interplay of communication, which flow within a system.

A better understanding of how people communicate is likely to support knowledge management and create competitive advantage. It is noteworthy that an improved understanding of the implications and the complexity of real work practices and related interactions, support a business develop and help people to achieve a more efficient information flow. However, professional development, as a consequence of the understanding of collaborative work practices as well as learning from each other, help people to make better decisions. In other words, organizations could benefit from fine-tuning their knowledge management systems to achieve business excellence. In addition, the authors argue that employees' knowledge of their work is of considerable relevance. Employees are acknowledged as experts in the experience of the business context in practice. If the business is consequence of the employees' work, we cannot afford to ignore their knowledge of activities in context.

The multi-proposal perspective comes from the consideration of these assumptions and encompasses different points of views. Actually, the research presented in this study aims to offer a different approach to understanding interactions in context rather than single viewpoints. Indeed, the nature of interactions entails an understanding of different context. The "joined perspectives" which underpin the paper, and support an understanding of interactions, are:

- Activities, actions, communications.
- Areas and levels of interaction.
- ICT maturity, technologies and competences.
- Coexistence and interplay of systems.
- Contexts.
- Diversification of businesses, company culture.
- Real-work practices.
- Employee's perspective.
- Socio-Technical perspective.

Hence, the authors have formulated an "*Interaction-Context*" schema as a practical proposition for the multi-proposal perspective described above. The start point of the "*Interaction-Context*" schema is to facilitate the understanding of interactions through an enriched analysis of interactions. Therefore, the schema seeks to identify the interaction among the coexistent systems which belong to; meanwhile, has special consideration on the ICT system. The authors pay significant attention to the impact of an ICT system on a business, as well as how the information systems could be affected. The logical of the ICT system can be evaluated in a socio-technical perspective, the authors therefore, insist on highlighting the strong connections to the study of interactions. Indeed, the "*Interaction-Context*" schema has also been developed to facilitate the categorization of the existing links between technologies and competencies required from the adoption of an ICT system that support these specific interactions, rather than others business activities.

The "*Interaction-Context*" schema consists of "Categorization" and subsequent "Contextualization" of interactions. The three main categories constitute a typology: "Coordination", "Operation", and "Control". These three contexts can be broken down into an interaction orientation: "Business", "Local" or "Individual".

It is also noteworthy that context analysis is a prerequisite when the dynamism of system activity and process flow of an organization viewed as a knowledge community is analysed [3]. The "*Interaction-Context*" schema, which belongs to the multi-proposal perspective, could afford an extended realization of the interactions that happen inside a business in order to define their reasons and purposes. Furthermore, the "*Interaction-Context*" schema helps both the researcher and business analyst to better understand the information systems that characterize a business, where significant interactions could support the information flow between different stakeholders involved. Moreover, the "*Interaction-Context*" schema supports analysis through the association of technologies and skills within each area of concern, in terms of interactions, core activities and business.

The next section presents the background to the work, and a brief overview of the research. The "Methodology" section that follow, outlines the different methods. In this research the authors have token an organic approach. The "Methodology" section will therefore provide a breakdown of the work done. In depth, two different methods divide the study presented in this paper into "Pre-analysis" and "Proposed Model". The Authors envisage that the "Pre-analysis" section represents the roots of the "Proposed Model" section, which has been developed until the focus changed to the development of the "*Interaction-Context*" schema (Proposed Model).

However, as a forerunner study, the "Pre-analysis" section outlines an empirical study related to interaction analysis. In this section, the authors highlight some of the findings from the interaction analysis conducted on several businesses, which aim to prepare the ground for the "Proposed Model". Additionally, the dataset analysed belongs to a large-scale project, which will be widely discussed in the specific methods section.

The "Proposed Model" section presents the core proposition of this paper. Indeed, the "*Interaction-Context*" schema emphasizes the "Pre-analysis" results throughout, using a graphical representation which seeks to address and resolve the issues presented in the study. Table 2 "Issues" and Table 3 "Reflections" of "Pre-analysis" section presents various considerations that have afforded the developed of the schema. It is worth noting that, the results (Findings 1,2,3,4) of "Pre-analysis" section supports the schema rationale and have triggered the abductive considerations to "Proposed Model" section. The authors have outlined four major "Abductive-Considerations" (5.1 Considerations from an Interaction Perspective, 5.2 Considerations from a Context Perspective, 5.3 Considerations from a Multiple Perspective, 5.4 Example Drawing on our Trial Study Case) at the end of Sect. 5 "Proposed Model", which seek to emphasize the multi-proposal perspective underpinned in the paper.

In the "Conclusion", areas of future research are suggested and included, as well as the strengths and weaknesses of the "*Interaction-Context*" schema (Proposed Model).

2 Background

"*The term interaction broadly encompasses all the exchanges needed to coordinate the relevant actors, resources, and activities*" [4]. Every organization consists of the people, the technical system and the environment [5] where a socio-technical approach supports the organization to establish an effective balance between those areas. A socio-technical approach is one that recognizes the interaction of technology and people and produces work systems that are both technically efficient and have social characteristics that lead to high job satisfaction [6]. Mumford defined the objective of the socio-technical approach as "*The joint optimization of the social and technical systems*" [7]. Mumford argued that humans' needs must not be forgotten when technical systems are introduced,instead, they should have more or at least the same value [7]. The socio-technical perspective explores one of the most significant interactions within a system: People and technologies.

People and technologies represent two interdependent systems. The intersection of them is the communication system that uses artefacts or tools for mutual collaboration. Bednar states that the essence of the information system lies in the way people use technology to support an action: "*Given that information systems link human activity systems and ICT systems, they should be considered as classic examples of socio-technical systems*" [8].

The development of technologies inside companies requires organizational changes and a re-design of the Human Activity System (HAS). Given this direct connection between interactions and systems, the changes made to a system also cause changes at the interaction level. Organized activities entail coordination that becomes achievable from a perspective of soft system development. The authors in this study suggest that, in order to facilitate the changes, the relationships between systems (ICT based or not) and interaction levels (intensity, stakeholders, business areas involved) need first to be well identified.

The innovation and the development of new or different technologies in a business related to the ICT system can be a double-edged sword. From a holistic approach, the change impacts on the whole business. For example, gaps could occur as a consequence of competencies and skills required from the system to the stakeholders. Gaps in ICT competences could be a significant weakness for a business when it comes to supporting effective quality communication among stakeholders. In practice, improved understanding also comes from the identification of ICT based practices, which are underpinned by the different levels and areas of interaction. Hence, these practices affect the exchange of information inside an organization. The development of an effective ICT system is one of the key factors supporting knowledge management. However, if the enterprise can manage development, benefits include competitive advantage to a firm.

Pham states that employees' usage of IT applications and user-friendly IT systems were found to significantly affect employee knowledge-sharing capabilities in the organizations [9]. Therefore, an organization should develop appropriate policies to support the information system, which could be identified through the "ICT maturity" level [10]. It is noteworthy that ICT competencies have to increase to overcome communications difficulties. An understanding of cultural, social, economic, and technological factors, which influence the adoption and diffusion of ICT systems are required to achieve high levels of global competitiveness [11]. Therefore, the authors contend that an improved understanding of context should consider the industry in which the SMEs operate and the size of the firm. "*Knowledge has become an essential resource that organizations need to manage effectively to get their competitive advantage and develop steadily*" [12].

Due to these factors, a company should not focus solely on the technical side but also on the managerial side. For this reason, them depend on both social and technical skills. Each organization chooses its own set of combinations amongst competences and ICT skills, which could originate inside or outside (outsourcing) the organization [8]. Ergo, those combinations reflect the context and the levels of interaction established for the communication across the company. Hence, ICT maturity is the state of an enterprise when it achieves the full development state in using ICT to support its business [12]. The Interactions associated with the efficiency of a high level of ICT maturity, are relying on the adoption and understanding of the socio-technical system related to the organization [13].

Since this study addresses two distinct subjects of interest considered hand in hand, an improved understanding involves on one side the investigation of interactions, and on the other the ICT maturity. Onward, the Authors noted two studies present in the literature which fits the proposition above-mentioned: "A non-linear, interaction-based development model for e-business" [4], and, "Socio-Technical Toolbox" [8].

As a deduction, "A non-linear, interaction-based development model for e-business" [4], allows analyst to split-up the information system of a business into different areas of operations where the interactions take place. The authors argue in their preposition that the analysis of interactions should carry on through the identification and breaking down of the core activity of business within different phases. Consequently, the various stages in which the economic activity is achieved, defines the interactions, the actors involved, and the self-same core activities. Indeed, the authors identified in their model [4] three major areas of interactions ("Input", "Core", "Output"), which help analysts to place interaction between one of those. Then, the level of general interaction ("Basic", "Low", "Medium", "High", "Complete") is defined through a bottom-up approach depending on the interplay of interactions amongst the areas previously identified.

Instead, The Socio-Technical Toolbox [8] is a collection of socio-technical methods supporting a human-focus analysis that reflects on social and technical factors in the design of organizational systems. The Socio-Technical Toolbox (STT) promotes the understanding of the business practices of a company focusing on learning about sustainability. Furthermore, STT originate on the socio-technical concepts determined by Edin Mumford [6, 7]. STT comprise thirty different types of methods of analysis and is divided approximately into eight main analytical spaces. Five different types of questionnaires support these methods, one of these types is the interaction questionnaires. This interaction questionnaire ends within a graphic representation (ICT-Related Competencies matrix [8], which support the understanding and investigation of technologies and ICT skills implemented by a company.

The authors have developed the "*Interaction-Context*" schema (Proposed Model) in order to offer a combined analysis' approach, which relays on the previously cited studies: "A non-linear, interaction-based development model for e-business" [4], and "Socio-Technical Toolbox" (in particular in the Sect. 2E. Interaction Analysis "ICT-Related Competencies" matrix, p.53) [8]. The "*Interaction-Context*" schema could support a multi-proposal analysis which underpins a joined understanding of different subjects of interest.

3 Methodology

The authors addressed this study through an organic approach. It is noteworthy that the original purpose of this research was to carry out an interaction analysis throughout a qualitative approach. "What potential do SMEs have in terms of ICT competencies required to develop organizational excellence?" was the first research question. Interactions analysis is the major purpose which underpins this research; however, the authors' focus ultimately moved to the development of the "*Interaction-Context*" schema. Since the authors went along open-ended investigations, were not aware of the potential findings achieved. For this reason, two different but strictly linked studies divide the research.

Henceforth, the authors claim two different main subjects of the research. "Pre-analysis" section describes the forerunner study on interaction analysis. Instead, "Proposed Model" section presents the primary purpose of this paper: the "*Interaction-Context*" schema. In addition, this distinction begins in this section where Method 1 explains approaches and the dataset in which interaction analysis rely on (Pre-analysis); while Method 2 presents approaches and foundation of the "*Interaction-Context*" schema (Proposed Model).

3.1 Method 1

As mentioned above, interactions analysis was the first purpose of this research; therefore, the authors developed a forerunner interaction analysis (Pre-analysis) which originated on a large scale project. This large-scale project is relying on the Socio-Technical Toolbox [8]. In other words, this large-scale project represents a practical implementation of the methods of analysis which underpin the STT. Hence, the large-scale project involved several people between trainee junior analysts and business analysts, which have encompassed a teamwork. Approximately 46 trainee junior analysts collaborated on this project, which started in October 2018 and ran until Easter (April 2019). Each trainee analyst worked in different business and undertook more than ten interviews over this period, sometimes one per week. Each conversation took approximately half an hour. Some interviews were semi-structured, and all the questionnaires run-out during the interviews, (as a reminder to the readers, five different types of questionnaire support the methods presented in the STT).

Additionally, in each company, the trainee junior analyst interviewed at least three people and the same three people throughout the project. One of these employees has been the main focus of this company. This employee has been interviewed often and in great detail about their job, unlike the other two. However, the interactions questionnaire solely, and related data underpin the forerunner study developed in the "Pre-analysis" section. Employees from approximately forty companies participated in the interaction interview. Trainee junior analysts also collected this interaction dataset (Raw-data, "Dataset-one") which were used to develop the analysis. In addition, the questionnaires have a predefined structure and were standardized. Indeed, those questionnaires have five major areas of interest. Since this research focuses on interaction analysis, the authors used the data concerning the interaction area only.

It is worth notice that the interaction area treated in the STT [8] finds own foundation on "A non-linear, interaction-based development model for e-business" [4]. Five subareas develop the interaction questionnaire. In addition, the relationships in an information system which are reflecting the interactions between the different areas are the self-same foundations of this questionnaire. Therefore, four subareas are representing the areas which underpin these relationships, which are: "Output Interaction Area", "Core Interaction Area", "Input Interaction Area", "Interaction across the board" [8]. The fifth and last subarea "ICTs competences" [8] identify the relationships between the different areas through the analysis of the enterprise' ICT system. This subarea supports the investigation of competences and technologies developed in businesses, related to an internal or external (outsourcing) provision: "ICT In-house", "ICT External", "Competencies External", "Competencies In-house" [8]. Moreover, "ICTs competences" subarea seeks to helps analysts to define a "Combinations" (A, B, C, D) as a final mark point of synthesis of that analysis.

Furthermore, an unobstructed view of the dataset analysed follows below. The dataset consisted of three files, the primary "Raw-data" (Dataset-one), which was a collection of questionnaires. These questionnaires were submitted directly at least to three employees for each different company. Since the questionnaires investigated several types of analysis, one of the interviews was controlled and lead by questionnaire (interaction questionnaire) through specific questions. The interaction questionnaires were developed to investigate the different areas of interaction, as well as analysing ICT maturity. While trainee junior analyst did the questionnaires, the interviews were conducted by the trainees through a semi-structured approach. The role or task of the interviewed is not specified within the business. The interaction questionnaire comprises at least two or at most four questions per each interaction areas defined above. The Table 1 below presents some examples of the interaction questionnaire outlined in the Socio-Technical Toolbox (Interaction Questionnaire, pp. 111–112) [8].

The second file was a collection of "Interaction reports" (Dataset-two). The trainee junior analysts developed those "Interaction reports" as a summary relay upon own perception of the business analysed. In addition, "Dataset-two" also comprised an initial identification of business' interactions divided by subareas (the five subareas defined above). Interaction levels (see p. 5), skills, and combinations were also highlighted (see p. 7). Each "Interaction report" of the "Dataset-two" is based on several interviews; at most five, they are neither structured nor semi-structured.

The third file was an additional file which constituted an integrative report "Businesses reports" (Dataset-three) developed by the authors. The "Dataset-three" originates from the authors' background research, supported by some European regulations, of whom: the "NACE" regulation (The European Classification of Economic Activities) [14], and the "SMEs: definitions and scope" [15]. The authors have

Table 1 Some examples of the Interaction questionnaire from Socio-Technical Toolbox 2018 v13 (p. 111)

Interaction questionnaire	
Interaction area	First question per each interaction area
Output int. area	What is the typical customer of the organization? Are there any key clients?
Core int. area	What are the main processes and activities in this area?
Input int. area	What is the typical supplier of the organization? Are there any key suppliers?
Int. across the board	How does the organization facilitate the alignment between customers' needs/satisfaction, the identifications and contracting of suppliers, and the processing activities of the organization?
ICTs competences	How does the organization keep abreast of the ICTs evolution?

observed these European regulations to segment businesses by size and by economic activity. "Dataset-three" represented a reorganization of a part of the previous files (Dataset-one and Dataset-two) plus further details about businesses identifications (brief businesses descriptions outlined by the authors). The authors have also compared both the data set provided by the trainees to develop their own "Businesses reports" (Dataset-three). Hence, this file was made up of the size, the economic activity, the economic sub-activity of each business plus some notes (brief businesses descriptions).

The authors noticed the necessity to develop an additional dataset as an "integrative" report ("Business reports", Dataset-three), because of inhomogeneity and disparity of the information between the different files gathered by the trainee junior analysts. Additionally, three different excel file constituted the whole Dataset (Dataset-one, Dataset-two and Dataset-three).

3.2 *Method 2*

The Method 2 section outlines approaches and foundations of the major purpose of this research, the "*Interaction-Context*" schema presented in the section (Proposed Model). A reasonable approach that could tackle the "*Interaction-Context*" schema is abductive reasoning. Hence, the authors believe that the "*Interaction-Context*" schema is the product of abductive reasoning which originated from theoretical roots ("A non-linear, interaction-based development model for e-business" [4], "Socio-Technical Toolbox" [8] then reflexed to the active analysis (Pre-analysis). In addition, Alvesson and Sköldberg argued that abductive reasoning originates from reflective research underpinned through interpretations and reflections [16].

Due to "Pre-analysis" section which belongs to the large-scale project (see p.7), the authors have developed the "*Interaction-Context*" schema (Proposed Model) in line in the complex relationship between the process of knowledge production and the various contexts of such processes of involvement of the knowledge producer (reflexivity) [17]. Consequently, the multi-proposal perspective which emphasizes the "Proposed Model" is also in line to an abductive approach. Therefore, the "Proposed Model" roots under the abductive method: systematic reflection, interpretation, self-exploration of empirical material towards considerations as far as possible to the perceptual, cognitive, theoretical, linguistic textual, political and cultural circumstances that form the backdrop to the interpretations [16]. Additionally, the overall research presented in this study is likely to fit the Hanson agenda, where "abduction" as the process that enquires pattern-finding on empirical material [18]. Besides, the abduction method is likely to support research processes over real practice case studies [19], such as could be the large-scale project underpinned this study.

As mentioned above in Method 1, the authors developed a forerunner study (Pre-analysis) through an organic approach, where, a holistic perspective underneath the businesses analysed. The authors also claimed the "Pre-analysis" as actual research in-line with the socio-technical assumptions argued by Edin Mumford [6, 7]. Furthermore, (Pre-analysis) was set up from the three files described above (Dataset-one, Dataset-two and Dataset-three) which rely upon the large scale-project (see p. 6) as real-world businesses investigations. In addition, the authors state an ethnographic effort which seeks to enhance an understanding of the different business took under analysis. Since the project involved several stakeholders, it is important to bear in mind that possible bias could occur between the information exchanged. Hence, the authors have developed the "*Interaction-Context*" schema trying to address these issues.

The "*Interaction-Context*" schema founds its foundation in "A non-linear, interaction-based development model for e-business" as well as the "Socio-Technical Toolbox" [8]. The "*Interaction-Context*" schema is expected to encompass a multi-proposal (see p. 2) understanding of interactions in consideration of open-ended investigations. The authors articulate a matrix schema where interaction investigation and ICT system get together in one only understanding. Generally, the schema supports simultaneous analysis of the interactions and ICT system, which broad to identify a "Category" and a "Context" for each subarea of interaction. The "*Interaction-Context*" schema fall under two major headings: "Categorisation" and "Contextualization" of the interactions. With regards to context, three categories constitute an interaction typology: "Coordination", "Operation", and "Control". On the other hand, despite these interaction typologies, three contexts can be broken down into an interaction orientation: "Business", "Local" or "Individual".

As far as is concerned the subareas of interactions the "*Interaction-Context*" schema envisages the same foundation (interactions areas) outlined in the studies mentioned above [4, 8] ("Output Interaction Area", "Core Interaction Area", "Input Interaction Area", "Interaction across the board"). The authors report, therefore, a particular emphasis to the last interaction subarea "ICTs competences", which forms an integral part of the analysis of the others subareas under the "*Interaction-Context*" schema, in spite to be considered as a singular subarea (see Fig. 4, p. 11). The authors have emphasised the "ICTs competences" subarea in order to facilitate the categorisation of the existing links between technologies and competencies inside the major interaction subareas. In addition, the adoption of an ICT system could support these specific interactions rather than other business activities. Forasmuch as a multi-proposal analysis underpins this study (see p. 2), this emphasis which took place in the "*Interaction-Context*" schema could be useful to better understand and analyse the relationships between the social and the technical.

4 Pre-analysis

So far, this paper has focused on the long-term ambition of the authors. The following section will discuss the forerunner study developed until the (Proposed Model) "*Interaction-Context*" schema emerged. The authors started the interaction analysis through two major studies foundation presented in the literature. The analysis, therefore, mainly followed the roots of "A non-linear, interaction-based development mod-el for e-business" [4] as well the combination's matrix of competencies and technologies, present in the interaction analysis of the "Socio-Technical Toolbox" [8]. The starting point was to understand and interpret the available dataset (Dataset-one and Dataset-two), through the same perspective as the theoretical models mentioned above.

Hence, the authors have investigated the interaction questionnaire (Dataset-one) in order to develop a clear understanding of each business interaction areas relationships. It is noteworthy that the major ambition of the authors at that moment was to define patterns and clusters among the analysis under a qualitative approach. Thus, the first overview of interactions relations was carried out in a business perspective. These interactions were then identified for each business across the whole dataset. The "Pre-analysis" has pursued the aim to identify for each company: the overall level of interactions, the competencies required (ICT maturity) and the combination of technologies and skills. Then, "Interaction reports" (Dataset-two) was analysed and overlapped to these first outcomes.

The authors were not able to meet the linearity from this first understanding which in spite outlined different information between "Raw-data" (Dataset-one), (which come from interaction questionnaire), and the Trainees' "Interaction-reports" (Dataset-two). However, these first investigations were unable to support a clear understanding useful to develop the intended analysis. These factors may explain why the authors have warned the need to develop the authors' "Integrative reports" (Dataset-three). Indeed, the authors intended to outline and categorise patterns and clusters through an ethnographic effort which would emphasise the size, the economic activity and the economic sub-activity of each business. Besides, the developing of (Dataset-three) enhanced the understanding of each business (see Fig. 3 and related Coding Tables 4, 5, 6).

Thereby, an abductive reasoning has influenced the authors through the identification of interaction levels (see Fig. 2), the combination and a brief overview for each company and, this more explanatory (Dataset-three). The authors questioned a series of Issues (Table 2) and Reflections (Table 3) which originated from abductive reasoning:

Table 2 Issues occurred after the identification of the interaction levels, the ICT maturity and a brief overview of each business

Issues	
No	Issue
1	Does the information collected in the specific areas concern the interactions, or do they explain an activity?
2	What is the purpose of this interaction?
3	Does the detected interaction support one of the core phases of the business? Alternatively, does it support the work activity of the individual employee?
4	For what purpose technologies and skills are required, if investigating ICT maturity?
5	Does the implementation of technologies support the interaction, business or work of the employee?
6	Is the business under analysis primarily developed by the introduction of ICT systems?
7	What is the perception of the interviewee regarding the introduction of ICT systems?
8	Does the interviewee actively participate in the interactions? Is he aware of being part of it?
9	How can we benefit from the knowledge and behaviour of the employee?
10	According to what we analyse, how could the business be affected by growth?
11	What interaction could or should develop?

Table 3 Reflections occurred looking forward across associations, correlations, patterns and similarities into the dataset

Reflections	
No	Reflection
1	High propensity to information loss
2	High tendency to change data in the various phases of analysis
3	High inhomogeneity of data
4	A high inclination for misinterpretation of data
5	High mismatching of the information offered by interviewed
6	High knowledge but low awareness of the instance being analysed
7	Complexity in segmenting the phases of the core business
8	Complexity in the association of technologies with specific interactions
9	The complexity of splitting between activities and interactions
10	Need to categorize interactions
11	Need to contextualize the interactions
12	Need to contextualize and place technologies and skills (ICT maturity)

Needless to say, that "Pre-analysis" has triggered a long-terms ambition at this stage. The authors stopped to develop the analysis to reasoning on how best pre-process and reorganise all the available information. The purpose of the study was the same, analyse interactions. However, the attention shifted from an overall perspective strictly connected from the theoretical studies [4, 8], to a more practical understanding (of real-work practices which rely upon the large-scale project).

Therefore, the investigation of associations, correlations, patterns or similarities led the authors to highlighted some reflections. Moreover, the above mentioned "Reflections" in Table 3, have laid down the conclusions of the "Pre-analysis" section. From this point forward, a multi-proposal perspective through multiple points of views invests the research contents.

Since the large-scale project which underpins this research comprises several small and medium-sized enterprises, the "Pre-analysis" outlined the need to identify different perspectives. Hence, a clear understanding of interaction relationships could not depend on only narrow interpretation. For example, size and type of business diversify the different realities, which could be enough to emphasize the complexity which belongs to interactions analysis. However, previous studies on interactions have not dealt with this kind of approaches.

Therefore, four (Finding 1, 2, 3, 4*)* constitute the results of "Pre-analysis" section, which highlight each of the relevant aspects. These findings foster the reader to understand a broad analysis potential where a multi-proposal perspective supports the interpretation of contextualization and categorization of interactions. Below the relevant aspects (Finding 1, 2, 3, 4):

Finding 1: This section "Pre-analysis" identifies the relevance of contextualising the interactions in consideration of a multi-proposal perspective of analysis. The major finding (Finding 1) emphasises how interactions could affect businesses throughout specific competencies and the use of technology. The specific case presented as an example concerns a small pre-primary school. Technologies and skills are present at multiple levels and for different purposes. Interactions and business development are both supported by the use of technology. Moreover, one of the managers of the business analysed in this section provided the following sentence in own interview (information present in the second file, Dataset-two, "Interaction reports"). Below is shown a brief sentence took from the interaction questionnaire (first file, Dataset-one, "Raw-data"): "*Technology has a significant influence on improving the employee-child relationship. Through advanced technology, they are capable of instructing children efficiently. The instructional technology emphasises on developing the business*". (Cit. provided from the mentioned interview).

Finding 2: This finding seeks to emphasise part of the "Pre-analysis" done in order to present practical examples related to the intended multi-proposal perspective underneath this research. Hence, to get close to the "*Interaction-Context*" schema (Proposed Model). A simple ring chart shows few of the clusters of interaction

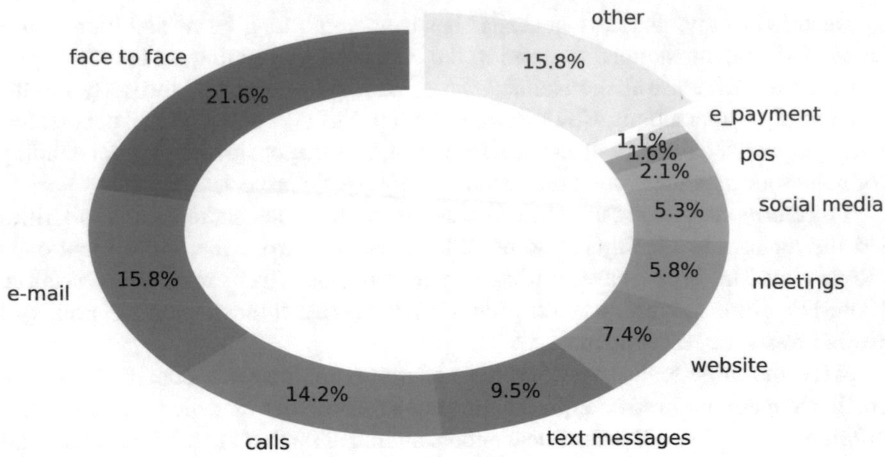

Fig. 1 Interactions-technologies labels of the output area, pre-analysis

relationships from the "Output Interaction Area". The "Pre-analysis" has identified approximately thirty-six different labels between various typologies interaction, technologies or competencies. These labels, drawn in Fig. 1., were reduced for simplicity of visualisation. However, percentages are analysed in comparison to the total of the businesses considered. For example, the "*Interaction-Context*" schema (Fig. 4.) could be useful to understand why interaction occurs in a specific area of a business with particular technology used. Below the "Output Interaction Area" ring chart:

Finding 3: This finding aims to shows the connection between technologies and competencies required from the adoption of an ICT system that supports specific interactions, rather than other business activities. The authors argued that the logic of the ICT system could be evaluated in a socio-technical perspective; therefore, insisted on highlighting the strong connections between ICT systems and the study of interactions.

Figure 2. shows the Interaction levels and the ICT combinations of the various companies analysed in "Pre-analysis". The pie chart draws the percentage of membership in each combination between the level of interaction and the level of combinations of ICT technologies and skills. The percentages level results in comparison to the total of the businesses considered. As an example, 20% of the total business analysed, is outcome as an organisation with competences and technology needed to manage "In-house" (combination A of combination's matrix in the interaction analysis of SST) [8], the relative hardware (personal computer, essential network devices) and software (web browser, basic content management systems to create a website). Besides, "medium" is the interaction level.

Those results (In-house; medium) means that the interactions in the 20% of the business cases analysed, commonly occurs in a specific area of the firm but two-way interaction (i.e., chat with customers in the output area; an online information

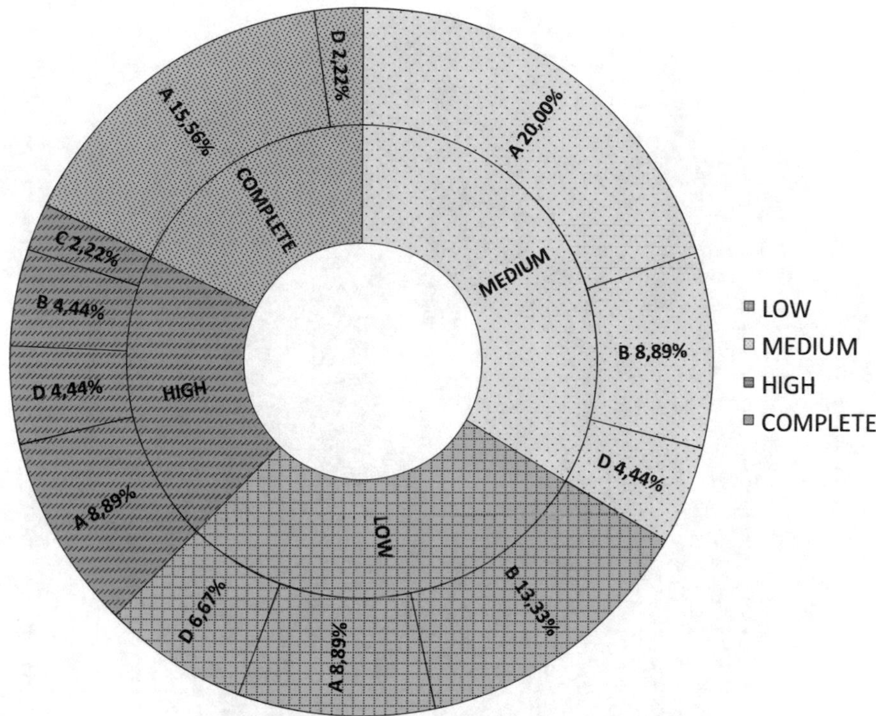

Fig. 2 Business levels-combinations analysed in pre-analysis

exchange with suppliers in the input area). Besides, the authors developed the "*Interaction-Context*" schema also to facilitate the categorisation of the existing links between technologies and competencies. Below the Interaction levels—ICT combinations sunburst chart:

Finding 4: This finding seeks to present in practice what the authors argued above. Thus, emphasise the complexity which belongs to interactions analysis. As an example of how many perspectives could be placed to a large-scale project; business size, economic activities, and sub-activities for each company analysed in "Pre-analysis" are shown in (Fig. 3). Furthermore, "Coding tables" (Tables 4, 5, 6), have also been created to enhance an instant view of the business variety enclosed in the dataset (see Appendix 1). The Coding tables outlines those three parameters mentioned above (business size, economic activities, and sub-activities), which in itself could classify each business.

Additionally, the plotted data are the result of the integrative reports, "Business reports" (Dataset-three) developed by the authors along with the analysis. As a reminder to the reader, European regulations [14, 15] were observed to perform this classification. Below the Economic-Activity and Business-size sunburst chart:

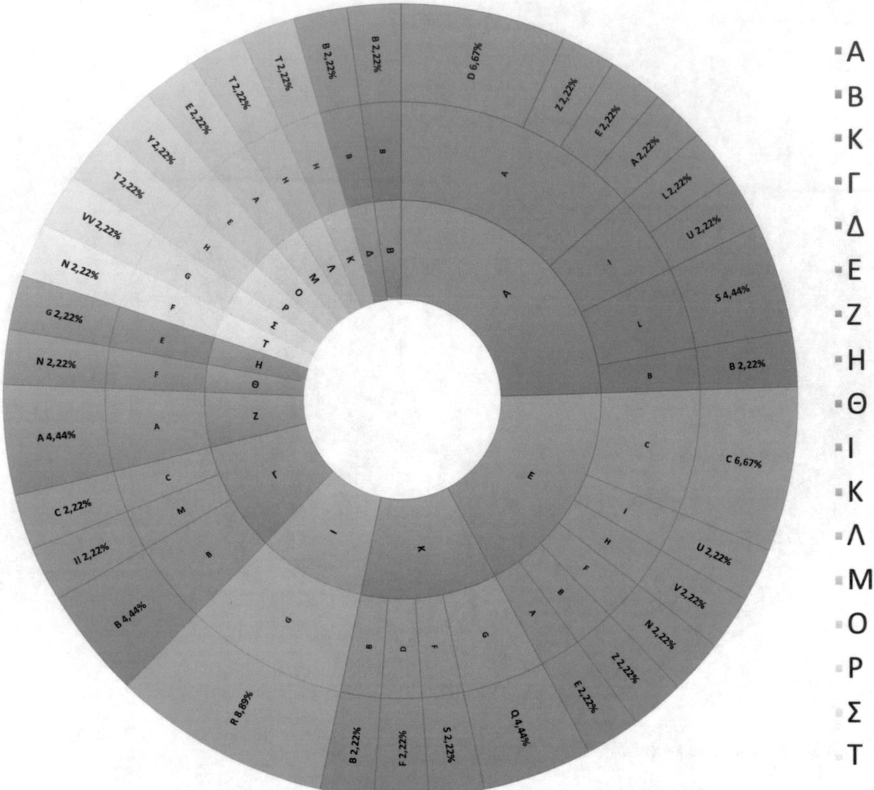

Fig. 3 Economic-activities (main caption in the Fig. above) and sub-categories partition of the business analysed based on business size

5 Proposition: Model-Proposal

The forerunner study discussed above in the "Pre-analysis" section has highlighted some interaction query related to real-work practices outlined across different businesses areas of several companies. The analysis took place in consideration of some theoretical foundation [4, 6, 8] needed to handle and access the Dataset as well to start the investigation. In addition, the "Pre-analysis" results (Finding 1, 2, 3, 4) have encouraged the authors to develop the "*Interaction-context*" schema which seeks to offer a multi-proposal perspective of interaction analysis, in order to support knowledge and management in practice.

Given the rise advancement of ICT and its relevance in the last decades, the authors offer the "*Interaction-Context*" schema as a different perspective to analyse organisational interactions within the context of ICT systems. Hence, the authors have placed particular emphasis on real-work practice as well as the employees' experience of the business context in practice. The "*Interaction-Context*" schema (Proposed Model), is rooted in a socio-technical approach which requires an improved understanding of the implications and complexity of interactions in real work practices. The simultaneous investigation of business activities, interactions, technologies and the interplay of systems could broaden our understanding of businesses. Hence, an enhanced understanding could support business to develop and help people to make better decisions. Furthermore, to pursue a more efficient information flow could optimise knowledge sharing, which could support companies to achieve business excellence.

Therefore, this multi-proposal conceptualisation accentuates the relevance to categorise the different types of interaction within its specific areas, which then must be contextualised. The "Proposed Model" aims to define and attribute a "Category" to all the interactions. Since specific interactions could occur, this proposition allows a better understanding of "Context". Three "Classes" seem to be enough of categorising the interactions: "Coordination", "Operation", or "Control". From this categorisation, we move on to the orientation of the interaction. Three "Contexts" contextualise the interaction within a specific orientation: "Business", "Local" or "Individual". These kinds of specifications could afford a more precise overview of the data, which could also support an improved understanding of real-work practices. However, the authors consider the use or not of ICT systems, in relation to the related skills required to use them. In this way, the same process described above to outline the relationships between the interactions areas, is then proposed to categorise and contextualise ICT systems, skills, and technologies.

This approach allows analysts to explore the interplay between technology and competences of an ICT system for each interaction relationship in own subareas of a business (see p. 7). From this perspective, it is possible to establish how, where, and if ICT systems develop a business. In this way, we will understand either these systems support interactions or a core business phase/activity. "*Interaction-Context*" schema is intended to simultaneously analyse interactions and ICT systems in order to identify particular ICT skills which support interactions in a particular system. At the same time the analysis could shows either interactions also support the development of an organisation. Furthermore, the schema also investigates the actual knowledge of an employee regarding the ICT systems or technologies used to carry out their work. As a consequence, should be evident if the employee's knowledge in terms of daily practices could affect the growth of the business.

Still rooted in the principal studies cited: "A non-linear, interaction-based development model for e-business" [4], and "Socio-Technical Toolbox" [8], the schema presents a structure which could increase our understanding of a multi-purpose line of inquiry.

Below in Fig. 4 a draft representation of the "***Interaction-Context***" schema (Proposed Model), then follows a preliminary approach description which pursues the schema.

The idea proposes to identify interaction in one of three "Categories":

COORDINATION, identifies an interaction or ***coordination*** activity.
OPERATIONAL, identifies an interaction or primary activity of the ***core business***.
CONTROL, identifies an interaction or ***control*** activity.

	Interaction Category	Interaction Context	ICT system / Technology Category	ICT system / Technology Context
OUTPUT				
CORE				
INPUT				
BOARD				

Fig. 4 The "interaction-context" schema

After that, identify one of the three "Contexts" for each category:

***BUSINESS*,** as a function and **business** support.
LOCAL, as a function and **local area** support.
INDIVIDUAL, as a function and **employee** support.

Thus, the same approach is proposed to understand "ICT maturity", then ICT System and technology.

The multi-proposal conceptualisation which underpins the Interaction-Context schema is likely to emphasise the potential of this preposition. Therefore, the simultaneous integration of different perspectives within interaction and ICT systems underpins a systemic approach. The authors argue that the Interaction-Context schema potential relies on the purposely try to integrate all these ideas. As a consequence, this integration represents all the reasons why the schema becomes systemic. Hence, this systemic conceptualisation, which reflects a business understanding, could help the analyst to carry out a better and broader understanding, which emphasises a socio-technical approach.

In this section, the authors discuss four major "Abductive-Considerations" (5.1 Considerations from an Interaction Perspective, 5.2 Considerations from a Context Perspective, 5.3 Considerations from a Multiple Perspective, 5.4 Example Drawing on our Study Case). Those "Abductive-Considerations" are proposed as a result of abductive reasoning (between theoretical studies [4, 8] and the "Pre-analysis") which try to emphasise some potentialities about the "Interaction-Context" schema. Additionally, the section also presents intuitive considerations and examples which rely upon real contemporary enterprises. Consequentially, the schema rationale originates from the results (Finding 1, 2, 3, 4) of "Pre-analysis", which aims to supports a broader understanding of the schema.

5.1 A Considerations from an Interaction Perspective

In "A non-linear, interaction-based development model for e-business" [20], the analysis of the company is carried out by deconstructing the core business. Significant business activities could be diverted by focusing precisely only on the core phases. The analyst's attention could be distorted if the information comes only and directly from the management (or the ownership of a business). Moreover, the primary emphasis should be given to the grassroots in the organization, precisely to the employee through everyday work practices understanding. All the information from managers as well owners could distort the real performance of the business. The owners of the company are in the same "handicap" of the managers because they are not doing the job in practice. Owners and managers could miss representing real business activity because they see the business from an abstract point of view. The experience gained doing a particular business job is not directly perceived by management.

Furthermore, even if owners and managers understand the theory the employee's job, because they are not doing the role of the employee, they are not as knowledgeable about the context of the actual job situation. Consequently, owners and managers are equally distanced from the job activity in context. However, management knows the job in principles, but in the real world, there are a lot of complexities, exceptions, and problems that have to be solved in everyday life to be able to do the job. Therefore, only the employee that is doing the job is considered problem-solving expert underpinned a real job situation. The "*Interaction-Context*" schema accommodates the relevance of the real-world employee engaging context of their career. Wherefore, management interpretation or guesses of actual work activities disconnect from the understanding of the business.

An example could be Italian historical management in small and medium-sized enterprises referring to the family businesses case. Traditionally, the enterprise's organization is unilateral. The ownership also appears like the management of its own company. Studies [21, 22], show that these cases have often been associated with the company's failure in the aftermath of the third generation. Often in family firms, the family system overlaps the business through the use of culture. When this overlap occurs, the role of family tradition can become a critical or success factor for the company [23]. Above all, the real issue is that the culture of change is missing. Thus, their perception of the business is not so clear to be able to identify crucial issues upon the company in the phase of the change. These "Family business" cases show how managers or ownership could affect the perception behind their own business. Recent researches [24, 25], have found that between father and sons, there is a particular sense of protection since the childhood phase. "Il ricorso al padre come figura di protezione e di conforto", "The recourse to the father as a Fig. of protection and comfort" [24]. The proposal is undoubtedly intended equally for the opposite gender.

The authors emphasize the purpose above in line with today's civilization where, although women from a relatively high percentage of the total workforce, the number of women in senior management positions is quite small, but principles for leadership stay the same. Progress is being made on this front, but quite slowly (in Italy) in comparison with some other European countries. Women tend to have a higher profile in some family-owned companies where standing within the family is the critical criteria for advancement [26]. Therefore, according to these cultural values, we could assume that a parent would typically protect and help their children, not push them in trouble. However, constant parental protection does not help the emancipation of the child.

The same phenomena do not support a successful generational change in leadership and management. This phenomenon demonstrates how cultural values are supporting or sabotaging the business. Despite that, the perception of the ownership of family businesses could distort understanding of business context and bring business failure. This kind of phenomena is not limited to Italy but is recognizable all over Europe [27]. Furthermore, in this paper, the authors emphasize the socio-technical foundations.

The employee should be considered as the expert of real work experience of a specific phase or activity of their work in the business context. Therefore, analysts should take into consideration the employee's knowledge. In this perspective, the business is the consequence of employee daily practices. The employee's knowledge needs to be considered as giving the added value of the business, where the agenda is to understand the workspace in its pure dynamism. Given that, the purpose is to identify how the business could be developed in practice drawing upon the employees' knowledge of the real-world business activity. In this research, the authors emphasize the relevance of system thinking to the problem. The study does not intend to ignore top management but insists that the real-world context provided by employees identifies a more precise understanding of the business needs. So that, a clear and specific overview provided by the top management or by ownership remains just as important. For this purpose, "A non-linear, interaction-based development model for e-business" model allows identifying in detail the core business.

However, for complete identification of the business, the experience and knowledge of context help by employees must be considered in equal measure. Thereby, the analyst should help the employees to reflect and investigate to develop a better understanding of their real-work practices. Conversely, employee perception can help the analyst, the opportunity to have a more developed view of the business. The "*Interaction-Context*" schema could support a better analysis. The information collected by employees could be better managed and designed with this schema.

5.2 A Considerations from a Context Perspective

The "*Interaction-Context*" schema presented above supports a specific classification which seems to meet the various difficulties and needs highlighted in both, Table 2 "Issues" and Table 3 "Reflections". So, the schema seeks to afford a more easily management of the many and diverse dataset available for the analysis. Additionally, a full understanding of a business starts from the identifications of interactions levels and ICT combinations, as Figs. 1 and 2. shows. Thereby, the "*Interaction-Context*" schema is intended to "Categorise" those starting point outcomes, and then, throughout the "*Interaction-Context*" schema (see Fig. 4.) "Contextualise" the overall set of information.

Hence, the analyst could be able to get a more detailed understanding of a business. This further step of the analysis could accentuate other secondary business activity, meanwhile, provide a more precise overview of the core business activities. Consequently, the schema investigates technologies which underpin the interactions. In the same way, analyse the competencies requested to employees for each subarea of the interaction previously identified.

5.3 A Considerations from a Multiple Perspective

Typically, a dataset holds several pieces of information, which is why "*Interaction-Context*" schema becomes relevant and useful. As this paper presents, mainly when the analysis is carried out through a multi-proposal perspective. Figures 2 and 3., enclose various aspects which could affect the reader's attention. At least as important as to compare and to match the data. For example, it would be interesting to identify the reason why interactions take place within various economic activities. Even though, seems even more appealing to combine the different analyses also related to the size of the businesses. From this perspective, the "*Interaction-Context*" schema allows matching a multiplicity of diverse data potentially analysable.

Indeed, if the interactions, as well as ICT skills and technologies, would be deconstructed by the "*Interaction-Context*" schema, this could make it easier to compare companies operating in the same business. For example, the purpose might be on the business' size, and the focus could be to detect why and how a company is more developed than the others. These initial observations suggest that the schema is in line with the aims of this proposition. Therefore, the schema seeks to analyse real-work practices that identify a company and indicate a trend towards development and organisational excellence.

5.4 Example Drawing on Our Study Case

Finally, in this section, the "*Interaction-Context*" schema is exemplified within a practical example using a subset of the "Raw-data" (Dataset-one) of the interaction questionnaire. Specifically, the authors remind that these data are the result of different questions that compose the interactions questionnaire (see pp. 7–8). The same example as described above in Finding 1 of the "Pre-analysis" is taken into consideration in-depth here. Besides, in this example, three different employees were interviewed, including a manager. The example which follows below shows the "Classification" of the interactions and their "Contextualization" using the proposed "*Interaction-Context*" schema and the data listed. Similarly, also ICT technologies and skills were identified. The authors intend to provide to the readers a trial study case useful for a better understanding of the "*Interaction-Context*" schema recommended in this paper.

	Interaction Category	Interaction Context	ICT system / Technology Category	ICT system / Technology Context
OUTPUT	Operational Coordination	Business Employee	Operational Coordination	Business Employee
CORE	Operational Coordination	Business Local Employee	Operational Coordination Control	Business Local Employee
INPUT	Operational Coordination	Business Local	Operational Coordination	Business Local
BOARD	Operational Coordination	Business	Operational Coordination Control	Business Employee

Fig. 5 Example based on Pre-analysis section

Follows a part of the collected data used as an example in (Fig. 5.):

Output Area: *Approximately 7–16 people. some of them are Deputy Manager, Group Leader, Key Worker, and Nursery Apprentice. They usually interact among themselves with setting up meetings. when it comes to customers, most of the time would be between these three ways; arranging meetings, phones, emails, sometimes Facebook. Picking the suitable way with customers would depend on the situation, what is it about and why.*
Core Area: *Educating children software, IT tool to help teaching activities, support the interaction between the main actors and customers (as users of the service).*
Input Area: *Issuing Checks, Contracts, Invoices, Track the orders, the delivery dates with Suppliers. Contacting with suppliers via emails, management software systems for foods, payments, contracts, etc.... Issuing Reports to every child at Nursery. Arranging Meetings for the Staff, Arranging workshops/training session for the Staff.*
Board Area: *Company Directors are responsible for Taking control of the Nursery Employees Progress, Activities, Salaries, Childcare, Suppliers, etc.... they have HR Software, and Management software in IT Dept, they can keep track of everything happens around.*

6 Conclusion

The authors have developed the "*Interaction-Context*" schema proposed in this paper trying to combine the previously cited studies: "A non-linear, interaction-based development model for e-business" [4], and "*Socio-Technical Toolbox*" in particular in Sect. 2E. Interaction Analysis ("ICT-Related Competencies" matrix) [8]. However, the "Proposed Model" underpins a long-term ambition which places a different perspective to analyse organisational interactions within the context of ICT systems.

Therefore, this paper proposes an "*Interaction-Context*" schema, which can be useful to better understand and analyse the interactions relationships between the social and the technical. The agenda of this study follows a multi-proposal perspective. Overall, the levels of interaction identified in "Pre-analysis" afforded the categorization of the core business. Technologies and ICT competencies required by the companies analysed defined the "ICT maturity". Further, in an in-depth analysis focused on those first findings, the employee's perspective being the primary purpose of the investigation. Therefore, looking at the organizations, more systems appeared to coexist. So, the focus of the research moved to follow a more detailed deconstruction of the business.

Furthermore, Bednar noticed: "*In order to take into account unique individual sense-making processes within an organizational problem arena, there is a need for analysts to explore multiple levels of contextual dependencies*" [28]. The in-progress analysis was conducted to develop the "*Interaction-Context*" schema (Fig. 4). An overview of the identified interactions has underpinned the assumptions described to create the schema, as well as ICT skills and technologies that support business interactions are associated with those assumptions.

The schema aims to pursue the employee's real-world practices, which support the company in it seeks towards organizational excellence. Additionally, in this paper, the authors contemplate of high relevance an employee's knowledge upon his work. Employees are acknowledged as experts in the experience of the business context in practice. Employees know crucial details based on their own experience that cannot be perceived by the management or ownership through their work. The purpose of the "*Interaction-Context*" schema discussed in this paper is to support investigation and analysis of elements that makes one business unique from another. In other words, if the business is the consequence of the employee's work, we could not afford to ignore their knowledge of activities in context. "*It is our view that organizations subsist through emergence from interactions among individual people who occupy particular roles and are charged with particular contextual tasks*" [29].

The "*Interaction-Context*" schema could support a better understanding of the interactions and technologies that make a business special. Meanwhile, seek to investigate which interactions or technologies are likely to develop the business. Thereby, the analysts could carefully orient is focussing on the research for uniqueness and hidden excellence in business. The proposal for the future is to develop an interaction analysis through the "*Interaction-Context*" schema. A revised and extended version of "Pre-analysis" according to the further perspective of the "Proposed Model" now only presented. The schema seems to be useful to investigate specific areas of interaction, including to analyse companies that use ICT systems to develop their business.

Moreover, this agenda for seeking excellence seems to be in line with Fourth Industrial Revolution's Real Innovation, "*The most substantial improvements start but do not finish with individual leaders: their beliefs, conduct, ways of handling people and understanding of strategy. A key part of the new mindset is to perceive the organization as a dynamic entity, not an inert set of assets*" [30]. There is growing evidence that the application of robotics and virtualisation throughout factories has concerned the main proposal of Industry 4.0 [31]. However, the human capacity for creativity and problem-solving are possible to waste, then replaced by "Smart" changes. Those changes are likely to support systems only from a technological perspective [32].

In this paper, the authors have discussed interaction in context, then put forward an "*Interaction-Context*" schema. Furthermore, this research, therefore, is likely also to fit the Industry 5.0 agenda. The "Proposed Model" aims to emphasise the contemporary socio-technical continuum approach which relays upon one whole integrated strand for examination (instead of two separate, social and technical) [28]. In addition, the long-term ambitions of the authors are probable in line in and similar to Industry 5.0 agenda. The "Proposed Model" is intended to support a better understanding of interactions, which emphasises the engagement and empowering of human beings in order to make a business stronger, instead of "automatic". After that, emphasise the synergistic relationships between such systems and people [33]. In conclusion, the authors believe that the "*Interaction-Context*" schema (Proposed Model) is likely to support organisational change for the better, which aims towards organisational excellence.

7 Appendices

1. Coding Tables (Tables 4, 5, 6)

Table 4 Various business-sizes codification

Business-sizes codification	
Code	Business-size
A	Micro SME
B	Micro SME-franchising
Γ	Small SME-franchising
E	Medium SME-part of a group
Z	Micro SME-part of a group
H	Macro
Θ	Medium SME
I	Medium SME-department in a big organization
K	Small SME
Λ	Micro SME-partnership
M	Small SME-part of a group
O	Macro-part of a group
P	Macro-partnership
Σ	Small SME-public sector
T	Medium SME-partnership

Table 5 Various economic-activities codification

Economic-activities codification	
Code	Economic-activity
a	Wholesale and retail trade; repair or motor vehicles and motorcycles
b	Accommodation and food services activity
c	Arts, entertainment and recreation
d	Financial and insurance activities
e	Manufacturing
f	Human health and social work activities
g	Education
h	Information and communications
i	Real estate activities
l	Non-profit
m	Wholesale trade, except motor vehicles and motorcycles/Other services activities

Table 6 Various sub-category of economic activities codification

Sub-category of economic activity codification	
Code	Sub-category of economic activity
A	Information and communication
B	Food and beverage service activities
C	Sports activities
D	Maintenance and repair
E	Retail trade, except of motor vehicles and mot. etc
F	Financial services activities except insurance. etc
G	Printing and reproduction of recorded media
N	Residential care activities
Q	Pre-primary education
R	Educational support activities
S	Social work activities
T	Information service activities
U	Real estate activities
V	Computer programming, consultancy and related, etc
Z	Accommodation and food services activities
Y	Manufacture of other food products
X	Fruit and vegetables
II	Wholesale of food, beverages and tobacco/Fun. etc
VV	Primary education
L	Real estate agencies

References

1. Sarker, S., Chatterjee, S., Xiao, X., & Elbanna, A. (2019). The Sociotechnical axis of cohesion for the is discipline: its historical legacy and its continued relevance. *MIS Quarterly, 43*(3), 695–719.
2. Jacucci, G. (2007). *Social practice design (spd), pathos, improvisation, mood, and bricolage: The mediterranean way to make place for it? mediterranean conference on information systems* (MCIS). p. 19.
3. Bednar, P. M., & Sadok, M. (2015). *A socio-technical toolbox for business systems analysis and design.* 1st International Workshop on socio-technical perspective in IS Development (STPIS'15). 1374, pp. 29–31. Stockholm, Sweden: CEUR
4. Depaoli, P., & Za, S. (2017). *SME E-business development: An interaction based approach.* Twenty-fifth European conference on information systems (ECIS). Spring 6 Oct 2017. Guimarães, Portugal: ECIS 2017 Proceedings.
5. Bartunek, J. M., Louis, M., Pasmore, W. A., & Woodman, R. W. (1988). *The interplay of organisation development and organizational transformation, Research in organizational change and development* (Vol. 2). Greenwich, CT: JAI Press.
6. Hickey, S., Matthies, H., & Mumford, E. (2006). *Designing human systems, an agile approach to ETHICS*. UK: Linghtning Source Uk Ltd.
7. Mumford, E. (2003). *Redesigning human systems.* PA, USA: IRM Press.
8. Bednar, P. M. (2018). *Socio-technical toolbox* (Vol. 13.2). Portsmouth, UK: Craneswater Press.
9. Pham, Q. T. (2010). Measuring the ICT maturity of SMEs. *Journal of Knowledge Management Practice, 11*(1), 1–14.
10. Benguria, G., & Santos, I. (2008). SME maturity, requirement for interoperability. In K. Mertins, R. Ruggaber, K. Popplewell, & X. Xu (A cura di), Enterprise Interoperability III (pp. 29–40). Uk: Springer, London.
11. Yunis, M. M., Koong, K. S., Liu, L. C., Kwan, R., & Tsang, P. (2012). ICT maturity as a driver to global competitiveness: A national level analysis. *International Journal of Accounting and Information Management, 20*(3), 255–281.
12. Kien, P. X., Son, L. N., & Giang, N. T. (December, 2013). Measuring the ICT maturity of enterprises under uncertainty using group fuzzy ANP. *International Journal of Machine Learning and Computing, 3*(6), 524–528.
13. Mohr, B. J., van Amelsvoort, A. D., Barrett, P., Bednar, B., … Ordowich. (2016). Co-creating humane and innovative organizations: Evolutions in the practice of socio-technical system design. Portland, ME: Global STS-D Network.
14. Nace 2. (2006). EUR-Lex—32006R1893—EN. Retrieved 2019 from EUR-Lex Access to European Union law: https://eur-lex.europa.eu/legal-content/EN/TXT/?qid=1566065636955&uri=CELEX:32006R1893.
15. Micro, S. A.-S. (2015). EUR-Lex—26026—EN. Retrieved 2019 from EUR-Lex Access to European Union law: https://eur-lex.europa.eu/legal-content/EN/TXT/?uri=LEGISSUM:n26026.
16. Alvesson, M., & Sköldberg, K. (2018). *Reflexive methodology, new vistas for qualitative research.* London, UK: SAGE Publications Ltd.
17. Alvesson, M. (2003). Beyond neopositivists, romantics, and localists: A reflexive approach to interviews in organizational research. *Academy of Management Review, 28*(1), 13–33.
18. Hanson, N. R. (1958). *Patterns of discovery: An inquiry into the conceptual foundations of science* (Vol. 251). Cambridge University Press.
19. Sköldberg, K., & Björnström, Y. (1991). *Reforms at a revolving stage: Organizational change in local government*. Lund, Sweden: Studentlitteratur.
20. Depaoli, P., & Za, S. (2019). *Designing e-business for SMEs: Drawing on pragmatism. organizing for digital innovation* pp. 237–246.
21. Chiesa, V., De Massis, A., & Pasi, M. L. (2007). Gestire la successione nei family business. Piccola Impresa/Small Business(1).

22. Cesaroni, F., & Sentuti, A. (2010). *Nuove generazioni ed evoluzione dell'impresa familiare: la sfida della successione imprenditoriale.* Analisi di alcuni casi di successo. Piccola Impresa/Small Business, 2.
23. Ruggeri, R., Pozzi, M., & Ripamonti, S. (2014). Italian family business cultures involved in the generational change. *Europe's Journal of Psychology, 10*(1).
24. Cescato, S. (2017). Una riflessione pedagogica sui padri, il loro ruolo educativo, la loro presenza nei servizi per l'infanzia. *Journal of Theories and Research in Education, 12*(2), 203–214.
25. Di Folco, S., & Zavattini, G. C. (2014). La relazione d'attaccamento padre-bambino: Una rassegna della letteratura. *Giornale Italiano Di Psicologia, 41*(1), 159–190.
26. World Business Culture, delivering global connections. Retrieved 2019 from Worldbusinessculture.com: https://www.worldbusinessculture.com/country-profiles/italy/culture/women-in-business/.
27. Brizi, M., Ercoli, D., & Trinari, C. (2017). FABUSS—An overview of the environment for family businesses—TUCEP. (F. B. Succession, Produttore). Retrieved 2019 from project eu, Project number: 2016–3-EL02-KA205–002673.: https://www.fabuss-project.eu/wp-content/data/IO1/FB_ENV_ITALY.pdf.
28. Bednar, P. M., & Welch, C. (May 3, 2019). *Socio-technical perspectives on smart working: Creating meaningful and sustainable systems. information systems frontiers* pp. 1–18.
29. Bednar, P. M., & Welch, C. (2009). *Paradoxical relationships in collaboration, competition and innovation: a critical systemic perspective.* The 10th workshop of Italian scholars on organization studies, 2009 (pp. 1–16). Cagliari: unica.
30. Gallo, P., & Hlupic, V. (May, 2019). Leadership strategy: humane leadership must be the fourth industrial revolution's real innovation. (Forbes Media LLC). Retrieved 2019 from forbes.com: https://www.forbes.com/sites/worldeconomicforum/2019/05/21/humane-leadership-must-be-the-fourth-industrial-revolutions-real-innovation/#64143835501b.
31. Vollmer, M. (2018). What is industry 5.0? Retrieved 2019 from LindedIn.Com.: https://www.linkedin.com/pulse/what-industry-50-dr-marcell-vollmer.
32. McEwan, A. M. (2013). *Smart working creating the next wave.* London, UK: Routledge.
33. Özdemir, V., & Hekim, N. (2018). Birth of industry 5.0: Making sense of big data with artificial intelligence, "the internet of things" and next-generation technology policy. *OMICS A Journal of Integrative Biology, 22*(1), 65–76.

Systemic Sustainability Analysis in Small and Medium-Sized Enterprises (SMEs)

Lucia Pascarella and Peter Bednar

Abstract Sustainability is rarely implemented in employee work practices in small and medium-sized enterprises (SMEs). The authors note that SMEs should implement sustainability practices as integrated part of work activities to ensure long term success. This paper describes an empirical study of SMEs sustainability on employee real work practices. A relevant perspective is offered by the triple bottom line approach (TBL) combined with sociotechnical theory. The attention to creating value for the future could lead to fewer sustainability issues. Furthermore, the analysis highlights the importance of the best use an employee knowledge and skills to ensure his satisfaction. The main issue that hinders the improvement of sustainability could be a lack of management attention to systemic integration of employee work practices. The authors argue to integrate technology and systemic perspective in TBL approach to achieve sustainability from sociotechnical perspective. The analysis aims to support enterprises to remain competitive in evolving contexts.

Keywords Systemic sustainability · Work practices · Triple bottom line · Sociotechnical approach · Contextual analysis

L. Pascarella (✉) · P. Bednar
University of Portsmouth, Portsmouth, UK
e-mail: luciapasc95@gmail.com

P. Bednar
e-mail: peter.bednar@port.ac.uk

L. Pascarella
Università degli Studi di Salerno, Fisciano (SA), Italy

P. Bednar
Lund University, Lund, Sweden

C. Metallo et al. (eds.), *Digital Transformation and Human Behavior*, Lecture Notes in Information Systems and Organisation 37,
https://doi.org/10.1007/978-3-030-47539-0_18

1 Introduction

Over the years, sustainability has taken on a key role in companies. The importance of sustainability has been underlined for many years but certainly explicit since 1987 [1]. Sustainable development in small and medium-sized enterprises (SMEs) is intended to support present needs without compromising the ability of future company generation to meet their own needs [1]. Elkington argues the need to integrate the sustainability agenda in real work practices of enterprise through the triple bottom line approach [2]. Since then, many studies [3–6] have focused on the relevance for enterprises to pursue sustainability based on the triple bottom line approach. This approach outlines a way of thinking that concerns corporate social responsibility so that it covers not only the profit of the enterprise but is also acceptable environmentally and socially fair [2]. Triple bottom line approach goes beyond the traditional business concept of the bottom line that pursued profit as its only goal [7].

In contrast, what is crucial for sustainability in the work practices of an enterprise is collaboration between stakeholders [3]. Usually, an enterprise is not made up of a single person, but rather it is a group of people working together to achieve a common goal. The impetus for a change towards sustainability should be driven by the company at all levels of the corporate hierarchy, especially among the grassroots employees. From this perspective, the company has to be aware of its responsibilities towards different stakeholder groups [8]. This approach is intended to improve a social and ecological performance of company taking into account sociotechnical issues [8].

A Sociotechnical perspective "*provides a new worldview of what constitutes quality of working life and humanism at work. It facilitates organizational innovation [...] with an organization and technology that enhances human freedom, democracy, creativity*" [9: 262], collaboration and participation among stakeholders. A sociotechnical approach concerns the technological and human system and their environment and how they affect human behaviors [10]. This approach focuses on human and technological sustainability and how the employee interacts with sustainability in work practices.

Practically, to make a real improvement, the managers should use their knowledge to understand real problems and provide guidelines for change; while at the same time always listening and considering the advice of the employee. According to sociotechnical theory, there should be more communication and exchange of information in the form of real dialogue between employees and management. Due to difficulties of communication, the latter could be simplified through meetings or with an analyst acting as a facilitator [11]. The facilitator would make communication constant, more comfortable and more productive. In any case, those who make sustainability in practice possible are the employees.

This paper describes the results from a project that analyzes systemic sustainability in work practices which draw on a sociotechnical and a triple bottom line approach in the SMEs. Some of the issues in the approach to systemic sustainability have been identified during the analysis of employee work practices. The main purpose of the paper is to analyze sustainable work practices of employee in SMEs with a sociotechnical approach. From the perspective of work practices, the pursuit of sustainability could be a way to achieve competitive advantages and long-term success. From a sociotechnical point of view focus on the respect of the environment, the well-being, and professionalism of employees and enterprise profit could lead to long term success. Sustainability is intended to support enterprises to reach business excellence towards competitive and in continuous evolution context. The factors that support business excellence are complex and not static [8]. From a sociotechnical perspective, over time value creation for companies is based not only on their intellectual capital and on "know-how" but also to the desire and the ability of their employees [8].

According to the agenda of industry 5.0, to be sustainable and competitive the focus should be on the relationships between employees and work systems [8]. In contrast, industry 4.0 was based on technological development and overlooked the human dimension [8]. Industry 4.0 appeared to lose the grounding that the sociotechnical perspective has traditionally provided.[8, 12]. In industry 5.0 there is a return to the importance of the sociotechnical approach, which is intended to lead to continuity and progress [12]. According to sociotechnical perspective, industry 5.0, through the support of its employee tries to reach business excellence in work practices [8]. The sociotechnical perspective is intended to lead enterprises to reach systemic sustainability.

Over the years, there has been a long interest in corporate sustainability but now it is not necessarily a choice. Since there is continuous social, cultural, economic and legislative pressure to move in a sustainability direction [13], sustainability has become mandatory thanks to European Directive 2014/95/EU [14]. The European Directive requires companies to include non-financial statements (for instance environmental matters, social and employee aspects) in their annual reports to encourage companies to develop a sustainable approach to business [15].

The next section will describe the background of the project and outlines how previous work provided the basis for the analysis. Following, in the methods section an overview of the dataset used in this analysis will be presented. The authors will then describe the initial analysis of the dataset and the way the data are studied. Finally, the second part of the analysis will be the core of the investigation, and focuses on three main areas of interest:

- Sustainability as dependent on management,
- Impact of paying attention to the future value,
- Employee satisfaction.

The paper will then discuss of the current analysis and key findings. The conclusion will provide an overview of future analysis and final thoughts.

1.1 Background

The project started in October 2018 and continued until April 2019. The engagement with each company was conducted by 40 trainee analysts. Each trainee analyst worked in a separate business. Trainee analysts interviewed a total of 148 employees. Typically, each trainee analysts would have had more than ten interviews with the same employees over this period. Each interview took approximately half an hour. Some interviews were semi-structured, and all trainee analysts completed questionnaires during interviews. In each company, a trainee analyst interviewed at least three people (3–5) who were the same three people throughout the project. In each company, the work practices of one employee are the main focus of the trainee analyst. This employee has been interviewed more often and in greater detail compared with the other two.

Sustainability analysis is only one part of the overall project. In this paper, the focus is systemic sustainability and development of the overall project based on the sociotechnical toolbox [STT]. "*STT is a collection of tools, techniques, and pragmatic methods which can be used to support organizational change*" [16: 3]. The main focus of STT is the work-system, which is the core of the organizational change [16]. This toolbox is useful to change organizational practices in order to reach business excellence [16].

The STT has approximately 30 different methods of analysis, which are divided into eight main analytical spaces [16]. Five different types of questionnaires [interaction, sociotechnical, sustainability, change-potential, information, and cybersecurity] support the methods of the analysis [16]. One of these questionnaires focused on sustainability, which is the subject of this research. The sustainability questionnaire has 24 questions divided into the following parts: economic sustainability, social sustainability and environmental sustainability.

Open and closed questions were used in the sustainability questionnaire. In addition, to add value to the research, part of the sociotechnical questionnaire was added. The reason why sections of the sociotechnical questionnaire were included was to investigate how enterprises integrate sustainability issues into work practices. In addition, it is essential to focus on how much an employee is involved and satisfied with their work. This integrated dataset intended to provide a better overview of sustainability.

1.2 Methods

The dataset collected by 40 trainee analysts is the basis of the analysis proposed in the current paper. The dataset contains all the open and closed answers of the 148 employees. This paper draws on a subset of the dataset that is focused mainly on sustainability and part of the sociotechnical questionnaire. Based on the content of the first dataset, to support the analysis, the following datasets were also created:

- The Enterprise Report. This contains the type, size, and economic activity for each company. The "NACE" standard was followed in order to connect each company to its economic activity [17].
- The Sustainability Report. This contains all the categorized answers of the employees related to and supporting sustainability.

2 Initial Analysis: The Dataset

The first step of the analysis concerns the meaning behind questions and raw data. A sustainability aspect that each question aims to uncover is the hidden meaning. The hidden meaning of each question, which aims to support the sustainability analysis was explored. Raw data are composed by open and closed response for each sustainability area. Each single question from an employee was categorized. During the categorization, most of the answers were not consistent with the questions. All open questions require explaining "how", and in contrast, the answers focus on "who" or "what". Only through a complete and coherent response can we understand whether the employee is involved and implements their sustainable work practices.

The following is an example of an answer given by an employee that does not address the question:

"Are you managing resources directly needed in your work? If yes how?".

"Yes. Stock, employees and my time are some of the resources that i need to manage in my work".

The first categorization is intended to lead to a clear vision of the true meaning of the data and their inconsistency. However, to compare businesses accurately with each other, there was a need to unify the data. Accordingly, there was the addition of the second categorization composed of the following categories and ranges:

The individual answer of an employee, based on the grade and coherence with the question, was placed in the category schema (see Table 1). To evaluate the whole business the mean percentage was calculated, based on the answers of employees from a single business. The mean percentage was calculated using the relative category range and then, by taking the middle range value of every single employee' answer which was in turn used to place the business into the appropriate category. This percentage was placed in the appropriate range for that category (see Table 1).

Table 1 Second Categorization' categories and percentages range

Category	Range
High	100–80
Medium–High	80–60
Medium–Low	60–40
Low	40–20
Absence	20–10

Table 2 Examples of questions that identify the problem in all sustainability areas

Sustainability Area	Problem (Example of question)
Economic	Is local budget surplus carried over to next year?
Social	Is there someone else who can do employee's job if he/she is away?
Environmental	Does the job require specific environmental considerations?

What is essential is the level of awareness and recognition of the problem. The problem is what compromises the ability of companies to meet their future needs. Examples of questions that identify the problem are below (see Table 2). If there is little or no recognition, then this is categorized as *High*. If there is significant recognition of the problem, this is categorized as *Low*. Therefore, the same previous categorization was used for the problem but in reverse. When the knowledge of the problem is high, the problem belongs to the low category and vice versa. This reverse connection is related to the company' lack of knowledge of the problems. If the company does not know that it has an economic, environmental and social problem, this could be the biggest problem for a company. In this way, all the data are uniquely placed on the same scale and can be compared for each single enterprise.

3 Second Part Analysis and Key Findings

3.1 Sustainability as Dependent on Management

Over the years, the theme of sustainability for companies has taken on a crucial role. Sustainable development is intended to meets "*the needs and aspirations of the present generation without compromising the ability of future generations to meet their needs*" [1: 292]. The triple bottom line is an approach that tries to achieve sustainability. Elkington intended to encourage a business vision based on the idea to control and coordinate economic, social and environmental value [7]. Focusing on these three aspects is a way to achieve sustainability [18] and is intended to bring value to the enterprise. The triple bottom line fits the agenda of Mumford on sociotechnical theory [9, 19, 20].

The basis of sociotechnical theory is technological and human sustainability through the attention to employees in their work practices [9]. Sustainability must be implemented in work practices, paying attention to employees and the human and technological system. Pursuing this idea, the first stage of the analysis was the identification of the level of the enterprise' attention to the future economic, environmental and social sustainability value. In this case, future value is understood as the extent to which companies are willing to meet their future needs. In other words, future value is what a company should care about for their long-term life and success. The attention to the future value is how much company support the ability to meet their future needs. Table 3 presents example of questions that identify the future value for each sustainability area (see Table 3).

Table 3 Examples of questions that identify the creation of future value in all sustainability areas

Sustainability Area	Future Value (Example of question)
Economic	Is the employee expected to keep spare financial reserves/resources?
Social	Does the employee get personal mentoring by an expert in his job?
Environmental	Does the employee get training/advice in environmentally friendly practices?

The analysis focuses on each question that aims to highlight the presence of attention to the future value presented in Table 3. Focusing on economic future value, only 22.30% of employees keep spare financial reserves/resources. This percentage underlines the low presence attention of enterprises to economic future value and, therefore, economic sustainability. The economic result seems to be low compared with the other sustainability areas. The analysis of social future value attention highlights that 47.30% of employees get personal mentoring by an expert in their job. This result underlines that most of the enterprises pay attention to social future value allowing the transfer of knowledge from an expert to a less experienced employee. Analyzing environmental future value attention, only 29.05% of the employees interviewed affirm that they get training and advice on environmentally friendly practices. Therefore, enterprises seem to do not pay enough attention to environmental future value creation.

In the investigation, none of the evidence from the dataset suggests that the enterprises interviewed achieve a maximum level of attention to future value in all sustainability areas. This lack of sustainability is the result of inadequate attention that is generally placed on the creation of future value and sustainability. All the firms that show the highest levels of sustainability, at least in two of the three areas are shown below in the graph (see Fig. 1). Only three enterprises out of forty achieved the highest level of sustainability, at least in the environmental and social area. These enterprises are different sizes (for example small, medium-sized), have different typologies (for example franchising, part of a group, department in a big organization), and different economic activities. However, sustainability does not appear to be entirely influenced by these factors.

Overall, there may be a correlation between size, typology, and economic activity. This is because depending on the typology, size and economic activity enterprises have different needs and problems to face. However, the similarities are not unequivocal, the graph below (see Fig. 2) shows that within enterprises with the same characteristics, there could be different results. Even if the enterprises "Beta", "Gamma" and "Kappa" have the same attention level to economic sustainability, they have different attention levels to social and environmental sustainability. This result indicates that the single most important thing that can influence the sustainability of an enterprise is management.

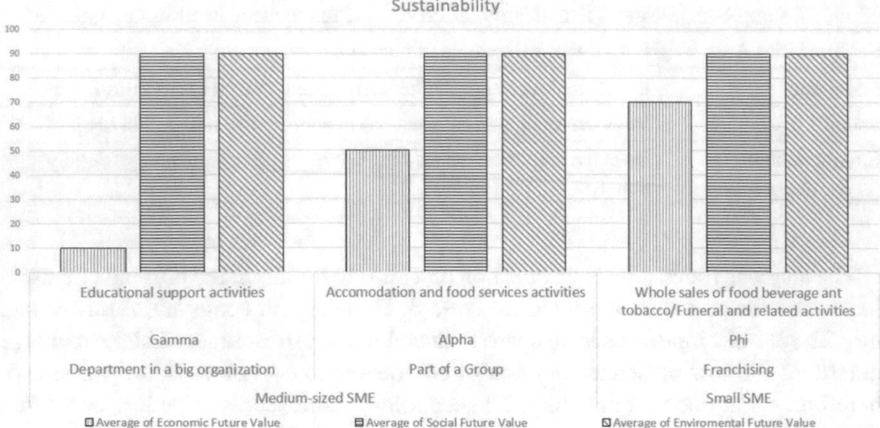

Fig. 1 Companies that show the maximum levels of attention to the creation of future value and sustainability

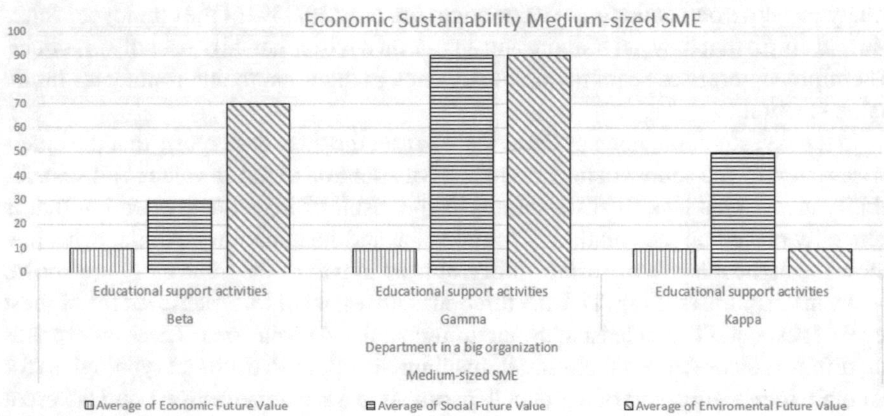

Fig. 2 Companies with the same size, typology, and economic activity have different attention levels to the creation of future value and sustainability

An overview of the levels attention companies devotes to future value creation of economic, environmental and social sustainability lead to the following considerations: the area that has achieved the highest result in terms of attention to the future value is social sustainability, with 25%. This may seem like a low result but in comparison with other areas it is the highest. Environmental and economic areas respectively are 5–10% of high attention to the future value (see Fig. 3).

In general, the expectation is that economic sustainability is the first aim pursued because it is a fundamental perceive of all economic activities. Managers tend to pursue only economic value and not future value, which leads to sustainable enterprise. The results suggest enterprises do not pay attention to the creation of surplus.

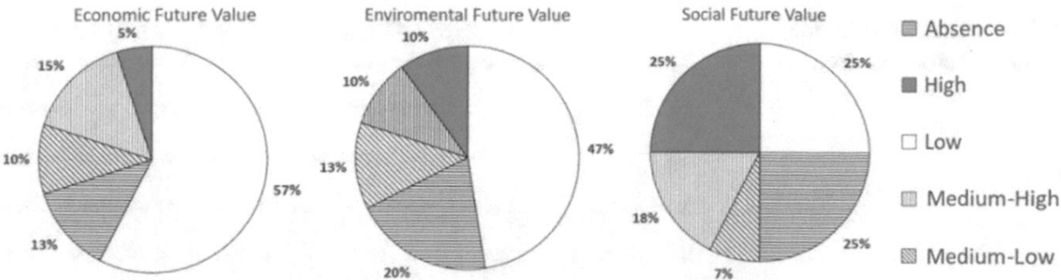

Fig. 3 Economic, environmental and social future value attention levels

This data can underline the lack of attention of managers to the future of their enterprises creating unsustainable development. The same thing happens in the environmental area. Those who manage the employees do not pay attention or raise awareness to environmentally friendly practices. An example of an employee' answer to the question about training in environmentally friendly practices was:

> "*Handbook to refer to but otherwise self-taught*".

This result supports the thesis that managers are lacking in this area. Managers do not direct work practices in a human activity system that should positively influence natural resources in their future. There seems to be insufficient culture and knowledge about sustainability in practice. Managers are not ready and prepared enough to lead sustainable development of an enterprise. Managers only pay attention to results in the present, and they do not have a broader view that leads to thinking about the future sustainability of an enterprise.

3.2 *Impact of Paying Attention to the Future Value*

To only focus attention on the analysis of future value (see Table 3) is reductive. Therefore, it is important to analyze the nature of the problem (see Table 2) that leads managers to pay higher or lower attention to the creation of future value.

From employee' perspective, the problem area that presents the significant uncertainty is the economic one (see Fig. 4). More than half of the employee does not know if the budget surplus is carried over the next year. This uncertainty could highlight that employee is little involved in economic issues. Even if employees are involved in the financial decision or have their budget to manage, they do not present the knowledge of surplus.

The 33.78% of employees affirm that there is no surplus carried over the next year and, in contrast, only 15.54% affirms the contrary. This result could be the consequence of top-down managerialism approach. Managerialism approach does not include employee; therefore, there is the decontextualization of the problem and the solution. In contrast, the sociotechnical approach proposes a bottom-up approach,

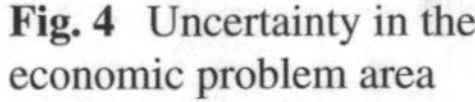

Fig. 4 Uncertainty in the economic problem area

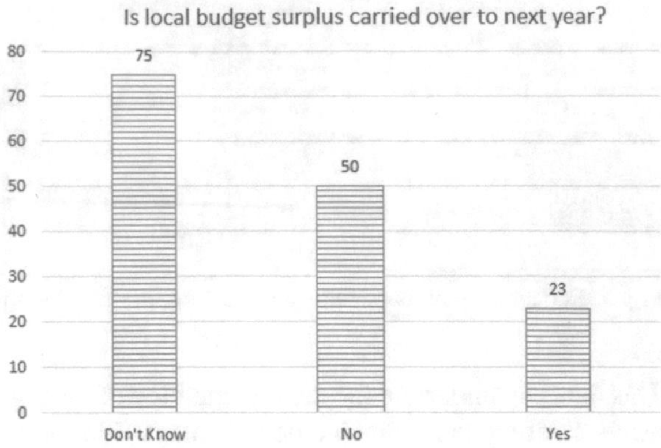

which includes the participation of employees who know how to afford the problem in practices.

Overall, the comparison of the actual problem and the attention to future value denotes that these two values are inversely proportional. When there is greater adoption of methods that focus attention on future value, the problem in that sustainability area is *low*.

The data in the figure (see Fig. 5) clearly show the inverse proportionality of the two factors. This result highlights the importance of paying attention to future value. When enterprises pay attention to future value and implement sustainable practices, they lower the problem. These practices are intended to lead to better results on all sustainability aspects. The attention to future value increases not only the prospects of the company but also its value.

The graph (see Fig. 5) does not only show this concept, for example, the case of "Delta" enterprise underlines that even if attention to future value is *medium–high*,

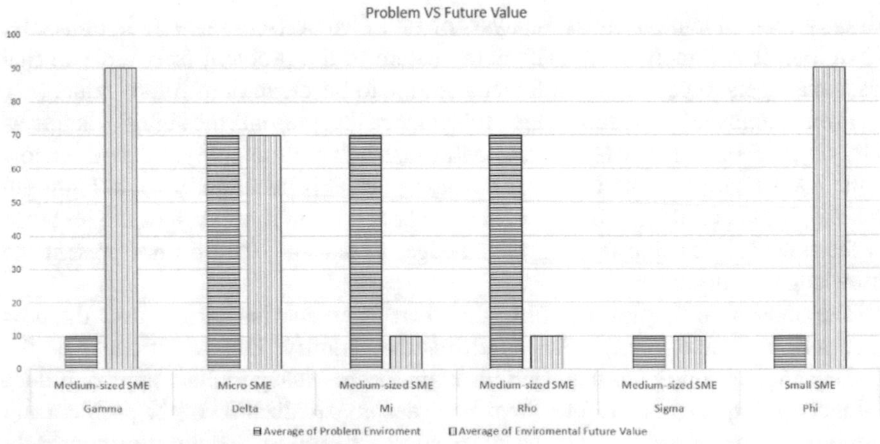

Fig. 5 Comparison between actual problem and attention to the creation of future value

the problem can remain *medium–high* and unchanged. This particular case leads us to suppose that it is not enough to pay generic attention to the problem. It is therefore essentially to pay proper attention to implementing adequate practices to solve the specific problem. In the environmental sustainability area, an example of best practice is to give employees training and advice on environmentally friendly practices. If the enterprise already implements these practices and it still has a significant problem, it should change their training methods because they may be inadequate for the context and employees.

Every problem is different because it comes from different conditions and contexts. Therefore, employee and managers together must analyze the problem, trying to understand its source and the causes. Only after they have achieved a clear vision of the problem can managers find the appropriate methodologies to solve it. Consequently, having a significant problem and high future value attention means that the management care about supporting their employees to develop sustainable practices. In this case, management is paying attention to the creation of future value but not in the right way.

Another particular case could be identified in the "Sigma" enterprise (see Fig. 5). "Sigma" enterprise has been categorized has having an *absent* problem and also categorized as having an *absent* future attention. At first, this result could lead us to thinking that the company does not have a problem and has no reason to worry about its present and its future. Even though the enterprise does not have the problem now, does not mean that it will not have in the future. Therefore, it can be assumed that an absent/low problem and a lack of attention to the creation of future value is a symptom of no interest in the future. In this context, the enterprise focuses on quantity and short-term results. This assumption leads to thinking that managers and employees have no knowledge of sustainable development and so they do not identify problem of sustainability as a real problem.

As a consequence, if managers do not prioritize the problem, it is unlikely that enterprises will achieve sustainability. In the area of social sustainability, there is a higher probability of finding this type of situation. In particular, managers tend to underestimate their employees and do not value their human value in terms of knowledge and experience. Managers do not consider the uniqueness of their employees, and they do not use their value to create competitive advantages for the future. Even if they do not have a social sustainability problem now, it can be expected that they will probably to have one in the future. Therefore, if there is not inverse proportionality between the problem and attention to the future value, it is a symptom of a problem.

3.3 Employee Satisfaction

In the future the long-term competitive advantage depends on human sustainability, in other words, the knowledge, creativity, work ethos that human beings bring to an enterprise. The concept of human sustainability is the basis of sociotechnical theory [16, 20]. If employees voluntarily make efforts to solve work-related problems, it is likely that the company will achieve work excellence [16]. The achievement of human sustainability can take place when the employee is able to enjoy and is satisfied with his/her work [20]. However, this condition is not only intended to benefit the employee but also the enterprise and its path to sustainability.

The general thought is that employee satisfaction only depends on economic factors. In contrast, the graph below (see Fig. 6) shows that this theory is not always valid. "*Workers want to be rewarded for their work and their contribution, but money is only one aspect (translated from Italian)*" [21]. In this context, the economic gratification refers to the economic bonus or surplus offered by the company to encourage better work from employees. What the graph (see Fig. 6) shows is that economic gratification is not the main key factor for employee' satisfaction.

A significant factor that could influence employees' satisfaction is the best use of their skills and knowledge. In this case, the best use of employees' skills and knowledge refers to the managerial ability to involve and encourage employee capability. Some data shows that even if economic gratification is higher than the best use of the employee' skills and knowledge, the level of employee satisfaction is the same as the best use of employee' knowledge and skills. Therefore, employees can be expected to be more satisfied and motivated to work better when their skills and knowledge are used in the best way. In this context, employees will feel involved and appreciated. Managers should focus on the employees, making them feel appreciated to earn their satisfaction and as a consequence, their trust.

From sociotechnical perspective, the importance of employee satisfaction is reflected in the analytic framework to evaluate employee satisfaction developed by the research unit at the Manchester Business School [20]. The first area of interest of this study is the knowledge "fit", where the knowledge and skills of the employee are collocated. Job satisfaction is based on the achievement of a good fit between job needs and expectations in different areas [20]. Employee satisfaction depends on multiple factors, for example task structure, ethics and efficiency [20]. Due to a lack of data, not all the multiple factors are the focus of this analysis. In this study,

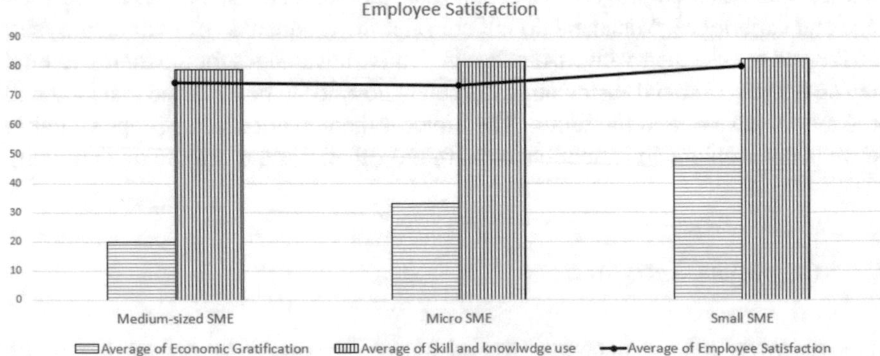

Fig. 6 Employee satisfaction compared to economic gratification and employee' skill and knowledge use

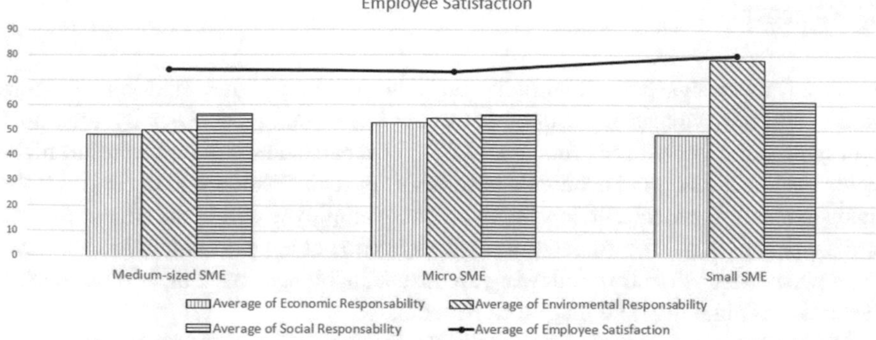

Fig. 7 Employee satisfaction compared to employee responsibility in all sustainability areas for each company size

it seems that employee satisfaction is the main result of the right use of employee skills and knowledge.

However, other factors could influence employee satisfaction, such as the amount or extent to which employees enjoy their work. Enjoyment of work mostly depends on the work environment and how the employee feels comfortable and integrated into it. In addition, the level of responsibility that an employee has in environmental, social and economic area could impact on his/her satisfaction. In this case, responsibility of employee indicates the economic, social and environmental issues that the manager gives to the employee as their responsibility.

Overall, the amount of responsibilities an employee has does not always have a positive influence on his/her satisfaction. The graph below (see Fig. 7) shows that economic responsibility is the one that has the least impact on employee' satisfaction. In contrast, environmental responsibility has a quite strong impact on satisfaction. Therefore, the responsibilities that can positively influence employee' satisfaction are those which can increase employee involvement and are voluntarily desired and not imposed.

Overall, employee satisfaction is a key factor in achieving sustainability. To achieve high level of sustainability the manager must be able to properly involve his employees, for example, allocating the correct responsibilities for each employee and not underestimating their potential. Once again, managers have a crucial role. In this analysis, managers could be defined as inexperienced because they do not know how to lead good sustainability leadership. Gaining trust and the attention of an employee is a complicated process, which leads to more satisfying and productive work. Employee satisfaction has a positive impact on whole enterprise. Furthermore, employee satisfaction helps to lead to an evident change in sustainability and competitive advantage for the future of the company.

4 Discussion

The analysis in this paper highlights the low attention to the creation of future value, especially concerning economic and environmental areas. Usually, the future economic value generally is fundamental for companies. However, the result highlights the low attention to economic sustainability. This result could derive from the managerialism approach and low involvement of employee within the economic area and the pursuit of short-term incomes. Managers do not appear to include sociotechnical perspectives therefore following an unsustainable approach and do not pursue systemic sustainability and long-term benefits.

Environment is commonly perceived as the first area associated with sustainability. In recent years, legislation and then the customer' perspectives pushed enterprises to have a green vision and having more respect for the environment. However, our analysis shows that enterprises still give poor attention to enviromental sustainability. Managers do not transfer environmental knowledge to their employees, and they do not involve them as the sociotechnical approach suggest. Employees are the ones that interface with the environment in their work practices. Therefore, employees should have proper training on best environmental practices to pursue sustainability as integrated part of their work. Overall, due to the lack of attention to future value as well as the maximum sustainable levels, there seems to be no presence of systemic sustainability.

The analysis identifies a correlation between the current problem with systemic sustainability and future value. The present problem of corporate sustainability could be addressed paying attention to the creation of value for future generations. Only through the contextualization and systemic understanding of the problem, could managers support employees to find the best solutions that lead to sustainability in work practices. However, the most critical issue that was noticed is the poor support and guidance that employees have from managers. In general, due to a lack of knowledge of sustainability practices in context, there is a low correlation of actual work practices and the ideal. The analysis of employees' sustainable work practices shows that the current approach of managers is incorrect. The Chartered Institute of Personnel and Development confirmed that the quality and approach of managers has not improved in the past decade [22]. Therefore, innovation is needed to develop sustainable enterprises [8]. Managers, as the cultivators of the enterprise' context, have a crucial role in sustainable work practices [8]. From sociotechnical perspective, developing both technology and human system is a way to bring innovation through an enterprise.

If managers follow the sociotechnical approach, focusing on employee' work practices, they can identify the main sustainability problems in the economic, social and environmental areas. Most of all, managers could detect and co-construct solutions with the employee to improve the implementation of sustainability with the triple bottom line approach [23]. In line with the Mumford perspective, and focusing on human sustainability the collaboration between manager and employee is essential. However, communication can be difficult in an enterprise context. Communication difficulties can hinder collaboration. To mediate and facilitate the communication the introduction of a facilitator could help the interactions and collaboration between managers and employees [11]. The implementation of collaboration and communication could be a benefit for better implementation of sustainability in work practices.

The analysis also highlights that it is important give attention to the experience of employees in order to improve employee satisfaction. Engaged employees are more likely to perceive that their knowledge is used in the right way. Therefore, if managers implement a systemic sociotechnical approach, this would be an overall improvement which could help the enterprise to move towards business excellence. From this perspective, managers should approach and understand employees and their work practices that are important for sustainability in practice. Furthermore, employees that feel valued for their efforts may voluntarily improve their relations with sustainable work practices. The desire of each employee to contribute to a change in the achievement of business excellence should be the bases of the companies work system [8]. Therefore, to remain competitive, managers should adopt a participative approach [22]. Instead of imposing directives, managers should combine individual and organizational needs, understanding their employees and learning about how to impact positively on them [22]. Overall, according to the industry 5.0 agenda, enterprises can be competitive by supporting employees work practices [8]. As a consequence, this could lead to a competitive advantage and sustainability, as a business is not sustainable if it cannot be competitive.

Triple bottom line together systemic sociotechnical approach seems to be a logical way to pursue sustainability in enterprises. TBL emphasizes the essential aspects of every business. The single areas included in the TBL approach are not relevant enough in isolation. The different sustainability' areas are systemically interconnected. The systemic perception of sustainability highlights that a change in a part of the system could affect the whole [16]. Sociotechnical system theory underlines the importance to focus on both technological and human systems to bring innovation and improve the performances of the whole system [16]. Even if it is not entirely developed in sustainability' practices, human sustainability is integrated into the TBL approach. Therefore, from a sociotechnical perspective, the authors argue the need to pursue a fourth bottom line creating the systemic sustainability model.

The model aims to achieve systemic sustainability with a sociotechnical perspective. Therefore, the model focuses on economic, environmental, social and technological aspects and their relationships (see Fig. 8). Previously, technology was not explicitly included in the TBL approach; however, it appears to have been assumed as part of each sustainability area. The technological area presents interconnections with other sustainability' areas and has the potential to afford systemic changes. Furthermore, technology is a part of the problem and part of the solution to achieve sustainability bringing innovation and competitive advantage in an enterprise. Therefore, there is a need to include technology and relationships with other areas as one integrated whole to achieve systemic sustainability.

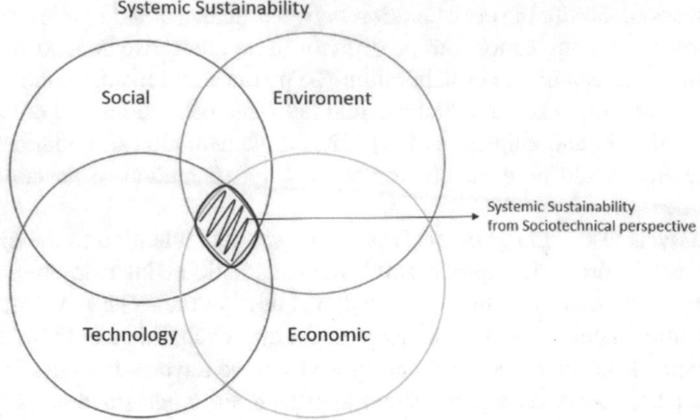

Fig. 8 Systemic sustainability

5 Conclusions

The sociotechnical approach helps to achieve business excellence and sustainable systems by focusing on human and technological capital. As Bednar and Sadok argue, "*Social and Human Sustainability are necessary to support loyalty and the development of quality work results and excellence in work practices*" [13: 24]. Sociotechnical system approach "*could provide support for companies to explore potential to incorporate future sustainability practices, involving changes in work systems design*" [24: 11]. Systemic sustainability model merge sociotechnical perspective focusing on economic, environmental, social and technological aspects. Therefore, sociotechnical and systemic sustainability could lay the foundations for the improvement of business activities and long-term systemic sustainability in business excellence. In addition, these approaches help enterprises to improve and verify corporate sustainability and also, they will be complying with the European directive [14].

In future analysis, in addition to these findings, it could be interesting to take further on investigation the involvement of individual employees in economic, environmental and social sustainability. Employee quality of involvement could be useful to understand the potential and future sustainable growth. The development of new categories could, for example, be intended to specify the level of employee involvement. This categorisation could support a complete overview of sustainability from the employee perspective. Furthermore, it could be interesting also to identify the systemic interconnection between different sustainability areas. The understanding and the hidden meaning of employees' perspectives that underpin the systemic perspective should be explored further to support a better-informed analysis. In addition, data related to cyber-security' aspects could be added to the raw dataset in order to explore and integrate IS security technology into the analysis. Overall, to analyse the level of systemic sustainability, there is the need to analyse the whole context deeper, starting with everyday employee work practices which are intended to implement sustainability practices, and expanding from there.

In conclusion, employees are the mirror which reflects enterprise. Only from the context of employees can we understand if sustainability is implemented in real work practices. Sustainability is not a concept that should remain abstract. Instead, systemic sustainability should be implemented day by day in real-world work practices under economic, environmental, technological and social aspects with the collaboration of both employees and managers. For this reason, when sustainability is integrated within the behavior and thinking of employees, the company can be considered sustainable.

References

1. Brundtland, G. H. (1987). Our common future Call for action. *Environmental Conservation, 14*(4), 291–294.
2. Elkington, J. (2004). Enter the triple bottom line. In A. Henriques & J. Richardson (Eds.), *The Triple Bottom Line: Does it all add up?* (pp. 1–16). London: Earthscan.
3. Elkington, J. (1998). Partnerships from cannibals with forks: The triple bottom line of 21st-century business. *Environmental Quality Management, 8*(1), 37–51.
4. Alhaddi, H. (2015). Triple bottom line and sustainability: A literature review. *Business and Management Studies, 1*(2), 6–10.
5. Zak, A. (2015). Triple Bottom Line Concept in Theory and Practice. *Research Papers of the Wroclaw University of Economics, 387*, 251–264.
6. Savitz, A., & Weber, K. (2006). *The triple bottom line: How today's best-run companies are achieving economic, social and environmental success-and how you can too.* San Francisco Calif: Jossey-Bass.
7. Slaper, T. F., & Hall, T. J. (2011). The triple bottom line: What is it and how does it work. *Indiana Business Review, 86*(1), 4–8.
8. Bednar, P. M., & Welch, C. (2019). Socio-technical perspectives on smart working: Creating meaningful and sustainable systems. *Information Systems Frontiers, 21*(1), 1–18.
9. Mumford, E. (2003). *Redesigning human systems.* Hershey: IRM Press.
10. Mumford, E. (2006). The story of sociotechnical design: Reflections on its successes, failures and potential. *Information Systems Journal, 16*(4), 317–342.
11. Stahl, B. C. (2007). ETHICS, Morality and Critique: An Essay on Enid Mumford's Socio-Technical Approach. *Journal of the Association for Information Systems, 8*(9), 28.
12. Sarker, S., Chatterjee, S., Xiao, X., & Elbanna, A.: Research commentary the sociotechnical "axis of cohesion" for the IS discipline: its historical legacy and its continued relevance12. *MIS Quarterly,* (2019).
13. Bednar, P.M. & Sadok, M.: A Socio-technical toolbox for business systems analysis and design", Proceedings of the *1st International Workshop on Socio-Technical Perspective in IS Development (STPIS'15) co-located with the 27th International Conference on Advanced Information Systems Engineering (CAiSE 2015)*, Stockholm, Sweden (2015).
14. *Official Journal of the European Union, L 330, 15 November 2014 eur-lex*, https://eur-lex.europa.eu/legal-content/EN/ALL/?uri=OJ:L:2014:330:TOC, last accessed 2019/05/27.
15. *Non-financial reporting ec.europa,* https://eur-lex.europa.eu/legal-content/EN/TXT/?uri=CELEX%3A32014L0095, last accessed 2019/05/27.
16. Bednar, P. (2018). *Sociotechnical toolbox: Information system analysis and design.* UK: Craneswater Press Ltd.

17. *Statistical classification of economic activities in the European Community ec.europa*, https://ec.europa.eu/eurostat/documents/3859598/5902521/KS-RA-07-015-EN.PDF, last accessed 2019/05/27.
18. Elkington, J. (2018). *25 Years Ago I Coined the Phrase "Triple Bottom Line." Here's Why It's Time to Rethink It. hbr*, https://hbr.org/2018/06/25-years-ago-i-coined-the-phrase-triple-bottom-lineheres-why-im-giving-up-on-it, last accessed 2019/05/27.
19. Mohr, B. J. &, Amelsvoort, P. van: Co-creating humane and innovative organizations: Evolutions in the practice Of Socio-Technical System Design. Global STS-D Network Press, Portland (2016).
20. Mumford, E., Hickey, S., & Matthies, H. (2006). *Designing Human Systems: An agile approach to ETHICS*. UK: Lightning Source UK Ltd.
21. "*Trattate bene i vostri dipendenti e loro tratteranno bene la vostra azienda" repubblica*, https://www.repubblica.it/economia/miojob/2018/12/26/news/_trattate_bene_i_vostri_dipendenti_e_loro_tratteranno_bene_la_vostra_azienda_-214622443/, last accessed 2019/05/31.
22. *"Humane Leadership Must Be The Fourth Industrial Revolution's Real Innovation" forbes*, https://www.forbes.com/sites/worldeconomicforum/2019/05/21/humane-leadership-must-be-the-fourth-industrial-revolutions-real-innovation/#42fce095501b, last accessed 2019/05/27.
23. Viscusi, G., Campagnolo G. M., & Curzi Y.: Phenomenology, Organizational Politics, and IT Design: The Social Study of Information Systems: The Social Study of Information Systems. IGI Global (2012).
24. Sadok, M., & Welch, C. E, (2019). Achieving sustainable business systems through sociotechnical perspectives. *27th European Conference on Information Systems (ECIS)*, Stockholm & Uppsala, Sweden (2019).

New Technologies for Preventing and Reducing Verbal and Non-verbal Assaults Against Healthcare Professionals Within Hospitals: The State of Art

Paola Briganti, Stefania Mele, and Luisa Varriale

Abstract This study investigates the main implications of new technologies within healthcare setting, specifically hospitals, in preventing and reducing verbal and non-verbal assaults, sometimes concrete violence, against healthcare professionals. New technologies significantly affect the way to work of healthcare professionals especially within hospitals taking into account, on one side, the need to strongly reduce the costs (spending review policy), and, on the other side, to provide effective services to citizens for making them to live in good health. Also, new technologies provide further innovative solutions for facing some specific challenges, such as the continuous and numerous episodes of violence and aggressions received by healthcare professionals during their work. This phenomenon is very spread, mostly within public hospitals in the world, above all in Italy. This study aims to analyse this phenomenon through a review of the main contributions of the literature on the topic and in the practice for building a clear and complete picture and give some useful suggestions.

Keywords Industry 4.0 · Healthcare setting · Verbal and non-verbal assaults · Hospitals · Violence and aggressions · New technologies

P. Briganti · L. Varriale (✉)
Department of Sport Science and Wellbeing, Parthenope University, Naples, Italy
e-mail: luisa.varriale@uniparthenope.it

P. Briganti
e-mail: paola.briganti@uniparthenope.it

S. Mele
Department of Management and Quantitative Studies, Parthenope University, Naples, Italy
e-mail: stefania.mele@uniparthenope.it

C. Metallo et al. (eds.), *Digital Transformation and Human Behavior*, Lecture Notes in Information Systems and Organisation 37,
https://doi.org/10.1007/978-3-030-47539-0_19

1 Introduction

Over the last three decades the healthcare setting aims to increase the effectiveness and the efficiency, especially responding to the pressures derived from the spending review policy at international level, above all in Italy. At the same time, healthcare organizations were completely and significantly transformed thanks to the spread and implementation of new technologies, typically connected to the Industry 4.0. The way to work within hospitals and any healthcare organizations significantly changed because of the automation and digitalization able to improve the efficiency of their organizational and managerial processes.

Drawing from a review of the main contributions in the literature and practice, this study aims to analyse the main implications of new technologies within healthcare setting, mostly hospitals, in preventing and reducing verbal and non-verbal assaults, especially concrete violence, against healthcare professionals. This phenomenon received an increasing attention by scholars and practitioners only in the last years giving the opportunity to think about and to search for innovative and also technologically advanced solutions for preventing and reducing this kind of behaviours by family members or caregivers of patients. Indeed, the studies, including press articles, show and describe episodes where healthcare professionals (nurses, doctors, physicians, etc.) are victims of verbal and non-verbal assaults, sometimes aggressions and violence actions. These episodes and also the existing high risks of threats represent sources of stress and very dangerous ills for healthcare professionals.

This conceptual study outlines the main implications and the crucial role played by new technologies (such as cameras, electronic control system, reporting tools, etc.) in preventing and reducing verbal and non-verbal assaults within hospitals. This research, which represents a starting research point, tries to systematise the existing contributions in the literature and practice, including press articles, especially with focus on the Italian context, for clarifying the current state of art in terms of studies and solutions proposed linked to new technologies.

The paper is structured as follows: Sects. 2 and 2.1 provide respectively a summary of the main studies in the literature focused on verbal and non-verbal assaults to healthcare professionals and existing proposals and effective solutions also related to new technologies. Section 3 evidences some major practices used for managing the phenomenon adopting new technologies. Last section provides some final considerations and future developments of the study.

2 Literature Review

During the last two decades, different studies outlined that hospital physicians, nurses, technical staff were at higher risk of verbal and non-verbal assaults by patients and their caregivers, also with negative effects on their psychological work safety and stress [1–4]. Because of this increasing phenomenon, there is an urgent need to adopt a well-being organizational perspective and, also, a cost-effective risk management strategy for preventing, managing and containing assaults in healthcare field, also using new technologies tools, and any innovative information technologies, such as camera, incident reporting systems, stress reporting, intranet aid request even to specific organizational counsellors [2].

At the beginning the phenomenon of violence against healthcare professional workers was mostly and primarily investigated within psychiatric structures, as shown from the broad documentation about evidences of continued occurrence of aggressive patient assaults on the staff, due to pathological characteristic of the target audience [2]. Furthermore, most cross-sectional studies didn't report relevant differences in terms of gender diversity showing that both male and female healthcare workers were had at the same highest risk. Indeed, Flannery and colleagues [2] in their 15-year longitudinal retrospective study analysed the same/different gender assaults over time, although in the psychiatric community, males were much more at risk from same male gender assaults compared to females with risk from assaults by both patient genders.

In recent decades, research and practice started to pay attention to verbal and nonverbal assaults against healthcare professionals in any organizations, going beyond the psychiatric structures, including general hospitals or rehabilitation structures.

Since the Nineties, scholars and practitioners outlined that healthcare employees mostly experience objective conditions, related to the psychosocial and physical environment, recognized as stressors, and indeed, perceived as harmful, threatening, and/or bothersome [5, 6]. Numerous factors may be conceived as stressors, including major life events (e.g. the death of co-workers on the job), ambient environment (e.g. exposure to noise or hazardous materials), daily hassles (e.g. meeting deadlines), chronic strains (e.g. ongoing work overload or sex discrimination), and cataclysmic events (e.g. toxic spills) [7, 8].

In the international domain, scholars and practitioners investigate, on one side, the main determinants, that is the objective and subjective factors related to verbal and non-verbal assaults of healthcare workers, and, on the other side, the major negative effects of increasing aggressions due to patients and their caregivers, especially in terms of psycho-social risks of work-related stress and burnout, and physical and psychological safety of healthcare professionals. Otherwise, this phenomenon and its negative effects don't have linear dynamics, particularly because different individual and organizational variables may moderate and mediate the negative effects. Thus, these factors, recognized as stressors, don't always have negative outcomes, also because it depends on how much people involved perceive these factors really stressful [4].

The major effects/reactions of healthcare workers as victims of violence by patients and their caregivers at workplace are very different including many elements, also depending by the personality traits of victims and environmental factors in general. It is possible to distinguish physiological (elevated blood pressure), psychological (tenseness), and behavioural (alcohol use, exercise, and use of protective equipment) reactions with also dangerous health outcomes for the victims, such as cardiovascular disease, anxiety disorder, or alcoholism [4]. These several factors as stressors for victims of violence can have several effects and can be modified, also depending on their relationship and on how individuals can experience the stress process, according to social, psychological, biophysical, behavioural, and genetic variables.

Israel and colleagues [4] developed a specific model focused on the effects of the stress process on individuals, but it is also applicable at group, organization, community, and societal levels. Thus, according to this stress model, the stressors, including personal and organizational/environmental factors with direct effect on short-term and long-term health outcomes, within a workgroup and organization, can be assessed considering their effects on such factors as social disintegration and organizational competence [4]. This stress model identifies five main elements as major stressor factors, that is social (e.g. social support control or socio-economic status), psychological (e.g. personality factors coping abilities), biophysical (e.g. age, gender, status), behavioural (e.g. exercise, relaxation response, nutritional diet), and genetic (e.g. family history of illness).

Other scholars focused their attention on the limited information and data about cases of verbal and non-verbal aggressions, especially violence, against healthcare workers within hospitals [9, 10]. For instance, one study evidenced that the incidence of workplace violence against nurses is underreported within hospitals [9]. Indeed, this study was able to show that the nature and frequency of violent incidents remains unknown making difficult to address the problem and also to propose some solutions. This study, using a phenomenological approach through focus group technique, identified the attitudes, barriers and enablers of emergency nurses to the reporting of workplace violence.

Most studies on the violence against healthcare workers within hospital focused on nurses at the emergency department (ED), because they are generally more exposed to assaults by patients and caregivers taking into account the high and continuative number of interactions with people affected by acute illness [10].

One recent study, using a qualitative descriptive exploratory design (a sample of 46 written narratives submitted by e-mail by emergency nurses and collected through the Emergency Nurses Association—ENA website) provided a clear understanding of the experience of emergency nurses who have been physically or verbally assaulted while providing patient care in US emergency departments [10]. Using the narrative analysis, where written narratives clearly described the experience of violence while providing care at work, three main emerging themes were identified, that is "environmental," "personal," and "cue recognition". These three broad themes, emerged from data, can be briefly described as follows: 1. the environmental theme clearly describes the institutional culture and the physical environment of ED, including the legal system/security, both inside and outside ED, including the legal system, law enforcement, and the judicial system. The personal theme concerns the impact of the event on nurses in terms of job performance, coping, and feelings, also interacting with the legal and judicial systems, law enforcement, or institutional culture. The cue recognition theme provides a clear description about the recognized or unrecognized antecedents to the violent event with focus on their characteristics of the perpetrator or the environment where the event took place.

Also, nurses believed that violence was something related to their workplace and, also, some specific barriers to mitigation were identified, such as limited recognition of cues indicating a high-risk person or environment and a culture of acceptance of violence.

An epidemiological study, always conducted in US, investigated the magnitude with the potential risk factors and consequences of work related violence against nurses in Minnesota [11]. The survey sent to 6300 Minnesota licensed registered (RNs) and practical (LPNs) nurses (78% response rate) allowed to collect relevant data showing high percentage of physical and non-physical violence, recording an increase in assault rates. Greater consequences concerned more non-physical than physical violence. The findings showed that especially the ED after experiencing severe violence should provide a clearer and deeper understanding of the phenomenon also regarding IT use (camera, information reporting systems of incident) for better preventing and managing it.

Our review shows that US nurses are widely exposed to assaults, for this reason most existing studies on the topic are focused on the US context, but other studies provide significant analysis of the phenomenon all around the world, including several countries, such as Iran or Italy, showing that the phenomenon is however independent from local culture and it depends mainly from individual and organizational factors.

Hassankhani and colleagues [12] investigated the consequences of violence against nurses working in ED in Iran, where the qualitative study outlined that serious consequences derived from workplace violence (WPV) in healthcare organizations with negative impact on nurses' lives and patient care. Also, research on the deeper underlying consequences of WPV for emergency nurses, particularly among emergency nurses in Iran, is still inconsistent and limited. Several specific themes, underlying consequences of WPV for emergency nurses, have been identified, that is "suffering nurses" (the primary theme), "mental health risks", "physical health risks", "threats to professional integrity", and "threats to social integrity" (For a summary see Table 1).

These findings should be useful for policy makers, healthcare leadership, and managers in order to better understand the phenomenon evidencing the main consequences of WPV defining and implementing effective prevention programs and support for nurses who already experienced WPV creating a safer workplace and patient care. Thus, this study, as other studies also in China [13], show that the consequences related to WPV for healthcare professionals include psychological, physical, emotional, professional, functional, social, private and financial effects (problems with their family and colleagues, impair daily activities, low morale, less work productivity, higher potential for medical errors, poor quality of care and safety, chronic health issues, sleeping problems, anxiety, depression and unpleasant emotions, physical injury and psychological damage, including chronic pain, disability, obsessive thoughts, flashbacks, and nightmares, dissatisfaction, lack of concentration at work, reduced quality of life, decreased job satisfaction, desire to

Table 1 WPV effects for nurses

Suffering nurses	
Mental health risks	Suffering from depression Anxiety and stress Unpleasant emotions
Physical health risks	Physical injuries Stress-related chronic conditions Sleeping problems
Threats to professional integrity	Loss of interest in work Poor nursing interactions Disruption in nursing care
Threats to social integrity	Family disruptions Problems especially Misunderstandings with colleagues Daily activity impairment

Source Our processing

leave the profession, increased burnout, raised organizational costs, high turnover) [10, 13, 14].

In conclusion, the findings outline that nurses who experience WPV suffer from multidimensional consequences (Table 1).

Therefore, it is necessary to change the workplace conditions in Iran, as well as in the overall world. This deep change of the workplace should be possible promoting and adopting violence prevention programs consisting of the administration's commitment and staff involvement, education and communication and adaptive skills improvement, and also through workplace analysis to find potential risk factors, risk prevention and control, continuing safety and health training and regular monitoring of the program [12]. In addition, supportive and helpful strategies, can be promoted and developed by policy makers, hospital administration, and healthcare managers, including psychological counseling and support, as well as the design and implementation of clearer reporting system for being able to identify and know facilitating factors.

In this direction, through a cyclical model of burnout and vulnerability to aggression, another study investigated anxiety, burnout and coping styles in general hospital staff exposed to workplace aggression [14]. Healthcare staff (375 workers) across professions completed the State-Trait Anxiety Inventory, the Maslach Burnout Inventory and the Coping Responses Inventory, according to the type and frequency of aggression experienced in the previous year. The results showed that there were no significant differences in levels of anxiety or in coping styles, as opposed to levels of burnout. Indeed, staff more frequently victimized presented emotional exhaustion and depersonalization leading to higher level of burnout.

As already outlined, although the aggression (physical assault, threatening behaviour and verbal aggression) within healthcare setting represents a very relevant and spread phenomenon which broadly and directly regards toward general hospital staff, and not only staff in psychiatric institutions, it is not still widely investigated.

Some interesting studies focus on the phenomenon in Italy. In particular, Winstanley and Whittington [15] investigated WPV against nursing students and nurses in Italy, by comparing the characteristics and effects of violence in nursing students and nurses for assessing the phenomenon and taking preventive action. This study conducted a retrospective survey on violence, mental health, job stress, and organizational justice in three Italian university schools of nursing (totally 346 students and 275 nurses from a general hospital).Most individuals presented at least one upsetting episode of physical or verbal violence during their lifetime activity in clinical settings (43% in nurses and 34% in nursing students). Nurses reported more physical assaults, threats, and sexual harassment during the previous 12 months more than students. Nurses evidenced assaults or harassments by patients, relatives and friends ("external" violence), whereas students mostly reported verbal and also physical violence on the part of colleagues, staff, and others, including teachers, doctors, and supervisors ("internal" violence). Also, in this study it was outlined that preventive actions are urgently needed to control patient-to-worker and worker-to-worker violence in clinical settings. In the clinical and organizational perspective, nurses and nursing students and hospital would benefit from multilevel programs of violence prevention.

Scholars and practitioners, as already evidenced, agree that the main barriers, also for making the preventing workplace violence programs successful and effective, concern the underreporting of workplace violence. Indeed, the lack of reporting doesn't allow to easily identify the trends and problem areas within hospitals [16]. Many reasons can explain the underreporting, like the feeling that violence is only one part of the job, and so although you report violence incidents, nothing can change, or the person responsible for receiving the report should be also the same perpetrator [16, 17].

As a consequence, formal reporting, through mechanisms utilizing incident forms, are not spread and common in these areas without any regulations. Fortunately, many state laws for violence prevention in healthcare recently imposed the formal reports, such as the New Jersey Department of Human Services (NJDHSS 2012).

Findorff and colleagues [17] outlined that escalation, injury, and repetition of events can be considered as key factors that increased motivation to report WPV incidents among healthcare workers. Several events/situations that can motivate more healthcare workers to report violence incidents can be distinguished, that is: the intention of the perpetrator not to stop; lost time in reporting the violent incident; the presence of an increased frequency in verbal and non-physical threats of violence; the use of the employee assistance program (EAP) services after an incident; the use of the healthcare system to treat the physical and mental wounds of violence by the employees [17].

In summary, WPV in hospitals represents and has been broadly recognized and clearly stated by scholars as a constant and increasing phenomenon among healthcare providers. Indeed, according to the Homeland Security Bulletin in February 2017, erratic patients, gang activities, and, an increased threat of terrorism make high risks for healthcare workers. In this report the victims of assaults are annually approximately 11,000 healthcare workers, and more than 50% of ED nurses regularly experience verbal or physical assault. Furthermore, violence against healthcare professionals at workplace in US annually accounts 1000 fatalities and over 20,000 non-fatal events in the United States [3]. Another report published in the Online

Journal of Issues in Nursing considered physical violence against nurses as "an endemic problem affecting nurses in all settings" across the globe. The emergency department and inpatient mental health units have been recognized as the two most dangerous departments in healthcare settings. ED presents the highest risk because of its characteristics and conditions for violent behaviour. Indeed, in ED numerous elements can motivate violent behaviours, such as long waits, delays, aggressive people, stress among people (patients, families, and visitors), substance and alcohol abuse, and unrestricted 24 h access. Otherwise, several sources evidence that ED security concerns are generally related to 3 sources: gang violence, dissatisfied patients, and behavioural health issues.

Therefore, WPV is seriously underreported, also due to the lack of organizational policy, the conceptualization of violence as a criminal act, or because healthcare providers justify the violent behaviour considering something outside the individual's control (medical problem, drugs, pain, altered mental status).

An effective resource for conducting a workplace safety assessment concerns the ASIS International's Workplace Violence Prevention and Intervention Standard. The healthcare staff, security personnel, and architects involved in the design process can follow these guidelines for ensuring best practices that need to be considered and integrated into healthcare facilities. Thus, hospitals should take into account WPV risks in their hazard vulnerability analysis (HVA), above all considering some crucial elements to define and implement, such as infrastructure, security response, policy response, staffing, case review, and interventions, and also the new technologies can really successfully and effectively support the development and adoption of preventing programs and interventions.

2.1 *Organizational Practices in the Literature Supported by New Technologies*

Even though numerous studies show that verbal and non-verbal assaults, mostly violence aggressions, represent one prevalent and serious problem for healthcare workers, especially in ED, significant contributions about of interventions and actions, addressed to prevent, reduce, and manage this alarming trend, are still scarce also including new disposable information technology systems.

Generally, specific efforts to prevent, reduce and manage violence and promote workplace safety tend to combine design solutions and operational protocols. Indeed, in this case prevention and management policies require a strong collaboration between organizational leaders, departmental staff, security officers, and law enforcement for being successfully developed and enforced. Adopting a multifaceted approach, taking into account environmental design, policy, enforcement of acceptable behaviours, and pre-empting escalating events, and activating a multi-actors perspective, where all the stakeholders and the overall community are involved, can allow to define and implement more effective and successful risk-preventing and reduction efforts.

The existing contributions in the research distinguish several interventions and forms of actions in order to prevent, reduce and manage verbal and non-verbal assaults against healthcare professionals, especially violent aggressions, that is physical and environmental design, education and training programs, advanced technology systems, and so forth.

Regarding the interventions related to physical and environmental design, which can positively affect the safety and efficiency of healthcare organizations, especially ED operations, it is possible to consider five main features, that is parking, entry zone, traffic management, care zones and room clustering, and specialized rooms. Indeed, in the pre-design stage several functional parameters are considered and understood for the final schematic design, that is space planning, work flows, and special adjacencies, as well as by including methods to secure high-risk departments or areas, cordon off (isolate) the ED entrance and limited access to the facility, safe spaces for staff, and rapid egress from secured spaces In this scenario regarding best practices for preventing and containing violence camera surveillance and intrusion alarms are recognised as standard features for all healthcare facilities.

One significant strategy and intervention for reducing the risk of violence is represented by education and training for prevention [18–20]. A quasi-experimental design study evidenced the learning outcomes of WPV educational program tailored considering the specific needs of 120 ED employees, consisting of a hybrid (online and classroom) educational intervention regarding [18]. Studies focused on the impact of training healthcare providers for violence prevention reported mixed results and significant limitations [17]. Most recently graduated nurses (83%) believed that education about violence prevention and bullying should be included in their nursing education curriculum compared to a few recently graduated nurses (22%) who actually received training during their academic preparation [21]. Both knowledge of how to report WPV and the use of personal cell phones increased the reporting of WPV incidents [22]. Also, an educational program among acute-care psychiatric nurses was positively and effectively assessed in reducing the number of assaults.

Gates and colleagues [23], using an action research model including six hospitals, implemented and evaluated a violence prevention and management intervention built through 12 focus groups with 97 individuals. To develop focus group questions by collecting data about the pre-assault, during assault, and post-assault time frames and by comparing these findings to planned strategies, it was used the Haddon matrix, which was very useful in identifying intervention strategies able to be successfully implemented and sustained by EDs (Table 2). Several themes were identified concerning the intervention strategies for patients/visitors, employees, managers, and the work environment by recognizing the relevance, feasibility, and saliency of the planned intervention strategies. Employees, managers and patients focused on themes like on improved staff communication and comfort measures and the need to introduce prevention violence strategies.

Violence and surveillance careful implementation of advanced technological systems, especially Close Circuit Television (CCTV) and alarm systems, have been

Table 2 Haddon matrix applied to ED violence prevention

	Host (employee) factors	Vector and vehicle (patient/visitor) factors	Physical/social environmental factors
Before assault	Education and training Policy and procedures Preventing aggressive behavior De-escalation and conflict resolution Managing aggression	Communication to patients and visitors of policy that violence will not be tolerated and potential consequences of violent behavior Minimize anxiety for waiting patients and visitors by communicating with them every 30 min	Develop and communicate policy to employees and management that violence is never acceptable Development and implementation of violence policies and procedures Manager education Security/police response/policies and education Monitor access to emergency department Develop mechanism to alert staff when patients and visitors who were previously violent visit the emergency department again Quiet environment/areas Special area for aggressive individuals/safe room for criminals Enforce visitor policies (ie, number of visitors)
During assault	Education and training Nonviolent crisis intervention	Isolate perpetrator from others	Security/police plan Implement procedures for dealing with violent event
After assault	Critical incident debriefing Mandatory reporting of all physical assaults and physical threats	Reporting to security/police Maintain patient's/visitor's name for alerting staff upon return visit	Create procedure for reviewing violent event

Source Gates et al. [23]

significantly investigated by scholars and practitioners providing contrasting results, as shown by numerous authors in relation to the appearing opposite nature of CCTV in terms of surveillance and privacy [14, 24–28]. In particular, on one side, CCTV cameras were introduced as a tool for managing safety especially within mental health hospitals all over the world, above all United Kingdom, recognized its relevant support to make the workplace safer and secure for everyone and also for providing a better care service. The major goal of CCTV surveillance is justified on the basis that they make hospital environments safer and much secure for patients, staff and visitors. Desai's review [29] aims to open up a debate about the main need for safety, mainly in mental health hospitals, reinforced, against privacy doubts, by the potential of CCTV monitoring to influence clinical mental health practices at broader level. Koskela [30] states that the fact that the 'camera itself has no eyes' and its gaze is therefore determined by whoever is undertaking the watching could be fundamental to prevent and manage violent situations, and to gain a better clinical understanding of mental health problems of patients, for more scientific observation of human behaviour, and the development of an evidence-based new psychiatrist approach.

On the other side, critical authors of CCTV claim about real and potential privacy violations: the implementation of CCTV cameras and other control systems technology systems has been negatively judged because of the restrictions of some countries in the regulation system with specific laws about the respect of privacy, the prohibition of surveillance at workplace in any organizational settings, the hierarchical power dynamics [30–33].

Also, using CCTV surveillance with some patients, very acutely unwell and subject to a wide range of cognitive distortions, evidences some doubts especially regarding the panoptic effects of CCTV in managing violent situations. For example, in the ward environment the presence of cameras has been somehow considered one factor able to incite a violent response because the cameras can increase levels of paranoia associated with their delusions and mental health problem [34]. Also, some patients use to see CCTV monitoring as limitations of their privacy.

In summary, new surveillance technology, such as CCTV, presents many advantages but also some disadvantages, but most studies which investigated the adoption of CCTV cameras and other technologies for surveillance, although they recognize their helpful and effective application, broadly agree that the efficacy for CCTV cameras in controlling and managing violence within psychiatric wards is still not enough and thus inconclusive. For this reason, it is necessary to further develop the research in this field.

In this direction to further develop the previous studies, Blando and colleagues [35] investigated barriers to effective implementation of programs for preventing WPV in hospitals, also considering new technologies. Although effective WPV prevention programs are essential, their implementation in healthcare is still limited and challenging. The authors evidenced seven themes as major barriers to effective implement WPV [35]: "lack of action despite reporting; varying perceptions of violence; bullying; profit-driven management models; lack of management accountability; focus on customer service; and weak social service and law enforcement approaches to mentally ill patients".

From the perspective of the impact of policies also from other industries than healthcare setting, such as educational institutions, comprehensive policies can be effective in reducing physical violence [36] compared to other results where policies and programs didn't have positive impact on the employees' perception of their risk of violence or their ability to respond to violence [37].

For implementing prevention and managing programs and interventions very successful and effective it is necessary to involve the overall management as well as any individuals within organizations, also for overcoming the main barrier, that is bullying, spread especially among new nurse graduates and nursing students [38, 39].

For being effective with WPV programs and interventions supported also by new technologies, scholars and practitioners still agree in needing to operate together and collaborate, especially for making and implementing creative innovations which are able to address these issues and improve WPV prevention programs.

3 Positive Impact of New Technologies Against Violence in Hospitals: Some Practices to Make Safer the Workplace

Some good practices could witness that a technologically improved workplace could be, on one hand, a way to control the environment and to give safety to it and, on the other hand, it should be a way to reassure patients who feel themselves protected by hospitals equipment. The results concern both organizational and psychological domains and it is a good experience as for healthcare staff as for patient centrality.

Two practical studies have been analyzed where ICT based hospitals gave good results in order to prevent and manage violence against healthcare professionals: the case of Humber River Hospital that is one of Canada's largest community acute care hospitals, serving a population of more than 850,000 people in the northwest Greater Toronto Area [40, 41] and the case of ten facility environmental evaluation reports along with staff focus group reports from these facilities of US hospitals [22].

In the first analysis, a research was conducted in Humber River Hospital a multi-site hospital with a total of 722 beds, just over 3800 employees, approximately 700 physicians and over 1000 volunteers, through a qualitative study in which data were collected through focus groups and semi-structured interviews with 11 nurses. Interviews were subjected to a content analysis to identify core themes.

Three themes were identified: a reassurance of safety through ICT technologies (camera monitoring, RFID, informatics procedures), an increase in proactive measures together with technology, that nurses held positive perceptions of the impact of technology-based interventions on violent incidents. The interventions were judged effective for the detection of potentially violent patients (before events), as well as for aiding from security staff when a violent incident occurs or appears imminent. However, nurses also acknowledged that technology cannot fully prevent violence from occurring without organizational commitment and adequate procedures. The way is to engage staff, patients and families in a digital and technology-enriched environment and try to rewrite hospital rules together with technologies.

The devices used in this case are a full camera monitoring especially for the first access areas, a RFID system to identify patients flow and a special flagging system, which is fully integrated into HRH's digital infrastructure, that involves the use of standardized symbols that can be seen in the patient's medical record, as well as on the digital signage next to the door of the patient's room.

One of the key advantages of the system at HRH is the use of digital signage over traditional paper-based signage as data automatically update once the information is added to the patient's medical record. The system also uses minimalist symbols, which avoids visual clutter and does not disclose more information on a patient than it is needed, while still supporting workers' "right to know" about potential dangers. The flagging system is also able to alert all staff, including maintenance workers and volunteers who do not have access to patients' charts, of any known risks before they enter a patient's room.

The second study was conducted in USA thanks to Federal policy recommendation on environmental strategies as part of a comprehensive workplace violence program in healthcare and social services.

The purpose of the study was to specifically contribute to the evidence–based guidance to the healthcare and social services employer communities regarding the use of environmental design to prevent violence. A review was conducted on environmental evaluations that were performed by architects through the methodology of Participatory Action Research (PAR). Ten facility environmental evaluation reports along with staff focus group reports from these facilities were analysed to categorize environmental risk factors and the link between technology structures and safe environments. The findings were organized according to their impact on the access control, ability to monitor patients and worker safety and activity support. The environmental assessment findings reveal the design and security issues that, if corrected, would improve safety and security of staff, patients, and visitors and reduce fear and unpredictability and the more technology is used properly the more the workplace is and it is perceived safe.

The settings for these studies were selected based on the state government agencies' interest in enhancing their existing violence prevention. The environmental surveys and focus groups described in this report are a part of the overall violence prevention intervention projects and were undertaken to identify environmental risk factors for violence, including sanitary staff perceptions of how the physical work environment contributes to safety at work. The findings from the staff surveys determined the enhancement of each facility's violence prevention program with the use of specific workplace design, especially for technological devices, ICT patient's identification, the applications distributed to nurses, physicians and employers to understand the high-risk event and to prevent violence. This study was especially interesting in mental healthcare departments.

The findings from these environmental surveys served as a baseline for environmental assessment and led to the development, implementation, and evaluation of feasible interventions. There was a total of 10 study sites: four psychiatric hospitals (two adult, one adult forensic, and one children's) and six inpatient addiction treatment centres within general purpose hospitals.

Data derived from ICT technologies could also be used for risk assessment activities and for improving all the system. In large structures through these technologies we could derive a set of big data and it is easy to upgrade risk management and redesign workplace for safety.

Focus groups were organized to understand not only the procedures and their impact on violence prevention but also to considerate how the organization must change in consequence of this technological design.

These two examples of research focused on practices related to measures and interventions for preventing and managing violence against healthcare workers can be considered as two interesting solutions which show that for being effective and efficient in this case it is necessary to follow several actions, that is: to create and implement a comprehensive reporting system of violence incidents able to record the incidents and analyse them; to identify the main risk factors of determinants; to deeply analyse the individual and organizational/contextual variables; to develop adequate prevention programs also through counselling services. All these actions can be significantly and successfully supported by new technologies.

4 Concluding Remarks

This research contributes to the existing literature and practice point of view providing a clear picture of the current state of art regarding the existing studies and practices that exist in preventing and reducing verbal and non-verbal assaults, especially any forms of violence, against healthcare professionals within hospitals with the support of IT. Indeed, this study mainly explores the experiences of nurses and healthcare staff regarding the implementation of technology-based violence prevention interventions.

The review of the main contributions in the literature and in practice shows that the adoption of new technologies, such as cameras or badge control system, represents effective solutions for supporting and defending healthcare professionals at workplace significantly reducing their stress and high risks. Unfortunately, this phenomenon is still under research and it is not very clear which frameworks can be adopted for clarifying the possible effective solutions and, also, how it is possible to take into account cultural, contextual and organizational factors.

This research consisting in a conceptual study represents a starting research point, as a working progress, with the specific aim to find the right way for giving a contribution from the organizational perspective in managing this interesting phenomenon still underrepresented.

In the future, for deeply and clearly knowing the determinants of the phenomenon and better identifying and implementing more effective innovative and technologically advanced solutions, we aim to build a complete portrait of specific experiences reported in the literature and in the press at international level and to create a clear research design model, including also contextual and cultural variables, making comparative analysis between several healthcare contexts, taking into account specific characteristics of the territory.

References

1. Lenaghan, P. A., Cirrincione, N. M., & Henrich, S. (2017). Preventing emergency department violence through design. *Journal of Emergency Nursing*.
2. Flannery, R. B., Marks, L., Laudani, L., & Walker, A. P. (2007). Psychiatric patient assault and staff victim gender: Fifteen-year analysis of the Assaulted Staff Action Program (ASAP). *Psychiatric Quarterly, 78*(2), 83–90.
3. Runyan, C. W., Zakocs, R. C., & Zwerling, C. (2000). Administrative and behavioral interventions for workplace violence prevention. *American Journal of Preventive Medicine, 18*(4), 116–127.
4. Israel, B. A., Baker, E. A., Goldenhar, L. M., & Heaney, C. A. (1996). Occupational stress, safety, and health: Conceptual framework and principles for effective prevention interventions. *Journal of Occupational Health Psychology, 1*(3), 261.
5. Lazarus, R., & Folkman, S. *Stress, appraisal and coping*. New York: Springer.
6. Selye, H. (1984). *Life stress, 1982*. New York: Van Nostrand Reinhold.
7. Israel, B. A., & Schurman, S. J. (1990). Social support, control, and the stress process. In K. Glanz, F. M. Lewis, & B. K. Rimer (Eds.), *The Jossey-Bass health series. Health behavior and health education: Theory, research, and practice* (pp. 187–215). San Francisco, CA, US: Jossey-Bass.
8. McPhaul, K. M., London, M., Murrett, K., Flannery, K., Rosen, J., & Lipscomb, J. (2008). Environmental evaluation for workplace violence in healthcare and social services. *Journal of Safety Research, 39*, 237–250.
9. Hogarth, K. M., Beattie, J., Morphet, J., & Koller, R. N. (2016). It could never happen here: Promoting violence prevention education for emergency department nurses. *Journal of Continuing Education in Nursing, 47*(8), 356–60. https://doi.org/10.3928/00220124-20160715-06.
10. Corey, D. M., & Wolf, G. D. (1992). An integrated approach to reducing stress injuries. In J. C. Quick, L. R. Murphy, & J. J. Hurrell (Eds.), *Stress and well-being at work: Assessments and interventions for occupational mental health* (pp. 64–78). Washington, DC: American Psychological Association.
11. Gerberich, S. G., Church, T. R., & McGovern, P.M., et al. (2002). A study of risk factors for violence among nurses (R01 OH03438). Final Technical Report, Centers For Disease Control and Prevention, National Institute For Occupational Safety And Health.
12. Hassankhani, H., Parizad, N., Gacki-Smith, J., Rahmani, A., & Mohammadi, E. (2018). The consequences of violence against nurses working in the emergency department: A qualitative study. *International Emergency Nursing, 39*, 20–25.
13. Zeng, J. Y., An, F. R., Xiang, Y. T., Qi, Y. K., Ungvari, G. S., Newhouse, R., ... & Tang, W. K. (2013). Frequency and risk factors of workplace violence on psychiatric nurses and its impact on their quality of life in China. *Psychiatry Research, 210*(2), 510–514.
14. Lanctôt, N., & Guay, S. (2014). The aftermath of workplace violence among healthcare workers: A systematic literature review of the consequences. *Aggression and Violent Behavior, 19*(5), 492–501.
15. Winstanley, S., & Whittington, R. (2002). Anxiety, burnout and coping styles in general hospital staff exposed to workplace aggression: A cyclical model of burnout and vulnerability to aggression. *Work and Stress, 16*(4), 302–315.
16. Magnavita, N., & Heponiemi, T. (2012). Violence towards health care workers in a public health care facility in Italy: A repeated cross-sectional study. *BMC Health Services Research, 12*(1), 108.
17. Gallant-Roman, M. A. (2008). Strategies and tools to reduce workplace violence. *AAOHN Journal, 56*(11), 449–454.
18. Findorff, M. J., McGovern, P. M., Wall, M. M., & Gerberich, S. G. (2005). Reporting violence to a health care employer: A cross-sectional study. *AAOHN Journal, 53*(9), 399–406.
19. Gillespie, G. L., Gates, D. M., & Fisher, B. S. (2015). Individual, relationship, workplace, and societal recommendations for addressing healthcare workplace violence. *Work, 51*(1), 67–71.

20. Gillespie, G. L., Gates, D., & Berry, P. (2013). Stressful incidents of physical violence against emergency nurses. *The Online Journal of Issues in Nursing, 18*(1).
21. Gillespie, G. L., Gates, D. M., Miller, M., & Howard, P. K. (2010). Workplace violence in healthcare settings: Risk factors and protective strategies. *Rehabilitation Nursing, 35*(5), 177–184.
22. Goertz, O., Hirsch, T., Buschhaus, B., Daigeler, A., Vogelpohl, J., Langer, S., ... & Ring, A. (2011). Intravital pathophysiologic comparison of frostbite and burn injury in a murine model. *Journal of Surgical Research, 167*(2), e395–e401.
23. Gates, D., Gillespie, G., Smith, C., Rode, J., Kowalenko, T., & Smith, B. (2011). Using action research to plan a violence prevention program for emergency departments (pp. 32–39). Copyright © 2011 Emergency Nurses Association. Published by Elsevier Inc.
24. Burkoski, V., Farshait, N., Yoon, J., Clancy, P. V., Fernandes, K., et al. (2019). Violence prevention: Technology-enabled therapeutic intervention. *Nursing Leadership (Toronto, Ont.), 32*(SP), 58–70.
25. Church, P. M., McGovern, H. E., Hansen, N. M., Nachreiner, M. S., Geisser, et al. (2004). An epidemiological study of the magnitude and consequences of work-related violence: The minnesota nurses' study. *Occupational and Environmental Medicine, 61*(6), 495–503.
26. Duncan, S. M., Hyndman, K., Estabrooks, C. A., Hesketh, K., Humphrey, C. K., Wong, J. S., et al. (2016). Nurses' experience of violence in Alberta and British Columbia hospitals. *Canadian Journal of Nursing Research, 32*(4), 57–78.
27. Ogloff, J., & Daffern, M. (2006). Dynamic appraisal of situational aggression: An instrument toassess risk for imminent aggression in psychiatric inpatients. *Behavioral Sciences and The Law, 24*(6), 799–813.
28. Papa, A., & Venella, J. (2013). Workplace violence in healthcare: Strategies for advocacy. *Online Journal of Issues in Nursing, 18*(1), 5. https://doi.org/10.3912/OJIN.
29. Desai, S. (2010). Violence and surveillance. Some unintended consequences of CCTV monitoring within mental health hospital wards. *Surveillance & Society, 8*(1), 85–92.
30. Koskela, H. (2000). "The gaze without eyes": Video-surveillance and the changing nature of urban space. *Progress in Human Geography, 24,* 243–265. https://doi.org/10.1191/030913200668791096
31. Park, M., Cho, S. H., & Hong, H. J. (2015). Prevalence and perpetrators of workplace violence by nursing unit and the relationship between violence and the perceived work environment. *Journal of Nursing Scholarship, 47*(1), 87–95. https://doi.org/10.1111/jnu.12112.
32. Wood, D., & Pistrang, N. (2004). A safe place? Service users' experiences of an acute mental health ward. *Journal of Community & Applied Social Psychology, 14,* 16–28.
33. Hinsby, K., & Baker, M. (2004). Patient and nurse accounts of violent incidents in a medium secure unit. *Journal of Psychiatric and Mental Health Nursing, 11*(3), 341–347.
34. Perreault, S. (2015). Criminal Victimization in Canada, 2014. Statistics Canada catalogue no. 85–002-X. Ottawa. Retrieved March 18, 2019.
35. Flannery, R. B., Rosen, J., Lipscomb, J., McPhaul, K. M., London, M., Murrett, K., & Gerberich, K. (2007). Environmental evaluation for workplace violence in healthcare and social services. *Journal of Safety Research Elsevier, 39,* 237–250.
36. Wilkes, L., Luck, L., Jackson, D., & Mohan, S. (2010). Development of a violence tool in the emergency hospital setting. *Nurse Researcher, 17*(4), 70–82.
37. Shields, M., & Wilkins, K. (2009). Factors related to on-the-job abuse of nurses by patients. *Health Reports, 20*(2), 7–19.
38. Stevenson, K. N., Jack, S. M., O'Mara, L., & LeGris, J. (2015). "Registered nurses' experiences of patient violence on acute care psychiatric inpatient units: An interpretive descriptive study. *BMC Nursing, 14*(1), 14–35. https://doi.org/10.1186/s12912-015-0079-5.
39. Phillips, J. P. (2016). Workplace violence against healthcare workers in the United States. *New England Journal of Medicine, 374*(17), 1661–1669. https://doi.org/10.1056/NEJMra150.

40. Blando, J., Ridenour, M., Hartley, D., & Casteel, C. (2015). Barriers to effective implementation of programs for the prevention of workplace violence in hospitals. *Online Journal of Issues in Nursing, 20*(1).
41. Burkoski, V., Farshait, N., Yoon, J., Clancy, P., Fernandes, K., et al. (2019). *Violence prevention: Technology-enabled therapeutic intervention in nursing leadership* 32 (Special Issue).

Digital Social Innovation

Technology Mediated Interaction for Users with Learning Disabilities: A Scoping Review

Nabil Georges Badr and Michele Kosremelli Asmar

Abstract Developers of computer systems and interfaces compete to produce tools that are usable and useful in the sense of assisting potential users to achieve the desired result. This usefulness angle of the discussion is what prompts us to look at existing knowledge on the potential of technology for improving social interaction and inclusion of people with learning disability (LD). We investigate how the extant literature guides conversation around premises of assistive devices and information technologies, in the context of improving interaction with people with LD for an inclusive value co-creation in our digital society of today. Through the lens of the DART framework, the four pillars of interaction of (Dialogue, Access, Risk, and Transparency), our approach seeks to explore how the current literature treats this contemporary topic.

Keywords Learning disability · Interaction · Value co-creation · Inclusion

1 Introduction

Assistive technology (AT) for social inclusion is becoming increasingly present in our connected digital societies. However, the full potential of AT to enhance the social inclusion and well-being of people with learning disability (LD) is yet to be realized.[1] By 2017, only about 10% of all people who require AT had access.[2] Those users with different type of disabilities including vision, hearing, mobility, learning problems, live in partial or complete isolation [1]. Social support and interaction

[1] WHO global disability action plan, 2014–2021: better health for all people with disability. 2015:32.
[2] WHO https://www.who.int/disabilities/technology/en/ Assistive devices and technologies.

N. G. Badr (✉) · M. K. Asmar (✉)
Higher Institute for Public Health, Université Saint-Joseph, Beirut, Lebanon
e-mail: nabil@itvaluepartner.com

M. K. Asmar
e-mail: michele.asmar@usj.edu.lb

C. Metallo et al. (eds.), *Digital Transformation and Human Behavior*, Lecture Notes in Information Systems and Organisation 37,
https://doi.org/10.1007/978-3-030-47539-0_20

is a key determinant effective use of AT. The more effective the interaction with society through AT is, the more inclusive becomes the experience of the users [2]. By examining what features are essential in functionality, and interfaces of personal or assistive technologies, this paper explores potential concepts that may enable social interaction of people with learning disabilities (LD), therefore stimulating the potential for value co-creation between these users and the social setting.

1.1 Motivation

Nowadays, assistive devices have crossed another threshold of value co-creation with the use of digital stories or technology enhanced learning for people with learning disabilities [3]. That said, in an era of rapid technological disruption, it remains true that, users should set the pace of an interaction with their assistive devices [4], especially in the case of users with LD. This user group has been seriously overlooked [5]. Human–computer interface expert, Jef Raskin, posited: "*users should set the pace of an interaction," meaning that a user should not be kept waiting needlessly, should not do more work than necessary and should not come to harm during its use*" [6].

Developers of computer devices and interfaces aim to produce tools that are usable and useful in the sense of assisting users in their interaction to achieve the desired result [7]. Beyond the principles of user interface design of visibility, simplicity and structure, intended to improve the quality and usability of user interfaces [8], we investigate how broad streams in the extant literature guide the conversation around premises of assistive devices and information technologies, in the context of improving interaction with people with LD. Consequently, we ask ourselves the following question: *What is the debate on the value created through promoting social interaction of people with LD through assistive technology?*

1.2 Approach

In our paper, we attempt to explore the existing linkages between assistive technology and social interaction for people with LD. This scoping review [9] is aimed at deepening our discovery of concepts of user centered design and human computer interaction as they relate to people with LD.

First, we frame our introduction in the context of people with learning disabilities and assistive technologies, noting the importance of personalized experiences for users with LD and the technology mediated value co-creation process.

We, therefore, conduct a scoping review of the literature on value co-creation with the use of technology for interaction and social inclusion. Our aim is to explore the depth and breadth of current knowledge on the topic. We search for papers written in the English language and including keywords of "value co-creation"; "social interaction"; "information technology"; "information technologies"; "human computer interaction"; "user interface design"; "user centered design"; "assistive technology"; "assistive technologies" in the context of LD. We pay attention to include all possible permutations in plural and singular form of the keywords. The set of target sources includes Scopus, Web of Science, PubMed, ScitePress, IEEEexplore and other available databases; we did not define a date range in order to capture most contributions.

After isolating 64 articles, we read them in full then check for relevance, rejecting patents and citations, removing duplicates, and restricting the review to papers relevant to our study. Consequently, we single out 47 papers for our work, as they relate directly to concepts of social interaction in technology designs for people with LD or related disabilities as opposed the remaining studies that pivoted around classroom settings, landscape, environment, or access for the physically disabled.

Understanding value co-creation for vulnerable consumers is an emerging area in service research [10]. In a service ecosystem, the literature refers to transformative service mediators as supporting value co-creation for vulnerable consumers in a service context. These transformative service mediators can contest and transform dominant social structures and stimulate social action [11], with implications that promote well-being among vulnerable populations. Technology is an example of transformative service mediators [12]. Technology-mediated interaction is essential for co-creation of value with users with learning difficulties [13]. This interaction then becomes a building block for creating value.

Prahalad and Ramaswamy [14] suggested that the fundamental building blocks of such interaction are four: dialogue and communication between stakeholders; ability stakeholders to access and share data; ability to monitor risk and gaps between stakeholders and the transparency among stakeholders eliminating information barriers. In our discussion, we deliberate value co-creation through technology-mediated social interaction for users with LD. Therefore, we categorize the extant case studies under the DART model.

This preliminary-descriptive study uses, as the basic units of analysis, papers and statements that address the mediating function of technology for value co-creation of people with LD for effective social interaction. We seek to understand how the current literature treats this contemporary topic of social interaction through assistive or other information technology for users with LD. Through lens of the 'blocks of interactions' of the DART model for value co-creation (Dialogue, Access, Risk, and Transparency) [14], we can focus on the perspective of the consumer perception of value co-creation, in their personalized experiences [15].

Finally, we propose directions for further research for inclusion of people with LD.

2 Background

2.1 Learning Disabilities

The term "*Learning Disabilities*" is an "*umbrella*" term describing a number of other, more specific LD, that affect a person's ability to understand numbers and learn math facts (Dyscalculia); or a person's reading ability and related language-based processing skills (Dyslexia); or a person's handwriting ability and fine motor skills (Dysgraphia). People with LD have a range of difficulties with communication. These difficulties include: Comprehension—not understanding what others are saying and/or understanding more abstract language; Expression—not being able to express thoughts and feelings, or not being verbal at all and social skills—not understanding social norms, and how to respond appropriately in social situations. Non-verbal individuals who have major learning difficulties or "severe" autism are often very difficult to interact with, placing a significant hurdle on their ability to express their own needs or feelings, further isolation. Children and young adults with a learning disability may struggle in society, school, and family. In adult life, LD can interfere with higher-level skills such as organization, time planning, abstract reasoning, long or short-term memory and attention, thus, influencing their life beyond academics and can have serious societal impact. One in 4 people with LD spend less than one hour outside their home each day and 93% of those interviewed by the Foundation for People with LD in 2012 said they felt lonely and isolated (mencap.org.uk).

2.2 Assistive Technologies

Assistive technology (AT) refers to devices used to compensate for disabilities. The US Technology-Related Assistance Act of 1988[3] defines an assistive technology as "*any item, piece of equipment, or product system acquired commercially off-the-shelf, modified, or customized, that is used to increase, maintain or improve the functional capabilities of individuals with disabilities*". Historically, in the non-medical literature, conversations around technology and users with LD address obstacles, successes and failures [16], adoption and abandonment of related assistive technologies [17] for reasons of ease of use, interface complexity and literacy levels [18]. In the early understanding of AT, researchers report that developers have sought ways to adapt mainstream technologies and modify them for the use of people who have disabilities [19]. Technology publications boast the existence of standards and guidelines for inclusive designs without directly addressing the social impediments of people with LD in the depth that is required [20]. These standards explore ways to transform AT that can result in new forms of social inclusion, transforming the thinking

[3]The US Technology-Related Assistance for Individuals with Disabilities Act (P.L. 108–364).

of technology developers to build technology for people, not disabilities [21]. Most frequently, technology feature and functionality standards for LD have transitioned focus from which technology to use to what interface to use for the technology for an improved value-added interaction and social inclusion [22].

3 Discussion

The scarcity of papers addressing the research question supports the use of a scoping review. We found rare evidence relating the potential varying degree of social interaction to features and functionality of technology and assistive devices. We present a sample of these papers in Table 1.

Our search has uncovered a use case for a project (LITERACY) with an aim to create an advanced online portal to support the inclusion of dyslexic youth and adults in society. The (LITERACY) project is a European effort to build a portal that

Table 1 Sampling of the literature on technology features that promote interaction and inclusion for persons with LD—through the lens of value co-creating social interaction (DART)

Pillars of interaction (DART) in relation to Topics of the Scoping Review [Reference]
Dialogue (D) • Dialogue promoters of valuable interaction: • Forums, online help tools and collaborative interfaces [23]; • Language and number processing assistance [24]; • Simple menus in native languages [25]; • Enriched experience through multidirectional communication [26–29]
Access (A) • Inadequate access to AT can disempower people with LD [30–32]; • Presenting readily accessible information in a usable and understandable format [33, 32]; short menus, sitemaps and breadcrumbs as navigation aids [34]; • Simplified visual aids [35]; • Larger fonts with associated illustration [25]; • Providing sequential steps are for improved experience [36]; • Devices that integrate touch technology [28] text-to-speech software (TIS) [37], or voice-over features [38] can lead to better interaction; • Training improves ability of people with LD to access technology and is an essential promoter of interaction [39]
Risk and Benefit (R) • Quick or unexpected screen responses may be upsetting, and strong, realistic visual feedback is important [30]; • Unpredictable system or interface behavior may introduce uncertainty in the interaction and lead to reluctance [40]; • Tactile interaction for learning real tasks by workers with mental deficiencies [41, 42]
Transparency (T) • Transparency through clarity, visibility and accessibility of interfaces to eliminate chances for confusion for people with LD [33, 42–46] • Integration and usefulness of assistive technologies [47]

supports social inclusion through the assistive attribute of information technology (literacyproject.eu). The scarce literature available has also indicated that efforts made to foster social inclusion through adaptation in technology features of many interfaces, most of which have involved users with learning disabilities in the design and testing process for this technology, as a best practice, leading to the success of the project [48].

Inclusion for physical disabilities is covered, to a certain extent [43], especially during the past decade. Covering disabilities related to aging [49, 50], or physical impairment [44, 51, 52]. In a nutshell, the literature proposes approaches for developing inclusive infrastructure [45]. Web accessibility standards prescribe guidelines for content, adapted for persons with disabilities [30]. Contributions address accessibility metadata for systems design with a focus on usability and fit for use [31], in the general term, with rare emphasis on the needs of people with LD [47]. These guidelines provide prescriptive paths to create content that can be presented in different ways to make it easier for users to see and hear content, and help users avoid and correct mistakes [33]. However, design guidelines addressing inclusion for people with LD are scarce, devoid of essential guidance on features that promote inclusion and create value through meaningful and facilitated interaction [30].

3.1 State of Technology for Users with LD

Technology platforms and devices have been a focal consideration for value co-creation in a variety of settings [53]. Physical disabilities including mobility, sight, and hearing impairments have received ample attention in the literature inside the social-technological context [54, 55]; leaving LD users in an underrepresented user group when it comes to value realization through interaction with assistive devices [52]. In general, for people with disabilities, assistive technologies provide a ramp for independence through the ability of self-reliance [30], work and productivity [51] and an elevated self-worth [56].

Assistive technologies (AT) for people with disabilities span a wide range of features adapted for the disability types and the different needs: Screen readers are available for the blind through text-to-speech software (TIS) [37], or voice-over [38] for example, or sent to a braille display to read by touch [28]. Such tools have the functionality of lowering the threshold of use of technology, thus facilitating social interaction. Other examples are screen magnifiers make text and graphics much larger for the vision impaired, or read aloud tools are available for people with reading disabilities such as dyslexia.

The AT industry has continued to evolve with defiance of the mainstream to support individual differences among users such as age, gender, literacy, culture, and disabilities [57]. The universal usability claim for inclusion in interface design [58] stipulates support for LD. This claim must apply to a broad range of hardware, software and network access in order to be effective—As demonstrated in the industry's prolific use of simplified menu structures, multimodal interfaces, visual cues and patterns, and use of audio and other multisensory means for promoting interaction [59].

Mobile applications, social media and well-designed assistive devices have the potential to boost the chances of social interaction and social inclusion of people with LD, however this potential is still unrealized [60]. Caveats of fitness for use are yet to be addressed in the design of technology [61]. Changes are required to the way we build technology; interact with each other through the technology, at the technical, social and legislative planes [62]. Tuning the available technology (computers, handheld devices, assistive devices, etc.) to these essential features has the prospect of improving social interaction at work, in society, for the wellbeing, business or personal fulfillment.

3.2 Designing with LD Users in Mind

Prahalad and Ramaswamy, [14] discussed the co-creation experience in a framework (DART) that outlines four blocks of interaction (Dialogue, Access, Risk, and Transparency). DART assumes a service dominant logic, and takes into account the interaction between actor in the value chain, placing importance on dialogic communication, transparent access to information by all parties, and the maintenance of a risk-benefits balance for a sustained added value for all actors of the interaction.

Dialogue—Dialogue is the foundational element for the co-creating process. It is the foundation of interaction, knowledge transfer and learning [63]. Forums, online help tools and collaborative interfaces would be dialogue promoters of valuable inter action especially for people with learning disabilities [23]. Persons with learning disabilities often have trouble processing language and numbers, deciphering auditory input, and with spatial orientation, especially when the information presented is in a compact, handheld format [24]. Target audiences prefer menus offered in the users' native language, which creates a welcoming environment for social inclusion of people with dyslexia [25]. Sometimes, it is necessary to move beyond guidelines that focus on one-way transfer of information, data entry, or search requests and to develop specific guidelines for enriching the experience through multidirectional communication [26]. Furthermore, some have argued that even 2D synchronous video-based communication tools such as Skype and FaceTime do not represent a satisfying alternative to personal contact [27]. Technology developers are exploring haptic feedback options [64] to enrich the dialog with a potential third dimension [28], for an improved and more gratifying interaction [29].

Access—Inadequate access to AT can disempower people with LD, obstructing their capacity to participate in community processes and to form and maintain meaningful interpersonal relationships [32]. As defined by Prahalad and Ramaswamy [14], the access block of interaction refers to the level of access to data provided to one or more entities in the value co-creating chain. This includes presenting readily accessible information in a usable and understandable format [32]. The use of short menus, sitemaps and breadcrumbs as navigation aids [34], simplified visual aids [35], larger fonts with associated illustration [25]. Sequential steps are often prescribed practices for an improved interaction experience [36]. Devices that integrate touch technology [28] text-to-speech software (TIS) [37], or voice-over features [38] can lead to better interaction. Notwithstanding, the ability for the users to receive training on the use and understanding of the visual interfaces of the technology which improves their ability to access technology and is an essential promoter of interaction [39].

Risk and benefit—Prahalad and Ramaswamy discussed risk and benefit gaps as the third block of successful interaction for co-creating value [14]. Reliability and predictability are essential. Quick or unexpected screen responses may be upsetting, and strong, realistic visual feedback is important [30]. Unpredictable system or interface behavior may introduce uncertainty in the interaction and may lead to the reluctance or refusal to use [40]. Tactile interaction that is coordinated with multisensory feedback is seen as a large benefit. The literature demonstrates the interest of a virtual reality tool associated with a tactile interaction for learning of real tasks by workers with mental deficiencies [41]. Therefore, the perceived value of the device in use and the ensuing risks of use are fundamental concepts to positive interaction [42].

Transparency—According to Prahalad and Ramaswamy, transparency is related to the level of clarity in objectives and actions between value creators [14]. Transparency is connected to the ease of collaboration using the tools. Attributes of clarity, visibility and accessibility of interfaces exemplify the definition of transparency [42], eliminating chances for confusion, which establishes the definition of a good design [65]. Rothberg [57] stipulates that, the participation of persons with LD in user testing is critical to a successful design, sometimes, using interactive machine learning to support interface development through workshops with disabled people [66]. This value co-creation activity has the premise of validation for an effective design for transparency [67] with the value-added consequence of richer features and innovative outcome [68].

4 Conclusion

Designing for inclusion has not been the focus of many authors, rendering our task anemic in matter of research depth and analysis.

Our review has not shown concrete patterns can be identified regarding the type of technology or technological trends that can be used to support the social integration of individuals with disabilities. Yet, under the lens of the DART framework, our effort was successful to underscore valuable input on the debate around features for technology-mediated interaction, for co-creation of value with users with LD.

We therefore, summarize our findings and present them as suggestions for the basis of "Good Design".

In summary, we have learned that in "Good Design" for users with LD:

1. Forums, online help tools and collaborative interfaces promote valuable interaction. The use of short menus, sitemaps and breadcrumbs as navigation aids. Menus offered in the users' native language create a welcoming environment for social inclusion.
2. Simplified visual aids, larger fonts with associated illustration and sequential steps are often prescribed practices for an improved interaction experience.
3. Clarity, visibility and accessibility of interfaces eliminate chances for confusion. Quick or unexpected screen responses can be disruptive, should be avoided.
4. The emphasis on strong, realistic visual feedback is important. Haptic feedback and 3D technologies enrich the dialog of people with LD for an interaction.
5. Multidirectional communication has the potential to enrich the experience.
6. Tactile interaction that is coordinated with multisensory feedback - as a large benefit (technology based on virtual reality a possible plus).
7. Reliability and predictability are essential to reduce anxiety levels and encourage a deeper, more involved experience.
8. Training on the use and understanding of the visual interfaces improves the LD user's ability to access the technology and is an essential promoter of interaction.

Furthermore, as "*the meaning of value and the process of value creation shifts from a product and firm-centric views to personalized consumer experiences*" [14], our exploration has demonstrated the criticality of including participants with LD in user testing for a successful outcome of validation and value-added innovation.

4.1 Contribution and Limitations

There is a plethora of assistive technology for people with LD on the market today. Most of them tackle the issue at hand from multiple directions. Abbreviation expanders, electronic dictionaries, alternative keyboards, audio books, speech recognition programs, screen readers, talking calculators and spellcheckers, etc.,[4] mostly used in education setting.[5] Technological innovations, aimed at promoting or facilitating social inclusion of individuals with disabilities, are still lagging [60].

Our work is a first step into the foray of assistive technology innovation, for better value co-creation in social interaction of the LD users. It is call to action for researcher and practitioners to accelerate the motion towards effective technology-mediated interaction for co-creation of value with users with LD.

We suggest that our work be a starting point in a deeper dive into improving technology usability, rendering more communication tools available, and reducing the acquisition barriers for users with LD. We therefore, present our findings as suggestions for the basis of "good design" [65].

---

[4]https://www.readingrockets.org/article/assistive-technology-kids-learning-disabilities-overview.

[5]https://www.masters-in-special-education.com/lists/5-examples-of-assistive-technology-in-the-classroom/.

Our exploration demonstrated the criticality of including participants with LD in user testing for a successful outcome of validation and value-added innovation. The user community can participate in the design and interaction as an evolution that supports a transformation toward more sustainable ways of living in the future [69].

Practitioners and solution providers have created what could be the dawn of a new era of meaningful and value-creating social inclusion, mediated by information technology for the learning disabled. The (LITERACY) project is one example and there are others; for instance, Telecentre (telecentre.org) is a global initiative that aims to establish and sustain personal and social improvement through Information Technology.

4.2 Limitations and Further Research

We understand that this sampling is not a full and complete set of scientific evidence. Yet, we find it sufficient to guide the conversation about value co-creation through technology-mediated social interaction for users with LD. By its nature as a unique and first approach, our review may have neglected the medical implications, psychological benefits and physical environment requirements.

The scarcity of the published material on the subject may have presented a limitation in the sampling, casting doubt on the scientific evidence of this work. Yet, we find it a good start of a necessary conversation about the value co-creation contribution of technology-mediated social interaction for the inclusion of users with LD. Another challenge here is that the scope of LD is so broad and varied that it is difficult to generalize the results. Therefore, the discussion is quite general. Though directional, most of the recommendations are not particularly innovative. For example, LD can be cognitive or depend on will and engagement (autism).

Nevertheless, maybe our findings will encourage future work that would treat subareas of the problem separately. Researchers are invited to use this paper as a springboard and icebreaker in a cross-domain effort to include, technology innovation and medico-social settings, for instance.

References

1. Hall, S. A. (2009). The social inclusion of people with disabilities: A qualitative meta-analysis. *Journal of Ethnographic & Qualitative Research, 3*(3).
2. Verdonschot, M. M., de Witte, L. P., Reichrath, E., et al. (2009). Impact of environmental factors on community participation of persons with an intellectual disability: A systematic review. *Journal of Intellectual Disability Research, 53,* 54–64.
3. Parsons, S., Guldberg, K., Porayska-Pomsta, K., & Lee, R. (2015). Digital stories as a method for evidence-based practice and knowledge co-creation in technology-enhanced learning for children with autism. *International Journal of Research and Method in Education, 38*(3), 247–271.

4. Rotondi, A. J., Sinkule, J., Haas, G. L., Spring, M. B., Litschge, C. M., Newhill, C. E., et al. (2007). Designing websites for persons with cognitive deficits: Design and usability of a psychoeducational intervention for persons with severe mental illness. *Psychological Services, 4*(3), 202.
5. Hoppestad, B. S. (2013). Current perspective regarding adults with intellectual and developmental disabilities accessing computer technology. *Disability and Rehabilitation: Assistive Technology, 8*(3), 190–194.
6. Raskin, J. (2000). *The humane interface: New directions for designing interactive systems.* Addison-Wesley Professional.
7. Mwanza, D. (2001). Where theory meets practice: A case for an activity theory based methodology to guide computer system design. In: *Proceedings of INTERACT' 2001: Eighth IFIP TC 13 Conference on Human-Computer Interaction*, July 9–13, 2001, Tokyo, Japan.
8. Constantine L., & Lockwood, L. (2001). Structure and style in use cases for user interfaces. In M. van Harmelan (Ed.), *Object modeling and user interface design.* Boston: Addison-Wesley (2001)
9. Peters, M. D., Godfrey, C. M., Khalil, H., McInerney, P., Parker, D., & Soares, C. B. (2015). Guidance for conducting systematic scoping reviews. *International Journal of Evidence-Based Healthcare, 13*(3), 141–146.
10. Johns, R., & Davey, J. (2019). Introducing the transformative service mediator: Value creation with vulnerable consumers. *Journal of Services Marketing.*
11. Blocker, C., Barrios, A. (2015). The transformative value of a service experience. *Journal of Service Research, 18.* https://doi.org/10.1177/1094670515583064.
12. Breidbach, C. F., & Maglio, P. P. (2016). Technology-enabled value co-creation: An empirical analysis of actors, resources, and practices. *IND Market Manage, 56,* 73–85.
13. Wass, S. V., & Porayska-Pomsta, K. (2014). The uses of cognitive training technologies in the treatment of autism spectrum disorders. *Autism, 18*(8), 851–871.
14. Prahalad, C. K., & Ramaswamy, V. (2004). Co-creation experiences: The next practice in value creation. *Journal of Interactive Marketing, 18*(3), 5–14.
15. Solakis, K., Peña-Vinces, J. C., & Lopéz-Bonilla, J. M. (2017). DART model from a customer's perspective: An exploratory study in the hospitality industry of Greece. *Problem Perspective Manage, 15*(2), 536–548.
16. Dikter, D. (2004). Outcomes and benefits-challenges in the assistive technology field. *Assistive Technology Outcomes Benefits, 1*(1), 6–7.
17. Butler, D. L. (2004). Adults with learning disabilities. In Learning about Learning Disabilities (3rd. edn., pp. 565–598).
18. Alper, S., & Raharinirina, S. (2006). Assistive technology for individuals with disabilities: A review and synthesis of the literature. *JSET, 21*(2), 47–64.
19. Brodwin, M. G., Star, T., & Cardoso, E. (2004). Computer assistive technology for people who have disabilities: Computer adaptations and modifications. *Journal of Rehabilitation, 70*(3), 28.
20. Gillespie, A., Best, C., & O'Neill, B. (2012). Cognitive function and assistive technology for cognition: A systematic review. *Journal of International Neuropsychology Society, 18*(1), 1–19.
21. Foley, A., & Ferri, B. A. (2012). Technology for people, not disabilities: Ensuring access and inclusion. *Journal of Research in Special Educational Needs, 12*(4), 192–200.
22. Giakoumis, D., Kaklanis, N., Votis, K., & Tzovaras, D. (2014). Enabling user interface developers to experience accessibility limitations through visual, hearing, physical and cognitive impairment simulation. *Universal Access in the Information Society, 13*(2), 227–248.
23. Shneiderman, B., & Plaisant, C. (2010). *Designing the user interface: Strategies for effective human-computer interaction.* Pearson Education India.
24. Brewer, J. (Ed.). (2005). How people with disabilities use the web: Working group internal draft, May 5, 2005. W3C.
25. Hagelkruys, D., & Motschnig, R. (2017). The LITERACY-portal as the subject of a case study on a human-centered design solution supporting users with special needs. *International Journal on E-Learning, 16*(2), 129–147.

26. Jaeger, P. T., & Xie, B. (2019). Developing online community accessibility guidelines for persons with disabilities and older adults. *Journal of Disability Policy Studies, 20*(1), 55–63.
27. Cohen, A., Goodman, L., Keaveney, S., Keogh, C., & Dillenburger, K. (2017). Sustaining a caring relationship at a distance: Can haptics and 3D technologies overcome the deficits in 2D direct synchronous video based communication? In *2017 23rd International Conference on Virtual System Multimedia (VSMM)* (pp. 1–6). IEEE.
28. Knochel, A. D., Hsiao, W. H., & Pittenger, A. (2018). Touching to see: Tactile learning, assistive technologies, and 3-D printing. *Art Education, 71*(3), 7–13.
29. Owuor, J., Larkan, F., Kayabu, B., Fitzgerald, G., Sheaf, G., et al. (2018). Does assistive technology contribute to social inclusion for people with intellectual disability? A systematic review protocol. *BMJ Open, 8*(2), e017533.
30. Harper, S., & Yesilada, Y. (2011). Web accessibility: Current trends. *Handbook of Research on Personal Autonomy Technologies and Disability Informatics, 1,* 172–190.
31. Sloan, D., Dickinson, A., McIlroy, N., & Gibson, L. (2006). *Evaluating the usability of online accessibility information.* University of Dundee.
32. Jiwnani, K. (2001). Designing for users with cognitive disabilities. Universal Usability in Practice. Available: https://www.otal.umd.edu/uupractice/cognition/.
33. Anderson, S., Bohman, P. R., Burmeister, O. K., & Sampson-Wild, G. (2004). User needs and e-government accessibility: The future impact of WCAG 2.0. In *ERCIM workshop on user interfaces for all* (pp. 289–304). Berlin: Springer.
34. Hudson, R., & Weakley, R., & Firminger, P. (2005). An accessibility frontier: Cognitive disabilities and learning difficulties. *Webusability—Accessibility and Usability Services.*
35. Rowland, C. (2004). *Cognitive disabilities part 2: Conceptualizing design considerations. Web aim—Accessibility in Mind.*
36. Hellman, R. (2007). Universal design and mobile devices. In *International Conference on Universal Access in Human-Computer Interaction* (pp. 147–156). Berlin: Springer.
37. Lazar, J., & Stein, M. A. (Eds.). (2017). Disability, human rights, and information technology. University of Pennsylvania Press.
38. Shokuhi Targhi, S. A. (2017). *Study of mobile accessibility for users of IOS voice over.*
39. Harper, S., & Chen, A. Q. (2012). Web accessibility guidelines. *WorldWideWeb, 15*(1), 61–88.
40. Jokisuu, E., Langdon, P. M., & Clarkson, P. J. (2012). A framework for studying cognitive impairment to inform inclusive design. In *Designing inclusive systems* (pp. 115–124). Springer, London.
41. Loup-Escande, E., Christmann, O., Damiano, R., Hernoux, F., & Richir, S. (2012). Virtual reality learning software for individuals with intellectual disabilities: comparison between touchscreen and mouse interactions. In *International Conference on Disability, Virtual Reality and Associated Technologies* (9; 2012; Laval) (pp. 295–303). The University of Reading.
42. Ahrar, N., & Rahman, A. A. (2012). Value co-creation attributes which influence on e-services: The case of UTM Institutional Repository. *IJERD, 2*(9), 46–50.
43. Pareto, L., & Snis, U. L. (2006). Understanding users with reading disabilities or reduced vision: Toward a universal design of an auditory, location-aware museum guide. *International Journal on Disability and Human Development, 5*(2), 147–154.
44. Rodriguez-Sanchez, M. C., Moreno-Alvarez, M. A., Martin, E., Borromeo, S., & Hernandez-Tamames, J. A. (2014). Accessible smartphones for blind users: A case study for a wayfinding system. *Expert Systems with Applications, 41*(16), 7210–7222.
45. Vanderheiden, G. C., Chourasia, A., Tobias, J., & Githens, S. (2006). The library GPII system. In *International Conference on Universal Access in HCI* (pp. 494–505). Cham: Springer.
46. Summers, K., & Langford, J. (2015). The impact of literacy on usable and accessible electronic voting. In *International Conference on Universal Access in HCI* (pp. 248–257). Cham: Springer.
47. Duhaney, L. M. G., & Duhaney, D. C. (2000). Assistive technology: Meeting the needs of learners with disabilities. *International Journal of Instructional Media, 27*(4), 393–393.
48. Hagelkruys, D., & Motschnig, R. (2014). Designing a web-portal supporting the social inclusion of a specific user group. A case study of the LITERACY-portal. In *EdMedia+ Innovate Learning* (pp. 267–277). AACE.

49. Picking, R., Robinet, A., Grout, V., McGinn, J., Roy, A., Ellis, S., & Oram, D. (2009). A case study using a methodological approach to developing user interfaces for elderly and disabled people. *The Computer Journal, 53*(6), 842–859.
50. Ashby, S., & Maslin-Prothero, S. (2010). Involving older people and careers in a research project: The 'virtual' steering group. *Healthcare Research*, 239.
51. Bodine, C. (2005). Cognitive impairments, information technology systems and the workplace. *ACM SIGACCESS Accessibility and Computing, 83,* 25–29.
52. Yi, Y. J. (2015). Compliance of Section 508 in public library systems with the largest percentage of underserved populations. *Government Information Quarterly, 32*(1), 75–81.
53. Wolf, M., Sims, J., & Yang, H. (2015). *Towards understanding of value co-creation on web 2.0 platforms: An assessment methodology*.
54. Jaeger, P. T. (2006). Assessing Section 508 compliance on federal e-government Web sites: A multi-method, user-centered evaluation of accessibility for persons with disabilities. *Government Information Quarterly, 23*(2), 169–190.
55. Ruiz-Olaya, A. F., & Lara-Herrera, C. N.: Enhancing e-accessibility of disabled people using low-cost technology. In *2016 8th Euro American Conference on Telematics and Information Systems (EATIS)* (pp. 1–5). IEEE.
56. Yeager, P., Kaye, H. S., Reed, M., & Doe, T. M. (2006). Assistive technology and employment: Experiences of Californians with disabilities. *Work, 27*(4), 333–344.
57. Rothberg, M. A. (2019). Designing for inclusion: Ensuring accessibility for people with disabilities. In Consumer informatics and digital health (pp. 125–143). Cham: Springer.
58. Shneiderman, B. (2000). Universal usability. *Communications of the ACM, 43*(5), 85–85.
59. Kodagoda, N., Wong, B. L., Rooney, C., & Khan, N. (2012). Interactive visualization for low literacy users: From lessons learnt to design. In *Proceedings of the SIGCHI Conference on Human Factors in Computing Systems* (pp. 1159–1168). ACM.
60. Manzoor, M., & Vimarlund, V. (2018). Digital technologies for social inclusion of individuals with disabilities. *Health and Technology, 8*(5), 377–390.
61. Louw, J. S. (2017). E-Inclusion: Social inclusion of young adults with intellectual disabilities-a participatory design. In *AAATE Conference* (pp. 269–272).
62. MacIntyre, G. (2008). *Learning disability and social inclusion.* Dunedin Academic Press.
63. Nonaka, I., & Konno, N. (1998). The concept of "Ba": Building a foundation for knowledge creation. *California Management Review, 40*(3), 40–54.
64. Sorgini, F., Caliò, R., Carrozza, M. C., & Oddo, C. M. (2018). Haptic-assistive technologies for audition and vision sensory disabilities. *Disability and Rehabilitation Assistive Technology, 13*(4), 394–421.
65. Jagger, P. (2018). Good by design. *ITNOW, 60*(1), 62–63.
66. Katan, S., Grierson, M., & Fiebrink, R. (2015). Using interactive machine learning to support interface development through workshops with disabled people. In *Proceedings of the 33rd Annual ACM Conference on Human Factors in Computing Systems* (pp. 251–254).
67. Hagelkruys, D., Motschnig, R., Böhm, C., Vojtova, V., Kotasová, M., et al. (2015). Human-centered design in action: Designing and performing testing sessions with users with special needs. In *EdMedia: World Conference on Educational Media and Technology* (pp. 499–508). AACE.
68. Magee, P., Ward, G., Moody, L., & Roebuck, A. (2017). Inclusive smartphone interface design in context: co (re) designing the PIS. In *AAATE Conference* (pp. 195–198)
69. Sanders, E. B. N., & Stappers, P. J. (2018). Co-creation and the new landscapes of design. *Co-Design, 4*(1), 5–18.

Social and Ethical Shifts in the Digital Age: Digital Technologies for Governing or Digital Technologies that Govern?

Paolo Depaoli, Maddalena Sorrentino, and Marco De Marco

Abstract Organizational efficiency and economic development has benefited significantly from the ubiquitous nature of information technology in today's governmental machinery and in society, but what of its serious implications at the macro and micro level? The argument of the paper is that technology-driven social changes require—and facilitate—a policy response. Exploring the wider implications of ICT used by governments through the lenses of two analytical frameworks (i.e., the 'tools of government approach' and the 'data-driven agency approach') elaborated in two seminal books allows us to formulate a number of information policy recommendations for contemporary decision makers seeking viable solutions to ethical concerns. The conceptual discussion aims to spur an early and pro-active engagement with the social impacts of technology.

Keywords E-government · Tools of government · Data-driven agency · ICT policy · Ethics · Social impacts of ICT

1 Introduction and Impetus of the Study

Handling the impacts and consequences of technology has become a problem of political, social and academic relevance since the Sixties [1]. Today, unlike the pre-digital era, the intertwining of 'society' and 'technology' [2] has acquired even greater importance and has no equivalence in terms of scale, scope, integration and

P. Depaoli (✉)
Sapienza University of Rome, Rome, Italy
e-mail: paolo.depaoli@uniroma1.it

M. Sorrentino
University of Milan, Milan, Italy
e-mail: maddalena.sorrentino@unimi.it

M. De Marco
International Telematic University Uninettuno, Rome, Italy
e-mail: marco.demarco@uninettunouniversity.net

C. Metallo et al. (eds.), *Digital Transformation and Human Behavior*, Lecture Notes in Information Systems and Organisation 37, https://doi.org/10.1007/978-3-030-47539-0_21

capability [3]. Many commentators are by now convinced that current developments may change the very fabric of society in a short period of time [4, 5].

A global issue with a far-reaching impact on public expectations is e-government. Many years have passed since the use of digital ICTs for the conduct of government stopped being a stand-alone issue to become a cross-cutting issue. At the 'government-society interface' level [6:17], the transformational impact of ICTs is manifested mainly in the way governments use digital technologies to gather information and influence individual and firm behaviour. But there is more at play. ICTs also involve a change in values or in the value system: according to Bannister and Connolly [3:119], almost any ICT implementation in the public sector will have implications for public values. Further, governmental technology policy creates obligations for everyone [7:21].

Hence, the transformative potential of ICT has truly become a game changer of the social context. Notable examples of new generations of ICT that enter the public arena bring with them unprecedented, ethically relevant questions and implications regarding, for example, analytics, artificial intelligence and virtual/augmented reality. And, while the main talking points of public opinion centre on key issues such as privacy and surveillance, the debate fails to address other, just as relevant cross-cutting issues. To date, far less envisaged and explored are the critical questions: How legitimate is the techno-regulation exercised by the private digital giants? Are the consumers truly aware of the rules embedded in the ICT artefacts or in the online services they use in the everyday lives?

Against this background, it is essential to understand what is happening and with which consequences. The OECD [8] very recently published a document stating that the role of public services is being questioned due to the effect of the increasingly pervasive presence of the global digital players in areas such as broadcasting, postal services, libraries and social meeting spaces. The OECD goes on to say that where the rationale for public intervention may have eroded, the governments and regulators need to apply a 'rethinking' [8:28].

Getting a clear and unobstructed view of the underlying nature of the changes spurred by digital transformation is prerequisite to ensure policy responses better tailored to the times we live in. Despite the crucial issues raised by privacy threats, public decision makers seeking to proactively address normative issues must push past the emotive response to news stories (such as the outrage sparked by the Cambridge Analytica scandal) to focus on what really lies beyond the immediate horizon.

The main purpose of this paper is to inform and increase awareness of the complexities of "moral and ethical concerns arising due of the social use of technologies" [9:21], and to sketch a range of recommendations for information policies. The need for brevity means that the approach taken here covers solely a handful of selected issues, building upon seminal studies that have addressed social and ethical shifts associated with the digital age from a variety of perspectives. Our interest is not the technologies *per se* but the generic interaction of ICT with society.

The article is organized as follows. After illustrating the research approach, the paper explicates the 'instrumental' and 'relational' perspectives of digital technology, followed by a nuanced analysis of the ICT tools available to government in their broader context. The next section hosts the discussion and summarises the policy implications. The paper closes with the authors' final remarks.

2 Research Approach

The paper draws on two ground-breaking studies that have problematized the role of technologies in the public sphere, namely, the book by C. Hood and H. Margetts, *The tools of government in the digital age* (2007) [6], and that by M. Hildebrandt, *Smart technologies and the end(s) of law* (2015) [10]. The interest in these contributions is twofold, and lies precisely in the diversity (and, at the same time, the contiguity) of the analytical frameworks that inform them (policy studies and the theory of cybernetics, respectively, and legal and ethical studies). The books were written at two distinct periods in the timeline of the development and public visibility of the digital technologies. The 2015 essay shows a far more complex networked ty landscape than that considered by Hood and Margetts just eight years earlier.

The exploration follows two parallel tracks with the aim of highlighting for each of the two essays the way the ICTs are designed and the ethical consequences for the action of governments and for the information policies. The guiding question can be summarised as follows: *In what way do the different ways of conceptualizing the intertwining of society and technology contribute to the practice of government in the digital age?*

3 Digital Technology: 'Instrumental' or 'Relational'?

Much has been written and debated on the social implications of digital technologies [11]. Here, we start to map the methods with which the two essays in question, *The tools of government in the digital age* (2007) [6] and *Smart technologies and the end(s) of law* (2015) [10], have addressed the theme.

3.1 Digital Technologies as Tools of Tools

To understand the viewpoint of Christopher Hood and Hellen Margetts ("H&M"), it is necessary to know that the 2005 book was developed from Hood's earlier publication, *The tools of government* [12], written in the pre-digital age. The focus of the H&M essay is the interaction of the state with the citizens and the organisations through two macro categories of exchange-action instruments: (1) the 'detectors' or the information flows from individuals/organisations to the government ("all the instruments government uses for taking in information", p. 3),and (2) the 'effectors', which are the influence flows that go in the opposite direction to the detectors (i.e. "all the tools government can use to try to make an impact on the world outside", ibid.).

The two macro categories use four basic types of tools of government policy. *Nodality* denotes "the property of being in the middle of a social network". *Authority* relates to "the ability to command and prohibit, commend and permit, through recognized procedures and identifying symbols". *Treasure* indicates "whatever positive incentives or inducements government can use to secure information or change behavior". Finally, *Organisation* denotes the possession of "stock of land, buildings and equipment, and a collection of individuals with whatever skills and contacts they may have", somehow arranged. The authors say that any public policy will involve some mixture of these four basic resources.

The basic question continually evoked, even before indicating the effects of the digital technologies on the nodality, authority, treasure and organisation ("NATO") instruments, is the way in which the authors consider such technologies. On the one side, H&M observe that, since the 1990s, Internet and the associated technologies have changed both the way in which many individuals behave in different social spheres and the way in which the governments interact with citizens and business. On the other, they argue that in many cases these (apparently) new instruments "can be understood as old instruments in a new technological context" (p. 14).

This position is resumed in the closing chapter of the book, in which the authors specifically reiterate the term 'digital age', confirming the instrumental role of digital technology: "we discuss the potential that the digital age may offer for a 'sharpening' of government tools, both to economize on governmental effort and to make government's interactions with individuals less obtrusive (p. 185)." Further, the instrumental role of the technologies (which allows this 'sharpening') seems not to be affected by the organisational solutions adopted. In fact, the authors state in the introduction that their work "pays little or no attention to what goes on inside government's organizational machinery" (p. xiii). Instead of considering the power games or the 'convoluted decision processes', their attention "focuses on the point where government meets individuals" (ibid.). Therefore, it would appear that the problem of the means-ends relationship can be solved only once the characteristics of the exchange instruments (opportunely updated to the state of the art of the digital technologies) have been defined, which happens at a certain point of interaction. In other words, it is a question of choosing the means best suited to the pursuit of a specific end.

To make this hypothesis hold water, we must assume that the technology plays a neutral role in social relations and, above all, in the organisations, and between these and the individuals that either belong to or have relations with it. In this respect, the authors state that:

> Digital technologies have been hyped by some as fundamentally reshaping all human relationships, dismissed and ignored by others as irrelevant to the fundamentals of law and government. To get any grip on that slippery but important question, we need a method of analysis that is *technology-free*. (p. xiv our emphasis).

In a nutshell, the authors claim that a technology-free approach allows us to skip over complex and never-ending diatribes on the nature of the digital technologies (on this point, see [13]. Further, given that it is also organisation-free, the H&M approach enables us to move with agility among the substantially unchanged instruments (i.e., the government tools) and the 'tools of tools' (the digital technologies) that 'sharpen' the former. A further advantage in adopting a similarly technology-neutral framework is that it would allow us to understand what changes occur in the government toolkit when technology changes (p. 183). This latter observation by the authors does not seem to stray too far from technological determinism.

3.2 *Digital Infrastructures and Data-Driven Agency*

The pace of technological developments, in particular the Information and Communication Infrastructures (ICI), accelerated significantly in the eight years between the publication of H&M's study in 2007 and Mireille Hildebrandt's ("MH") in 2015, when, taking a net position on the issue considered 'slippery' by H&M in 2007 (see above citation), the latter opined that: "Big Data is not a hype. It is here to stay. It is, however, a threat" (p. 226).

Hildebrandt maintains that the intertwining of relations between the diverse categories of actors and agents that use the new digital technologies whilst unknowingly being used is problematic. Although MH's research was conducted in fields not strictly connected to the public sector, it is just as relevant because it concerns the consequences of the development of the ICTs that have caused the human agency to be affected by the 'data-driven agency'.

Also for the purposes of this paper, the effects of such a development serve to understand how the ICIs are capable of conditioning not only the nature of the information exchange interface (detector), but also the influence (effector) of the four tools considered by Hood and Margetts. As a result, Hildebrandt argues that the digital technologies cannot be conceived as neutral tools.

MH suggests surpassing the instrumentalist and neutralist conception that disregards the values incorporated in technological devices to favour the view that sees technology—like the law—as a means of regulating the interactions between individuals and organisations and the behaviours of the various actors.

According to MH, conceiving technology in merely instrumental terms is problematic because it does not allow us to easily understand how a certain technology enables or impedes certain behaviours. Just as problematic is the explanation of how the interaction between individuals and environment changes when the technology used changes (p. 162). Rather, MH maintains that the technology itself already contains a normative and relational component and that the attention on and the research into the impacts of a technology must extend to the affordances, i.e., the potential of the tools or the artefacts, concluding that the assessment of technology cannot be limited to its intended usage or foreseeable functionalities (p. 172).

This aspect is particularly valuable in the case of the ICIs because many of the affordances that characterise them are *hidden* and concern ‘pre-emptive computing’, i.e., a computing based on predictive analytics combined with computational interventions that shape the human action, orienting it, supporting it or forcing it, before the human being can arrive at a conscious decision (p. 263). Here, Hildebrandt is referring to the configuration of a *digital unconscious,* i.e., a complex interweave of hidden inferences that increasingly reconfigure our digital environment (p. xiii), which, among other things, is increasingly integrated with the non-digital environment through the ubiquity of interconnectedness (p. 110).

The digital unconscious proposes real-time solutions-actions based on the preferences expressed unknowingly by the individuals during their online interactions and harvested, for example, through the practices of web profiling. Hence, MH maintains that we are witnessing a reduction of personal autonomy and, therefore, a growing difficulty in identifying responsibility at the individual level.

4 Digital Technologies for Governing or Digital Technologies that Govern?

These two different ways of thinking generate two different conceptions of the technologies used in the public sphere, prompting a much closer look.

4.1 NATO Tools and Digital Technologies for Governing

H&M’s broad definition of tools of government (Nodality, Authority, Treasure, Organization, or “NATO”) responds to two primary needs: the first is to include the different ways of use shaped in different political and cultural domains. The second derives from the first and is the possibility to make comparisons in time and among the different forms of government (p. 192). In terms of the digitisation processes, the authors note that, on one side, “… the government is aiming to ‘lead’ digital developments in the society at large” (p. 195). On the other, the possibility of adding the digital technologies to the existing toolkit varies according to the level of digitisation and digital knowledge in the society, for which the governments can follow or accelerate the pace (p. 193).

This precise definition is prerequisite because excessive misalignment—i.e., one that greatly anticipates the effective take-up level of digital skills—tends to overestimate the potentially positive effects of public leadership on de-bureaucratisation and the participation and empowerment of the citizens.

Conversely, the conditions of alignment of the governmental action with the social patterns are maintained constantly, and it can be reasonably expected that the digital age will produce its effects in terms of the ‘sharpening of the government’s tools’

(p. 196). In this respect, the authors claim that a government that sets as its goal a limited intrusion into the lives and business of its interlocutors will prefer, where possible, to use the tools of 'nodality' and 'treasure' as opposed to those of 'authority' and 'organization' (p. 196). A government "will generally aim to maximize the precision and scalability of its detecting and effecting tools, so that it hits only its intended targets and hits them only as hard as they need to be hit to achieve the desired effect" (ibid.).

Hood and Margetts point out that digitisation allows governments to extend scalability and directness. The former is the capacity to use the effectors at variable degrees of intensity. The second is the ability to tailor the effectors to specific categories of interlocutors that the government intends to engage in either positive or negative terms without triggering spillover effects (ibid.). Below, we provide some examples for each of the four tools identified by the authors.

Nodality This tool allows the government to 'detect' relevant information to get an overall picture and to intervene in "softer" and less costly ways than those employed by more traditional tools. For example, the analysis of traffic records in the telephony networks and online channels can generate potentially useful information flows. Likewise, the web-based technologies have strengthened the ability of governments to provide personalised messages directed at specific groups of recipients (p. 42). However, the positive aspects, such as the ability to conduct cheaper direct surveys, are accompanied by negative aspects, including the de facto exclusion of the more disadvantaged categories, such as the poor, the vulnerable, the elderly, and the marginalised. The internet age makes nodality-based tools sharper while making others less efficacious (p. 41). In definitive, the nodality of government "will depend upon government's ability to compete successfully in the online space, something that many governments find challenging" [14].

Authority The ability to command and veto and to command and permit is exercised through the so-called 'tokens of authority' that are ubiquitous, both in the gathering of information and in the changing of behaviours (p. 50). These tokens translate into "[o]rders, bans, requisitions, vouchers, warrants, coupons, licences, quotas, certificates (digital or otherwise)—once you start looking, you see them everywhere." (ibid.). And so, also in this macro-tool environment, digital technology has led to changes in both the tokens used and their degree of usage. Internet influences government's ability to wield authority, both in terms of how citizens use the Internet to challenge or circumvent authority, and how governments use the Internet and related technologies to respond. On the other hand, the new business models and the activities developed via internet are technically hard to 'detect' (and, therefore, to 'effect') also by those governments with the required resources. Like nodality, the digital technologies also enable the authority to accurately target the interventions (the tokens) to the different categories of interlocutors (p. 72).

Treasure Like the 'authority tokens', the government uses the 'fungible chattels' it has at its disposal to gather information and to promote or discourage certain behaviours. Such examples (see pp. 78 and following) include tax rebates, public procurement, and grants to incentivise businesses to set up in certain locations. The digital age amplifies the possibilities for government to become a customer of the private companies that produce the e-government tools, platforms and services. The digital age facilitates the implementation of specific incentivising or non-incentivising actions, as well as increasing its ability for group-targeting to encourage behaviours deemed virtuous (p. 97). Treasure was, not by chance, the earliest resource to move online from the 1950s onward.

Organization Organization denotes the entire stock of tangible and intangible resources the user has at their disposal to carry out detecting and effecting activities. According to H&M, of all the NATO tools, organization has brought the most change to the digital age (p. 119). The greatest impact underlined by the scholars is, not surprisingly, labour saving and the increasingly manifest use of intellectual capital and equipment since the early twenty-first century. Basically, the new digital technologies allow the public resources to be used in a more precise and discriminating manner than the "previously 'unintelligent' forms of physical effectors such as walls and barriers" (p. 120).

In short, the technological advances do not change the actual content of the government toolbox and, in a digital age as any other, the fundamentals remain "nodality-authority-treasure-organization" (p. 181). Instead, the changes triggered by the digital age affect the costs and practicality of different modes of action. In particular, the most visible effects can be seen in the information-gathering tools available to government, for instance, with the near-universal ownership of mobile phones. Hence, it is the detector that has changed more than the effector part of the operation (p. 182).

4.2 Digital Technologies that Govern

As outlined in §2.2 above, Hildebrandt favours a relational conception of technologies. This same view is transposed into law. In the words of MH:

> A relational conception of law sees law neither as instrumentalist nor as autonomous. First, it denies that law is a mere instrument, because its instrumentality depends on the legal subject that enacts, administers or adjudicates the law, and on the ends it aims to achieve. Second, it denies that law is independent from its societal, scientific and professional environment, because its existence depends on the performative nature of the social fabric it constitutes and by which it is constituted. The latter indicates that in so far as this social fabric is articulated by means of particular ICIs, the mode of existence of the law co-depends on the ICIs that institute the society it aims to regulate (p. 172).

In addition to the impossibility of considering digital technology, as it is being developed today, neutral to policy objectives, three important consequences ensue from the inseparable interweave of society, law and ICIs. The first is that the conscious ability to deliberate is conditioned by the digital *unconscious*. The second is that the affordances of the online world lead to an instrumentalisation of the law (meaning that the technical regulation ends up supplanting the legal regulation). The third is that the 'pre-emptive computing' takes on a deterministic nature (pp. 184–185). To better understand the relevance of these concepts, it is necessary to delve deeper.

Conditioning the ability to deliberate The critical characteristic of the law, in addition to being binding, is that it is based on a long and careful consideration or discussion. Interaction with smart technologies creates a situation of 'rushing to judgment', reducing the need to stop and think about what we are doing and discouraging the thought process that delays judgement until we have considered different views or positions that counter the initial arguments. The result is a reduced capacity to deliberate (p. 184).

Instrumentalisation of the law The reduced capacity to deliberate may lead people to see the law as merely a tool to influence social actors. If the design and engineering of the digital world, inasmuch as it is unconscious-oriented, are directed at achieving policy goals to replace the legal precepts in all those cases in which the law is deemed less efficacious and less efficient, then the meaning of the law is hollowed out. The law thus becomes a tool like any other, used or not according to preferences. The question then becomes: but of which actors? (p. 185).

Deterministic effects of the ICIs Even if we deny the deterministic nature of the technology, we cannot deny that the ICIs shape the human action to a certain extent. As indicated above, this is precisely what happens when the law is perverted. With the growth of a deterministic ICI "the online world becomes saturated with invisible detection and decision mechanisms that manage to redress our behaviours instead of addressing us with regard to our actions (ibid.).

MH clarifies that the intention is not to anthropomorphize the ICIs and excludes attributing them with the capacity of agency. Rather, the point the author is making is the need to for us to condition this 'data driven agency' and to not let it condition us: "It is up to us to design and engineer this mind in a way that does not pre-empt us such that we become the cognitive resource of the ICI instead of the other way round" (p. 185).

For MH, the push to intervene on the ICI in the design phase is based on the fundamental right to privacy, which consists of freedom from illegal interference as a prerequisite for the freedom to develop one's own identity (p. 189). Hence, we are talking about a design inspired by the EU's General Data Protection Regulation (GDPR), which at the time of Hildebrandt's writing (2015) was still in the proposal stage but was later approved in 2018. The author's orientation is based on Legal Protection by Design (LPbD) and on Data Protection by Design, the meaning of which is basically: "LPbD seeks a methodology capable of translating legal conditions into technical requirements, taking into account the fundamental requirements of 'resistability' and contestability." (p. 218). Is this perhaps a question of techno-regulation? "On the contrary, designing legal protection into an ICI means that mechanisms to steer people into certain behaviours must be made *visible* and *contestable*." (p. 219, our emphasis).

Hildebrandt envisaged that this perspective would generate the following consequences. First, data-driven systems "will force existing technology developers to include a new set of requirements at the *starting point of their design process*, while at the same time creating a market for new technologies that help to render data processing systems compatible with the GDPR" (p. 221, our emphasis). But that is no simple task: "The challenge of translating these rights into technical and organizational requirements is intimidating". However, if opportunely promoted and supported by appropriate human machine interfacing technologies, the solution may lead to user empowerment.

Second, MH suggests developing counter-profiling tools and skills with respect to data-driven agency. Counter-profiling must not be confused with anti-profiling (p. 223). Hence, "At this moment there is no legal obligation to provide the socio-technical infrastructure for counter-profiling, whereas this seems to be a critical requirement for achieving the compensation that is called for by technology neutral law. The importance of such an infrastructure for the ICI of pre-emptive computing can hardly be overstated …. To figure out how to actually fabricate smart technologies that enable counter-profiling is no mean feat" (ibid.).

5 Discussion and Policy Implications

The foregoing discussion offers valuable ideas for interpreting and assessing current and foreseeable developments of the intertwining of society and technology. The two books reviewed address similar yet different points that we cannot go into here due to space limitations, which is why we have narrowed our focus to a selected set of issues. Nevertheless, drawing on both works together helps us to make sense of the complexity of the contemporary digital landscape.

The response to the guiding question posited at the beginning of the article—*In what way do the different ways of conceptualizing the intertwining of society and technology contribute to the practice of government in the digital age?*—can be articulated in three points.

First, it is now accepted that the ICT artefacts and their use in the government machinery and in society offer great promise but pose new challenges in reshaping government-society connections. In the words of Henman, ICTs "are part of the complex mix which defines our social realities and its dynamics" [15:19]. Nevertheless, it is one thing to acknowledge the organisational and societal relevance of ICT, but another to identify *the* source of an autonomous rationality, i.e., capable of providing universal "plug-and-play" solutions, in the potential impact of the technologies. In other words, it is illusory and misleading to treat ICT in isolation, i.e., as a variable divorced from the context, also when viewed through the lens of soft determinism, as in the case of H&M.

Second, to develop an adequate understanding of the potential of the relevant ICT tools and applications, it is necessary to consider their variety and diversity. For example, the category of social media technologies comprises "a conglomeration of web-based technologies and services" that vary dramatically in their purposes and approaches [11]. Further, their affordances, or 'action possibilities' [5] can be the conscious or unconscious fruit of design choices.

Third, ICT is in need of political attention. The ability of the technologies to regulate is inherently political: technology can be designed (consciously or unconsciously) to open certain social options and close others [2]. The transformative effects move faster than the policy-making process [8]. Further complicating matters is the fact that the socio-technical nature of the change makes it unpredictable, while the intertwining of society and technology excludes the possibility of implementing 'straightforward solutions' [16].

The above response pulls techno-regulation away from the streamlined vision of law held by the mainstream. Many public policies date back to the pre-digital era and the difficulty of comprehending the changes underway may delay the review and adaptation of old policies [8]. Information policies can come from a large number of sources, including legislations, regulations, norms, circulars and recommendations. Italy, for example, has had a regulatory compass for its e-government policies and machinery since 2005, when the Codice dell'amministrazione digitale (CAD), or the Digital Administration Law, came into effect. Basically, CAD aggregates the norms in a similar way to the Austrian law that allows the federal government to define standard products in the ICT field [17]. In general, the law primarily gives principles and guidance in areas such as safety, trust, security, ownership rights, archiving and record keeping, but fails to address crucial issues related to human agency, equity, democracy, inclusion, equal access, etc.

The critical importance of resolving such unanswered questions, and the potential risks that stem from the excess of power wielded by the digital giants, was confirmed by a journal article [11] on the USA context: "By adopting the use of specific social media tools, government agencies appear to be tacitly endorsing the privacy, security, and other policies employed by those social media providers as adequate". The kick in that citation is the observation that, even in an advanced country such as the USA, there is a de facto disconnect between existing information policies and the public agencies' ongoing use of social media services.

According to a recent paper [4] on technology developments that are likely to have significant social impact in the next 10–15 years, we need better ethics for emerging technologies. Also, given the likelihood that the ICTs of tomorrow will continue to be affected by the problems of today, the public agencies must pay greater attention to information policies in their ICT-related decisions [11]. This gives policy makers the crucial task of ethically grounding the ICTs by devising an appropriate and relevant mix of regulatory framework and infrastructure.

A project funded by the European Community's Seventh Framework Programme (FP7/2007–2013) concludes that such a framework should cover at least the following three main areas of policy activity [4:152–3]:

(a) *Provide regulatory framework* to: support ethical impact assessment for ICTs and e-government. A techno-ethic regulatory framework would help to both raise awareness and identify and address ethical issues.
(b) *Set up an ICT ethics observatory* in order to: provide a community-owned publicly accessible repository and dissemination tool of research on ICT ethics; give examples of approaches and governance structures that allow the addressing of ethical issues; disseminate past and current research ethics and ICT including relevant work packages and deliverables and relevant National Ethics Committee opinions.

(c) *Establish a forum for stakeholder involvement* to: allow and encourage civil society and its representations, industry, and other stakeholders to exchange ideas and express their views. For example, policy consultation by responsibility ethics can take place in the preparatory phase of legislation relevant to technology [7] or in the software development phase.

6 Final Remarks

Guided by the 'tools of government approach' and the 'data-driven agency approach', this paper has explored concisely some of the crucial issues for the information policy design and implementation process. The relatively institution-free approach of the 'tools of government approach' can lead to a more nuanced vision of the digital tools available to government. It also underlines the governments' capacity to use the tools the 'data-driven agency approach' helps to capture and comprehend not only the current technological developments by going beyond appearances, but also the complexity of the social impacts of the digital age.

Drawing on the combined insights of both lenses can help to upgrade existing axioms and chart the ethically best way forward. The review of a selected set of contributions (a limitation of this study) strongly implies that the change underway requires a change in pace and tack that the public decision-makers need to be alert to. The paper also has outlined how the ensuing tentative recommendations can aid the development of more responsible and integrated information policies.

Further, to deny the neutrality of the technology does not necessarily mean that the effects of the ICT will be always ethically relevant [5]. Importantly, the ethical or regulatory concerns posed by most developments (for example, in the area of artificial intelligence) are not markedly different from those posed by existing IT solutions [18].

In definitive, as Grunwald rightly observes, in the digital era it is necessary to know how to distinguish [19] between 'business as usual' and the need for ethically-informed reflection. In countries with a legalistic tradition, like Italy, a potential risk that needs to be addressed is to avoid dealing with the ethical concerns by force-feeding society with, yet again, a further mishmash of normative measures—that would be like "jumping from the frying pan into the fire".

References

1. Grunwald, A. (1999). Technology assessment or ethics of technology? *Ethical Perspectives, 6*(2), 170–182.
2. MacKenzie, D., & Wajcman, J. (1999). *The social shaping of technology*. Buckingham: Open University Press.
3. Bannister, F., & Connolly, R. (2014). ICT, public values and transformative government: a framework and programme for research. *Government Information Quarterly, 31*(1), 119–128.

4. Stahl, B. C. (2011). IT for a better future: how to integrate ethics, politics and innovation. *Journal of Information, Communication Ethics in Society, 9*(3), 140–156.
5. Leenes, R. (2011). Framing techno-regulation: an exploration of state and non-state regulation by technology. *Legisprudence, 5*(2), 143–170.
6. Hood, C. C., & Margetts, H. Z. (2007). *The tools of government in the digital age*. Basingstoke: Palgrave Macmillan.
7. Grunwald, A. (2011). Responsible innovation: Bringing together technology assessment, applied ethics, and STS research. *Enterprise Work Innovation Studies, 31,* 10–19.
8. OECD, "Vectors of digital transformation," in "OECD Digital Economy Papers," 2019, Available: https://www.oecd-ilibrary.org/content/paper/5ade2bba-en.
9. Stahl, B. C., et al. (2010). Identifying the ethics of emerging information and communication technologies: an essay on issues, concepts and method. *International Journal of Technoethics, 1*(4), 20–38.
10. Hildebrandt, M. (2015). *Smart technologies and the end(s) of law*. Cheltenham: Edward Elgar.
11. Bertot, J. C., Jaeger, P. T., & Hansen, D. (2012). The impact of policies on government social media usage: Issues, challenges, and recommendations. *Government Information Quarterly, 29*(1), 30–40.
12. Hood, C. (1983). *The tools of government*. London: Macmillan.
13. Leonardi, P. M., & Barley, S. R. (2008). Materiality and change: Challenges to building better theory about technology and organizing. *Information and Organization, 18*(3), 159–176.
14. Margetts, H. (2009). The Internet and Public Policy. *Policy and Internet, 1*(1), 1–21.
15. Henman, P. (2010). *Governing electronically*. Basingstoke: Palgrave Macmillan.
16. de Bruijn, H., & Janssen, M. (2017). Building cybersecurity awareness: the need for evidence-based framing strategies. *Government Information Quarterly, 34*(1), 1–7.
17. Pollitt, C. (2013). *Governments for the future*. Main Report. Helsinki: Ministry of Finance.
18. Renda A. (2019). *Artificial Intelligence. Ethics, governance and policy challenges*. Brussels: CEPS
19. Grunwald, A. (2000). Against over-estimating the role of ethics in technology development. *Science Engineering Ethics, 6*(2), 181–196.

Power Relationships in the Co-production of Smart City Initiatives

Walter Castelnovo and Mauro Romanelli

Abstract Participatory smart cities promote urban development and transformation by involving citizens and communities in participation and co-production exercises. However, to take advantage of the citizens' contribution to the success of smart city initiatives, interaction-defined and participation-based governance infrastructures should be implemented that return power to the people. An exploratory study shows that how the smart city collaborative/participatory governance questions the traditional power relationships between city governments and citizens is a still underexplored topic. The paper aims to help bridge this theoretical gap by discussing citizens' co-production in smart city initiatives from the point of view of the power relationships. The main point of the paper is that to leverage the citizens' smartness to develop a smart city, the power relationships between the city government and the citizens should be rebalanced, which entails a shift from a power-over domination-based logic to a power-with interactive and collaboration-based logic.

Keywords Co-production · Participation · Power relationship · Smart city · Interactive governance

1 Introduction

In the digital era, cities can become smart by promoting investments in human and social capital, technological infrastructures for sustainable economic growth, higher quality of life and opening up to participatory governance [1, 2]. Promoting smartness in urban context means to plan the urban future, to develop social and economic growth, and to foster new knowledge and intelligence that enables designing and

W. Castelnovo (✉)
University of Insubria, Varese, Italy
e-mail: walter.castelnovo@uninsubria.it

M. Romanelli
University of Naples Parthenope, Naples, Italy
e-mail: mauro.romanelli@uniparthenope.it

C. Metallo et al. (eds.), *Digital Transformation and Human Behavior*, Lecture Notes in Information Systems and Organisation 37,
https://doi.org/10.1007/978-3-030-47539-0_22

implementing processes to support innovation and learning within urban communities. Smart cities contribute to reinventing the urban community, enabling people to understand how to use and interact with technology to promote urban transformation and change in power structure and organisational patterns [3]. Hence, promoting smartness in a city helps advance and support a human-centred design to drive sustainable and smart urban development [4].

Developing the smart city paradigm requires cities to drive urban development involving public and private partners in multi-stakeholder participatory practices and co-production exercises to support local development. This entails promoting a smart mindset, developing a continuous dialogue with civil society and involving public and private stakeholders in a networked distribution of power and resources using the potential of ICT to support community building, capacity building and citizens' engagement in local decision-making [5, 6]. To this end, smart cities have to deal with power discourse and structures and changes in organisational and governance patterns in order to promote urban transformation and support co-production of services and value co-creation [3, 7].

While citizens' participation and co-production in smart city initiatives are topics widely discussed in the literature, how the smart city collaborative/participatory governance questions the traditional power relationships between city governments and citizens is a still underexplored topic, as evidenced by the exploratory study reported in this paper.

The paper intends to contribute to bridging this theoretical gap by investigating how the citizens' involvement as co-producers in smart city initiatives, as exemplary of the citizens' active participation, impacts on the power relationships between city governments and citizens. More specifically, by considering smart cities as social systems characterized by interdependent power relationships [8], the paper argues that to take advantage of the citizens' contribution to the success of smart city initiatives interaction-defined and participation-based governance infrastructures should be implemented that return power to the people [9]. This requires city governments to shift from the traditional power-over to the new power-with and interactive governance style as exemplified by the involvement of citizens in co-production. The paper thus concludes that co-production represents the most effective strategy for developing the city smartness by capitalizing on the citizens' smartness, at the condition that the city government agrees to play the game under the rules of power-with governance.

The paper is structured as follows. Section 2 contains an essential discussion of citizens' participation in smart cities that points to the need of considering the rebalancing of the power relationships in participation exercises. Section 3 describes the survey of the literature we perform as a basis for our exploratory study. Section 4 discusses the results of the survey highlighting a theoretical gap that Sect. 5 tries to bridge by discussing co-production in smart city initiatives as a 'power-with' strategy. Finally, Sect. 6 drives some conclusions, highlights the limitation of the study and describes some further research directions.

2 Smart Citizens as Active Participants

In the public sector, co-production can be considered as an enhanced form of participation in which citizens are actively involved in the design, implementation and evaluation of public policies [10–12]. In smart city initiatives, the collaboration between those who design and implement public policies (policy makers, public sector professionals and private subjects acting on behalf of public agencies) and those who will benefit from them (the citizens, as playing different urban stakeholder roles) is the essential condition to yield the desired results. Engaging citizens in smart city initiatives as co-producers leads to a view of smart cities as organic ecosystems in which end-users and relevant urban stakeholders collaboratively contribute to public value creation and delivery. Governance is an important building block for smart cities. In the smart city literature, governance often refers to citizen participation [8, 13, 14] and collaboration among stakeholders [15–17]. Implementing smart city governance could require transforming to some extent (more or less radically) government structures and operations [18] to both enable and exploit stakeholders' engagement and participatory governance [19]. Although successful smart city initiatives are based on multi-stakeholder governance [15], citizens play the most important role since the city smartness strictly depends on the smartness of its citizens who are asked to participate in the development of the smart city and are implicitly considered as responsible for this objective [20]. For this reason, while acknowledging the fundamental role that different stakeholders (e.g. solution vendors, professionals, advisors, universities, research centers and communities among others) can play in smart city initiatives, the paper focuses exclusively on citizens' participation and on the relation between the citizens and the city government.

Within the literature, citizens are most often conceptualized as the direct or indirect beneficiaries of the smart cities initiatives. However, besides this view of citizens as passive recipients of the services delivered to them by the city, there is a different view that postulates an active role of citizens in the achievement of the smart city objectives. Under this view, citizens not only benefit from the services delivered by the city but also participate (with different modalities) to the development of the smart city since, despite how innovative it is, every smart city initiative is deemed to failure if citizens do not collaborate.

Citizens' participation is most commonly viewed as an attempt to influence the formulation of public policies by taking part in the decision-making processes, which is what political participation (under different forms) usually amounts to. However, citizens can exert important influences on policy also through their participation in the execution of public programs [21, 22]. These more intensive processes go beyond engagement and contribute to involving the individuals in a wide variety of activities in which they work together with public officials to produce benefits [3]. This is what co-production in the public sector amounts to in its broader sense [23–26].

Co-production could be defined as "the provision of services through regular, long-term relationships between professionalized service providers (in any sector) and service users or other members of the community, where all parties make substantial resource contributions" (p. 847) [10]. Co-production invariably requires the co-producers to exert an active role. While participation can also refer to passive involvement, co-production tends to be a broader concept because it focuses on the establishment of a partnership relation between citizens and public officials as an enhanced form of participation [27].

Citizens' participation is often little more than a formality since "while citizens are given the opportunity to provide input, their suggestions rarely change the outcomes of the process because the most critical decisions have been usually made already" (p. 87) [28]. This brings to the foreground the problem of how power and authority are distributed in citizens' participation exercises. In fact, participation should be considered as the process "by which members of a society (those not holding office or administrative positions in government) share power with public officials in making substantive decisions related to the community" (p. 5) [29].

The concept of co-production, and the somewhat related concept of co-creation, is often cited within the smart city literature to refer to the citizens' active involvement in initiatives aimed at making cities smarter. However, as shown in [30], very few cases can be found in the academic literature that describe 'on the ground' implementations of co-production and co-creation exercises in smart cities and even less are the cases that consider how the implementation of co-production exercises impacts on the power relationships between citizens (and other urban stakeholders as well) and public officials. In fact, out of the 37 academic papers in the sample considered in [30] only 6 papers consider the problem of how to redefine the power relationships between public authorities and citizens, which is critical for making co-creation and co-production effective. Moreover, 3 papers in the sample only mention the problem without discussing it in any detail. This is quite surprising since the problem of how to rebalance the power relationships between citizens and public officials has been widely discussed both in the citizens' participation literature [27–29, 31, 32] and the public service co-production literature as well [10, 14, 33–36].

3 Objectives of the Paper and Research Methodology

The results reported in [30] highlight what appears to us a relevant theoretical gap within the literature that, from different disciplinary perspectives, refers to the concepts of co-production and co-creation to describe the role of citizens in smart cities. For this reason, in this paper we perform a systematic (although still limited in coverage) survey of the literature with the aim of investigating whether and how the relationship between the concepts of co-production and co-creation and the rebalancing of the power relationships between citizens and public officials has been discussed in the smart city academic literature.

From a methodological point of view, the paper adopts an exploratory survey methodology [37, 38] with the aim of laying the basis for further in-depth investigations on the power relationship in smart city co-production and co-creation exercises. The study is based on the results of a search performed on *Scopus* and *Web Of Science* on April 2019. The search is based on a combination of keywords, namely *smart city/smart cities* combined both with *co-production/coproduction* and *co-creation/cocreation* and using the term *power* as a filter on the results. The search found 116 academic papers containing one of those combinations of keywords. After deleting duplicates, a set of 72 papers has been identified. All the 72 papers have been considered by analyzing the abstract and, when needed, the whole paper to identify papers in which power is referred to the relationships between citizens (and communities) and public officials. At the end of this refinement process, a set of 17 papers has been identified as relevant for the exploratory study. Due to the exploratory nature of the research, no iteration of the search through backward or forward snowball has been performed. This means that neither the references of the selected papers, nor works citing them have been considered for possible relevance. For the same reason, the results of the search do not include papers in which the key-terms occur only within the references. All the papers considered are listed in the Annex.

4 Exploratory Analysis of the Sample

Most of the studies in the sample identified with the literature search do not directly discuss power in relation to co-production but stress the role of technology in stimulating power shifts and decentralization of roles and tasks in smart city initiatives that increasingly involve local communities, groups and people in services co-production and value co-creation processes.

According to (C3) public service delivery relies on inclusive participatory governance that enhances the co-design between the city and the citizens, with regards to specific capacities and skills provided by users. Value co-creation relies on the involvement of all the members of a community and on the engagement of citizens who should be empowered in order to contribute to digital service co-production and innovation (C12).

(C2) distinguishes co-production and co-management. Co-production relates to citizens that, with public resources, produce the services they use without necessary involving public officials in the production process. Co-management implies that representatives from different organizations work together to deliver services and requires that different actors (e.g. civil society, public and private stakeholders) use resources and expertise to contribute to planning and implementing specific initiatives. Viewing service development as a process of co-management maintains a focus on practical, tangible actions. While issues of power, institutional structures, control and accountability are important drivers of the service management process, the concept of co-management allows to pay particular attention to the actions that are embedded in complex institutional environments.

Smart cities as urban third places (where first place is referred to as home; second place as work) help to empower people to develop social networks and community engagement and enable them to develop behavioral and community loyalty (C14).

Smart cities can be considered as systems of stakeholders looking at the strategic change in the future and that nurture various interests and powers. As such, smart cities should promote a multi-stakeholder analysis that leads to value co-creation in smart city management (C6). Sustaining a networked governance implies to consider capacities, resources, policies and information of all the actors involved in the interaction (C5). Strengthening citizen participation helps empower citizens to contribute to decision-making issues (C9) and relies on promoting collective action supported by participatory practices that contribute to redefining power structures within urban ecosystem (C8).

In smart cities, innovation processes need to be integrated with shared governance processes that enable the sharing of power in decision making, allowing citizens to experience autonomy in self-organization, which opens up to more democratic participation and entails shifting some power away from public officials (C1). Power relies on governance structures and emerges as a source for user-driven innovation and co-creation of services as an urban collective power. Sustaining positively an orientation towards shared power in the smart city vision relies on enhancing cultural, technological and human energies existing within the urban ecosystems. This requires developing collective actions crossing the organization boundaries, empowering individuals and valuing their interests, goals and objectives.

Smart city projects are urban experiments that serve to construct political power and reflect public engagements to influence the audience about the economic and social benefits of a city as a sustainable and smart urban community (C16). In the smart city discourse, there is a shift from domination to influence. Power can be intended as influence, leadership and reciprocity, and citizens are considered as stakeholders in the smart city design and implementation. Involving citizens in smart cities means to encourage them to play an active role using and mobilizing their skills, competences and experience for public or voluntary services delivery, and support co-production that relies on cooperation, co-commissioning and co-delivery of services (C4).

Sharing power within the smart city ecosystems contributes to sustaining freedom, no-constraints and independence as attributes that help people to promote value and services co-creation processes in order to pursue a common good view that enriches value creation within business ecosystems. Attention to power should be paid in order to enhance and support people as autonomous actors in constructing loyalty, to develop social capital and value creation within the community. Empowering people helps value co-creation and services co-production. It drives managers to support the relationship with customers by improving customer patronage through community engagement, local business practices via customer-owner friendship and by encouraging meaningful customer experiences (C8).

Understanding the role of power requires to consider the role of the institutional context where people, groups, public and private institutions tend to deal with questions of power. In (C5) the authors propose the notion of *improstructure* as a conceptual model that explains the infrastructure of governance in terms of improvisational processes of call and response involving diverse sets of actors. The constituents can take the role of creative *provocateurs*, discovering opportunities and developing new practices that cities and utility managers have to respond to. *Improstructure* seems to refer to a mode of fluid and participatory governance infrastructure, where decisions are implemented immediately, but are at the same time historically contextualized in an environment structured by social conditions and power relationships. Designing the cities of tomorrow implies to consider managerial and production aspects in terms of both co-production and co-management.

Technology enables a power shift towards local communities (C13) and helps support a smart approach that contributes to reconsidering the role of citizens in driving knowledge co-creation, collaboration and empowerment and to sustaining user-engagement (C7). According to (C2), the advancements in technology help create digital platforms that enhance the role of citizens as co-creators of smart city design and contribute to supporting transformative power within smart and sustainable cities to develop long-term solutions, to engage citizens in participatory activities and offer them an increasing role in the co-design, co-creation and co-delivery of public services and policies. The design and use of technology influences the distribution of power and enables citizen participation. Moreover, according to (C11) it helps develop transformative power, enables citizen participation and services co-production, and promotes a transition from a top-down government-centric approach to a more decentralized and citizen-centric approach to smart governance.

Technology supports life and sustainability of cities that employ the participatory methodologies of urban informatics to avoid technocratic solutions and to promote a cultural shift in policy and governance style in order to encourage collaborative city-making and to strengthen the abilities of citizens (C17). According to (C15), Information and Communication Technologies are driving the citizens to contribute to sustainability and to the evolution of cities by developing a smart city governance that enables citizen participation and co production of public services and policies. Smart cities initiatives contribute to promoting the city as a governance platform that supports decentralized participation and innovation by involving and encouraging citizens via networks. A new technology-driven and technology-enabled era makes the citizens ready to play a direct role in co-producing services and policies, with consequences on both the services and the political and policy processes. This will promote changes or potential shifts in power relationships and enhance the voice of the city in the urban life and environment.

Power can emerge also as a barrier in smart city value co-creation. Promoting collective action for developing power relies on the involvement of people, groups and organizations in urban development processes. New participatory practices should be developed because the existing ones tend to be a barrier for innovation and change (C8). In particular, the use of technology should help empower citizens to have voice in decision-making and play an active role in participatory practices (C9). According to (C10), smart city vision and policies open up to the need to develop a new balance of power by using information technology that helps connect and promote dialogue and cooperation between business, government, communities and the public. Strengthening networking and collaboration among urban stakeholders thus helps to remove existing power structures and promote new sources for changing the urban landscape and to develop more participatory and democratic patterns that enable value creation within urban ecosystems.

5 Bridging the Theoretical Gap

The results of the survey reported in the section above clearly show that in the smart city literature there is a quite scarce awareness of the relationship between co-production and power. In fact, only 5 papers out of our sample of 17 papers discuss with some details how co-production exercises can impact on the power relationship between citizens and public officials. The most interesting elements that emerged from the survey seems to be the suggestion that effective co-production exercises in smart cities need to be based on influence instead of domination. However, in the papers in the sample this idea, which entails reciprocity (C15), common understanding (C8) and collective power (C17), has not been further elaborated. In this section we suggest a possible explanation of that idea based on the concept of 'power-with' as it has been elaborated in [39].

In the extended literature on power, two essentially contrasting views of power have traditionally been studied: *power-over*, largely characterized as domination, and *power-to*, frequently theorized as empowerment [40, 41]. When designing and implementing public initiatives, public officials exert the power-to decide that derives them from authority. Power in this case refers to a social actor's ability to attain an end or a series of ends [39]. However, by exerting their power-to, public officials can constrain the choices available to the citizens in a nontrivial way, thus exerting also power-over citizens (at least indirectly), which entails (more or less overt) domination over citizens. When they are not exploitation disguised as participation [42], effective co-production exercises challenges both these views of power.

Bovaird and Loeffler [43] consider co-production as a "negotiative relationship between public service professionals and managers, on the one hand, and citizens (…) on the other hand" (p. 254). According to their view, co-production is "a particular set of practices within the wider category of interactive governance" (*ibidem*), which refers to "the complex process through which a plurality of social and political actors with diverging interests interact in order to formulate, promote, and achieve common objectives by means of mobilizing, exchanging, and deploying a range of ideas, rules and resources" (p. 14) [44]. From this point of view, in the public sector, co-production entails social interactions and interdependency, which influences the power relationships by reframing an actor's power to act so as to attain some end (power-to) as the collective ability or capacity to act together so as to attain some common or shared end, which Allen [39] defines power-with. Power-with reflects "an empowerment model where dialogue, inclusion, negotiation, and shared power guide decision making" (p. 6) [39]. It "highlights the values of interaction, dialogue, cooperation, and relationships" (p. 16) [39] and "emphasizes shared power with stakeholders that is achieved through dialogue, negotiation, collaboration, and substantive relationship building" (*ibidem*). Interaction, dialogue, negotiation, cooperation and relationship building are the basic tools for implementing a power-with strategy, but according to the marketing literature on co-production they are also the building blocks for effective co-production and co-creation experiences [45–47].

According to Grönroos and Voima [48] interaction is a dialogical process in which three value spheres are involved: the provider's sphere, the users' sphere and a joint sphere between the provider and the users. In the interaction, the interacting parties are involved in each other's practices and merge their processes into a coordinated, interactive process in which both actors are active. Through interaction, the service users can directly influence the service provider's production process and the service provider simultaneously can influence the users' value creation process. On the one hand, in the interaction the service users are co-producers in the service provider's production process, thus influencing the provider's value sphere. On the other hand, since the interaction potentially enables a merged and coordinated value creation process, it may provide the service provider with access to the users' value sphere [48]. Authority cannot orient value co-creation and co-production that rely on dialogue and negotiation. Sharing values requires dialogue and negotiation, hence in the value creating interaction power can be exercised only as power-with, which means that in the interaction both parties should be ready to redefine their value creation processes (which depend on priorities, preferences, objectives, etc.) in order to create a joint value sphere.

This is a critical point for every smart city initiative based on the active involvement of citizens, for instance through citizens sourcing exercises [14, 49, 50]. As pointed out in [51], if the city government does not consider and put into practice the results of a citizen sourcing exercise, which means that the city government keeps its value sphere closed to the citizens, the government citizens relations can be undermined. Citizen sourcing exercises might result in choices conflicting with the goals and policies of the city government (the provider's value sphere), which indicates a gap between the city and its citizens. This is a problem for the city government, but it could also be an opportunity if the city government and policy makers resort to citizen sourcing as a way to share with them priorities, preferences and objectives (the joint value sphere), which is a fundamental aspect in the process of cities becoming smarter [47].

Without the emerging of a joint value sphere from power-with interactions between the city government and the citizens and without the perception that things are happening within a joint value sphere, there cannot be co-creation of value nor co-production. It can thus be concluded that co-production can represent an effective participation strategy allowing the city to take advantage of the citizens' contribution to the success of smart city initiatives, but at the conditions that interaction-defined and participation-based governance infrastructures are implemented based on the concept of power-with.

6 Conclusions, Limitations and Further Research Directions

The smart cities of the (near) future are expected to design and implement a strategic vision that promotes citizens and communities' participation in policy making, public service co-production and urban value co-creation as drivers of urban and local sustainable development and growth. However, to implement this collaborative and multi-stakeholder vision, smart cities should redefine the power map in urban landscape. This implies opening up to redesigning the power relationships between citizens and city governments by strengthening the role of citizens as proactive stakeholders and decision-makers that interact and dialogue with city government agencies and management.

Power distribution between the agents involved plays a critical role in every participation exercise. In the case of co-production this role is even more critical since, without a rebalancing of the power relationships between governments and citizens co-production can be perceived as exploitation disguised as participation, with negative consequences on the citizens' trust toward governments.

In the paper it has been argued that the smart city collaborative and participatory governance should be based on the values of interaction, dialogue, cooperation, and relationships building typical of the power-with relationship in which power is not exercised as 'domination' but as peer-to-peer influence. The identification of the concept of power-with as the basis for a participation-based governance infrastructure that can return power to the citizens and allow them to contribute their smartness to coproduce the smart city can be considered as the main result of the paper. By discussing citizens' participation in smart city initiatives from the point of view of the rebalancing of power relationships the paper contributes to bridging a theoretical gap, since this topic is still underexplored in the in the smart city literature. A notable exception is the academic literature that studies smart cities from the point of view of the 'governmentality theory', although the governmentality perspective is quite different from that assumed in this paper.

The paper presents some limitation as well, especially in the way in which the papers in the sample have been selected. As observed, in the selection phase no iteration of the search through backward or forward snowball has been performed. Moreover, the search has been limited to papers listed in Scopus and Web of Science. We plan to overcome this limitation in a future research by considering also papers listed in Google Scholar to extend the coverage.

In the paper we did not consider the subjective conditions that can allow, or prevent, citizens to exert influence in smart city initiatives, first of all the role that citizens' knowledge and competences (and of other urban stakeholders as well) can play in the power-with interactions with government. This is a potentially critical limitation that need to be overcome.

However, despite these limitations, which are in part inherent in its exploratory nature, this study clearly identifies a theoretical gap within the smart city literature concerning the role of the power relationships in participation and co-production exercises, and highlights some directions that can be taken to reduce it.

Annexure

C1	Bifulco, F., Tregua, M., Amitrano, C. (2017). Co-governing smart cities through living labs. Top evidences from EU. *Transylvanian Review of Administrative Sciences, 13*(50), 21–37
C2	Schlappa, H. (2017). Co-producing the cities of tomorrow: Fostering collaborative action to tackle decline in Europe's shrinking cities. *European Urban and Regional Studies, 24*(2), 162–174
C3	van der Graaf, S., Veeckman, C. (2014). Designing for participatory governance: Assessing capabilities and toolkits in public service delivery, *16*(6), 74–88
C4	Granier, B., Kudo, H. (2016). How are citizens involved in smart cities? Analysing citizen participation in Japanese smart communities. *Information Polity, 21*(1), 61–76
C5	Offenhuber, D., Schechtner, K. (2008). Improstructure—An improvisational perspective on smart infrastructure governance, *Cities*. *72*, 329–338
C6	Mayangsari, L., Novani, S. (2015). Multi-stakeholder co-creation analysis in smart city management: An experience from Bandung, Indonesia. *Procedia Manufacturing, 4*, 315–321
C7	Bull, R., Azennoud, M. (2016). Smart citizens for smart cities: Participating in the future. *Proceedings of the Institution of Civil Engineers. Energy, 169*(EN3), 93–101
C8	Artto, K., Kyrö, R., Ahola, T., Peltokorpi, A., Sandqvist, K. (2016). The Cuckoo's nest approach for co-creating business ecosystems in smart cities. *Technology Innovation Management Review, 6*(12), 26–37
C9	Mukhopadhyay, C. (2017). Transparency in planning practice: Contemporary urban reform in India. *Italian Journal of Planning Practice, 7*(1), 213–233
C10	van Waart, P., Mulder, I., de Bont, C. (2016). A Participatory approach for envisioning a smart city. *Social Science Computer Review, 34*(6), 708–723
C11	Anttiroiko, A.-V. (2016). City-as-a-platform: The rise of participatory innovation platforms in Finnish Cities. *Sustainability, 8*(9), 1–31
C12	Bertot, J., Estevez, E., Janowski, T. (2016). Universal and contextualized public services: Digital public service innovation framework. *Government Information Quarterly, 33*(2), 211–222
C13	Scekic, O., Nastic, S., Dustdar, S. (2019). Blockchain-supported smart city platform for sociavalue co-creation and exchange. *IEEE Internet Computing, 23*(1), 19–28
C14	Meshram, K., O' Cass, A. (2013). Empowering senior citizens via third places: Research driven model development of seniors empowerment and social engagement in social places. *Journal of Services Marketing, 27*(2), 141–154
C15	Webster, C.W.R., Leleux, C. (2018). Smart governance: Opportunities for technologically-mediated citizen co-production. *Information Polity, 23*, 95–110
C16	Levenda, A.M. (2019). Thinking critically about smart city experimentation: Entrepreneurialism and responsibilization in urban living labs. *Local Environment*, 1–15

(continued)

(continued)

C17	Foth, M. (2018). Participatory urban informatics: towards citizen-ability. *Smart and Sustainable Built Environment, 7*(1), 4–19

References

1. Giffinger, R., Fertner, C., Kramar, H., Kalasek, R., Pilchler-Milanović, N., Meijers, E. (2007). Smart Cities: Ranking of European Medium-Sized Cities. Vienna, Austria: Centre Centre of Regional Science (SRF), Vienna University of Technology. Available from https://www.smart-cities.eu/download/smart_cities_final_report.pdf.
2. Caragliu, A., Del Bo, C., & Nijkamp, P. (2011). Smart cities in Europe. *Journal of Urban Technology, 18*(2), 65–82.
3. Eger, J. M. (2005). Smart communities, universities, and globalization: Educating the workforce for tomorrow's economy. *Metropolitan Universities, 16*(4), 28–38.
4. Lara, A. P., Da Costa, E. M., Furlani, T. Z., & Yigitcanlar, T. (2016). Smartness that matters: Towards a comprehensive and human-centred characterisation of smart cities. *Journal of Open Innovation: Technology, Market and Complexity, 2*(2), 1–13.
5. Allwinkle, S., & Cruickshank, P. (2011). Creating smart-er cities: An overview. *Journal of Urban Technology, 18*(2), 1–16.
6. Lombardi, P., Giordano, S., Farouh, H., Yousef, W. (2012). Modelling the smart city performance. *Innovation: The European Journal of Social Science Research, 25*, 137–149.
7. Dameri, R. (2013). Searching for smart city definition: A comprehensive proposal. *International Journal of Computer & Technology, 11*(4), 2544–2551.
8. Piven, F. F. (2008). Can power from below change the world? *American Sociological Review, 147*, 1–14.
9. Johnston, E. (2010). Governance infrastructures in 2020. *Public Administration Review, 70*(s1), s122–s128.
10. Bovaird, T. (2007). Beyond engagement and participation: User and community coproduction of public services. *Public Administration Review, 67*, 846–860.
11. Bovaird, T., Loeffler, E. (2012). From engagement to co-production: The contribution of users and communities to outcomes and public value. *Voluntas: International Journal of Voluntary and Nonprofit Organizations, 23*(4), 1119–1138.
12. Alford, J. (2009). *Engaging Public Sector Clients: From Service-Delivery to Co-production*. Basingstoke: Palgrave Macmillan.
13. Castelnovo, W., Misuraca, G., & Savoldelli, A. (2015). Smart cities governance: The need for a holistic approach to assessing urban participatory policy making. *Social Science Computer Review, 34*(6), 724–739.
14. Webster, W., & Leleux, C. (2018). Smart governance: opportunities for technologically-mediated citizen co-production. *Information Polity, 23*, 95–110.
15. Nam, T., Pardo, T. (2011). Conceptualizing smart city with dimensions of technology, people and institution. In *Proceedings of the 12th annual international digital government research conference: digital government innovation in challenging times* (pp. 282–291). ACM.
16. Chourabi, H., Gil-Garcia, J. R., Pardo, T. A., Nam, T., Mellouli, S., Scholl, H. J., Walker, S., & Nahon, K. (2012). Understanding smart cities: An integrative framework. In *Proceedings of the 45th Hawaii International Conference on System Sciences (HICCS 2012)*, IEEE Press. pp. 2289–2297.
17. Pereira, G. V., Parycek, P., Falco, E., & Kleinhans, R. (2018). Smart governance in the context of smart cities: A literature review. *Information Polity, 23*(2), 143–162.

18. Bolívar, M.P.R. (2016). Mapping dimensions of governance in smart cities: Practioners versus prior research. In *Proceedings of the 17th International Digital Government Research Conference on Digital Government Research*. ACM.
19. Paskaleva, K., Cooper, I., Linde, P., Peterson, B., & Götz, C. (2015). *Stakeholder engagement in the smart city: Making living labs work. In Transforming city governments for successful smart cities* (pp. 115–145). Cham: Springer.
20. Vanolo, A. (2014). Smartmentality: The smart city as disciplinary strategy. *Urban Studies, 51*(5), 883–898.
21. Sharp, E. B. (1980). Toward a new understanding of urban services and citizen participation: The coproduction concept. *Midwest Review of Public Administration, 14*(2), 105–118.
22. Whitaker, G.P. (1980). Coproduction: Citizen participation in service delivery. *Public Administration Review, 40*(3), 240–246.
23. Nabatchi, T., Sancino, A., Sicilia, M. (2017). Varieties of participation in public services: The who, when and what of coproduction. *Public Administration Review, 77*(5), 766–776.
24. Pestoff, V., & Brandsen, T. (2006). Co-production, the third sector and the delivery of public services. *Public Management Review, 8*(4), 493–501.
25. Verschuere, B., Brandsen, T., Pestoff, V. (2006). Co-production: The state of the art in research and the future agenda. *Voluntas: International Journal of Voluntary and Nonprofit Organizations, 23*(4), 1083–1101.
26. Voorberg, W.H., Bekkers, V.J.J.M., Tummers, L.G. (2015). A systematic review of co-creation and co-production: embarking on the social innovation journey. *Public Administration Review, 17*(9), 1333–1357.
27. Arnstein, S. (1969). A ladder of citizen participation. *Journal of the American Institute of Planners, 35*(4), 216–224.
28. Timney, M. (2011). Models of citizen participation: Measuring engagement and collaboration. In: M. E. Sharpe (Ed.), *Government is Us 2.0* (pp. 100–114). London: Routledge.
29. Roberts, N. (2008). *The Age of Direct Citizen Participation*. London: Routledge.
30. Castelnovo, W. (2019). Coproduction and cocreation in smart city initiatives: An exploratory study. In M. P. R. Bolívar & L. Alcaide Muñoz (Eds.), *E-Participation in smart cities: Technologies and models of governance for citizen Engagement* (pp. 1–20). Cham: Springer.
31. Roberts, N. (2004). Public deliberation in an age of direct citizen participation. *The American Review of Public Administration, 34*(4), 315–353.
32. Kweit, M. G., & Kweit, R. W. (2008). *Implementing Citizen Participation in a Bureaucratic Society: A Contingency Approach*. New York: Praeger.
33. Linders, D. (2012). From e-government to we-government: Defining a typology for citizen coproduction in the age of social media. *Government Information Quartely, 29*(4), 446–454.
34. Bovaird, T., & Downe, J. (2008). *Innovation in Public Engagement and Co-Production of Services*. Cardiff Business School, Cardiff: Department of Communities and Local Government.
35. Joshi, A., & Moore, M. (2004). Institutionalised co-production: Unorthodox public service delivery in challenging environments. *Journal of Development Studies, 40*(4), 31–49.
36. Brandsen, T., & Honingh, M. (2016). Distinguishing different types of coproduction: A conceptual analysis based on the classical definitions. *Public Administration Review, 76*(3), 427–435.
37. Yin, R. (1984). *Case Study Research: Design and Methods*. Beverly Hills: Sage.
38. Kothari, C.R. (2004). *Research Methodology: Methods and Techniques*. New Age International.
39. Allen, A. M. Y. (1998). Rethinking power. *Hypatia, 13*(1), 21–40.
40. Haugaard, M. (2012). Rethinking the four dimensions of power: domination and empowerment. *Journal of Political Power, 5*(1), 33–54.
41. Pansardi, P. (2012). Power to and power over: Two distinct concepts of power? *Journal of Political Power, 5*(1), 73–89.
42. Cova, B., & Dalli, D. (2009). Working consumers: the next step in marketing theory? *Marketing Theory, 9*(3), 315–339.

43. Bovaird, T., & Loeffler, E. (2016). What has co-production ever done for interactive governance? In J. Edelenbos & I. Van Meerkerk (Eds.), *Critical reflections on interactive governance. Self-organization and participation in public governance* (pp. 254–277). Cheltenham: Edwar Elgar.
44. Torfing, J., Peters, B. G., Pierre, J., & Sørensen, E. (2012). *Interactive Governance: Advancing the Paradigm.* Oxford: Oxford University Press.
45. Etgar, M. (2008). A decriptive model of the consumer co-production process. *Journal of the Academy of Marketing Science, 36*(1), 97–108.
46. Prahalad, C. K., & Ramaswamy, V. (2004a). *The Future of Competition: Co-Creating Unique Value with Customers.* Boston: Harvard Business School Pres.
47. Prahalad, C. K., & Ramaswamy, V. (2004b). Co-creation experiences: The next practice in value creation. *Journal of Interactive Marketing, 18*(3), 5–14.
48. Grönroos, C., & Voima, P. (2013). Critical service logic: Making sense of value creation and co-creation. *Journal of the Academy of Marketing Science, 41*(2), 133–150.
49. Schuurman, D., Baccarne, B., De Marez, L., & Mechant, P. (2012). Smart ideas for smart cities: Investigating crowdsourcing for generating and selecting ideas for ICT innovation in a city context. *Journal of Theoretical and Applied Electronic Commerce Research, 7*(3), 49–62.
50. Baccarne, B., Mechant, P., & Schuurman, D. (2014). Empowered cities? An analysis of the structure and generated value of the smart city Ghent. In R. P. Dameri & C. Rosenthal-Sabroux (Eds.), *Smart city: How to create public and economic value with high technology in urban space* (pp. 157–182). Cham: Springer.
51. Nam, T. (2012). Suggesting frameworks of citizen-sourcing via government 2.0. *Government Information Quarterly, 29*(1), 12–20

Strategic Issues of the Current Context of Smart Cities and the Industry 4.0. Case Study: Trends on the Romanian Market

Alina Mihaela Dima and Maria Alexandra Maassen

Abstract The industry 4.0 has become one of the main strategic issues globally in terms of automation and interconnectivity of several sectors, being considered the fourth industrial revolution. Industry 4.0 factors, such as cloud computing, internet of things as smart metering or smart traffic lights, but also cyber physical systems have emerged in different regions of the world sustaining more efficient business, infrastructure, city and cost management, but also interconnected systems to make decentralized decisions regarding these matters. Such elements support numerous parties involved, including users, companies, institutions and municipalities, in managing waste reduction, more effective cost, energy consumption and information transparency, leading to a dynamic environment of adaptation to contextual and environmental situations, that otherwise could be difficult to manage. While there is a trend of automating and interconnecting systems in all sectors of activities, there are still challenges and limitations in regard to the implementation of these industry 4.0 factors, especially in terms of smart cities. Through the Delphi method based on interviews and questionnaires we inquired the implementation degree, needs and costs of some of the most important Smart City and Industry 4.0 tools in the Romanian market, as well as expected trends for the coming years. While there is still a significant gap between the needs of the population, infrastructure and city and the current implementation level of these tools, significant progress has been made though. The relevance of the study lies in the novelty of the practical approach for the Romanian market referring to the industry 4.0 and smart city tools, that have not been inquired previously.

Keywords Industry 4.0 · Smart city · Internet of things

A. M. Dima (✉) · M. A. Maassen
The Bucharest University of Economic Studies, Calea Grivitei, No. 2-2A, Bucharest, Romania
e-mail: alinamihaeladima@yahoo.com

M. A. Maassen
e-mail: maria_nichifor@hotmail.com

C. Metallo et al. (eds.), *Digital Transformation and Human Behavior*, Lecture Notes in Information Systems and Organisation 37,
https://doi.org/10.1007/978-3-030-47539-0_23

1 Introduction

The concept of Industry 4.0 has become a global issue as the need for interconnectivity and data automation systems intensified in recent years. While there are numerous applications of the concept in home automations, urban areas, companies, workplaces and other, there are few studies, that describe this concept, as well as its link to the smart city term in the current context of economic and technological development.

Industry 4.0 has been described by several authors as the fourth industrial revolution, referring mostly to interconnectivity of systems and data automation [1–3]. Increasing urbanization trends caused by demographics explosion led to several challenges in city planning, forcing practically governments and municipalities to find innovative solutions, where the smart city initiative has brought efficient tools and applications to solve many of these strategic issues in developed and developing countries [4].The smart city concept is directly linked to the term of industry 4.0 as the intelligent city with enough development, that is able to ensure quality of life, competitiveness, resource availability for present and next generations [3]. Currently industry 4.0 and smart city applications and tools are used in several sectors of activity, but also in homes of the citizens, leading to quick information transfer, information transparency and better opportunities to manage time and costs in the sense of efficiency increase.

In the current study the main objective was to determine which main types of industry 4.0 and smart city tools and applications citizens use within Romania and which are the main expected trends until 2025, as several changes are expected, especially in terms of smart infrastructure from the municipality. Through the Delphi method based on interviews and questionnaires the practical part of the research offers an overview of the expansion of industry 4.0 and smart city applications, that have encountered significant progress in recent years.

The novelty of the study lies in the fact, that these concepts have not been inquired before in the case of Romania and the scientific literature still offers plenty of research space for inquiring these concepts and their link practically.

2 Literature Review

In recent years the industry 4.0 has expanded tremendously globally, as the need for interconnectivity and data automation has increased in all sectors of activity. The concept Industry 4.0 was first used at the Hannover Fair 2011 and was described as ''a collective term for technologies and concepts of a value chain organization which creates together Cyber-Physical Systems (CPS), Internet of Things Internet of Services, Internet of People, and Internet of Energy" [1]. It is also currently considered the fourth industrial revolution. A main factor contributing to the development of Industry 4.0 tools and smart city was the increase in demographics globally and higher urbanization rates, that made it necessary to find innovative solutions to managing several aspects of the every day life through interconnectivity of machines, people and institutions. A significant characteristic is that the transfer of information does not occur only between persons or persons and machines, but between machines themselves. Machines are transferring information via wireless sensors and transferring the data to the smart service/product providers' centers, that process large amounts of data [2].

An important factor linked to the concept of industry 4.0 is the concept of smart city. Smart cities are described mostly as a city with enough advanced progress that ensures quality of life, competitiveness, resource availability for present and next generations [3]. Figure 1 illustrates the main principles of the industry 4.0 applied for the smart city concepts, referring to: interoperability, virtualization, decentralization, real time capability, service orientation and modularity. In terms of service orientation of smart cities, which is a main characteristic, this refers to interconnectivity of city systems, neighborhoods, intelligent buildings and infrastructure, public transformation and other such systems with multiple parties, such as: citizens, business institutions and others.

Smart cities are mostly evaluated from the point of view of quality of life and ensuring urban services, which practically define what an intelligent city means and connects as previously mentioned more systems to produce synergy effects and better efficiency results.

Figure 2 illustrates the basic principle of interrelationship of core city systems, which is a basic characteristic of the smart city concept. Cities are defined by different

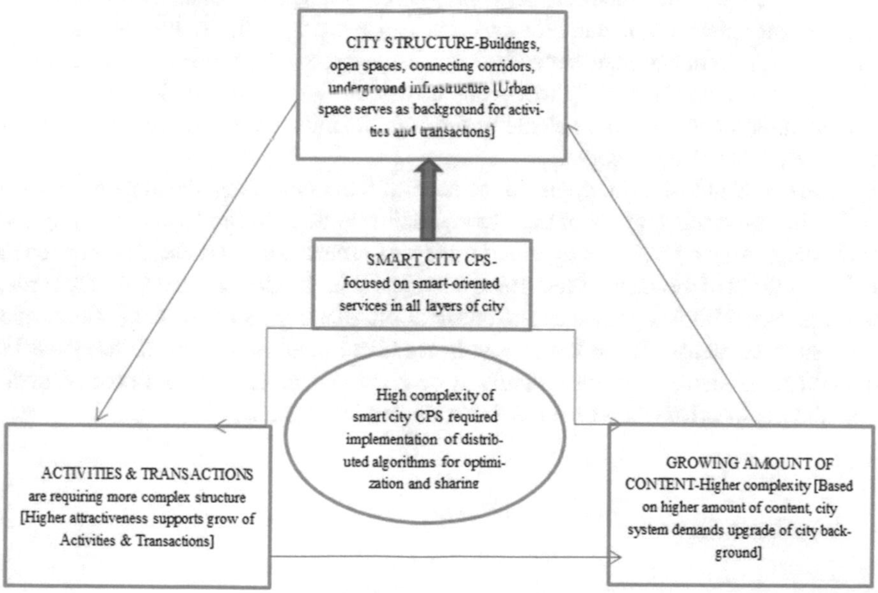

Fig. 1 Smart City shifting focus on smart-oriented service domain *Source Postránecký and Svitek (2017)* [5]

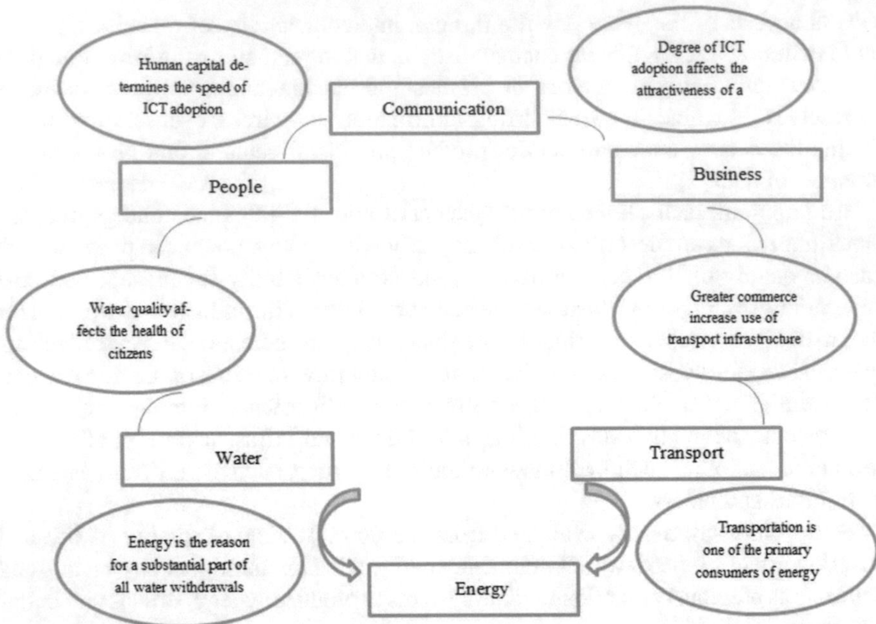

Fig. 2 An example of interrelationship of core city systems *Source Nowicka, 2014* [6]

systems, such as infrastructures, networks and environment, which are affecting the activity and existence of numerous parties and sectors, namely: people, business, transport, communication, water and energy. The effectiveness and efficiency of these systems determines how a city works and how successful it is at delivering its goals through interconnecting these elements through the industry 4.0 interconnectivity of machines, systems and people.

In terms of industry 4.0 applications several tools have been developed, that are visible in numerous regions of the world, such as: smart traffic lights adjusting the traffic depending on its intensity, smart transport, smart parking sensors connected to mobile devices of the users to determine free spaces in the city, smart rentals for cards, bicycles, smart home appliances and automation, identity management systems and other such elements. These have brought a radical change of information transfer and editing of data, allowing systems to be managed more time and cost efficient from the perspective of users, municipalities and institutions.

3 Methodology

For the practical part we used the Delphi method based on interviews and questionnaires as a main tool to ensure a practical approach. There were two sections of questionings between the 1st March 2019 until 20th May 2019 with 61 selected participants from Romania.

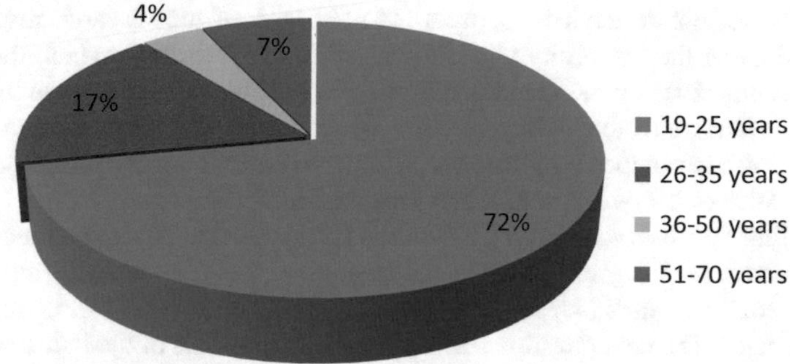

Fig. 3 Participants classification based on age

The first part of the questioning regarded the used smart city and industry 4.0 tools in the city, at home, at the workplace, as well as observed implemented applications and devices in the city of residence of the participants, while the second part of the questioning referred to the availability of the respondents to pay for improving the city infrastructure with smart city tools and applications and expected trends until 2025. The majority of the respondents were from Bucharest as a city of residence (72%), while 13% from Brasov and the rest from more other cities.

Most of the participants were people between the ages of 19–25 years old (72%), while 17% were between the ages of 26–35 years old, as shown in Fig. 3.

Regarding the occupation of the respondents: 34% were employees, 56% were students, 7% were freelancers and the rest were retired. Most of the participants had graduated Bachelor studies (42.6%), 16.4% had graduated master studies and 37% had high school studies. The rest of the respondents had graduated Ph.D. studies.

Practically, the study targeted mostly the observance of differences of more respondents also depending on age, but also the development of smart city and industry 4.0 applications in Bucharest mainly, but also throughout Romania.

The relevance of the study lies in the novelty of the subject, as this topic has not been previously been studied for

4 Findings and Analysis

The first part of the study as mentioned inquired the used applications, tools and devices in the case of the research participants at home, at work or at the study place and in the city.

The majority of the respondents used a local application for mobile phones, that determined routes, arrival times and other information on public transport options, Info STB developed by the municipality of Bucharest in March 2019 (41%), while 16.4% used another application of the same institution Parking Bucharest, that determined through sensors the free parking spaces of the city hall and transmitted the information to mobile devices of users (16.4%).18% of the research respondents mentioned using the smart city application Traffic alert, through which they could alert local authorities by mobile phone of illegal parking, irregularities in the traffic, issues of the roads and other such problems. 23% of the questioned persons mentioned they did not use any of these applications, while the rest used other international smart city tools, such as Moovit, Lime, Waze, Google Maps.

Regarding the observed tools of industry 4.0 respondents observed already being implemented in their city of residence, the most important ones were the smart transport tool, such as smart bicycle renting and systems to recharge electric cars, as Fig. 4 indicates. The next question referred to necessary tools of the industry 4.0 and smart city tools from the perspective of the respondents, but that had not been implemented yet in the city. As Fig. 5 illustrates most respondents 57% mentioned sensors

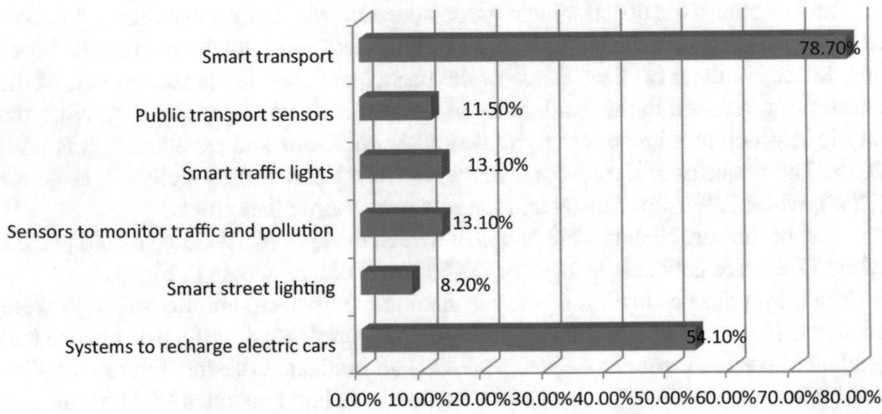

Fig. 4 Industry 4.0 and Smart City tools implemented in the residence city of the participants

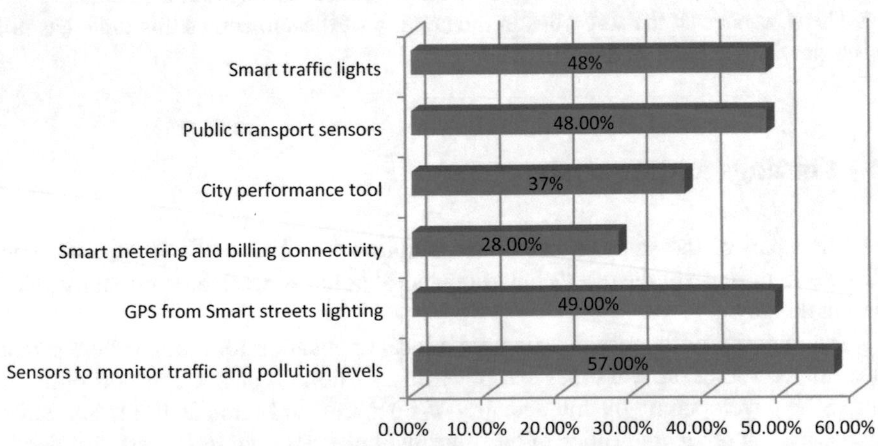

Fig. 5 Industry 4.0 and Smart City tools considered necessary by respondents in the city of residence

to monitor traffic and pollution levels as necessary elements, while 47% considered public transport sensors and smart traffic lights adjusting light signals according to the traffic intensity as important ones. Respondents have selected multiple tools when answering this question.

Another important aspect underlined by the participants of the study were the industry 4.0 tools used at the workplace or at the study place. For example, applications that connect mobile phones or other devices of your daily use to your work or study place information were used already by 67% of the respondents, while smart building tools (for. ex. security systems and other appliances connected to your mobile phone or other devices or to the service companies, etc.) were used by approximately 14% of the participants of the study. An interesting fact was that there were employees of the study, whose institutions or companies already used identity management software for the office, such as for facial recognition of employees (8%) and 16% of the study participants used smart applications to book conference rooms and other spaces, as shown in Fig. 6.

When asked about the industry 4.0 tools used at home 48% of the respondents mentioned home automation, such as smart TVs, turning on and off lights and appliances by phone or voice, SIRI, Google Home, Amazon Echo, 21% smart WiFi security cameras connected to the mobile devices, 51% paying bills through 5G, 28% smart car appliances (for ex. mobile applications managing car), 18% smart thermostats. 75% of the respondents also mentioned they did not have any costs with the tools or applications of industry 4.0 they used.

The second part of the research inquired first the availability of participants to pay an extra amount for improving the city infrastructure with Industry 4.0 and Smart city tools and applications.

55% of the respondents were willing to pay between 5 and 50 Euros maximum a year extra to add to this sector, while 19% were willing to pay between 100–200 Euros per year. This aspect was related to the income levels of participants and also

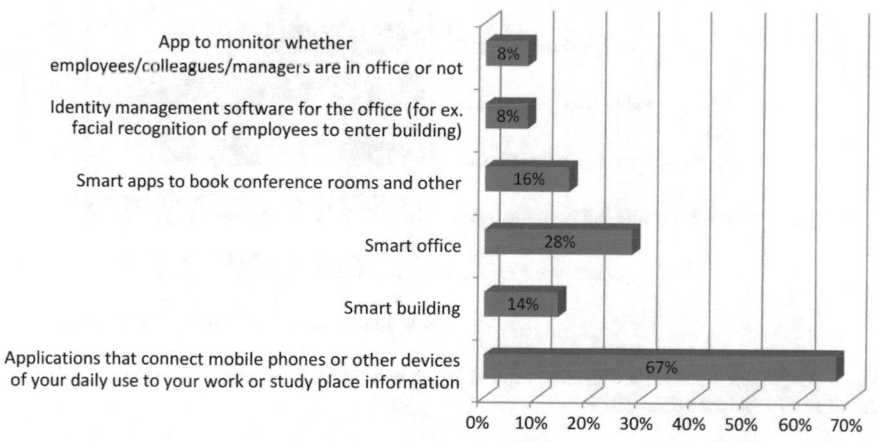

Fig. 6 Industry 4.0 tools implemented by research participants at the workplace/study place

to the interest in this sector. Only 7% of the respondents were either not willing to pay extra or did not know yet as they did not think about the subject (Fig. 7).

The last part of the research inquired the expected trends until 2025 on implementation plans of municipalities or institutions for industry 4.0 and smart city tools that respondents were aware of. The most mentioned tools, that were expected to be implemented in the cities of residence of the participants were sensors to monitor traffic and pollution levels as mentioned by approximately 51% of the respondents and smart street lighting as mentioned by 49.2% of the participants (Fig. 8).

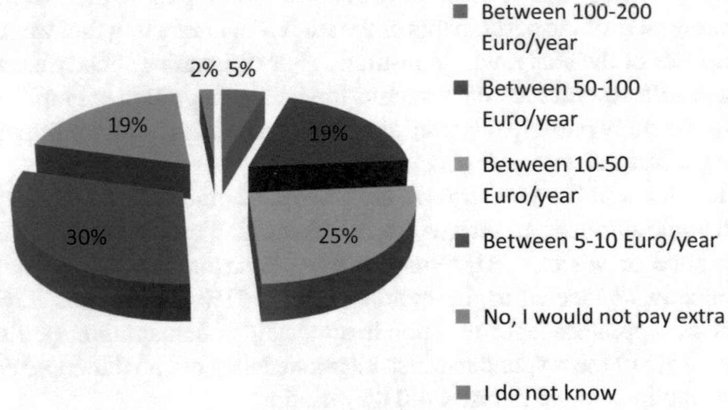

Fig. 7 Amounts participants would be willing to pay extra to ensure a better infrastructure of the city through implementation of Industry 4.0 tools

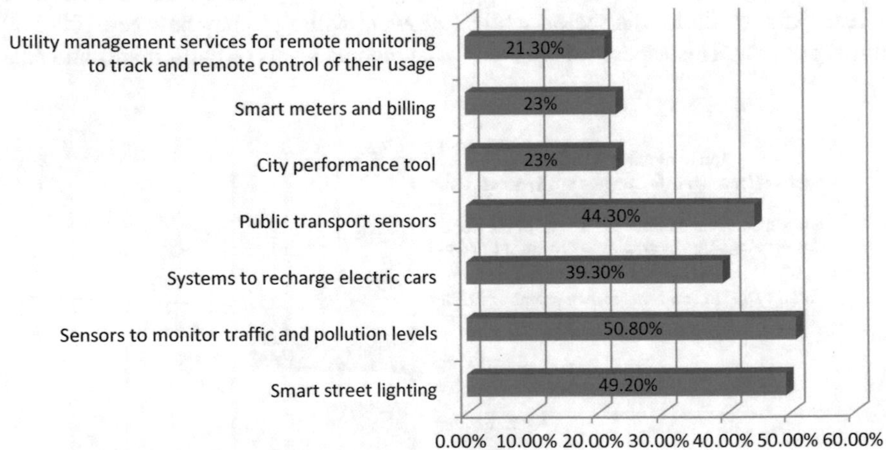

Fig. 8 Expected tools of the Industry 4.0 and Smart city concepts expected to be implemented in the cities of residence until 2025

The current research indicated through the responses of the participants an advanced knowledge of the participants of the industry 4.0 and smart cities concepts, as well as several uses in the urban areas, at workplaces and at their homes.

5 Conclusion

As a conclusion, although there are several improvements awaited in terms of implementing the industry 4.0 and the smart city concept within Romania, a significant progress has been made in terms of usage of these type of applications in all sectors of work, study and living for the citizens as mentioned by the participant of the study. The study revealed today mostly smart transport tools, such as bike rentals or smart steps and charging stations for electric cars are used today in most cities of residence of Romania, numerous other tools are expected to be installed by 2025. The limitations of the study refer to the sample of participants included, however the research is one of the first done on this subject as it is a new field starting to be implemented in Romania. Practical implications of the study imply the analysis based on this sample of participants of current developments in the smart city concept in Romania, trends expected to be implemented until 2025, as well as the willingness of participants to invest in this field. The research showed already the usage of mobile smart applications as some of the preferred methods for users, as well as smart transport and smart recharging systems for electric cars as some of the most implemented instruments for the development of the smart city concept in the cities of residence of the involved participants.

The practical research also revealed the expansion of usage of home and workplace applications of the industry 4.0, such as applications that connect mobile phones or other devices of your daily use to your work or study place, identity management software for the office and other smart applications, as well as for home automation at the living spaces of the respondents.

Most respondents (93%) were also eager to pay an extra amount per year to ensure a better infrastructure for their city through the installment of industry 4.0 and smart city applications, indicating a high level of interest for this aspect of urban development.

While the Industry 4.0 has implemented a high interconnectivity of the people, municipalities, companies and machines, there are still numerous developments expected on all levels of transporting, living, activity and urbanism. The fourth revolution has challenged multiple fields of the social and economic levels and has imposed a new way of acting through quick information transfers and transparency, that has brought a new level of independence for machines and individuals as well. The current study can serve as a basis for future research in the field of the smart city and industry 4.0 concepts, that are expected to develop and will offer new possibilities of inquiry.

A future research object for the present study is to expand the research for the next five years regarding the implementation of industry 4.0 elements in homes, workplaces and cities of Romania, as several programs and applications are expected to be developed.

References

1. Lom, M., Pribyl, O., and Svitek, M. (2016). Industry 4.0 as a part of smart cities. In *Smart cities symposium prague* (pp. 1–6), Prague.
2. Roblek, V., Mesko, M., and Krapez, A. (2016) A complex view of industry 4.0. SAGE open, (pp. 1–11).
3. Gocmen, E., and Erol, R. (2018). The transition to industry 4.0 in one of the Turkish logistics company. *International Journal of 3D Printing Technologies and Digital Industries*, *2*(1), 76–85.
4. Irnazarov, F., and Kayumova, M. (2017) Toward smart city development in Central Asia: A comparative assessment, *Brill Journal 4*(1). https://doi.org/10.1163/22142290-00401003.
5. Postránecký, M. and Svitek, M. (2017). Smart city near 4.0-an adoption of industry 4.0 conceptual model. Prague: Springer International Publishing AG.
6. Nowicka, K. (2014). Smart city logistics on cloud computing model. *Procedia-Social and Behavioral Sciences, 151,* 266–281.

Smart GOALA: An Alternative Marketing Channel for Connecting the Peri-urban Marginal Dairy Farmers with the Urban Consumers in Bangladesh

S. M. Mokaddes Ahmed Dipu and Tunazzina Sultana

Abstract The objective of this paper is to present a mobile-based conceptual model of marketing channel for connecting the peri-urban marginal dairy farmers with the urban milk consumers in developing countries, particularly in Bangladesh. It reports the results of one quantitative survey and four qualitative focus group discussions. The survey reveals that the farmers are deprived of getting fair prices of their product due to inefficient marketing channel. The study also explores that a technology-based marketing channel might help the farmers to overcome the problems. Based on these findings, the study proposes a mobile-based channel—'Smart GOALA'—for connecting the peri-urban farmers with the urban consumers which will ensure them to get a better and fair price.

Keywords Smart GOALA · Efficient marketing channel · Developing countries

1 Introduction

Information Communication Technology (ICT) is the fuel of economic growth of all the nations in the world [2, 4, 30]. Focusing on developing countries, researches have been conducted to explore the benefits of ICT in the development of those countries [3, 29–31, 37]. Dramatic increase in the usage of ICTs in the developing countries, which is measured by several indicators such as fixed-line telephone and mobile cellular subscriptions, number of Internet users, and number of broadband subscriptions [17, 38], has made the researchers interested in this field of research. Most interestingly, this rate of usage of ICTs is higher than that of the developed countries

S. M. M. A. Dipu
Department of Agricultural Economics and Social Sciences, Chattogram Veterinary and Animal Sciences University, Chattogram, Bangladesh
e-mail: smmadipu@cvasu.ac.bd

T. Sultana (✉)
Department of Marketing, University of Chittagong, Chattogram, Bangladesh
e-mail: tunazzina@cu.ac.bd

C. Metallo et al. (eds.), *Digital Transformation and Human Behavior*, Lecture Notes in Information Systems and Organisation 37,
https://doi.org/10.1007/978-3-030-47539-0_24

which attracts the attention of both the researchers and designers for exploring the opportunities of different use of ICT.[1]

The contribution of telecommunication technologies particularly mobile phone and internet to the development of economy of both developed and developing countries has been identified in many studies [5, 15, 16, 19, 36]. The role of mobile phones in agricultural sector has been found in many research studies [13, 24]. Particularly, [3] emphasized on the role of mobile phone in "*improving agricultural and labor market efficiency and producer and consumer welfare in specific circumstances and countries*" through communication cost reduction. Moreover, information asymmetry which is considered as one of the main problems for low growth rates and low productivity in agricultural sector can be solved with mobile technology [25]. Similarly, [27] suggested using technology for "*new organizational models, new management of channel relationships, as well as new models of communication*".

In this light, we are motivated to investigate how a technology-based distribution channel can help in adding value by improving the efficiency of the marketing channel of dairy milk in developing countries by addressing the following research question:

Can a mobile app-based distribution channel model add value to the existing milk marketing channels in Bangladesh?

In this paper, we report a survey and subsequent focus group discussions that was done to assess the profitability and marketing efficiency of the marginal backyard dairy farmers of the peri-urban villages in a developing country, namely Bangladesh and the requirement analysis phase for designing and developing mobile app based conceptual model for connecting the peri-urban marginal dairy farmers with the urban unprocessed milk consumers. From socio-technical perspective, this work involves different stakeholders of dairy milk distribution channel including the milk producers, channel members and end users for eliciting the requirements and the designers for designing and developing an app for increasing the efficiency of the marketing channel for dairy milk.

In what follows, we first give the background and motivation of this research, and then describe the methodology adopted for this work. We then report and discuss the main findings of a survey and four focus group discussions that are done to conceptualize a new marketing channel model and to design and develop a prototype for serving our purposes. We then summarize the insights and the next step of our research in the conclusion.

2 Background and Motivations of the Study

Bangladesh is a South Asian country having more than 165 million people. Of them, around 80% people live in the rural areas. The economy of the country is based mainly on agriculture, and livestock is an essential component of the rural economy and the livelihood of the poor farmers.

[1] ITU. (2015). https://www.itu.int/en/ITU-D/Statistics/Documents/facts/ICTFactsFigures2015.pdf.

Bangladesh Investment Development Authority [6] reported that 90% of the dairy farmers have 1–3 cows, 6% dairy farmers have 3–10 cows and the rest 4% dairy farmers have more than 10 cows in the country. But due to the wake of price-hiking of cow's feed items, medicines and other requisite inputs, dairy farming has now become expensive for that huge number of poor farmers. On one hand, most of the dairy farmers are small with low milk production; on the other hand, the price of their dairy milk is not fixed under traditional marketing system. Moreover, due to the involvement of intermediaries; lack of bargaining power and infrastructure facilities for collection, storage, transportation, and processing of raw milk, the farmers do not get the expected price for their milk [23, 33]. These are common problems to the milk marketing channel in most of the developing countries. Bangladesh is not an exception. Here, many of the farmers abandoned their business due to lack of marketing facilities incurring huge financial loss [34]. Small-scale farmers face many constraints that obstruct them from taking advantage of market opportunities [11]. However, the marginal milk producers of many developing countries like India, Bangladesh are enjoying the advantages of cooperative. On one side, in cooperative, the price is fixed, and the marketing channels are more efficient than other channels [23]. On the other side, it offers a secured permanent market for supplying any quantity of milk.

Researches also suggested for improving marketing facilities "*by establishing milk processing plant in the milk producing area or by making provision for collection of milk through well-organized marketing channel*" [22].The development of new, more sophisticated marketing channels by adopting technology can help to increase productivity in domestic milk [12]. Proper milk marketing scope could be a way to make dairy farmers' business profitable and sustainable which will lead to an improved standard of living of those farmers [35]. Hence, we are motivated to develop an alternative marketing channel with the help of mobile app which we named Smart GOALA[2] for connecting the Peri-urban[3] [1]. Marginal dairy farmers with the urban consumers by adopting technology for improving its efficiency.

3 Methodology

To serve our purposes, we adopted a mixed approach: a survey and four focus group discussions on the development of a mobile-based alternative channel. Firstly, we conducted a survey in the ten adjacent villages (peri-urban) to Chittagong City [10]. Specifically, these villages are situated in the entrance of the City. Then, we organized and moderated four exploratory Focus Group discussions in March 2019; farmers, DLS (Department of Livestock Services) Officials, University Teachers,

[2]In Bangladesh, the term Goala is used for milkman who delivers milk, often directly to customers' houses, in bottles, cartons or packets.

[3]Peri-urban refers to the areas between urban and rural area.

Dairy Association leaders and potential consumers were invited for fruitful discussion and brainstorming. The group discussions were conducted by adopting the methodology proposed by [8] and used by [8] as well as by [7]. This method helps the researcher in two ways: it helps to refine and improve in the design through exploratory focus groups (EFGs) and to confirm or evaluate of the utility of the design through confirmatory focus groups (CFGs) by involving actual and potential users. Moreover, this method was considered as the best one for this project since it will allow the researchers to go for a further rigorous investigation of the design in case of future development.

3.1 Survey

Study Area: This is a quantitative study where the data were collected from field visits in the ten adjacent villages (peri-urban) to Chittagong City [1, 14] Specifically these villages are situated in the entrance of the City e.g. Chikondondi, Shikarpur, Burirchor (Hathazari Upazilla); Urkirchar, Noapara (Raojan Upazilla); Gomdandi (Boalkhali Upazilla); Char Pathorghata, Shikalbaha, Kolagaon (Patiya Upazilla) and Salimpur (Sitakund Upazilla) We have selected Chittagong City as our sample area for few reasons: it is the second biggest Metro City in Bangladesh where fresh untreated raw milk is packaged in non-branded polyester packet and sold directly to the consumers [9], geographically a convenient location having peri-urban villages which are better matched with the definition given by [1]; and it has a dairy zone in one of the selected Upazillas (Paitya Upazilla).

Sample Size and Data Collection: Snowball sampling method was used to collect data from four to seven marginal dairy farmers from each village totaling a sample size of 51 out of 560 farmers (9.11% of the population). There was no farmers' database available and hence the population size was determined by personal observation of the authors and discussion with the local vets, Upazilla Veterinary Surgeons and Livestock Officers. The farmers were given token gift for giving their time. Structured questionnaire and personal interviews were used for the survey which aimed at farm data as well as demographic, socioeconomic and technological data of the farmers. Besides, local and near-by town markets were also visited during the study time to collect market information. Moreover, data was collected from few random buyers of raw milk in Chittagong Metropolitan Area by using a structured questionnaire to know about their buying behavior on some specific issues.

3.2 Exploratory Focus Groups Discussions

We organized and moderated four focus group discussions in March 2019. Farmers, DLS Officials, Teachers from Dairy Science and other relevant departments of Chittagong Veterinary and Animal Sciences University, Dairy Association leaders, potential consumers were invited for participating in the discussions. The overall focus groups involved thirty-two participants, lasting around 8 hours altogether. The participants were divided in 4 focus groups of 8 participants each, so that the groups were all homogeneous with respect to gender, age and profession. We considered and maintained the procedures of a focus group discussion in every discussion regarding environment, moderator, observer, record keeping, and timing [20, 21, 26, 32]. One of the authors transcribed the records and summarized them in a list.

4 Results and Discussions

4.1 Survey Results

Demographic, Socio-Economic, General Farm, Business and Technological Factors: To understand the present status of the farmers, demographic and socio-economic data were analyzed. Among the participants, 88% were male and married. Among them 43% farmers have small family whereas 52% families have equal or less than two children. Concrete sanitation facilities are used by 31% farmers compared to 51% farmers use semi-concrete or mixed sanitation facilities. Dairy farming is the main income source for 33% dairy farmers in the study area whereas business (29%) is the second in rank. By mere observation it was found that 24% farmers were solvent (middleclass) and 33% farmers were not solvent (poor), 10% of the farmers were very poor and the rest of the 33% farmers were very solvent.

The survey revealed the average purchase price of the buyers; the highest price is 70.00 Taka paid by Consumer/Household customers in urban area and the lowest price is 45.00 Taka paid by Big Bulk Buyer in urban area. From the field survey, it has been found that the farmers get on an average of 54.00 Taka. Hence, there is a bigger opportunity in the urban consumer market for improving marketing efficiency which has not reached the optimum level due to lack of market linkage and market knowledge. Again, production constraint (average 3.74 liter/day/smallholder) is another bottleneck to improve the efficiency level.

Table 1 shows that lack of finance, getting unfair price of the milk and facing unstable price of the milk are the major problems faced by the farmers during milk marketing.

'Location' (around 71%) is considered as major selection criteria used by the buyers of raw milk whereas 'irregular supply' (approximately 22%) is the major prevalent problem faced by the buyers. Around 58% buyers report that they also face some other miscellaneous problems.

Table 1 Problems faced by the farmers during milk marketing

Problems	Minimum	Maximum	Mean	Std. deviation
Farmers lack market information	1	5	2.47	1.189
Farmers lack market linkage	1	5	3.02	1.086
Farmers lack storage facilities	1	5	3.94	1.448
Farmers lack transportation	1	5	3.35	1.197
Farmers lack finance	**1**	**5**	**4.53**	**1.120**
Farmers get unfair price of the milk	**1**	**5**	**4.00**	**1.166**
Farmers face unstable price of the milk	**1**	**5**	**4.27**	**1.218**
Farmers can't pack the milk	1	5	3.51	1.206
Farmers feel gap with the consumer	1	5	2.59	1.023

Interestingly, in one hand, 98% of the farmers showed positive attitude towards technology and around 92% of the respondents expressed their high interest regarding the use of technological intervention particularly mobile-based system for increasing marketing efficiency. On the other hand, the buyers (94%) also preferred any 'easy to use' technology to procure raw milk directly from the farmers (Fig. 1).

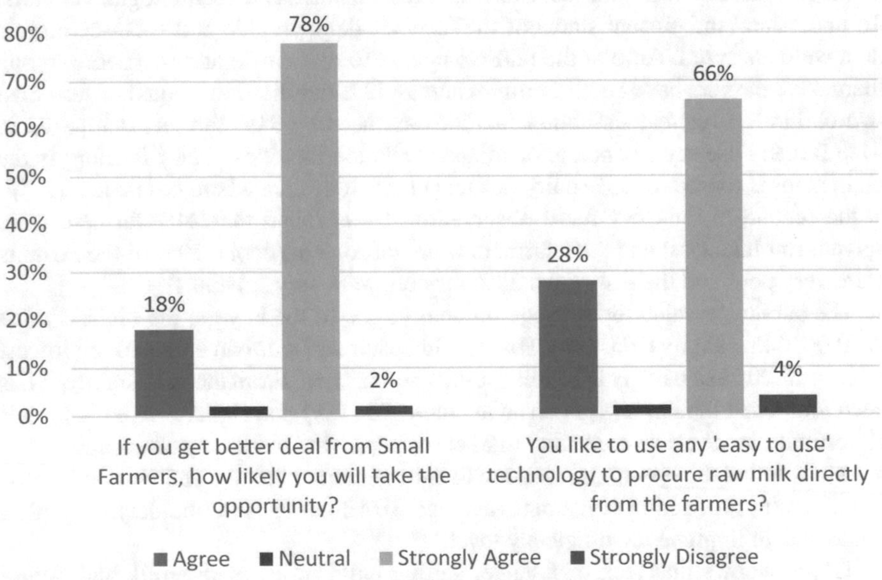

Fig. 1 Buyers' feedback on smallholder and use of technology

4.2 Exploratory Discussions

The findings of the focus group discussions are listed below:

- To overcome the issue of the production constraint of the smallholder peri-urban dairy farmers, there should have group activity or cooperatives aligning the nearby farmers.
- To ensure the fair price for milk by establishing mainstream market linkage, the peri-urban smallholder farmers can be connected directly to the urban consumers by using information and communication technology (ICT). To be specific, GPS location-based mobile application, which connects the urban consumers with the nearest farmers' group, can be a good option.
- There should have a facilitator/organizing body (usually a non-business partner who works for dairy development) which will organize the farmers' group, develop and maintain the mobile app, promote the cause (safeguarding the smallholders), market the product (high quality pure raw milk) and train-up the farmers' group.
- To safeguard the profitability of the farmers' group, dependency on one product (milk) should be lessened and other milk/dairy products should be introduced gradually. And these products should be made available on the app to sell.
- As urban consumers are highly quality conscious, proper quality control procedures are to be maintained.
- The mobile app should be capable of creating a customer database with necessary information e.g. name, contact no, location address, GPS location, National Identification No etc.
- The mobile app should have the necessary payment options with payment updates. Mobile banking can also be incorporated in the app.

The following table summarizes the main issues/ideas and their subject matters as they came out from the analysis of the group conversations. The detailed analysis and description of all the identified issues reported in the next paragraphs (Table 2).

Technological Intervention and Design Issue:

All the participants were agreed on the fact that technological intervention is highly needed in the marketing channel of raw milk to make it more efficient. In this case they opined for a GPS location-based system that can connect the producer and consumer easily even when they are not close to each other and this system could help the customers get immediate access to product information. Consequently, the farmers also get access to urban and mainstream market where better opportunities are lying.

Regarding design issue, few participants suggested for payment option in the mobile app as such kind of option would make the transaction easier and customer might feel it more comfortable. Since Smart GOALA is expected to be used by both dairy farmers and urban consumers, some participants asked for provision for customer databases. Particularly, their discourses emphasized on security issues and they asked for an essential provision for National Identification Number.

Table 2 Issues and subject matters of FGD

Technological intervention and design issue	Organization	Necessity of cooperatives	Mechanism of smart GOALA	Expected benefits
– Connection through ICT – GPS location-based mobile application – Payment option in mobile app – Customer data-base enabled mobile app – User friendly	– One administrative body – Facilitator of core activities – Training provider	– Grouping nearby farmers	– Facilitate the cooperative to organize farmers' group for milk collection – Policy formulation for different activities (quality control, packaging, promoting etc.) – Conducting the set activities	– Linking the market actors – Increasing productivity – Ensuring fair price

Necessity of Cooperatives:

Since the peri-urban dairy farmers are poor and the quantity of their daily production of milk (average 3.74 liter/farmer) is not enough to commercialize efficiently, it is essential to form cooperatives to make them stronger. The advantages of cooperatives were reflected by the opinions of the participants. Most of them believed that such cooperatives are a must to develop an alternative marketing channel-Smart GOALA for smallholder and marginal dairy farmers.

Organization:

The required activities like organizing the farmers group, designing the system, implementing it and other activities related to Smart GOALA should be facilitated and monitored by an administrative/facilitator body. Almost all the participants agreed on the fact that these activities should be administered by any non-business partners who are involved with dairy development. In this connection, they all named Chittagong Veterinary and Animal Science University would be the best organization as administrator in this case.

Participants also agreed on the fact that necessary training to the cooperatives and their members should be provided by this organization. In addition to this training, formation of cooperative, safeguarding the dairy farmers, protecting consumers rights, formulating the policies, designing and implementing the system, developing, maintaining and promoting the mobile app should also be ensured by this administrative body.

Mechanism of Smart GOALA:

After the thorough discussion of the role of the administrative body, the fourth issue emerged regarding the mechanism of Smart GOALA and the way how the new model will work. Most of the participants suggested that administrative body should formulate the rules and regulations regarding the total activities, and it should monitor the activities as well. The farmers will deposit their milk in their nearest cooperative and they will freeze up the milk and pay to the farmers at a predetermined price. Packing and branding will be done at the cooperative office with the necessary supports from the facilitator body. However, few of them opined for local collector instead of cooperative for milk collection. The idea is to develop an entrepreneur in the cluster area, and he will organize the farmers from whom the milk will be collected. By work or functionality principle, there is no difference between the cooperative and local milk collector (entrepreneur) but the only difference is the formation of that milk collection point. As a result, the discussion came up with two alternatives for the new distribution model. However, in either case, the cooperative/local milk collector (entrepreneur) will be regulated by the administrative body.

Next comes the 'way' to be used for connecting the producers to the consumers. As a good number of urban consumers are habituated with internet, Smartphone and mobile app, the facilitator body will develop a mobile application as a technological intervention. This app will be branded as Smart GOALA and will be marketed online by the facilitator body targeting the urban milk consumers. The consumers will place their orders on the app and the orders will be relayed to the nearest cooperative using GPS location. In the cooperative end, order summary can be generated day-wise. Afterwards, the respective cooperative will take the initiative to fulfill the order.

Expected Benefits:

The expected benefits of the new model were out of question. All the participants agreed on the fact that this model would help the channel members reduce the gap between them. Currently, the smallholder and marginal dairy milk producers sell milk to their neighborhoods or local markets at a poor price. If they failed to connect the consumers or if there is no demand for their product, they get compelled to through away/dispose their product due to lack of storage facilities. If the model works properly, it will help the producers in different ways. Broadly, it connects the urban consumers with the smallholder and marginal farmers, which will help to increase the marketing efficiency of the farmers by capitalizing the urban market opportunities. To be specific, it is expected to guarantee a better and stable price by establishing linkage to the mainstream market. As there will be storage facilities in the cooperative, the unwanted products disposal by the farmers is supposed to be lessened substantially. On demand side, the urban consumers get easy and immediate access to product information as well. It helps the consumers get the quality raw milk at their doorstep. In a nutshell, the model ensures a win-win situation by securing fair price for the farmers and by delivering quality milk at doorstep for the consumers.

The objective of this research is to develop a mobile-based conceptual model of marketing channel for connecting the peri-urban marginal dairy farmers with the urban milk consumers in Bangladesh. This research came up with some results that help develop a conceptual model of marketing channel which will be helpful to establish a market linkage which is currently absent, and which will enable the marginal and smallholders to get access to the mainstream market.

Considering these insights, the distribution model can be drawn as below: (Fig. 2)

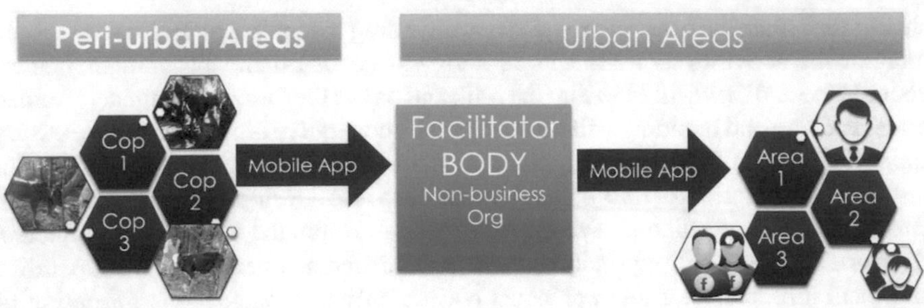

Fig. 2 Proposed distribution model

Here, cluster-based cooperatives of the smallholder and marginal dairy farmers will be formed in the peri-urban areas. The farmers will deposit their milk in their nearest cooperative and they will freeze up the milk and pay to the farmers at predetermined price. Packing and branding will be done at the cooperative office with the necessary supports from the facilitator body. Alternatively, the cooperative can be replaced by local milk collector who will be developed as entrepreneur by the facilitator body. By work or functionality principle, there is no difference between the cooperative and local milk collector (entrepreneur) but the only difference will be the form of its organization.

As a good number of urban consumers are habituated with internet, Smartphone and mobile app, the facilitator body will develop a mobile application as a technological intervention. This app will be branded as Smart GOALA and will be marketed online by the facilitator body targeting the urban milk consumers. The consumers will place their orders on the app and the orders will be placed to the nearest cooperative using GPS location. In the cooperative end, order summary can be generated daywise. Afterwards, the respective cooperative will take the initiative to fulfill the order. Thus, the model connects the urban consumers with the smallholder and marginal farmers which will help to increase the marketing efficiency of the farmers by capitalizing the urban market opportunities. Hence, it is expected to guarantee a better and stable price by establishing linkage to mainstream market. In the following, we described the features of Smart GOALA which was designed and developed based on the requirements elicited through focus group discussions and inserted few screenshots of the interface of the app.

Features of the 'Smart GOALA' Mobile Application: Mobile application usability refers to nice and functional interface which acknowledges all usability issues such user friendliness, well integration of functions, ease of navigation, simplicity and consistency of the design [28, 39]. According to [18], the usability features can be of two types namely hardware (physical) and software (system). Physical attributes e.g. indicator, screen display, button and overall presentation of the app are related to physical features which are the subject matter to describe in this paper for the Smart GOALA mobile application.

To ensure the user friendliness of the app, Bangla has been used as the language of the app so that the users find it self-explanatory to navigate to different options. The functional utilities of the app are described in below heads for clarification of the physical features of the Smart GOALA.

Home Page: When the users hit the application button on their Android Smart device, the home page will appear which clearly depicts the selling proposition and the purpose of Smart GOALA in very short and simple language. The page also shows the Menu button both on top and bottom. Either way, the users will be navigated to different tabs.

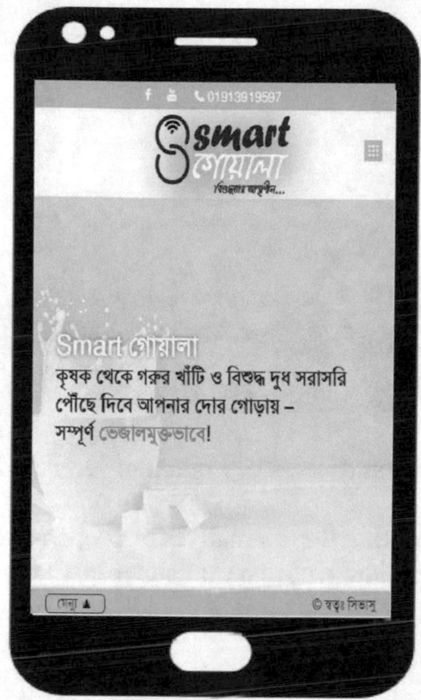

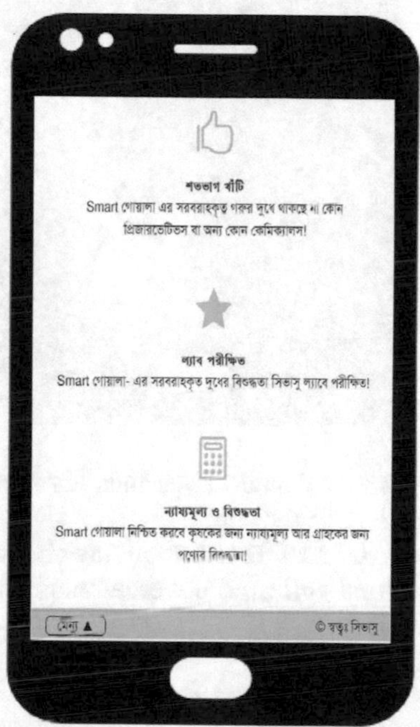

Menu: In Menu tab, the unregistered users will see lesser information and are given the registration option to use the full utility of the app. When the users go for registration, they are asked very basic information regarding their identity, location and contact details. The app will also take their device location with the due permission from the users. After registering to the app, the users will be able to browse all the relevant tabs such as Profile, Order Setting, Previous Orders, Bill, Information and Recipe.

In 'Order Setting/Placing' tab, the consumers can place their order as per their requirement. Their placed orders can be viewed and edited on 'Previous Orders' tab. In 'Bill' section, the users can check their bill for any given period. This section will also reflect the payment status of the consumers.

To make the app more interactive and useful, some worthwhile information and relevant exclusive recipes will be posted periodically in 'Information' and 'Recipe' tabs respectively.

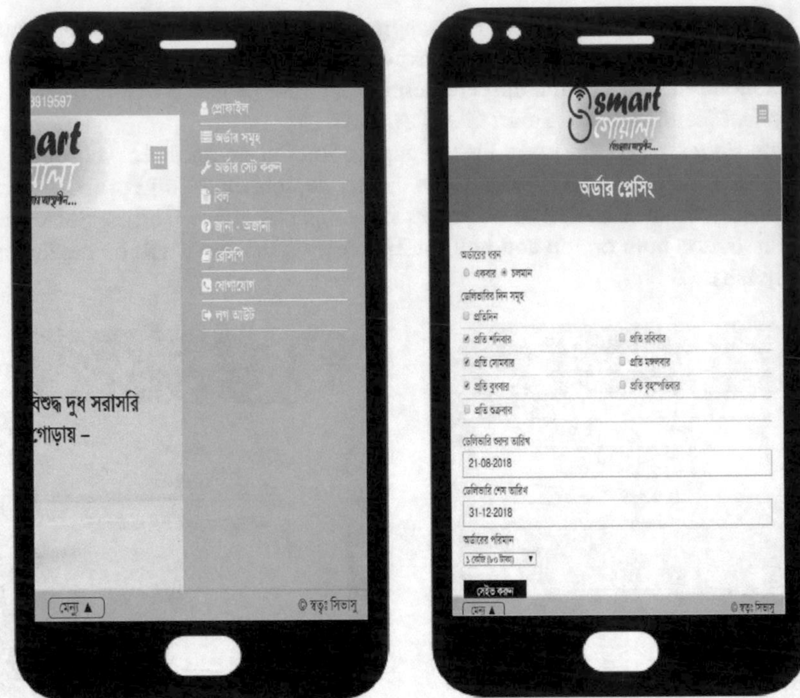

Others: Contact hyperlink, log in remember and necessary brand materials will be placed in the app.

Order and distribution flowchart: Considering the alternatives of cooperatives and local collector, the order and distribution flow chart can be either of the two below:

Alternative 1:

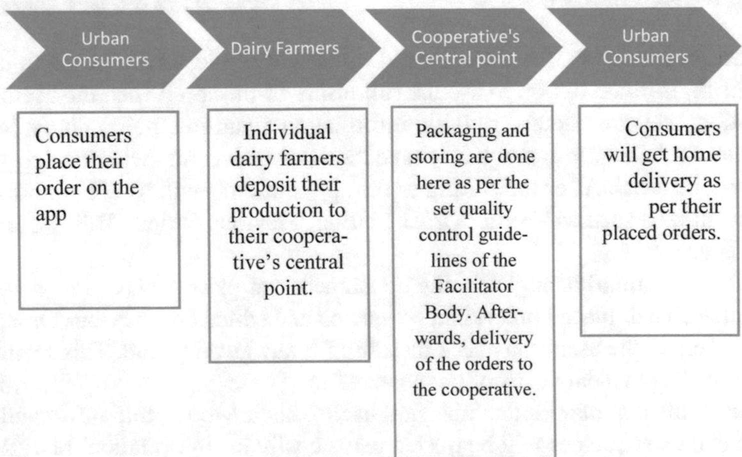

Alternative 2:

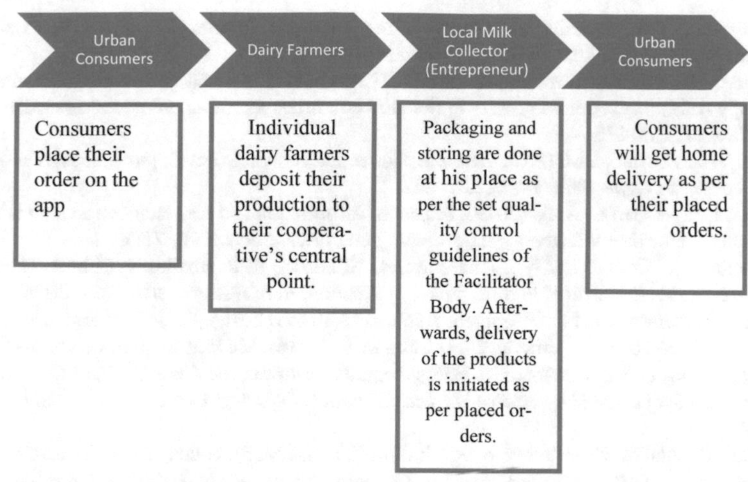

5 Conclusions

In this paper, we attempt to explore the opportunities of ICT in developing countries to improve the efficiency of marketing channel for dairy product, unprocessed milk in particular. To this aim, we develop a mobile-based distribution channel for raw milk marketing where we suggest using a mobile app Smart GOALA-for connecting the peri-urban marginal dairy farmers with the urban consumers in Bangladesh. This study has given a first look at the potential of a mobile-based marketing channel for connecting the urban consumers with the smallholder and marginal farmers in order to increase the marketing efficiency of the farmers by capitalizing the urban market opportunities. However, we consider the limitation of this research: not assessing and validating the functionalities of the app. This limitation provides us with the future research direction. In the next phase, the current prototype of Smart GOALA will be tested by the potential users through confirmatory focus group discussions for assessing the user experience and complying with the design research methodology [8]. We consider that this research shows potential to identify a new way to be introduced as a socio-technical solution for the development of dairy sector in developing countries. This work can then be a contribution towards developing and introducing an alternative marketing channel which could play a significant role for connecting the peri-urban marginal dairy farmers with the urban consumers and for increasing the efficiency of the channel.

References

1. Adell, G. (1999). Theories and models of the peri-urban interface: A Changing Conceptual Landscape. London, UK: Development Planning Unit, UCL.
2. Aghaei, M., & Rezagholizadeh, M. (2017). The impact of information a communication technology (ICT) on economic growth in the OIC countries. *Environmental and Socio-Economic Studies, 17,* 255–276.
3. Aker, J. C., & Mbiti, I. M. (2010). Mobile phones and economic development in Africa. *Journal of Economic Perspectives, 24*(3), 207–232.
4. Bahrini, R., & Qaffas, A. A. (2019). Impact of information and communication technology on economic growth: Evidence from developing countries. *Economies, 7*(1), 21.
5. Bhavnani, A., Chiu, R. W. W., Janakiram, S., Silarszky, P., & Bhatia, D. (2008). The role of mobile phones in sustainable rural poverty reduction. *Retrieved November, 22,* 2018.
6. Bangladesh Investment Development Authority (BIDA) (2010). Dairy in Bangladesh.
7. Cabitza, F., Locoro, A., Simone, C., & Sultana, T. (2016). Moving western neighbourliness to East? A study on local exchange in Bangladesh. *Presented at the The 19th ACM Conference on Computer-Supported Cooperative Work and Social Computing*, Feb 27–Mar 2, San Francisco, USA.
8. Chiarini Trembley, M., Hevner, A. R., & Berndt, D. J. (2010). Focus groups for artifact refinement and evaluation in design research. *Communications of the Association for Information Systems, 26*(27), 599–618.
9. Das, S. (2009). A study on quality of milk from farm to shop in Chittagong Metropolitan area.
10. Fink, A. G. (2002). *The survey handbook*. Sage Publications.
11. Fischer, E., & Qaim, M. (2012). Linking smallholders to markets: determinants and impacts of farmer collective action in Kenya. *World Development, 40*(6), 1255–1268.
12. Fuller, F., Huang, J., Ma, H., & Rozelle, S. (2006). Got milk? The rapid rise of China's dairy sector and its future prospects. *Food Policy, 31*(3), 201–215.
13. Ganesan, M., Karthikeyan, K., Prashant, S., & Umadikar, J. (2013). Use of mobile multimedia agricultural advisory systems by Indian farmers: Results of a survey. *Journal of Agricultural Extension and Rural Development, 5*(4), 89–99.
14. Gizaw, S., Abera, M., Muluye, M., Aliy, M., Alemayehu, K., & Tegegne, A. (2017). Validating the classification of smallholder dairy farming systems based on herd genetic structure and access to breeding services. *Agricultural Sciences, 08*(07), 545–558.
15. Gruber, Harald, & Koutroumpis, Pantelis. (2010). Mobile communications: Diffusion facts and prospects. *Communications and Strategies, 77,* 133–145.
16. Inklaar, Robert, O'Mahony, Mary, & Timmer, Marcel. (2005). ICT and Europe's productivity performance: Industry-level growth account comparisons with the United States. *Review of Income and Wealth, 51,* 505–536.
17. International Telecommunications Union. (2017). *ICT facts and figures 2017*. Geneva: International Telecommunication Union.
18. Jakimoski, K. (2014). Analysis of the usability of m-commerce applications. *International Journal of U-& E-Service, Science and Technology, 7*(6), 13–20.
19. Koutroumpis, P. (2009). The economic impact of broadband on growth: A simultaneous approach. *Telecommunications Policy, 33,* 471–485.
20. Kitzinger, J. (1995). Qualitative research: Introducing focus groups. *BMJ, 311,* 299.
21. Krueger, R. A., & Casey, M. A. (2009). *Focus groups: A practical guide for applied research.* Sage.
22. Mandate, G. K., Mandal, M. A., & Rahman, M. S. (2009). Production and marketing of milk in some seelected areas of serajgonj district. *Bangladesh Journal of Agricultural Economics, 32*(454–2016–36444), 105–115.
23. Mishra, K. V. (2015). Marketing strategies of small-scale milk producers: A study in azamgarh district, uttar pradesh. *IUP Journal of Marketing Management, 14*(2), 63.

24. Mittal, S., & Mehar, M. (2012). How mobile phones contribute to growth of small farmers? Evidence from India. *Quarterly Journal of International Agriculture, 51*(892-2016-65169), 227.
25. Mittal, S., & Tripathi, G. (2009). Role of mobile phone technology in improving small farm productivity. *Agricultural Economics Research Review, 22*(347-2016-16874), 451.
26. Morgan, D. L. (1996). *Focus groups. Annual Review of Sociology*, 129–152..
27. Musso, F. (2012). Technology in marketing channels: Present and future drivers of innovation. *International Journal of Applied Behavioral Economics (IJABE), 1*(2), 41–51.
28. Nielsen, J. (1993). Usability engineering: Morgan Kaufmann Publishers. *Inc.*
29. Papaioannou, S. K., & Dimelis, S. P. (2007). Information technology as a factor of economic development: Evidence from developed and developing countries. *Economics of Innovation and New Technology, 16,* 179–194.
30. Pradhan, Rudra P., Girijasankar, Mallik, & Bagchi, Tapan P. (2018). Information communication technology (ICT) infrastructure and economic growth: A causality evinced by cross-country panel data. *IIMB Management Review, 30,* 91–103.
31. Pradhan, R. P., Arvin, M. B., & Norman, N. R. (2015). The dynamics of information and communications technologies infrastructure, economic growth, and financial development: Evidence from Asian countries. *Technology in Society, 42,* 135–149.
32. Stewart, D. W., Shamdasani, P. N., & Rook, D. W. (2007). *Focus groups: theory and practice.* Newbury Park, CA, USA: Sage Publications. The Asian Age. (2017). Dairy farmers look for milk marketing scope.
33. Tavera, J. A., & Mónago, T. O. (2018). *Milking the milkers: A study on buyer power in the dairy market of peru* (No. 2018–470). Departamento de Economía-Pontificia Universidad Católica del Perú.
34. The Asian Age Online, Bangladesh. Retrieved February 28, 2018, from https://dailyasianage.com/news/64117/dairy-farmers-look-for– milk-marketing-scope.
35. The Daily Star. (2016). Bangladesh dairy: Challenges and opportunities| The Daily Star. Retrieved Apr 21, 2018, from https://www.thedailystar.net/round-tables/bangladesh-dairy-challenges-andopportunities-1337251.
36. Vu, K. M. (2011). ICT as a source of economic growth in the information age: Empirical evidence from the 1996–2005 period. *Telecommunications Policy, 35,* 357–372.
37. Wamboye, E., Kiril, T., & Sergi, B. S. (2015). Technology adoption and growth in sub-Saharan African countries. *Economic Studies, 57,* 136–167.
38. World Bank. (2017). *World development indicators*. Washington, DC: World Bank.
39. Zhang, D., & Boonlit, A. (2005). Challenges, methodologies, and issues in the usability testing of mobile applications. *International Journal of Human-Computer Interaction, 18*(3), 293–308.

Author Index

C. Metallo et al. (eds.), *Digital Transformation and Human Behavior*,
Lecture Notes in Information Systems and Organisation 37,
https://doi.org/10.1007/978-3-030-47539-0